Canadian Economic
Development

CANADIAN

Fourth edition

From the French regime to the present-day
Canada of ten provinces

ECONOMIC

DEVELOPMENT

A. W. CURRIE,
Dr. Com. Sc.,

*Professor of
Commerce
University of Toronto*

Printed and bound in Canada by

THE HUNTER ROSE CO. LIMITED, TORONTO

FOREWORD

Foreword

The purpose of this book is to set forth the main features of Canada's economic development. The emphasis throughout has been on underlying elements, on trends, on fundamental forces. For this reason the book cannot be expected to be up-to-date on every small detail of the current situation. It is believed, however, that an understanding of the basic forces will lend a broader meaning to the detailed information on current economic conditions as depicted in the daily press and annually summarized in that invaluable compendium, *The Canada Year Book.*

The book makes little claim to presenting original material. Instead it has tried to synthesize the scattered publications on Canadian economic history which have appeared in recent years. The author's indebtedness to the authorities listed in the "Selected Readings" at the end of each chapter is gratefully acknowledged. In particular, he is obligated to Professor H. A. Innis of the University of Toronto who first applied the theory of the staple to Canadian conditions. The author has assumed that the reader already possesses some knowledge of the general history of Canada such as that contained in the sixth volume of the Cambridge "History of the British Empire" or any recent High School text.

The manuscript has been read in its entirety by Professors W. N. Sage and F. H. Soward of the University of British Columbia, by Mr. Eric Kelly of John Oliver High School in Vancouver, and the chapter on **Labour** was read by Professor C. W. Topping, also of the University of British Columbia. The author has benefited greatly from the advice generously given by these gentlemen. He wishes also to record his obligation to his wife for encouragement on many occasions.

A. W. Currie.

FOREWORD TO FOURTH EDITION

Very profound changes have occurred in Canadian economic life since this book was first published and so a special effort has been made to bring this edition up to date. Our economy is now so complex, however, that only the more significant facts could be presented if the book were to be kept down to the modest size which is, the author hopes, one of its main advantages. *The Canada Year Book* (annual), the *Encyclopedia Canadiana* (1957–8) and numerous publications listed in the Selected Readings at the end of each chapter should help the interested reader to enlarge his knowledge beyond what a single text can provide.

A. W. Currie

Contents

INTRODUCTION

ECONOMIC history is the story of how man through the years has earned a living. It is concerned with how he has fed, clothed and housed himself and his family: it deals with products such as fish, furs, lumber, wheat, minerals and manufactured goods: it discusses production methods and how they have changed through invention and superior business organization: it covers such topics as labour problems, transportation, foreign and domestic trade, public and private finance, banking and currency: finally, it considers in what ways economic activity has been controlled by governments. In brief, economic history inquires into the activities of the common man in his daily work and the factors which affect his prosperity.

In order to deal with all these topics in a brief compass, even for a single country like Canada, it is necessary to generalize, to theorize, to pull into a single pattern the tangled threads of the activities of thousands of men and women whose work has covered a period of more than three hundred years. Now the general pattern of Canadian economic history lies in the theory of the staple and arises out of the fact that throughout most of her history Canada has been in the pioneer or colonial stage of development. A pioneer community is defined as one where there is plenty of land but a scarcity of labour and capital. By the term "land" we mean "all the natural forces which assist man in his productive efforts". The term includes not only the soil and its fertility but rainfall and sunshine, forests, fisheries, minerals, water power, natural harbours and, in fact, all natural resources. In a colonial economy natural resources are plentiful.

On the other hand labour, i.e., human workmen of all types, is scarce. There are few people relative to the natural resources and such labour as does exist, although energetic and ingenious, is not likely to be highly trained or to have the background of accumulated skill of the older, more mature economies. Similarly there is a scarcity of capital. To the economist, capital is not money because money in itself is of little value; it will not by itself keep one fed or housed. Money is important only for what it will buy. Some money is used to buy consumer's goods like food, houses, clothing and other articles which yield satisfaction directly to the user. Other money buys producer's goods such as machinery, office buildings, farm implements and railway rolling stock. Such goods are used in further production; they do not give satisfaction directly to the consumer but indirectly. For example, shoe machinery confers no benefits on consumers except in a roundabout manner, that is, when it is used to make shoes which, in turn, do give satisfaction to their wearers. It is these producer's goods, called capital by economists, which, along with labour, are comparatively scarce in a pioneer community.

In view of this situation a colony is always anxious to bring in labour and capital in order to "fill up its great open spaces and develop its untapped natural resources". To secure labour the Southern States brought in slaves. Virginia got indentured servants—impoverished Europeans who wanted to start a new life in America but lacked the funds with which to pay their fare across the Atlantic. Accordingly they entered into a contract (indenture) whereby in return for their fare, they undertook to work on a tobacco plantation for their board, room and clothing or, perhaps, at very low wages for a period of from four to seven years. By the end of that time the indentured servants were considered to have recompensed the employer for the advance of passage money he had made for them, and they became completely free to work for themselves if they wished, or to re-engage themselves to the same or another employer for a reasonable money wage. In the more northern colonies, including Canada, labour has nearly always been free but the problem of inducing labour to come to the new world, of assisting it in paying transportation charges across the ocean, of settling it in fairly prosperous circumstances when it did arrive, in short, the entire matter of immigration occupied the attention of political and business leaders up to the present day.

Similarly the pioneer community must bring in capital. This involves the annual payment of interest and the eventual repayment of principal. The frontiersman is apt to think that he is enduring all the hardships of a pioneer existence, working from daylight to dark in order to pay toll to a distant capitalist who lives in luxury off the interest, the fruits of the strenuous toil of the settler. Thus the frontiersman, being acutely conscious of the burden of interest, is likely to advocate radical changes in the financial system and to confuse the need for capital with the need for money. The effect of acquiring capital is frequently to create friction between borrowers in the pioneer region and lenders in the older communities.

Partly as a result of this factor, investment in a pioneer region is typically risky. Wealthy people and institutions may be unwilling to lend to individuals in a new land or may consent to lend only on onerous terms. On the other hand, they are more ready to lend to a government. Thus the capital equipment in a new region is often provided either by the government itself, or under government auspices. If the equipment cannot earn enough to pay the interest charges, the government is left burdened with a heavy debt. In our study of Canadian economic history we shall see several different attempts to deal with immigration, more than one instance of zeal for monetary reform on the part of pioneers, and several cases of government attempts to supply capital equipment. It would be well to keep in mind that these events are aspects of the essential nature of any pioneer community—abundant natural resources, but insufficient labour and capital to develop these resources properly.

Every community, no matter where situated, must apply the available labour and capital to the natural resources at its disposal. The standard of living of the community, i.e., the total goods and services which each individual can enjoy, depends on how efficiently this application is made. The pioneer region may, if it likes, become self-sufficient. In this event its standard would be comparatively low. The people can use only those things which they can produce by their own efforts without the help of much capital equipment. Moreover there is little chance of specialization: every man is a jack-of-all-trades and master of none. No matter how skilled a carpenter may be in his trade, he cannot spend all his time at carpentry work unless he can trade the products of his skill—buildings, furniture and the like—for other goods which he and his family require. Other specialists are in the same position. Thus specialization involves both exchange and the existence of considerable numbers of people. Specialized labour is skilled labour because of such factors as repetition leading to the acquisition of skill (practice makes perfect), the use of better tools, the selection of trades to suit the aptitudes of the worker, and so on. When a pioneer community tries to live by itself, the lack of a large population limits the extent of specialization and the amount of skill that can be used, reduces the output of industry, and these factors, along with the lack of machinery, transportation facilities and other capital equipment, lower the standard of living.

But the colony may follow a different plan. It may export some article, called a staple, which it can produce easily and, in return, import the manufactured goods which it requires. The staple should have certain characteristics: it must be an article whose production involves the use of the natural resources which the colony has in abundance; it must have a comparatively easy technique of production, that is, not require expensive capital equipment nor a great deal of labour nor labour of a highly skilled character. The staple ought to be in general demand abroad; it must be of such a nature that it can be exploited quickly, for colonists want to attain a high living standard as soon as possible after they arrive in the new land; it should be concentrated, i.e., have a high value in proportion to bulk in order to stand the high cost of transport, because colonies are commonly far distant from their markets. Finally, the staple must be comparatively imperishable since it may be a long time in transit to the market.

In short, the staple is the article which the colony can produce and export most effectively. Manufactured goods, requiring as they do relatively large amounts of labour and capital, are what the mature economies can produce most cheaply. Thus there are mutual advantages to the trade. To be sure the colonial economy, because it is largely dependent on one commodity, is exposed to great risks, such as a drastic decline in price or the complete loss of markets for its chief export. Nevertheless colonies invariably attempt to concentrate their productive efforts on a staple and to import the other articles they require. In this way the colony ordinarily obtains a higher standard of living than would have been possible had a programme of self-sufficiency been adhered to. No colony, of course, completely discards its self-sufficiency and, particularly in times of economic stress, it may revert to it. Even so the most distinctive feature of the economic development of new areas is adherence to the staple theory. It is to be noted that the colonists do not adopt the theory consciously; they are practical men and do what seems to them to be advantageous, but the effect of their actions is to concentrate their efforts on a staple and to avoid self-sufficiency as much as possible.

Examples of the staple theory in operation are numerous. In the early Spanish colonies in Central and South America the staples were silver and, to a lesser extent, gold; in the West Indian colonies the staple was sugar; in Virginia, tobacco; in New France and Rupert's Land, furs; in Newfoundland, salt fish. In other colonies now comprised in the Dominion of Canada the early staples were fish, furs and lumber. At a later period of time the staple was wheat, first in Ontario and then in the West. In more recent years Canada has produced a number of staples—wheat, apples, potatoes, lumber, pulp and paper, minerals—each one of which is important in one or other of the regions of the country. Furthermore, we have created our own financial markets which supply funds for businesses and governments at home, and to some extent abroad. In other words, Canada, or at least certain parts of it, is approaching a mature economy.

Despite our growing maturity, our stake in world trade is very substantial even to-day and if one looks back over our economic history as a whole, reliance on a few staples dominates the course of development. One effect of this reliance has been that economic growth has progressed in successive waves of prosperity and depression. This is sometimes called a "boom and bust" economy. These waves may be caused by rises in the price of the staple, a lowering in the cost of transportation, new techniques of exploitation, or the discovery of new resources. When any of these events occurs and particularly when more than one take place at the same time, the pioneer community booms, capital and immigrants flow in, everything proceeds in a spirit of boundless optimism. Should any or all of these factors cease to be favourable, the economy is plunged into the depths of depression and burdened with the necessity of paying back, with staples selling at low prices, the debts which were accumulated during good times. For this reason depressions have often been particularly severe in Canada. Of course it would be a mistake to believe that all Canadian economic history can be written in terms of the staple theory, but a clear understanding of that theory, along with its implications, illumines many aspects of Canadian economic development. It may be re-iterated also that the words, colony or pioneer, are not used in any disparaging sense but merely to describe an economic organization with peculiar features with respect to land, labour and capital.

It will be observed that most of the staples of North America which have been listed are those of tropical or semi-tropical areas on the one hand, or of northern regions (furs) on the other. They are articles which Britain cannot produce for herself: they are complementary or supplementary to the products of Britain. To be sure, wheat is listed but this commodity did not become important until the mother country became industrialized, until people began to flock from the farms into the new factories in the cities neglecting agriculture at home and creating a demand for Canadian food-stuffs.

Initially, colonies which supplied articles readily produced in Britain were not as favourably regarded as those producing complementary goods. Indeed, the New England colonies, which had substantially the same climatic conditions as Britain, would have been compelled to adopt the alternative of self-sufficiency had not a way been found to offset the basically competitive nature of their products with those of old England. The method which was followed was to send grain, fish, and lumber for casks to the plantations in the West Indies. The slaves on the plantations produced sugar which was sent to Britain. Thus the agricultural, forest and fisheries products of the central and northern colonies were exported to Britain indirectly in the form of sugar. By means of this roundabout technique the fundamentally competitive character of the products of the northern colonies and of Europe was evaded. Moreover, the same ships which carried food to the West Indies took sugar to Britain and brought back manufactured goods to New England. This triangular trade was an important element in the commerce of certain of the early colonies. The important point is that the staple theory could be followed either directly or circuitously with almost equally satisfactory results to the colony concerned.

Before proceeding to consider the economic history of Canada in detail, it is necessary to pay some attention to another factor in its development, namely, the physical stage on which the significant movements in our economy have operated. It is nature which determines to a considerable degree how man earns a living, what articles he may produce, how he produces them, how he transports them, with whom he trades and so on. The study of economic history properly begins with geography.

To its discoverers, North America was essentially an obstacle to be overcome, an impediment on the western route to the Far East. The explorations of Magellan, Cortez, Cartier, Hudson and others show the many efforts to go round or through this obstacle in order to secure direct access to the riches of Asia. Only slowly was it realized that North America had resources which in themselves were worth while to develop. It is this geographic fact that largely explains why, although the discovery of parts of present-day Canada took place in 1497, the first permanent settlers did not arrive until more than one hundred years later.

When economic development did begin in North America it was greatly influenced by the existence of several extensive networks of rivers. The greatest of these is the Mississippi, the natural north-south highway of the huge interior plain. Somewhat less extensive is the St. Lawrence, including the Great Lakes and the Ottawa river, a natural east-west route to the American Middle West and the Canadian North-West. The economic significance of this route is modified by the Mohawk-Hudson, a kind of side door between the Great Lakes region and the Atlantic at New York City. In the northern part of the central plain there is the Nelson-Saskatchewan providing access to the interior through Hudson Bay. Even farther northward is the Mackenzie, still of minor but growing economic importance.

Before the railway era, transport by land was exceed-ingly difficult and consequently the rivers provided the only means of transportation and communication. The trade in furs and lumber centred along the rivers; later, settlement clung to them. Thus the river basins became economic units. Sometimes the economic organization in one river basin spread over the watershed invading the region which was economically as well as geographically tributary to another drainage system. The conflict in the fur trade between the Hudson's Bay Company and the fur-traders, both French and English speaking, in Montreal was essentially a struggle between the economic systems of the St. Lawrence and Hudson Bay. Some-times attempts were made to link up adjacent economic-geographic areas in a political way. The French tried to join the St. Lawrence and Mississippi regions by a series of forts. Such a union, if successful, would have restricted the English colonists to the relatively narrow plain between the Appalachians and the Atlantic. The fear of this political as well as economic encirclement accounts for the enthusiasm with which the English colonists attacked the French in the Seven Years' War.

On the Pacific coast the significance of the river basins is less clear cut because the rivers are, generally speak-ing, shorter, less navigable and drain smaller areas. Nevertheless after its initial stage of development, the fur trade of British Columbia centred either at Astoria, near the mouth of the Columbia, or at Victoria, near the mouth of the Fraser River. Later on, the fear that busi-ness areas north of the forty-ninth parallel would be pulled down by river boats to cities south of the line led to the construction of an important railway through the Crow's Nest Pass. These illustrations of the importance of drainage basins in Canadian economic development are given, not because they exhaust the subject, but because they furnish clues to the intelligent understanding of Canadian economic history.

The most important inter-relationship between geography and economic history, however, lies in the fact that Canada is not one, but five distinct economic regions. Newfoundland, a separate dominion until it entered Confederation in 1949, will be dealt with by itself. The Maritime Provinces are an area jutting far out from the main body of the continent, an area of relatively barren rock with a few fertile agricultural regions in Prince Edward Island, in the Annapolis-Cornwallis valley and elsewhere, an area concerned with staples like apples and potatoes and a coal and steel industry operating under considerable handicaps. In the St. Lawrence valley or lowland, including peninsular Ontario, there is another region, populous, with a reasonably prosperous agriculture of the mixed farming type, with extensive manufacturing, in short an area with a fairly well diversified economy. Racially, culturally and religiously, it is divided in two but economically, it is an entity. On the western plains there is another Canada, where wheat is the typical product. On the Pacific coast is another distinct geographic area with mining, lumbering and foreign trade as the chief occupations. To the north, in the Mackenzie River basin and the Laurentian Shield which circles Hudson Bay, is a new Canada creating its economic structure on the basis of minerals and pulp and paper.

Each of these five Canadas tends to be a distinct entity having a marked similarity of economic interests within itself, and differing from adjacent regions either in the nature or urgency of the economic problems which it faces. Each region is separated from the adjoining ones by wide stretches of unproductive rock. There is little blending of occupations along the boundary lines except, to some extent, between the Laurentian Shield and the St. Lawrence Valley. Yet in the main, the important businesses of one area do not merge gradually into the economic life of the next so as to give a well-knit national economy. Moreover the economic boundaries rarely coincide with provincial boundary lines. The Gaspé peninsula in the province of Quebec, has strong economic affiliations with the Maritimes because its terrain and products more closely resemble those of that region than they do those which are typical of the province to which it belongs in a political sense. Similarly, the business man in the Lake of the Woods district in Ontario looks not to Toronto, but chiefly to Winnipeg, the metropolis of the plains region, in which he sells his lumber and paper. The Peace River block of British Columbia is obviously part of the wheat economy. The economic region of the Canadian Shield cuts across the boundaries of all the provinces except the Maritimes. In other words, each of the five Canadas is distinct economically but its boundaries are not conterminous with provincial lines.

Until railways provided cheap means of transportation and Confederation supplied a practical mechanism of control, each of these areas pursued its own economic existence without much regard to its neighbours. With the setting up of a superior governmental organization an effort was made to unify the five Canadas in an economic sense. The process of integration is by no means complete even yet, but the separate development of the five areas and then the attempt at their unification provides another illustration of the close relationship between economic history and geography, and outlines another pattern which pulls together the isolated facts of our development.

This chapter had three objectives. First, to set forth the scope of the book; second, to explain the staple theory; third, to point out some of the relationships between economic history and geography. It was not expected that the treatment of these topics would be exhaustive. It was, however, necessary to sketch some of the underlying trends in our development in order to lend unity to the pages that follow. We have painted the background; now let us fill in the details.

SELECTED READINGS

CURRIE, A. W., *Economic Geography of Canada*, Toronto, 1945.

INNIS, H. A., *Problems of Staple Production in Canada*, Toronto, 1933.
"Significant factors in Canadian economic development" *Canadian Historical Review*, December 1937, pp. 374-84.

LOWER, A. R. M., "This island nation" in *Canadian Defence Quarterly*, Spring, 1937, pp. 489-507.
"Geographical determinants in Canadian history", in Flenley R., ed., *Essays in Canadian History*, Toronto, 1939.

MACKINTOSH, W. A., "Economic factors in Canadian history" *Canadian Historical Review*, March 1923, pp. 12-25.
"Some aspects of a pioneer economy", *Canadian Journal of Economics and Political Science*, hereafter referred to as C.J.E.P.S., November, 1936, pp. 457-63.

PLUMPTRE, A. F. W., "The nature of political and economic development in the British Dominions", *C.J.E.P.S.*, November, 1937, pp. 489-507.

PUTNAM, D. F., *Canadian Regions*, Toronto, 1952.

SAGE, W. N., "Geographical and cultural aspects of the five Canadas", Canadian Historical Association, *Annual Report*, 1937, pp. 28-34.

SIEGFREID, A., *Canada*, London, 1937.
Canada: An International Power, Toronto, 1949.

TROTTER, R. G., "The Appalachian barrier in Canadian history", Canadian Historical Association, *Annual Report*, 1939, pp. 5-21.

1

The French Regime

THE detailed economic history of Canada opens with the trade in fish. John Cabot, a Venetian, the first explorer (1497) under the English flag of what is now called Canada, was astonished at the great wealth of fish off Newfoundland. Before long fishermen ventured across the Atlantic with the object, not of exploring the new world, but of catching fish and returning to Europe with their cargoes. In 1578 nearly four hundred vessels of French, English, Portuguese and Spanish nationality were engaged in this trade.

As a staple, fish was reasonably satisfactory. It was an abundant natural resource, quickly exploited without the use of a great deal of capital or of highly skilled labour. It found a ready market among the Catholic countries of Europe as well as in England, for everywhere fish formed a more important part of the diet than at present. The primitive farming methods of the sixteenth and seventeenth centuries made it difficult to keep many cattle throughout the winter, so that a continuous supply of fresh meat was not available. In the absence of refrigeration or canning, meat soon decayed and, in spite of liberal applications of spice and strong sauces, rapidly became unpalatable. Hence fish, fresh or salted, introduced a welcome variety into the diet and was always in demand.

Unfortunately, fish lacked two of the essentials of a good staple—it was bulky and perishable. These defects were offset by cleaning and salting the fish. There were, in general, two methods of salting. Under the first, green salting, the fish were cleaned on board ship and each day's catch spread out in the hold with heavy layers of salt between each layer of fish. After standing for three or four days the fish were repacked in another part of the vessel with rather less salt. As can be imagined, this technique required large quantities of salt, but this article was readily obtained by the French and Spanish, through the evaporation of sea water in huge pans set up in the bright sun along the coasts of the Mediterranean and the Bay of Biscay. In England the cloudy weather prevented the use of this cheap method of producing salt, and for a time English fishermen were handicapped in their competition with the French. The other method of salting, dry salting, was to place the cleaned fish on racks erected along sheltered inlets in the new world so that the sun could evaporate some of the moisture and allow the salt to "strike in". When the fish were partially dried out they could be stored away in the vessel's hold with the use of a comparatively small amount of salt. This method was favoured by the English who could obtain sufficient salt for this process either by importing it from France, or by evaporating in vats heated by coal, brine which had been obtained from the sea or from salt springs. The saving of salt under the dry method was so great that by the end of the sixteenth century, the dry technique was used even by the French.

It is important to note that neither method of curing resulted directly in any important permanent settlement in the new world, at least not during the French regime. One method did not require any landings on the new continent at all and the other, although it did involve the use of land and frequently also the storing of small boats or unused supplies until the next season, did not lead to settlement. The outlook of the European fisherman was almost entirely toward the sea. The land near the Banks was inhospitable—so inhospitable, in fact, as to discourage not only settlement but exploration of the immediate area except in so far as a casual search for precious metals was concerned. Doubtless whenever landings were made, the fishermen would exchange trinkets for furs, but the largest supplies of furs came from regions other than those adjoining the fishing banks. Before long men came to trade for furs alone, ignoring the fish. Fishing was important because it introduced the French to the fur trade which dominated the economic life of the northern half of North America for well over two hundred years, but fishing in itself did not lead to settlement.

Although fishing continued to be important throughout the entire period of French control in America, it always stood somewhat remote from the agriculture, industry, and trade of the French colonies. The situation was different in New England. In that region the settlers, who came as early as 1620, soon realized that prosperity could be obtained more easily from the cod and halibut of the Grand Banks and along the coast of New England and Acadia, than from the rocky soil. By 1675 New England had six hundred vessels in the fishing industry and exported the products to Europe and, increasingly, to the sugar plantations of the West Indies. As these plantations developed, the prosperity of New England became more and more intimately bound up with the West Indian economy. Codfish and some agricultural products were sent out in ships built in New England and manned by the New Englanders themselves. The demand for salt was stimulated and vats for evaporating sea water were set up along the shore. Local lumber was used to manufacture barrels and casks which were needed to handle the sugar. Molasses, a by-product of sugar manufacture, was brought into New England and made into rum, then considered a necessary of life. Most important, perhaps, was the fact that business with the West Indies was part of the triangular trade which enabled New England to get around the difficulty that most of her products were competitive with those of the mother country. Fishing was an integral part of New England's prosperity—the basis of her ship-building, lumbering, trading and some of her manufacturing activities.

On the other hand, in the French colonies fishing was never integrated into the general economic scheme. This was true in spite of the fact that the French had farming communities in Quebec and Acadia, and sugar plantations in the West Indies. French agriculture in the St. Lawrence Valley was never very important, as we shall see. French farmers in the Annapolis Valley found their chief outside market in the fortress of Louisburg. Industry was hampered by the pre-occupation of the French with the fur trade. Ports on the St. Lawrence were open only part of the year; they were more distant from the West Indies than English colonial ports and, therefore, transportation costs were higher and vessels were more exposed to shipwreck or enemy attack. Finally the French preferred brandy from their native land to West Indian rum. For these reasons fishing was not pulled into the economy of the French colonies in America as was the case with the English colonies. To be sure, French fishermen frequented the Banks but their economic connections remained with France and not with the industry or the temperate or tropical agriculture of the new world. On the whole trade in fish did not, during the French regime, have a significant influence on economic development except in so far as it opened the door to another staple, furs.

As just indicated, by far the most important article of trade during the French period was furs for the reason that they fulfilled substantially all the requirements of a good staple. They were imperishable, valuable in proportion to bulk, and were in great demand in Europe where they were used for clothing and especially for the heavy beaver hats which every gentleman then wore. Furs did not compete with European goods to any considerable extent. They were of excellent quality because of the severe climate, and were numerous because the extensive forests and water-ways supported a great many animals.

A final advantage of furs was that they could be secured readily and without the use of elaborate machinery or scientifically trained labour. The native population knew the ways of the woods. They could easily obtain the pelts and, what was more, by means of their canoes they could quickly bring the furs along the extensive water-ways to points where contact could be made with Europeans. Moreover, the Indians were anxious to trade for they lacked such things as kettles, blankets, knives of metal, guns, ammunition, beads and other trinkets dear to the hearts of a primitive people. In order to get these articles—all of which Europeans could easily provide—the Indians were prepared to exchange furs and to exchange them without expecting much in return. In the course of time the Indians found that furs were rather more difficult to secure from the old hunting grounds. Hence they had to be given more goods in order to entice them to go farther afield for the pelts, or to hunt in the old regions more diligently. Nevertheless the natives were still under the whip hand of the Europeans for, by this time, they had become accustomed to the new commodities and refused to go back to their more primitive habits of life. The Indians were now dependent on Europeans for supplies and in order to obtain the goods, they had to get the furs. Even if the Indians had not been prepared to bring the furs to market, Europeans could have secured them for themselves because white men, especially the French, proved extraordinarily skilful in adopting the Indian mode of life, hunting and trapping on their own account. Thus until lumbering and agricultural settlement pushed back and destroyed the fur-bearing animals, a good, though variable supply of this excellent staple was available either through Indian or direct European exploitation.

Now it is obvious that no natural resource can be used profitably without some measure of control and direction. The organization used for this purpose was the joint stock company which was already well established in foreign trade when the French began to contemplate trading with North America. These companies, such as the English and Dutch East India Companies, were formed by royal charter, and members of the companies were given the right to trade in a certain area to the exclusion of other subjects of the monarch who issued the charter. The company would be composed of wealthy merchants, nobles of the court, and sometimes the king himself. These individuals subscribed various sums to the capital stock of the company. The money so received was invested in trading posts (factories) and warehouses, used to buy supplies for trading purposes, to hire employees, and so on. Commonly also, it was necessary to spend money to erect forts and maintain an army abroad in order to put down troublesome natives, or to keep out

foreigners and even people of the same nationality as
the company who might attempt to poach, or interlope,
on the company's exclusive territory. Sometimes, too, the
company had to support a navy or, at least, arm its trading
vessels in order to protect shipping between the pioneer
region and the mother country. In brief, the company
was more than a simple trading concern: it had to perform many functions which are now-a-days undertaken
by the government.

Now that the French had in North America an excellent
staple and a suitable type of organization, they were
faced with a further problem. They wanted to establish
a colony, a large settlement which would serve as an
outlet for the surplus population, provide a permanent
market for French goods, and supply all the temperate
zone commodities and also minerals which France could
not provide within her own borders. Finally, and perhaps most important, they wanted a colony that would
add to the prestige of the mother country. Thus the
French wanted a company to carry on both trade and
colonization. In the mind of the French Government the
two things were tied together. But economically the two
objectives were opposed to each other. Fur trading was
exceedingly profitable; it gave immediate financial returns; it did not require large numbers of Europeans.
Colonization was the very opposite in these respects and
to the extent that it succeeded, it would push back and
ultimately destroy the fur trade. Nevertheless the government of France insisted that the trading company
assume responsibility for settlement also.

It was partly in order to make the proposition of com-
bining business and colonization attractive to the company that the government granted a monopoly of the fur
trade. It was realized that the company needed all the

profits it could get from furs in order to enable it to establish the unprofitable permanent settlements. It was appreciated too, that the Indians did not clearly distinguish between one Frenchman and another. If one French trader deceived them, all fur-traders of that nationality suffered. In order to protect French interests as a whole, it was essential to keep out certain types of traders and to maintain certain standards of ethics for the others. The easiest way this could be accomplished was to grant a monopoly to a group who would have a definite interest in maintaining good relations with the Indians over a long period of time.

It was for these reasons that, beginning in 1608, monopolies were given by the French Government to companies trading in Quebec and Acadia. By 1627 four companies had succeeded each other in the trade and all had followed an almost identical course. In the first year of its monopoly the company would send out a number of settlers. Because it was expensive to bring farmers to Canada, profits of the fur trade would be eaten up in encouraging settlement. In the following year it was only natural that the company would cut down the number of settlers and concentrate on the fur trade in order to increase profits. Before long settlement would be entirely neglected except in so far as it aided the fur trade through providing some local supplies of food. Then a competing group, usually merchants from another town in France, would complain to the king that the company was not fulfilling its obligations to send out settlers. The charter of the original company would be cancelled; the new group would get a charter on substantially the same terms. In a few years the cycle would be repeated. No matter what group was in control, settlement suffered.

In 1627 the famous Cardinal Richelieu, then practically prime minister of France, made a strenuous effort to rescue the colony from stagnation. He created the Company of New France, or as it is sometimes called, the Company of One Hundred Associates, and managed to stir up a good deal of enthusiasm for the new colony. The new Company undertook, as usual, to bring in settlers but the profits of the fur trade soon lured the shareholders away from the prosaic and expensive task of fostering immigration. The loss of vessels and supplies when the English captured Quebec in 1629 caused the remainder of the original enthusiasm for the colony to evaporate. To be sure, the Company under various forms dragged on for several years but it cannot be said that settlement was ever aggressively pursued, although profits from the fur trade were reasonably satisfactory.

The colony continued in a backward state until at least 1663. There were many reasons for this lack of progress. The various companies and individuals were always much more concerned with the profitable fur trade than with settlement. The French had made the mistake of allying themselves definitely with certain Indian tribes— the Algonquins and the Hurons. This lead the Iroquois, who were the traditional enemies of both these tribes, to attack the French settlements periodically, pillaging the farms and destroying whatever agriculture did exist. Furthermore, Europeans felt that the climate of Canada was too severe for comfort. Those who were persecuted for their religion in France could not come to Canada as the Puritans did to New England. France was almost continuously at war with her neighbours in Europe. She had to maintain a large standing army and an extravagant court, both of them drains on her resources. Also she lacked the sea power necessary to protect Acadia and

give New France a trading outlet free from English interference.

In an effort to speed up settlement the French introduced the seigniorial system. This was the typical method
of land tenure in France. Under it each head of a family
held his land from some superior—a knight, lord, duke
and so on up to the king. Each land-holder had to swear
fealty to his immediate superior and also pay him certain
goods or perform certain services as a kind of rent. The
method of introducing this system into New France was
simply to grant large tracts of land (seigniories) along
the St. Lawrence River, and one or two of its tributaries,
to officers, merchants, younger sons of the nobility, court
favourites and generally to persons of some financial or
social standing in France. In return for the land the
seigniors undertook to send out settlers, develop their
land and eventually, it was hoped, they would reproduce
in Canada the social structure of old France. From an
economic standpoint the important thing is that the
seigniorial system was a means of encouraging immigration. Unfortunately the scheme was not a success. Some
of the seigniors preferred the pleasantries of the French
court to the arduous task of developing a new colony.
Other seigniors found that bringing out settlers was
expensive, and that developing their land involved too
heavy an initial capital investment and then too long a
wait for returns. They found that some of the settlers
they did bring ran off to the woods where quick profits
could be made in furs. Thus, in spite of the seigniorial
system, settlement languished, a sickly adjunct to the
fur trade.

In view of the backwardness of the colony the Government of France, in 1663, completely changed its administration. Canada was made a royal province or, as we

would say, a crown colony, and control of almost all its
activities was put in the hands of government officials.
The monopolistic fur trading company was not immediately abolished but it ceased to have any effective voice
in directing colonial activities. The new administration,
especially under the intendant Talon, adopted a vigorous
policy of development. Troops were sent out to give protection against the Indians. On the expiration of their
term of service, the regiments were settled on farms and
in case of attack could be easily called up to provide a
trained militia. New settlers coming to Canada were put
on cleared land so that they could provide for their own
needs with the least possible delay. They were supplied
with the necessary tools, with grain for seed, and with
sufficient food to last until the first crop was harvested.
The seigniories which had been granted earlier but had
not been settled were given to other persons who it was
thought would be more likely to bring in people. The
administrators in Canada encouraged large families and
early marriages. Prospective wives were brought in for
single men already in Quebec. The local officials asked
that village girls be not sent but only country girls inured
to hardship. The girls "should not be disagreeable by
nature and . . . not bad looking. They should be healthy
and strong for work in the country or, at least, should
have some training in the handicrafts". As for the men,
they should not be "gentlemen but only poor men who
know how to work". The quality as well as the numbers
of immigrants was a matter of concern for Canadians
even at this early date.

Not all the schemes of the new administration were
successful. For example, the effort to develop trade with
the French West Indies, the search for mines, the growing of hemp, the building of ships turned out to be of

little importance in spite of continued efforts in these directions. The lack of skilled labour, of capital and of suitable resources, and the greater profit-making possibilities in furs accounted for the situation. On the other hand, the colony steadily developed agriculturally. By 1700, there were 15,000 people in Quebec and about 40,000 acres of land under cultivation. Almost all the farm land abutted either the St. Lawrence or the Richelieu, for the rivers provided the only means of transportation. Every habitant wanted access to the river and hence the farms were long and narrow, typically about 468 feet wide and perhaps a mile and a half deep—so ribbon-like that it did not pay to cultivate the land far back from the river front. Since the houses were close together, each side of the river between Quebec and Montreal looked like a long straggling village street. Because of intermittent wars in Europe and considerable turmoil within France itself, there was little immigration after 1700. The population within Canada, however, increased steadily as a result of natural increase and by 1760, that is at the time of the Conquest, there were about 62,000 French-speaking persons in the St. Lawrence Valley. Agriculture, especially after 1740, was far from prosperous but a small proportion of the colony's inhabitants was firmly rooted to the soil.

The living conditions of the habitant were primitive but not unattractive. The houses were built of timber or later of stone, whitewashed, with a single door and projecting roof with dormer windows. Behind the house would be a log stable, a root-house, and an outside oven where a week's supply of bread would be baked at one time. The houses were usually kept scrupulously clean, with a brightly coloured rug on the floor. The food was rough but wholesome—pea soup, coarse wheat or rye

bread, salted meat, fowl, fish, and game. The clothing was made at home from wool or deerskins. The proximity of the houses to one another encouraged social life, and dancing, card playing and gossiping filled the long winter evenings. On the whole the settlers were religious, thrifty and carefree, especially after the Conquest when the danger of war with the English and Indians was removed.

In the meantime the fur trade of the colony enjoyed considerable though uncertain prosperity. The first exchanges in Canada, of furs for European goods had taken place between Indians and French fishermen chiefly at Tadoussac at the mouth of the Saguenay. Before long Frenchmen, interested primarily in furs, had pushed up the St. Lawrence to Quebec, Three Rivers and Montreal. From the latter point, exploring traders such as La Salle and the Vérendryes, went farther along the St. Lawrence to Fort Frontenac where Kingston now stands: they penetrated up the Ottawa, to the head of Lake Superior, down the Mississippi and, in the 1730's, into the Great Plains themselves.

Steady expansion into new territories was a most important characteristic of fur trading under the French regime. In part this extension was due to the decrease in the supply of furs, especially beaver, in the areas adjacent to the trading centres. In addition, the Huron tribe, which had formerly acted as middlemen in the trade with the Indians to the west, had been annihilated by the Iroquois in 1649-50 and the French found it necessary to send their own traders farther afield. More particularly, French traders were compelled to penetrate inland in order to meet the competition of the Dutch who, until 1664, operated from New Amsterdam, now New York, and of the English who came in from the south, and also

from the north through Hudson Bay. Competition forced fur-traders to go farther and farther along the rivers and lakes into the interior of the continent in order that they might intercept the furs as they were going from their original source to traders of an alien race. The effect of this competition was threefold. It led to the exploration of the country. It brought larger numbers of Indians into direct contact with Europeans, thus breaking down their native culture and increasing their dependence on European goods. Finally the extension meant that more and more Europeans were engaged in hauling supplies and furs along the lines of communication and in actual trade with the Indians. As time went on an increasing proportion of the people in New France were engaged directly or indirectly in the fur trade and as a result the agriculture of the colony suffered.

The trade in furs was one of considerable instability. Demand fluctuated with changes in style and suffered badly when there was a shift to smaller, lighter types of men's felt hats. The frequent wars in Europe, as well as in America, disorganized the trade. Supplies of furs varied with the seasons. The smuggling of furs to the English and the activities of interlopers of both nationalities were a constant problem to French colonial administrators. As the routes along which furs were brought from the interior to Montreal lengthened, the cost of transportation increased. Also supplies and furs spent longer in transit and thus the risk of price changes increased. The inadequacy of the records makes it difficult to trace the history of the fur trade in great detail, but the trends toward expansion and instability are clear. The fur trade illustrates some of the economic problems which arise when a community bases its economy upon a staple.

In a broader sense and from the standpoint of the colony
of New France as a whole, dependence on the fur trade
was of doubtful value. The fur trade was, in large measure,
responsible for the colony's lack of agricultural and industrial development. The trade involved a scattering of
the population. It created a jovial, irresponsible class,
the coureurs-de-bois, "dare-devils of the wilderness", who
spent the summer in trade and travel, who caroused for
a few short weeks in the towns during the winter, and
who then returned in the spring to life with the Indians.
The excitement of their life discouraged young people
from the hum-drum of farming. In consequence agriculture was neglected or left in the hands of women. In
the early years of the colony the exodus of men in the
summer exposed the settlements to the depredations of
the Indians more than would otherwise have been the
case. In the later years agriculture was purely self-
sufficient, without the exports which characterized the
English colonies. As the trade routes stretched into
more distant regions the number of colonists engaged in
the trade became relatively greater. The energies of
the colony were more and more drawn into the fur trade,
and into the intermittent wars with the English and the
Indians which the fur trade involved.

In addition the fur trade led to difficulties in the administration of the colony. The colonial governors were
forced to concern themselves with defence, to the neglect
of the economic welfare of the community. Some of the
government officials were themselves financially interested
in the trade, and there was a good deal of favouritism and
corruption on this account. The church wanted to prevent the sale of brandy because of its demoralizing effect
on the Indians. The traders insisted that the traffic in
liquor was essential in order to meet the competition of

English rum. Endless, and sometimes unsavoury, quarrels developed between the two groups. As a result of these factors confidence in the colonial government was gradually weakened, and during the Seven Years' War it broke down completely.

Fundamentally, the relationship between the fur trade and the broad economic development of New France was a reflection of geographic factors. The St. Lawrence River gave relatively easy access not only to its own extensive basin, but also to the Great Plains and the Mississippi valley. It was natural that the French should conceive the idea of linking up the St. Lawrence and Mississippi valleys by a string of forts. It was natural, too, that over this enormous region the chief business activity should have been the one which involved the largest immediate returns and, relatively, the smallest number of men. On the other hand, the English-speaking colonies were hemmed in between the Appalachian barrier and the sea. Prevented by geography from extending themselves broadly over the western region, they were forced to develop a more diversified economy, to consolidate their position before they expanded westward. Also they had the advantages of a better climate and a superior trading position with respect to Europe and the West Indies. Their agriculture was progressive and largely on an export basis. Their fishing was extensive. Their manufacturing and ship-building were developing. Taken together the English-speaking colonies had a population of over two million in 1763, compared with about sixty-two thousand in New France.

In short, the geographic structure influenced the English colonies toward a solidly established, well-rounded economy but geographic factors induced the French colony to a wide-spread and, in the long run, exhausting extension of its economic life-line and an undue dependence on the fur trade. The English planted in America what was essentially a progressive European settlement, slightly modified to suit the requirements of the new world. The French economy was fundamentally an adaptation of native techniques—the collection of furs, the use of the birch-bark canoe, life in close contact with the Indian. Agriculture was self-sufficient and unprogressive. The colony was basically a fur-trading and military dependency of France.

SELECTED READINGS

BROWN, G. W., ed., *Readings in Canadian History*, Toronto, 1940, pp. 1-186, 289-368.

CREIGHTON, D. G., *Dominion of the North*, Toronto, 1957.

DE CELLES, A. P., "The habitant, his origin and history" in Shortt, Adam, and Doughty, A. G., ed., *Canada and its Provinces*, Toronto, 1920, Vol. 15, pp. 17-117.

EASTERBROOK, W. T. and AITKEN, H. G. J., *Canadian Economic History*, Toronto, 1956, pp. 23-134.

FAUTEUX, J.-N., *Essai sur l'industrie au Canada sous le régime français*, Quebec, 1927.

CLARK, S. D., *The Social Development of Canada*, Toronto, 1942, pp. 21-94.

GRANT, RUTH F., *The Canadian Atlantic Fishery*, Toronto, 1934, pp. VII-XXI, 1-4.

INNIS, H. A., ed., *Select Documents in Canadian Economic History*, 1497-1783, Toronto, 1929, pp. 1-149, 269-430.
The Fur Trade in Canada, New Haven, 1930.
The Cod Fisheries, Toronto, 1940.

INNIS, M. Q., *An Economic History of Canada*, Toronto, 1954, pp. 1-52.

MACKAY, DOUGLAS, *The Honourable Company*, Toronto, 1936.

MUNRO, W. B., *The Seigneurs of Old Canada*, Toronto, 1914.
The Seigniorial System of Canada, Cambridge, 1907.

RICH, E. E., *The History of the Hudson's Bay Company*, London, 1958.

2

Early British Rule

WHEN the French capitulated in 1760, the colony of New France was in a wretched position. During the winter of 1759-60, the inhabitants of Quebec were in such misery that the British soldiers donated cash and a share of their own rations to their relief. Agriculture in the colony had been badly neglected because almost all the men had been called up to serve in the militia. The fur trade had been disorganized by the intermittent wars on land and by the difficulty of maintaining connections with France by sea through the British blockade. The machinations of the intendant Bigot had destroyed confidence in the colonial government. The excessive issues of paper money had led to depreciation of currency and the demoralization of trade. Finally, at the end of the war, almost all of the officials and many of the seigniors and business men returned to France. In short, the colony was not only in the depths of depression but it lacked the type of people who might have given it intelligent business leadership.

Close upon the heels of the British army came English-speaking traders, mainly from Boston. These traders were at first concerned only with providing the army with supplies, but their acute commercial instinct quickly led them to take the places of the French business men who had gone. They re-established the wholesale trade in Montreal and Quebec. The retail trade continued in the hands of the French for an intimate knowledge of the language and customs of the mass of the population was more essential there than in wholesaling. In any event, there was a cleavage between the wholesalers and the rest of the community. Wholesalers were constantly being blamed by the habitants for charging too much for manufactured goods and paying too little for whatever produce the habitant had to sell. This very natural economic discontent within the colony was buttressed by the fact that the wholesalers were of a different race and religion from the bulk of the people. Moreover, the merchant class was a source of embarrassment to the government in London for they demanded a legislative assembly to which they felt, as British-born, they were entitled. The mother country was reluctant to grant this privilege, however, because it would involve either excluding the French-speaking majority from the government, thus putting control in the hands of a small clique of about five hundred men or it would mean admitting the French, placing control with the newly acquired colonists and, perhaps, discriminating against Anglo-Saxon merchants. In brief, the existence of a distinct wholesaling class accentuated the economic, racial and political difficulties of the next few decades.

With the conquest, Canada became an integral part of the British mercantile system. The essential feature of this system, in so far as colonies were concerned, was that the overseas possessions should be used to increase the prestige and economic prosperity of the mother country. Each European nation wanted to amass all the gold and silver it possibly could. Today, we understand that the important matter in a country's prosperity is not its stock of precious metals, but the total volume of goods and services available for distribution among its inhabitants and the equity with which the distribution among the various classes is made. But in the sixteenth to eighteenth centuries, when the possibility of borrowing enormous sums from the general public was unknown, a supply of gold was essential to prosecute the interminable wars. In addition, one country, Spain, was exceedingly prosperous due to the fact that she was drawing huge amounts of silver from the new world, and other countries naturally felt that they must emulate her. Accordingly each nation tried to appropriate a large supply of precious metals.

This policy of acquiring all the gold and silver possible involved the search for mines at home and abroad. It led to the stimulation of exports and the reduction of imports of goods, that is, to the creation of a "favourable" balance of trade in the expectation that foreign countries would have to offset the "favourable" balance by sending in gold. The mercantile system encouraged domestic manufacturing because it would at the same time reduce imports and increase the value of exports, since manufactured goods sent out of the country are worth more than raw materials. Mercantilism aimed to develop shipping with the objects of heightening the prestige of the mother country, more adequately providing for national defence, enabling the country to control its foreign trade more effectively, and keeping within the country the carrying charges which, it was assumed, would otherwise be paid in gold to foreign ship owners.

A final tenet of mercantilism was to encourage the establishment of colonies. They would supply a market for goods. In addition they would provide a source of raw material, especially of precious metals, and of commodities which the mother country herself could not produce and which she would otherwise have to buy with gold from foreign nations. The ideal situation would have been to have an adequate supply of every important commodity produced at home but if this were impossible, it was better to keep trade "within the family" than to deal with outsiders.

Now if colonies were to fulfil these functions it was necessary that their economic life be controlled. Their trade must not be handled in foreign ships. They must not be allowed to buy goods from foreign nations if these articles could possibly be supplied by the mother country. They must not manufacture to meet their own needs and they must produce agricultural commodities which were complementary, not competitive, with those of the mother country. Regulations to attain these objectives had already been applied by Britain to the English-speaking colonies in America. When the colony of New France was ceded to Britain it automatically came under the same system. By this time, however, the older British colonies were beginning to chafe against the trade restrictions. When, therefore, the fear of French assault from the north and west upon the Atlantic coast colonies was removed, when it appeared to many that under the Quebec Act (1774) Britain had treated the newly conquered French-speaking Catholic settlement too generously and had tried to keep English-speaking settlers out of the Ohio valley, when Britain tried to extend her control by taxing the colonies largely in order to pay the cost of their defence during the Seven Years' War, when these things happened, the thirteen English-speaking colonies revolted and set up an independent country of their own.

Fortunately, the appeal of officials of the new nation to the French-Canadians fell on deaf ears. The habitant felt little interest in such matters. He was little concerned with foreign trade and hence was not disturbed by restrictions upon it. The British leaders offered him solid gold and silver for his produce instead of colonial paper money, a medium of exchange about which he had unhappy memories dating from the last days of the French regime. Finally the church opposed revolt. For these reasons the French-speaking farmers and traders, for the most part, gave little encouragement to the emissaries of rebellion. On the other hand the English-speaking merchants were more conscious of the hampering effects of the trade regulations. Also many of them had but recently come from the mercantile communities of Boston and New York. Though few of them became active supporters of rebellion, the merchant class was fairly sympathetic toward those who, by force of arms, opposed the mercantile system.

After the termination of the American Revolution, the colonies in Canada continued, of course, within the framework of British mercantilism while the United States was excluded from its benefits as well as its drawbacks. The trade between New England and the British West Indian colonies was forbidden, but a great deal of smuggling was carried on because the trade was too well established to be shattered by decree. Officially an effort was made to put Quebec and Nova Scotia in the place of New England in the West Indian trade. The effort was only moderately successful. It failed for substantially the same reasons as had held when France had tried to follow a similar policy for her colonies.

One other aspect of mercantilism after the American Revolution was to forbid trade between Canada and the newly established republic to the south. The volume of such trade would not have been great in any case because of the difficulties of land transportation and the similarity in production between the two regions. On the other hand, the Richelieu River and Lake Champlain provided a

natural outlet for the products of Vermont. Trade along
this route was considerable and for a time was legalized
by the Quebec council as well as winked at by the mother
country. As will be pointed out later mercantilism slowly
withered away and was abolished completely in the 1840's.
In the meantime, Canada remained within the system
enjoying certain advantages such as tariff preferences in
the British market and, at the same time, suffering somewhat from the restrictions requiring that all trade be
carried on in British ships and through Britain alone.

During the early years of the British regime, trade
operated under other handicaps, some of them more
serious than the restrictions of mercantilism. For example, there were complaints by merchants of the difficulty of securing commercial credit from London, of
delays in the adjustment of marine insurance, of the
danger of fire to their warehouses in Quebec. More serious were complaints about the coinage and the "infamous,
Scandalous, Ignominious and Shameful practice of Clip-
ping, Mutilating and Debasing" gold coins. In particular
there were bitter protests against French civil law which,
according to the Quebec Act, was to prevail in the colony.
This law was unfamiliar to the English-speaking merchants and was interpreted by judges who were completely
untrained in the principles they attempted to apply. Often
times bothersome, expensive litigation was stirred up
throughout the country by bankrupts and discharged
soldiers who hoped to pocket large fees. Altogether, the
legal system was a cause of considerable annoyance to
the English merchants. The difficulty was solved in part
by the division of the valley into Upper and Lower Canada
in 1792, in part by the slow assimilation of the two
systems, and in part by the accumulation of knowledge
of the law by merchants and judges.

A marked improvement in the economic position of the colony became apparent in the 1770's and 1780's. In 1768 the governor, Sir Guy Carleton, later Lord Dorchester, reported to London that the severance of trade relations with Europe during the wars had forced the people in Canada to become more self-sufficient. The habitants manufactured a rough linen cloth, a coarse combination of linen and wool, a crude type of pottery, and poorly tanned leather. He went on to say, in effect, that the colonists would be better off if they concentrated their productive efforts on staples and abandoned manufacturing. The official reply from London was that manufacturing should not be prohibited, but that the attention of the people might be well diverted to occupations less likely to operate to the detriment of Great Britain.

Accordingly, the British fostered industries which were more advantageous to the development of the colony and less apt to interfere with the mother country. In order to secure a supply of rope for the sailing vessels for their navy and merchant marine, the British tried to induce Canadian farmers to grow hemp. Despite offers of free seed, a cash bounty and expert advice, the efforts to make hemp a staple were unsuccessful. This was due to the lack of mills to prepare the product for market, and the competition of wheat whose growth was more profitable to the farmer. Another British project of doubtful value was the production of rum and of oak staves, so that Canada might fit in more completely with the West Indian trade. This attempt was of relatively little value to the colony because of the lack of suitable timber in the lower part of the St. Lawrence Valley.

A British innovation of much importance was the manufacture of pot and pearl ash to be exported to

Britain for bleaching textiles. As explained later, potash was a staple of considerable significance in the development of both Ontario and Quebec until slowing down in the rate of clearing land reduced supply, and the development of chemical bleaching powders eliminated demand. Equally noteworthy was the improvement in agricultural methods generally. The Quebec *Gazette*, the first newspaper published in the St. Lawrence Valley, had a long series of articles on types of ploughing, the use of fertilizer, the culture of new vegetables such as onions, "coliflower, celeri and spinage" to supplement the traditional peas and beans of the habitant. In effect, the English brought to Quebec knowledge of the agrarian revolution which had been developing in Britain during the preceding half century. The advanced techniques seem to have been adopted fairly quickly by the habitants even though later, from 1800 to 1850, farming methods in Quebec stagnated again. In any case freedom from war gave farming in Quebec an opportunity to develop which it had never before possessed. In 1771, the colony exported nearly 200,000 bushels of grain and thereafter the export of food was fairly regular. What had been unusual under the French regime now became typical. Much of the farming in Quebec remained of the self-sufficient type, but the production and export of an agricultural surplus allowed the farmer to enjoy greater prosperity than he had ever previously experienced.

It was the fur trade, however, which was the most important factor in the business life of the northern half of North America under early British rule as it had been under the French regime. The acquisition of Canada by Britain did not mean that the British came into contact with the Canadian fur trade for the first time. In fact, for a great many years they had operated from New

York by way of the Hudson-Mohawk valley. In this trade they had the advantage of cheap supplies, but were handicapped by the fact that they had entered the field to the south of the French and so were cut off from the better quality furs to the north. The English traders never associated with the Indians, were never absorbed into native culture to the same extent as the French or the Scots. They held more or less aloof from Indian life and most of their furs were brought to them by the Iroquois or by outlaw coureurs-de-bois from the French colony.

The English also approached the fur trade from a different and more important front, that is, through Hudson Bay. Two French traders, Radisson and Groseillers, became disgruntled at the interference with their trading operations by colonial administrators. The two went to Boston and later to London where they were able to interest Prince Rupert, the brother of the reigning monarch, in the possibility of carrying on the fur trade through Hudson Bay. Two vessels were dispatched to test out the plan and after their successful return the Hudson's Bay Company or more accurately "The Governor and Company of Adventurers of England trading into Hudson's Bay" was formed in 1670. This joint stock company was given a grant of all the land drained by rivers flowing into Hudson Bay, and a trading monopoly of the region. In return the Company agreed to pay "to us [the king], our heirs and successors, for the same, two elks and two black beavers, whensoever and as often as we, our heirs and successors shall happen to enter into the said countries, territories and regions hereby granted".

From the start the Company was successful. Dividends of 50 per cent were common and of 100 per cent not unknown. The original capital of £10,500 owned by nineteen shareholders increased, solely out of earnings, to £100,000 in 1720. At first the English were handicapped by lack of knowledge of the type of goods required in trade, the method of sale and, generally, by lack of experience. However, they were able to engage French deserters for much of the actual trading with the Indians and gradually they built up a solid trading organization of their own. Most of the actual traders in the country were Scots who often intermarried with the Indians. The chief advantage which the Company possessed was that of cheap supplies of goods for trading purposes. The competition between the English and the French operating out of Montreal became so intense that raids for possession of the trading posts on Hudson Bay occurred towards the end of the seventeenth century. British control of the region was not finally acknowledged by France until 1713.

The general policy of traders of "the Bay" was to remain at their posts along the coast, and encourage nearby Indians to take goods into the interior for trade and then bring out the furs. In other words, the policy of the Hudson's Bay Company was to use the coast Indians as middlemen with the Indians of the Plains who had no knowledge of canoes. This arrangement broke down when the French pushed from the Great Lakes into the Plains region, erected forts around Lake Winnipeg and even beyond, and intercepted the Indians on their way to the Hudson's Bay Company posts. To meet this competition the English were forced to establish their own posts in the interior. The competition between "the Bay" and Montreal traders was temporarily solved by the Seven Years' War which crippled the French fur trade.

During the Seven Years' War the French fur trading

posts, along with Quebec and Montreal, capitulated to the British but the colony was not formally ceded to the conquerors until 1763. Meanwhile the French traders were leaving the west for the farming communities along the St. Lawrence; a few joined the service of the Hudson's Bay Company; many remained with the Indians waiting for British traders to come from Montreal. The British, however, were reluctant to enter the trade out of Montreal until the colony was officially ceded to Britain. Then shortly after the cession the Indians under Pontiac waged war on the British traders. The natives feared destruction of their mode of life by encroaching settlers who might come from the English-speaking colonies along the Atlantic seaboard, as well as from the newly acquired colony. The Indians also hoped for the return of their friends, the French. As a result of these disorders and uncertainties, the trade through Montreal was practically suspended. In the late 1760's it revived and now had the advantage of cheap goods of English manufacture. These goods were obtained originally through Boston and New York but after the American Revolution they had to be obtained directly from London. In the course of time the trading organization settled down into a system whereby London merchants handled the sales and extended credit; Montreal merchants, mainly Scots, directed the trade; and traders in the west, often French, carried on the actual barter with the Indians and shipped the furs to Montreal. The trade through Montreal was open to every British subject on payment of a license fee. A great many people came to Montreal after the annexation of Canada to share in the profits of the trade. As a result competition was cut-throat, often taking the form of supplying drink to the Indians and skirmishing between traders themselves. The intense rivalry threatened

profits, but little effort was made to amalgamate for
mutual benefit until after the establishment of an independent American republic introduced the possibility of
well organized competition from a new quarter.

Under the treaty which ended the war between Britain
and her former colonies in America, British fur trading
companies were required to withdraw from American
territory. Instead, they retained the posts at Ogdens-
burg, Oswego, Detroit and other points. The ostensible
reason was that the American states had failed to live
up to their obligations under the treaty, because they did
not compensate the Loyalists for the loss of their property
during the Revolution. The fundamental reason was that
the British wanted to keep hold of the fur trade which
centred along the St. Lawrence basin, without regard to
the newly established and more or less artificial international boundary. The dispute between the two countries was amicably settled in 1796 when, as a result of
Jay's treaty, the trading posts south of the border were
abandoned by Canadian fur-traders.

Conflict between the two nations over the fur trade
revived in the first decade and a half of the nineteenth
century. When settlers came over the Appalachians into
the valleys of the Ohio and the Mississippi, they created
apprehension among the Indians and fur-traders who
feared that the advance of settlement would destroy their
means of livelihood. For their part the settlers saw no
reason for leaving the rich agricultural area in the hands
of a few savages who were developing almost none of
the region's resources. As a result, there was a good
deal of ill feeling between the natives and the new
settlers. Indians often menaced American settlers and,
since these Indians were supplied with guns and ammunition through Montreal, it was easy enough to charge

that Canada was actively urging the Indians to make war on the settlers. In fact the settlers felt that it was necessary to go to the extent of annexing Canada in order that agriculture might progress. So strong was this feeling along the American frontier that, in 1812, the "War Hawks" were successful in forcing the United States to wage war on Canada in spite of the fact that the New England States were opposed to war, and the original trouble regarding British interference with American ships was in the process of being cleared up. The "War Hawks", of course, failed to annex Canada. Neither did the animosity of the Indians halt settlement. Indeed settlement in the Great Lakes region progressed so rapidly that the larger part of the American fur trade, except that of the Pacific coast, was soon destroyed. In 1812 the firm headed by John Jacob Astor, the most important American trader, was sold to the Montreal Company. The sale was made by the partners of the firm who were trading on the Columbia River and without the consent of Astor himself. The Columbia partners seem to have been afraid of British competition or even of attack by Britain—fears which Astor, who remained in New York city to look after the wholesale end of the business, did not share.

Meanwhile in 1783 the fur-traders in Montreal—the Frobishers, McTavish, McGill and others—formed an association eventually known as the North-West Company. Each member contributed his quota of supplies and the profits of each expedition were divided according to the individual contributions. At first the arrangement was for only one year at a time but later was extended to twenty years. The Company revived the policy of French traders in establishing trading posts in the Plains in order to intercept furs on their way to Hudson Bay.

The Montreal group gave better terms of barter to the
Indians of the Plains who had been badly exploited by
middlemen of their own race dealing in goods for the
Hudson's Bay Company. The Montrealers also built
boats for use on the lakes in order to get cheaper transportation than that previously provided by canoes. Each
spring the traders from Montreal proceeded westward
with the supplies for next year's trade, while the so-called
wintering partners came down from the west with the
furs obtained in the year just past. The two groups met
near Fort William, interchanged the furs and supplies,
discussed the coming year's operations and in a few days
began the long return journey. The lines of communication between Montreal and the actual traders in the west
were lengthy and the problem of effective control of employees exceedingly difficult. In order to get the whole-
hearted support of its employees, the Company followed
the practice of promoting subordinates as soon as they
had proved their worth and of paying them on a commission basis, that is, giving them a share of the profits on
the business they handled. Loyalty to the Company was
also generated by the forceful personalities of the men
who directed its affairs.

The result of these two stimuli was an enthusiasm
among the North-West Company men which the Hudson's
Bay Company could not equal. Unfortunately in 1799
the ranks of the "Nor'Westers" were split by a personal
quarrel between Simon McTavish and Sir Alexander Mackenzie who set up his own concern. In 1804 the two
firms were re-united but the North-West Company never
recovered its original strength. It was exposed to competition from the north by the Hudson's Bay Company
which had adopted the commission system of payment to
encourage its men and which, in addition, had begun to

establish more of its own posts in the interior in order to prevent interception by the Montreal group. Toward the south the North-West Company was subject to intense competition from the Astor interests. The purchase of the latter gave the Company little financial relief for the supply of furs in the northern parts of the United States was beginning to dry up with advancing settlement. Within the Company itself, *esprit de corps* was greatly weakened since the inability to expand into new territories limited the possibility of rapid promotion which had been a vital factor in maintaining morale. As a consequence of its long lines of communication the North-West Company needed nearly three years to complete a venture, that is, from the time the goods were sent out through Montreal until the furs for which they were exchanged were received back in London and sold. During this period—about a year longer than the "Bay" required —the Company ran the risk of price declines and also soon ran short of working capital. By 1821 the power of the North-West Company was at an end. It amalgamated with the Hudson's Bay Company but the union was really a "submersion" as one of the partners said.

For the next fifty years the Hudson's Bay Company was the only important factor in the Canadian fur trade. The traffic was carried on almost entirely through ports on Hudson Bay, the Montreal-Winnipeg route being abandoned. The abandonment severed, for the time being, all business connections between the British colonies in the East and the Plains. By 1860 steamer connection had been made with St. Paul and cheap American-made goods were brought in. The Company, especially under the administration of Sir George Simpson, was well managed and dividends were paid regularly. Even so there was a steady decline in the number of furs due to over-trapping and the slow advance of settlement. The Company was fighting a rearguard action but it fought with extraordinary skill. In 1869, it sold its exclusive trading privileges and most of its land in the drainage basin to the British Government for transfer to the newly created Dominion of Canada. It has, however, continued as a fur trading company and remains an extensive landowner. It now competes with other concerns. Beaver, once almost the sole pelt in the trade, has lost its paramount position. The use of money has replaced barter. The wireless, the airplane, the tractor train have introduced new features into carrying on trade.

While these events were taking place in the St. Lawrence Valley and on the Plains, the fur trade was developing also along the Pacific coast. When Captain James Cook arrived at Nootka Sound in 1778, he carried on a valuable trade in furs with the natives. On the return of the expedition to England, Cook's journals were published and great interest was aroused in the profit-making possibilities of the region. By the turn of the century a number of English and American ships were engaged in the trade. The furs, chiefly sea otter (now almost extinct), were secured cheaply from the Indians who had a passion for collecting anything made of metal. The furs were sold in China. By 1810 the boom days were over due to the exhaustion of the supplies of sea otter and the collapse of the Chinese market.

Meanwhile the North-West Company, ever eager for new sources of supply, had pushed beyond the mountains from the Plains, and John Jacob Astor had established a trading post at the mouth of the Columbia River at which he collected furs from its extensive drainage basin. The purchase of the Astor interests by the North-West Company in 1814 and the amalgamation of the latter with the

Hudson's Bay Company in 1821, left the entire region in the hands of one concern. Under Dr. John McLoughlin, a domineering, energetic but at heart a generous man, the operations were extended over the Columbia and Fraser basins and along the coast. Anticipating the transfer of the southern part of this region to the United States whose citizens had poured into the Oregon country after 1830, the Company in 1842 ordered McLoughlin to have established a new post in territory which would be indisputably British. The new post, Victoria, was founded by and governed by (Sir) James Douglas who exercised a powerful influence on the development of the region. After the official cession of the present states of Idaho, Oregon and Washington to the Republic, the Hudson's Bay Company gradually withdrew all its operations from the Columbia to the Fraser. Since navigation on the latter river above Yale is difficult, pack-horses were used to carry supplies over mountain trails to interior posts such as Kamloops, Fort Okanagan and Fort Alexandria. Sailing vessels and then steamships, beginning with the *Beaver* (1836), were used in trading operations along the coast. The furs were exported around the Horn to Britain or, to a less extent, across the Pacific to China.

SELECTED READINGS

BROWN, G. W., ed., *Readings in Canadian History*, Toronto, 1940, pp. 187-250.

BURT, A. L., *The Old Province of Quebec*, Minneapolis, 1933.

EASTERBROOK, W. T. and AITKEN, H. G. J., *Canadian Economic History*, Toronto, 1956, pp. 135-89.

HENRY, ALEXANDER, *Travels and Adventures in Canada*, J. Bain, ed., Toronto, 1901.

HOWAY, F. W., "An outline sketch of the maritime fur trade", Canadian Historical Association, *Annual Report, 1932*, pp. 5-14.

INNIS, H. A., ed., *Select Documents*, Toronto, 1929, pp. 153-265, 431-578.
The Fur Trade in Canada, New Haven, 1930.
Peter Pond, Toronto, 1930.

INNIS, M. Q., *An Economic History of Canada, Toronto*, 1954, pp. 57-81, 112-118.

MACKINTOSH, W. A., "Canada and Vermont", *Canadian Historical Review*, March, 1927, pp. 9-30.

MCARTHUR, DUNCAN, "The new regime", in Shortt, Adam, and Doughty, A. G., *Canada and its Provinces*, vol. III, pp. 21-49.

RICH, E. E., *Hudson's Bay Company, 1670-1870*, Toronto, 1960.

SAGE, W. N., *Sir James Douglas and British Columbia*, Toronto, 1930.

3

The Maritimes
to Confederation

FISH in Acadia and furs in Quebec were the first two steps in Canadian economic development. The establishment of British rule and complete British control over the fur trade were the next. These were followed, and to some extent overlapped, by the creation and slow development of English-speaking colonies bordering the Atlantic, along the Upper St. Lawrence and Lower Lakes, in the Red River valley and on the Pacific coast. Still later, very much later in fact, economic penetration took place in the Laurentian Shield. Although a number of colonial governments were set up in these areas, only five economic groups existed,—the Maritimes, the St. Lawrence Valley, including both the French and the English-speaking settlements, the Prairies, the Pacific, and the Laurentian regions. In 1867 a federation of some of these governments was formed. One of the aims of Confederation was promotion of inter-regional trade and development of a national consciousness. But the economic cohesion of each region has persisted.

In view of this situation the logical arrangement in a book of this nature is to trace the development of each region to Confederation (though in view of the smallness of the growth in the Prairie, Pacific and Laurentian regions, consideration of economic beginnings there, except in furs, will be deferred, and a separate chapter will be devoted to Newfoundland). The date of Confederation is not selected because it forms a distinct change in the type of economic life. As a matter of fact, however, 1867 is not more than ten or fifteen years removed from the date on which the Industrial Revolution may be said to have begun in Canada. The real reasons why the date was chosen are that it is convenient, and that it marks, or ought to mark, the beginning of a national economy. Confederation, of course, did not mean the submersion of all local problems. Hence it is necessary to trace the economic history of each region since Confederation, as well as the development of the country as a whole. This, then, is the plan of the remainder of the book—two regions to 1867, five regions after 1867, national problems.

In the Maritime region under the very early years of the French regime, the sea alone provided a living and fish was the staple product. In the course of time, however, the land was settled and, in addition to fish, other staples became important—furs, agricultural products, timber, minerals but all these were on a limited scale. Outside of the mighty fortress at Louisbourg, the most populous settlement was in the Annapolis-Cornwallis valley—the Land of Evangeline. Under French rule this area developed rapidly. Ceded to the British in 1713 its progress continued but the persistent loyalty of the Acadians to France caused Britain, in 1755, to expel them from the area in order to remove a serious potential threat to the British flank in both Nova Scotia and New England. Though widely dispersed, some of the Acadians eventually came back to the Maritimes, settling around the Bay of Chaleur and in other areas in present day New Brunswick and in Prince Edward Island.

Until 1749 the British themselves neglected settlement of the area. At last they were stirred into action by the need of a counterpoise to the powerful fortress at Louisbourg in Cape Breton Island, which the French had retained. Accordingly, Halifax was founded as a military settlement. Because retired soldiers proved to be mediocre settlers, Swiss and Germans were encouraged to take up land in Halifax and elsewhere, especially in the district around Lunenburg. Moreover a steady stream of settlers came from New England to the Annapolis valley, with smaller groups elsewhere. In 1775 there were in the Maritime region about 18,000 people of whom at least two-thirds were New Englanders.

The greatest influx of people came in 1783, after the American Revolution when perhaps 30,000 United Empire Loyalists found refuge in the area now known as the Maritime Provinces. This sudden migration overwhelmed the facilities of the region to accommodate them, especially in the previously almost unsettled St. John River valley. The situation was made worse by the fact that many of the newcomers were inexperienced in meeting the problems and bearing the hardships of pioneer life. Wide-spread suffering, particularly in New Brunswick, was the result and there were many weary years before even reasonable prosperity was achieved.

The population of the Maritimes was enriched by still another race of people. In 1774 Scots arrived in the ship "Hector" at Pictou, and early in the nineteenth century they came in large numbers to Cape Breton, and to Prince Edward Island. They came because conversion of their beloved Highlands into huge sheep pastures had destroyed their means of livelihood, and frequently had led to eviction from their cottages. In the 1840's and early 1850's many more people came from Britain and other parts of Europe. The history of immigration into the Maritimes is extraordinarily complex and cannot be easily summarized. At all events, by approximately 1860 the immigration into the Maritimes was practically complete for the region did not participate in the later waves of migration into Canada. In general terms, it can be said that the Maritimes were settled by people of many national origins and largely as the result of war or misfortune.

Many of the newcomers earned a living from the sea, the traditional source of wealth. They turned to the sea either because they were fishermen by trade or, more commonly, because they found the soil infertile. Until nearly twenty years after Confederation, Maritime fishermen confined their activities to the fisheries close to shore. They farmed or worked in lumbering or ship-building part of the year, and during the remainder fished along the Bay of Fundy, the Atlantic coast of Nova Scotia and the Gulf of St. Lawrence, and even along the Labrador coast. Maritime-owned fishing schooners did not, at this time, frequent the Grand Banks of Newfoundland, though the latter were still visited, as they had been in the late sixteenth and seventeenth centuries, by ships from Europe which returned there with their catch. Some vessels from New England also went to the Grand Banks, but for all North American fishermen the inshore fisheries were by far the most important.

There were two chief markets for fish caught by Maritime vessels. One of these was controlled by the Robin family from Jersey, which is one of the Channel Islands. This family came in at the close of the Seven Years' War, appropriated the old French fishing stations along the Gaspé peninsula, and built up a lucrative trade in salt cod especially with Spain and Brazil, and, in general, created a kind of economic empire along the Gaspé coast. The other and more important market for Maritime fish was among the slave population on the West Indian sugar plantations. After the Thirteen Colonies had obtained their independence this market was, theoretically at least, reserved for British ships. It was expected that Nova Scotia would replace New England in the triangular trade, but the expectation was never fulfilled for the Maritimes were too distant from the Indies and lacked the supplies of food and oak staves necessary to the trade. In order that supplies essential to the prosperity of the plantations could be obtained, smuggling from American vessels into the West Indies was resorted to. Sometimes also, American goods were re-loaded into British ships at such ports as St. Andrew's and St. Stephen, thus putting them into the category of British goods for customs purposes. In 1791 direct United States-West Indies trade was allowed by the Imperial Government.

Meanwhile American vessels fishing off the shores of Nova Scotia were smuggling in tea, coffee and rum and selling them to the inhabitants more cheaply than the same articles could be brought in legally, i.e., by British ships which had paid duty on such commodities. Colonial merchants objected to the loss of trade, and quoted the principles of mercantilism to justify their position. In the fishing trade itself, Maritime fishermen were handicapped in competition with the Americans for the latter had cheaper provisions, a better system of taking and curing fish, and they received bounties from their government. Nova Scotia and New Brunswick attempted to offset the disabilities of their fishermen by means of bounties and, in the case of the latter government, by a remission of duties on supplies for the fishery. Another difficulty was that American vessels were alleged to fish in Canadian territorial waters, that is, in the waters which are within three miles of the shore-line and which, according to the principles of international law, belong

solely to the country owning the littoral. Disputes regarding smuggling and complaints of unfair competition in
the fishing industry in general, and in the off-shore
waters in particular, gave rise to a good deal of ill feeling
against Americans.

This feeling was not lessened by the instability of
general conditions in the industry. As has been pointed
out, American vessels were excluded from West Indian
markets after the Revolution. A few years later the
trade was thrown open to them much to the detriment of
Nova Scotia. Then, in 1807, the Embargo Act of the
United States forbade American vessels to leave for
foreign ports. This restored the original position to the
great benefit of the Nova Scotians. The War of 1812
gave another similar fillip to the industry and opened up
the possibility, not by any means neglected, of privateer-
ing on American shipping. After the War the renewal
of competition with American fishermen again depressed
conditions. The situation regarding inshore fishing was
relieved slightly by a convention in 1818, which debarred
American vessels from fishing within Maritime territorial waters. The convention, however, was regularly
violated. In 1825 trade with the West Indies was again
reserved to British vessels, but five years later United
States ships were legally re-admitted. The re-admission
of American vessels was made by the government in
London in spite of the protests of Nova Scotia fishermen.
The fishing industry was disturbed again in 1833, when
the abolition of slavery in the West Indies reduced the
market. Altogether, the fisheries suffered from instability
in markets, an instability created in large measure by
government action and foreign competition.

After 1833 the industry continued its erratic course.
It was assisted by an expanding market among the grow-

ing population of the United States and by diversification, that is, by the sale of haddock, alewives and salmon in addition to cod. The fisheries thrived exceedingly when the Reciprocity Treaty of 1854 admitted fish to the United States free of duty. The abrogation of the Treaty again brought depression. As a staple, fish was only moderately successful chiefly because changes in tariff policies alternately raised the industry up to a pinnacle of hope, and then plunged it into the depths of despair.

The expansion, erratic though it was, of the fisheries encouraged the growth of ship-building in both Nova Scotia and New Brunswick. The chief raw material, lumber, was abundant and cheap and, after the immigration of the Loyalists, skilled labour was available. Almost every sea-port—St. Andrew's, Saint John, Moncton, Digby, Yarmouth, Liverpool, Lunenburg, Halifax, Pictou, New Glasgow and many more—had its ship-building yard. Ships were constructed by families or by an informal syndicate of neighbours. The ship would be used in the fishing or local carrying trades, or laden with lumber and sailed to Britain where both ship and lumber would be sold. At first the ships were poorly built and Lloyd's, the marine insurance exchange in London, refused to give them a good rating. Gradually the quality improved and by 1850, ships built in the Maritimes had achieved such a high reputation for speed and general performance that they literally sailed the seven seas, and were known the world over. The California and Australian gold rushes, the Crimean War, and the growth of Maritime trade with the United States under the Reciprocity Treaty created a great demand for Maritime built ships. An industry which had grown slowly since the early days of settlement enjoyed a tremendous boom in the 1850's and early 1860's. After 1865, the industry declined steadily because of the re-entry of United States built ships into the world's carrying trade after the American Civil War, and especially because of the competition of the much more efficient iron steamship. By 1885, ship-building in the Maritimes was a sorry remnant of its former greatness.

Lumbering, another important Maritime industry, was stimulated by the construction of ships and, even earlier than this, by the rapid increase in settlement. Small sawmills, operated cheaply by water-power, were built at numerous points to supply the locality about the mill with lumber for houses and other buildings. In addition, the mills near seaports exported some lumber to the West Indies. Chiefly, however, the forest resources were used for ship-building and for the export of logs and squared timber to Great Britain. The export trade fluctuated greatly in accordance with the general business conditions abroad, and with such events as the Napoleonic Wars, the existence and then the abolition of tariff preferences in the British market, the Reciprocity Treaty and so on. The obvious instability of this trade, coupled with fluctuations in ship-building, made lumber a gener-ally unsatisfactory staple. Other economic aspects of lumbering will be considered when dealing with the St. Lawrence Valley, the chief centre of the industry.

When they arrived in the Maritimes most of the Anglo-Saxon settlers probably contemplated earning a living from agriculture. Unfortunately, they found that over large areas, in fact over most of the region, the land was infertile. Even the Annapolis-Cornwallis valley, previ-ously the most prosperous farming community in the Maritimes, languished for a time, mainly because the incoming New Englanders found themselves incapable of managing the dyked lands as effectively as their French-speaking predecessors had done. In New Brunswick, the settlers were interested chiefly in the hope of quick profits to be made in ship-building and lumbering. For them agriculture at best was only a side issue. In Prince Edward Island farming was handicapped by absentee landlordism. This was a system whereby certain individuals, proprietors, were given land on condition that they bring out settlers. Frequently, however, the proprietors remained in England refusing to work their island estates or to bring out settlers. In other cases, they were so insistent on collecting rents that they destroyed all incentive on the part of the settler to improve the land on which he lived. The whole scheme was a constant source of complaint until, in 1875, the proprietors were bought out by the Government and the land sold outright to the former tenants.

In view of these handicaps agriculture could develop only on a restricted scale. To be sure, the growth of the fishing, ship-building, lumbering and trading interests provided a local market but, before 1867, there was never any important surplus available for export. Before the end of the period, the production of some of the present day Maritime agricultural exports, such as apples and potatoes, was beginning, but in the pre-Confederation era Maritime agriculture was concerned almost solely with supplying the local market.

Mining was an industry which was developed to an even smaller extent than agriculture before 1867. The presence of coal in Cape Breton Island had been known during the French regime, but little exploited. In the early British period, following the tenets of mercantilism, the production of coal was not encouraged. In 1826, King George IV, acting on the principle that all mineral resources belonged initially to the crown, transferred the

Nova Scotian coal fields to his brother, the Duke of York, who in turn gave them to his creditors in payment of all his debts. The creditors formed the General Mining Association which began to mine coal on a moderate scale. The output was at first mainly used for household purposes, about half of it being sold in the United States. Gradually the industrial market was enlarged by the introduction of steamships and railways, and by the shift from water-power to the steam engine in factories. In order to carry the coal from the mines to the ships for transport to market, the Association, in 1840, built a railway, the first in the Maritimes, from the Albion Mines to Pictou. In 1858, the General Mining Association transferred most of its coal bearing lands back to the Province and thereafter, until 1892, coal mining was carried on by a great many small companies competing intensely with each other. In addition to coal, gypsum which was used for fertilizer, and grindstones were exported to the United States. In the 1860's a small amount of gold was mined by relatively primitive methods. Altogether, mining in the Maritimes before 1867 was more important for its prospective, than for its actual output.

The activities of the colonists in fishing, ship-building, lumbering and mining gave rise to a considerable volume of trade. Because of the difficulty of transportation by land, trade between various parts of the region was carried on by sea with a great many small ports participating in it. In addition there was the export traffic in lumber, fish and coal, through ports such as Halifax, Saint John, Lunenburg, and Pictou. The exports were sent to Great Britain, the West Indies and the United States. The imports from Britain consisted of hardware, ship-chandlery, manufactured goods generally, and luxuries for the

officers and officials at Halifax. From the United States
(especially in the latter part of the period), came the
cheaper grade of manufactured goods, such as small hard
ware, clocks, knick-knacks—Yankee notions they were
called. From the West Indies came sugar, molasses and
rum. As already pointed out, there was a good deal of
smuggling from American fishing vessels which often
operated close to shore. In order to prevent this smuggling and facilitate the collection of duties, an attempt
was made to have all goods entered through three or
four ports. The smaller trading centres protested, however, and smuggling actually increased. The total volume
of trade, legitimate and otherwise, grew considerably as
time went on but the instability of the entire economy
created a good deal of variation from year to year.

The growth of trade created financial problems. A
wide variety of silver coins and paper money—Spanish,
British, American and French—was used in ordinary
transactions. Most of the sterling and other gold coins
which were sent to Halifax for the purpose of paying the
officers and men of the military garrison and the naval
station got into the hands of merchants, and were returned
at once to England to pay for imports. Thus there was a
scarcity of sound money and a multiplicity of other types
of currency. For the purposes of governmental and private book-keeping, the pound "Halifax currency" was
used. This was a purely fictitious currency, never coined
and arbitrarily considered to be worth four Spanish
dollars of five shillings each. As a matter of fact, the
British Government often paid the troops in Spanish
dollars at the rate of 4s.6d. each, but Halifax merchants
accepted the actual coins at the higher and mathematic-
ally more convenient rates. Other coins were accepted at

fictitious values also, for the need of carrying on trade quickly and easily was more important than the rules of arithmetic.

These elaborate accounting arrangements are indicative both of the wide-spread areas with which Nova Scotia carried on trade and also of complications involved. Of course much local trade was still carried on by barter of goods for other goods or services but in the towns, where the use of money was more common, trade suffered from the lack of good, sound money. In order to relieve business of some of the monetary handicaps, attempts were made to form banks. The early efforts failed because of opposition of the legislature but in 1825, the Halifax Banking Company came into existence. Its founders were seven important merchants and shipowners. These men had more money than any one else in the community, conducted a good share of the external trade and foreign exchange, and individually were, probably, already making loans on their own account to retail merchants and small manufacturers. Two of the business men in the group were Samuel Cunard of steamship fame and Enos Collins. The latter had been a privateer in the war of 1812, and had then settled down in Halifax importing brandy, silks, spice, ammunition, and a great many other products, even handling wampum and beaver skins. When Collins died in 1871 at the age of 97, he was the richest man in British North America, worth between six and nine million dollars.

The Halifax Banking Company issued notes which circulated at par thus facilitating trade considerably; it made loans, handled remittances to and from Britain and especially the West Indies, and accepted deposits though it made no effort to solicit them. The Company had close connections with the governing clique in Halifax and was also alleged to make large profits. For these two reasons a rival firm, the Bank of Nova Scotia, was incorporated in 1832. Meanwhile other banks had been established in New Brunswick, and later in Prince Edward Island. The decimal or American system of currency was adopted in two provinces in 1860, but the English system of pounds, shillings and pence continued on the Island to 1881. The development of banking in the Maritimes was more or less duplicated in the St. Lawrence Valley. In both cases there was an urgent need for banking institutions, a close connection of banking with the wholesale trade and, finally, for the establishment of a number of local banks.

Prior to 1867 the Maritimes enjoyed considerable prosperity based mainly on fishing, lumbering, ship-building and trade, with mining and farming in secondary position. It is important to note that the economy was unusually well integrated, one part of it being closely dependent on the others. All was well so long as every phase of economic life was prosperous but collapse of one aspect might lead to the break-down of the entire structure. It is to be noted too, that the prosperity of the Maritimes was typically uneven because of instability in markets abroad. The period of the Reciprocity Treaty, that is, from 1854 to 1866, was particularly bright, for the American market was thrown open to Maritime fish, lumber and coal. In addition, during the Civil War when American sailing vessels were engaged in war operations, a larger volume of business was left to Maritime ships, and a few Nova Scotians made fortunes running the blockade which the Northern States threw around the South. Perhaps the prosperity of the Maritimes under the treaty was no greater than elsewhere in British North America and the depressing effects of the abrogation of the treaty no more

62   Canadian Economic Development

severe. At all events, the increasing use of the steamship threatened to upset the nicely balanced economy and the prospective abrogation of the treaty forced the re-direction of trade into other, and geographically less natural channels. Under these conditions, the minds of the people were turned first to a legislative union of the Maritimes and then to the federation of all the colonies. The fact that the beginning of a permanent decline in Maritime prosperity happened to coincide with the date of Confederation lead to political problems in later years.

SELECTED READINGS

BREBNER, J. B., *New England's Outpost*, New York, 1949.
  The Neutral Yankees of Nova Scotia, New York, 1927.

BROWN, G. W., ed., *Readings in Canadian History*, Toronto, 1940, pp. 253-63.

EASTERBROOK, W. T. and AITKEN, H. G. J., *Canadian Economic History*, Toronto, 1956, pp. 227-52.

ELLS, MARGARET, "Settling the Loyalists in Nova Scotia", Canadian Historical Association, *Annual Report*, 1934, pp. 105-09.

HANSEN, M. L., *The Mingling of the Canadian and American Peoples*, New Haven, 1940.

INNIS, H. A., *The Cod Fisheries*, Toronto, 1940.

INNIS, H. A., and LOWER, A. R. M., ed., *Select Documents in Canadian Economic History, 1783-1885*, Toronto, 1933, pp. 387-729.

INNIS, M. Q., *An Economic History of Canada*, Toronto, 1954, pp. 53-57, 83-89, 122-129.

SAUNDERS, S. A., *Studies in the Economics of the Maritime Provinces*, Toronto, 1939.

WHITELAW, W. W., *The Maritime Provinces before Confederation*, Toronto, 1934.

4

The St. Lawrence Valley to Confederation

SETTLEMENT of the St. Lawrence Valley proceeded in two quite different ways during the period between the Conquest and Confederation. In the French-speaking half, that is, Lower Canada or Quebec as it was later called, the population grew as a result of natural increase. The early British administrators in Quebec discouraged settlement of English-speaking people, even of Loyalists, in the belief that all the unoccupied land should be reserved for the French and that, in particular, the Eastern Townships should be kept as a buffer between Canada and the United States. This policy was abandoned after 1792 and large numbers of people from New England and New York entered the area. This immigration was supplemented later by farmers from Scotland and by merchants who settled in the cities. Nevertheless, the entire English-speaking population in 1871 numbered only 300,000 compared with 700,000 French, the descendants of the 62,000 persons in the province at the time of the Conquest a century before. As there was no immigration from France, it is obvious that the main reason for the increase was the excess of births over deaths.

On the other hand, in Upper Canada or Ontario, the population grew to a total of 1,600,000 in 1867 chiefly as a result of immigration. As invariably occurs, immigration came into the country in waves, so to speak. The first wave came in 1783, when United Empire Loyalists flowed into Ontario as they did into the Maritimes. They overwhelmed the government organization designed to assist them in establishing new homes. Poor management, rather than lack of good intentions, prevented the Loyalists from being supplied promptly with the necessary food, tools and stock to tide them over until they were able to support themselves. In consequence, there was a good deal of suffering which was aggravated by the unfamiliarity of the new-comers with conditions of pioneer life. In the course of four or five years, however, the Loyalist families were usually able to supply their own requirements on a modest scale for the reasons that land was fertile, fish and game were abundant, and neighbours gave what help they could. Besides the Loyalists, a considerable number of settlers came independently from the United States during the 1790's, in order to improve their economic positions. So important was this influx, that it was estimated that in 1813, three-fifths of the population of Upper Canada was of non-Loyalist American origin.

The Loyalists and the others from the south had settled almost entirely along the St. Lawrence River, the northern shores of Lake Ontario and in the Niagara peninsula. The next task was to fill up the back country, that is, the Lower Ottawa Valley, the district around Peterborough and Lake Simcoe, and the peninsula of Western Ontario. The settlers in the back country came under a number of different auspices. Individual leaders such as Bishop Macdonnell, Colonel Thomas Talbot, Peter Robinson and "The McNab" brought settlers to Glengarry county and the areas about St. Thomas, Peterborough and Arnprior. Commercial firms, chiefly the Canada Company, occupied the so-called Huron Tract, the north-western quarter of Western Ontario, and the British American Land Company peopled part of the Eastern Townships.

Finally settlers came under government auspices, for example, the settlement of military units brought in to defend the newly constructed Rideau Canal.

The influx of some of these groups of settlers began in the late eighteenth century but was cut off by the outbreak of the Napoleonic Wars. Immigration revived in the 1820's, reaching a peak in the decade after 1830 when the population of Upper Canada increased from 213,000 to 430,000. After falling off in the depression of 1837, immigration recovered in the 1840's, reaching peaks in the latter years of this decade when the potato crop failed in Ireland, and again in the early 1850's and 1860's, when prosperity was exceptionally great in Canada. In the latter years immigration was offset by the outflow to the United States of newly arrived immigrants and also, of young men born in Canada. This outflow first became a feature of Canadian settlement in the early years of the century, and increased steadily until, in 1866, two-thirds of the British arrivals at Quebec, in addition to many native born Canadians, went on to the United States. They were attracted to the south by the growing industries and especially by the fertile lands of Michigan, Ohio and neighbouring states then being opened up. In spite of this unfortunate drain the expansion of the province of Canada was rapid. In fact, by 1867 almost all the valuable farm land had been settled and industries were being steadily developed as well.

In coming to Canada, these settlers were not motivated by any desire to escape religious persecution as was the case with the Puritans in New England, nor were they impelled by the wish to live under more desirable political circumstances as were the United Empire Loyalists. Instead they came in order to better their own economic position. There was wide-spread suffering in Britain during the nineteenth century, when the full effect of the agrarian and industrial revolutions which had started earlier came to be felt. Many farmers were unable to adjust themselves to the changes in agricultural methods and the use of machinery. Others were evicted from their farms because of the desire of landlords to make more money out of their huge estates by converting them into pastures for sheep. At the same time, as a result of the Industrial Revolution, many scattered cottagers were deprived of a large part of their livelihood by the invention of power-driven spinning machines and looms which produced goods so cheaply and in such large quantities, that household workers using the older hand methods could not compete. Large numbers of those from the "deserted villages" went to work in the new factories, but thousands of the "unemployed" turned their eyes to new lands beyond the seas where they could expect to earn a decent living.

Before these prospective settlers could establish themselves in the new world, someone, an individual, company or government, had to supervise the movement and perhaps give financial assistance to it. A few individuals, for example Lord Selkirk, were genuinely interested in relieving the distress of the unfortunate victims of economic progress, and were prepared to sacrifice their own personal wealth to help their countrymen. But most of the individual leaders, along with the companies, hoped to make money for themselves by reserving some of the land, bringing out settlers to develop the remainder, thus increasing the value of the reserved land which could be sold at a price more than enough to cover the initial costs. In short, they hoped to profit from land speculation. Incidentally, in this hope they were usually disappointed but at least they built up the country.

As far as the Government itself was concerned, in Great Britain there were two attitudes during the nineteenth century. The one regarded emigration as a drain on the resources of the mother country. It considered that as soon as the emigrants had built up a strong colony they would inevitably rebel against the Motherland as the Thirteen Colonies had done. In other words, when the colony "matured" it would drop from the parent tree like ripe fruit to the ground. The "ripe fruit" theory was widely held. The other opinion maintained that colonization was necessary to relieve suffering at home. Also, it believed that with proper management colonies would become a source of strength rather than weakness to the mother country. This opinion was held by a few enthusiasts. On the whole the British attitude toward immigration was one of indifference, not apparently caring whether people went to the colonies or not.

Within the colony itself there was a very natural enthusiasm for increasing its population and wealth. Land speculators wanted more settlers so that the value of their property would increase. Moreover, after the war of 1812, colonial administrators felt that it was essential to populate Canada with a large number of people of unquestioned loyalty in order to repel any possible invasion. The administrators believed that these people might be secured from members of the Anglican Church in England for they considered that the main cause of dissatisfaction in Upper Canada arose out of the fact that many of the settlers were members of one or other of the nonconformist Churches, who had come from the United States.

Europeans were anxious to come, the colony was anxious to have them, and the British Government did not oppose. There remained then the practical business problem of handling the transfer. Throughout the entire period many persons, especially artisans, were able to pay their own way but a very considerable number, we cannot tell what proportion, had to receive financial assistance. In the early 'twenties this assistance was given on a limited scale by the Imperial Government. This scheme was soon abandoned, so far as immigrants generally were concerned because it was too expensive, though some aid continued to be given to naval and army officers. Even so, the English parishes, which were responsible for poor relief, often paid the fare of their unemployed to Canada in order to rid themselves of the cost of further relief. Some of these groups were cared for until they were settled on their land but many, after suffering misery on the voyage, were left stranded at Quebec, Montreal or Kingston to be looked after by local charity organizations. One result of government assistance was to direct to Canada the less desirable type of immigrant. Persons with capital or skill tended to gravitate to the United States where the spirit of enterprise was stronger than in Canada and development was more rapid. All travellers in North America at this time were impressed by the difference in tempo in the economic life of the two countries. Notwithstanding the fact that Canada received many worth-while settlers in the 1830's and 1840's, the country as a whole became notorious for having poor business prospects and for attracting the less suitable type of settler. Not before the end of the century was this unfortunate reputation entirely overcome.

Even under the best of circumstances immigration is a heart-rending business, but conditions in the first half of the nineteenth century made it doubly so. Dilapidated ships, "coffin ships" carrying timber one way, brought back emigrants who struggled for weeks and months—

and with sailing vessels the Atlantic voyage often did take months—under conditions of almost indescribable filth, disease and immorality. Epidemics, especially of cholera, were common both on board ship and in the ports. Government regulation and private charity did what they could to prevent disease and lend succour to the destitute but in spite of this, suffering was wide-spread.

Having arrived in Canada the immigrants had to travel to the lands allotted them. Sometimes they lacked the means to do this and became charges on the Emigration Societies in the ports, or worked in lumber yards until they had acquired a "stake". Commonly they were badly disillusioned, for they had been led to believe that Canada was a land where wealth could be suddenly acquired, where gold could very nearly be picked up off the streets. They were chagrined to learn that industry and thrift were the only roads to a decent living. Frequently, while farmers were complaining of lack of labour for harvest, some immigrants were loafing in the cities because they were unable or unwilling to go to the farms. There were good and bad workers, honest as well as dishonest persons among the new-comers as among all classes, but the vast majority went directly on the land and became good citizens.

The Colonial Government was generous in its grants of land to immigrants, especially to the Loyalists or anyone who had the remotest connection with them. Up to 1815, the head of each family was given two hundred acres. This policy led to so wide a dispersion of settlement that the size of the free grant was reduced to 100 acres. In 1826 a system of land sales was introduced and the land auctioned off at nominal figures. The terms of sale varied considerably from time to time but, generally speaking, the purchaser undertook to clear part of the land, erect a house on his property and build a road in front of his grant within a specified period, otherwise the land would revert to the Crown. Liberal credit was given purchasers both by the Government and the land companies. In fact, the terms of sale and even payment for the land were often evaded with impunity.

Land settlement was hampered by a number of factors. Private individuals and government officials personally acquired large tracts of land which they withheld from immediate sale, hoping that they would be able to sell later when settlement of the adjacent farms would have increased their value. Frequently the land held by such speculators was scattered among that sold to *bona fide* settlers. This made the construction of roads difficult, and kept people apart at a time when consolidation of the population would have been desirable in order to facilitate the maintenance of schools and churches. Also, this land often harboured wolves and other wild animals which preyed on live-stock. Finally, because some of this land had been given to friends of the Government, political animosity was created. The honest settler who worked so hard to get a living for himself and improve his farm felt that someone else was trying to profit unfairly from his strenuous labours. Attempts of the legislature to limit to twelve hundred acres the amount of land which could be purchased or granted to any one individual and, also, to tax wild lands proved ineffective in checking the evils of speculation.

Another obstacle to settlement was the Clergy Reserves. Under the Constitutional Act (1791), one-eighth of all the crown lands thereafter granted was to be set aside "for the support and maintenance of the Protestant Clergy". The lands granted for this purpose were interspersed among lands being actually settled, thus giving rise to an economic problem identical with that created by speculators. Also, the term "a Protestant Clergy" was taken by legal advisers to mean only the clergy of the Church of England and the Established Church of Scotland. The Methodists who formed the largest Protestant denomination in Upper Canada, the Baptists and some Presbyterians were excluded from benefits of the grant. As a matter of fact, in practice, the members of these denominations were excluded also from the civil service for the governing clique was almost entirely Anglican. In brief, the Reserves created both economic discontent and political ill-feeling. The problem of the Clergy Reserves was not completely settled until 1854.

Another restriction on land settlement was the opposition of Lower Canada, the present province of Quebec. This opposition was caused partly by the expense of caring for thousands of destitute immigrants dumped ashore at Quebec, and partly by the danger of disease brought by these persons spreading to the general populace. But mainly the opposition came from the political fear that as the number of English-speaking settlers increased the continuance of the language, customs and religion of the original French settlers would be imperilled. Experience has shown that this fear was unfounded but the attitude of Lower Canada constituted a brake—perhaps a worthwhile one—on wholesale immigration.

No matter at what time or place agricultural settlement in the St. Lawrence Valley took place, the problems presenting themselves to the pioneer were essentially the same. The first task which the new settler faced was to provide shelter, usually a log cabin, for his family. Then he cleared some land by cutting down the trees with an axe, and burning them when the wood dried out. Alternatively, he girdled the standing timber, that is killed the tree by cutting through the soft inner bark thus preventing the flow of life-giving sap. Thus the sun was able to shine through the leafless limbs upon the growing crops until such time as the dead trees could be burned. The final important problem was to grow grain and vegetables for his own use.

The pioneer had to undertake all these tasks unaided by modern machinery. His only weapon for attacking the forests was the axe; his farming methods were crude. He used oxen for draft purposes. His farm implements were few and mainly of wood. He cut his grain by means of the sickle and later the "cradle", a scythe with a light framework above the blade to hold the grain which had just been cut until it could be deposited on the ground in a loose sheaf. The pioneer farmer threshed with a flail; he spread sheaves on the barn floor; then he swung a piece of wood a couple of feet long, in a circular manner so that a second piece of wood, bound loosely to the first with a leather thong, beat upon the sheaves, separating the grain from the ears. Finally he had to winnow the grain. He made flour by pounding grain into bran with a wooden pestle, in a hardwood block in which a bowl-shaped cavity had been burnt, and then sifting the bran through a cloth. Frequently the pioneer's wife did the baking in an outside oven. Almost invariably, she operated a spinning wheel and made candles from grease and tallow either by "dipping" or by using a mould.

Typically the pioneer family in Ontario lived in a one-storey house, roughly fifteen by twenty feet in size, made of logs notched at the corners, with the cracks plastered with clay. The furniture—benches, chairs, table and beds—was made at home from wood. The clothing was of "homespun" or leather. The food was monotonous and scarce, especially in the first few winters, for the difficulty of clearing the heavily forested land limited the acreage which could be used to produce sustenance throughout the year for the farmer and his family. As time went on the quantity and variety of food improved. The struggle to secure a living was a hard one. What social life there was usually followed a day of work in which the community joined. A clearing "bee", barn-raising or quilting party was the occasion not merely for doing collectively what one farmer and his family were unable to do singly, but also for square dancing to the tunes of a fiddler, card-playing or, too frequently, for heavy drinking.

In the early years of settlement each farmer, or at least each farming community, tended to be almost entirely self-sufficient. The pioneers supplied with their own labour most of their own requirements of bread, meat, sugar (from the maple tree), clothing, leather, furniture, kitchen utensils and tools. There was very little surplus for sale, because the farmer did not have enough land cleared to produce anything beyond his own needs and, besides, his farm was commonly remote from market, and transportation was inadequate and expensive. As soon as possible, however, the farmer began to produce a staple, a commodity which, as we have seen, had to have certain characteristics. The first staple was potash whose production, fortunately, could be combined with the clearing of the land. Before long wheat had become important. Exports on a per capita basis were considerable during the Napoleonic wars when European wheat prices were high. They declined with the arrival of peace, but soon revived again increasing steadily to Confederation. Wheat was the staple of the St. Lawrence Valley long before it became a staple of the Prairies.

There were many reasons for the predominance of

wheat. It was relatively imperishable, valuable in proportion to bulk, easily produced. The increasing industrialization of Britain provided a ready market. In addition, until 1840, Canadian grain was given a substantial tariff preference over grain from other areas. Also the cost of its carriage to Britain was greatly lowered by the use of Durham boats (described later), the construction of canals and later of railways, and the use of steamships across the Atlantic. The building of roads and then of railways in Canada opened up new lands, and permitted the self-sufficiency of previous settlements to be replaced by the staple economy. In brief, from the 1830's up to 1867 and, indeed, up to the turn of the century, wheat was the cash crop of Upper Canada and, to a lesser extent, of Lower Canada too.

Although farmers produced a staple they still remained much more self-sufficient than they are to-day. It is substantially correct to say that in the early nineteenth century, the farmer either produced all his requirements at home or did without. In the middle and latter parts of that century he produced a staple plus many articles for his own needs. He sold the staple to buy only those commodities which he could not conveniently produce on the farm. At present, a Canadian farmer tends to be a specialized producer of one product which he sells to buy substantially everything else he needs in the way of food, clothing, shelter and fuel.

To put the matter in other terms, in the early nineteenth century the typical Ontario and Quebec farmer produced large amounts of vegetables, milk, wool, hogs and beef, poultry and eggs primarily for his own use. Some of these products he or his wife exchanged at the local store for limited amounts of tea, spice, molasses, tobacco, cotton prints, drugs and hardware. Occasionally he could sell some farm goods to the military garrisons, professional men and artisans in the growing towns, or disposed of them in the lumber camps. Sometimes he was able to export horses to the United States. Gradually the settler sold more and more wheat, and the farm economy became one of self-sufficiency on which a staple was super-imposed. The staple was important for it allowed the farmer a higher standard of living and made it profitable for him to clear more land, to purchase more and better implements and live-stock and generally to improve his farm and his home. By the middle of the century the staple became still more significant and self-sufficiency slowly began to wither away, but it was still strong by 1900. Incidentally, improvement in farming conditions was very rapid in the decade and a half before Confederation, for the Reciprocity Treaty (1854-66) opened up a large market in the United States and the construction of railways created one at home.

The new settlers were not concerned solely with agriculture, nor was wheat the only staple. Lumbering was a basic industry in the St. Lawrence Valley before Confederation. The thick stands of hardwood, and especially of pine, were a natural resource quickly exploited without the use of expensive machinery or highly skilled labour. Unfortunately, lumber was bulky, a factor which was all the more important because the chief market, England, had access to much closer supplies of timber in the Baltic countries. To overcome the bulkiness, the timber was concentrated into potash by the simple process of burning hardwood logs, gathering the ashes, putting them in a tub in which water was poured at intervals over a period of several days and, finally, evaporating the resulting liquid or lye in an iron kettle. The potash, or if it were refined further so as to become crystaline, the pearl ash, could be mixed with fat to make soft soap for domestic purposes, but most of it was exported to England to be used for bleaching textiles. The trade in potash, which reached a peak in the 1830's, declined due to the increasing use of other types of bleaching powders and because, as the land became cleared, settlers found it more profitable to produce wheat. While it lasted the trade was highly important to the economy of the St. Lawrence Valley, since it provided cash income at a time when the pioneer farmer could produce no other product in quantities much beyond the needs of himself and his family.

Nevertheless, the production of potash only partially solved the problem of lumber's bulkiness because even at the height of the trade, only a small part of the total resource could be exploited in this way. The original difficulty of large volume in proportion to value and of long distance to market remained, as far as lumbering as a whole was concerned. To some extent the difficulties were offset by changes in technique. Floating logs downstream, that is, timber "drives", "rafting" down the St. Lawrence to Quebec, "squaring" to eliminate the less valuable edgings, and in the early 'fifties construction of huge mills with complicated machinery, loading in second or third class sailing vessels which could be purchased and operated cheaply, handling large shiploads of immigrants on the return voyage across the Atlantic so that their fares would increase revenue on the round trip—all these factors reduced costs and enabled Canadian lumber to be sold in Britain more cheaply. Even so, the Canadian product could not be marketed in the United Kingdom in competition with that of nearby Baltic countries. Accordingly, Canadian lumber was given a tariff preference in Britain, that is, it paid much lower duties than lumber from foreign countries. This preferential treatment lasted from 1808 until the late 1840's. The preference was in line with the general principles of mercantilism and gave the navy a supply of cheap lumber for constructing ships and for masts and spars. It was essential that the source of supply be located so that it could not easily be cut off during war time, as had happened with Baltic lumber during the latter part of the Napoleonic Wars. In short, by means of better production methods and artificial protection, Canadian lumber had an assured market in Britain during the first half of the century.

The method of carrying on the lumber trade in Canada was simple. The Admiralty purchased through London firms who had agents in Saint John and Quebec. These agents either got out the timber under their own direction or purchased it from lumbermen. There were also a number of so-called "free traders" who shipped substantial quantities of lumber to Britain for sale to the general public. In any event, lumbering involved the employment of considerable numbers of men and horses in the woods during the winter. It involved also advancing money for food, feed and wages, for the purchase of timber rights in large areas and, as time went on, for the construction of large saw-mills. In short, as the scale of operations increased, lumbering became "big business" and the "lumber kings" were the tycoons of the time.

The centre of the export lumbering industry was the valley of the Ottawa and its tributaries, with smaller amounts cut north of Lake Ontario. Little exportable lumber was obtained elsewhere in the economic region of the St. Lawrence Valley, since the lower stretches of the river valley had been denuded of their pine years

before by the French-speaking settlers, and the lumber
in Western Ontario was too difficult to get down to Montreal before the days of railways. As a matter of fact the
forest resources of Western Ontario were used mainly for
local purposes or ruthlessly destroyed to make way for
farms. On the other hand, the Ottawa Valley was almost
ideal for the export lumber trade. The river and its tributaries provided a natural highway extending toward the
market. Its headwaters drained a huge heavily forested
area whose soil was incapable of supporting agriculture.
Also the lumber, chiefly pine, was of excellent quality. The
Ottawa, therefore, became a lumbering river in a sense
the St. Lawrence never was. The same circumstances
applied to the valley of the St. John River which became
the most important, but by no means the only, lumbering
centre in the Maritimes.

After 1850 there were several significant changes
in lumbering. The construction of railways, particularly
in the Ottawa Valley, opened lumbering areas which had
not been easily accessible by water. There was an influx
of capital, mainly American, under Eddy, Perley and the
Bronsons for the erection of huge saw-mills. These mills,
along with a great many smaller ones, tended to locate
up the rivers near the source of raw material, and thus
the "drives" became relatively less important. The
decline in wooden ship-building reduced the market available. The export of square timber was gradually replaced
by "deals" which are planks usually, but not always, of
pine and three inches or more thick. Finally, just before
1850, the British preference on Canadian lumber was
abolished. Further economies in production and the
superior quality of their product enabled Canadian lumbermen to retain a share of the British market for a
time, but gradually exports to Britain declined in impor-

tance. Canadian lumbermen tried to offset declining sales in Britain by expanding their markets in the United States and within Canada itself.

Lumbering was an industry of uncertain prosperity. As the timber in one area was cut down, the people and equipment dependent on the industry had to move. The reduction of costs coincident with new techniques of production displaced poorly located or inefficient plants. Since lumber was used mainly for construction and ship-building, its demand varied with general business conditions. The market also enlarged or contracted with reductions and increases in ocean freight rates. The abolition of the preference in Britain dealt a blow to the industry, but the rapid construction of railways in Canada in the late 'fifties and the opening of the American market under the Reciprocity Treaty permitted a quick recovery. This prosperity was followed by a recession in 1866, and after a short recovery, by the more serious depression of 1873. The entire industry was one of ups and downs in the short run with a long-run trend, after 1865, that was generally downward. At the date of Confederation, lumbering was still an important industry in Canada but coming events had cast their shadow before, and lumbering was already beginning to decline.

As a staple, lumber was not entirely satisfactory. Apart from its bulkiness, it was subject to pronounced cyclical fluctuations and, like minerals, was a resource which was sooner or later depleted. On the other hand, lumber's very bulkiness involved the return from Europe of a large number of otherwise empty ships which gave low rates on imports of manufactured goods and low fares to immigrants. In this way lumbering encouraged settlement. Lumber also supplied a basis for ship-building at Quebec city, and at ports in the Maritimes. It gave an outlet for agricultural goods, particularly salt pork, flour, beans and feed. In Upper Canada it gave the immigrant a chance to earn some ready cash until he could establish himself on a farm. Unfortunately, in many cases the earnings of a hard winter's work were wasted in a few days' debauchery after the drive was over. Particularly in the Maritimes, lumbering drew men off the farms permanently and thus tended to retard agriculture, probably because agricultural opportunities were less bright in any event. Essentially in Ontario, lumbering bridged the gap between furs and general farming, and in the Maritimes, between early settlement and specialized agriculture, the iron and steel industry and foreign trade. In both regions lumbering was not displaced; instead, it was overshadowed by other occupations.

Manufacturing, another industry in the St. Lawrence Valley, is distinguished in the period from, roughly, 1820 to 1867, by the transfer of operations from the home to the local shop. The rapid increase in population in Lower, and especially in Upper Canada, led to the growth of towns. Each town would have one or more of gristmillers, blacksmiths, wagon-makers, cabinet makers, tanners, cobblers and weavers. In general terms, each one of these craftsmen used much the same production methods as the pioneer farmer had used but, because he specialized in one task and had superior equipment, he was able to acquire greater dexterity and produce a better article. He sold his output almost entirely in the local community and used local raw materials. Often he was paid in produce not in cash. In the main, these craftsmen did for the farmer what the farmer, under the previous conditions of self-sufficiency, had had to do for himself but they did the job much more effectively. All that had happened was that a gradual, but by no means complete, shift had taken place from the "jack of all trades" to the specialist, from a pioneer farm to a small mill or shop in the nearby town. The shift proceeded more rapidly in Upper than in Lower Canada.

To this general statement there were exceptions. Before the end of the period some plants were selling in markets in other countries, or were using imported raw materials, or were following involved production methods. Flour mills along the St. Lawrence, large saw-mills along the Ottawa, cotton mills at Sherbrooke, a sugar refinery at Montreal, railway car and locomotive factories at Toronto and Kingston, iron works at Les Forges and Marmora and, later, agricultural implement plants at Newcastle, Guelph and elsewhere—these were exceptions to the prevailing conditions as well as forerunners of a new era. For the most part, manufacture was still tied closely to the farming communities.

Trade, both domestic and foreign, showed a steady expansion. Early in the period trade was almost entirely with Britain and through the port of Quebec. Timber, potash, furs and then wheat and flour were the main exports and hardware, textiles, sugar, salt, tea and spirits were the chief imports. Not all the goods imported were used in Canada. Many of them were shipped up the St. Lawrence to the rapidly growing settlements in the states south of the Great Lakes. Goods could be brought into upper New York State more cheaply this way than through the United States itself, for the route was more direct, customs duties on imports into Canada were much lower than those in the United States, and the articles were easily smuggled across the border.

Most of the export, import and transit trade was in the hands of wholesalers in Quebec and Montreal working closely with firms in London. In the early years of the nineteenth century, internal trade was limited in volume and was carried on mainly through local merchants, each one of whom handled a great many types of goods and accepted produce for them. The local merchants were largely under the control of the wholesalers who sold them goods on credit, and purchased some of the produce from them. When a trade depression occurred and the wholesale merchants attempted to collect the debts due them, the merchants in the towns complained bitterly that the wholesalers sold at the highest prices and bought at the lowest. This situation created a good deal of ill-feeling between the rural districts and the cities, and in Quebec, between the French-speaking habitant and the English-speaking wholesaler.

As time went on the volume of trade increased. Britain remained the chief market, partly because of the influence of mercantilism, and partly because Canada and her only near neighbour produced substantially the same type of articles. Yet, as the forest in the Eastern States disappeared, Canadian lumber was sent across Lake Ontario. Starting on a modest scale in 1830, wheat, barley and cattle were also exported. The volume of such trade varied considerably from year to year, though under the Reciprocity Treaty it was very great. Goods of British manufacture continued to be smuggled over the American border but were offset, in later years, by cheap American cotton textiles and hardware smuggled in the opposite direction. The establishment of new trade connections and the improvement of navigation along the St. Lawrence led to the growth of trading centres at Kingston, later at Toronto, and especially at Montreal, with a relative decline at Quebec.

The wholesaler continued to control the local merchant who, in turn, was alleged to control the community through his extension of credit to farmers and lumber-men. These latter groups obtained what they required throughout the year "on account" and then paid for them in produce when the crops were harvested or, in the case of the lumberman, after the spring drive. Because the rivers, then the only practicable means of transportation, were open only during the summer, goods for trade were brought in in the spring and fall. Commonly, the merchants in the larger towns like Perth, Brockville, Kingston, Belleville, Cobourg, Hamilton, Guelph, London (Ontario) and Chatham travelled to Montreal once or twice a year to make their purchases. These towns in turn were visited periodically by merchants from smaller communities. The wholesalers in Montreal, and indeed the exporters in London, England, adjusted themselves to this cycle. So long a period of time elapsed between the sale of goods on account and their eventual payment in produce, that the risks of price declines and credit losses were great. From the standpoint of the merchants concerned, a stringent credit policy was doubtless essential but the local merchants, and especially the farmers, felt they were the victims of a vicious system. Complaints were wide-spread until the increased use of money and improvements in transportation replaced the barter system with a cash economy, and introduced more competition among merchants. Thus the farming community was gradually freed from its trading disabilities.

The expansion of trade led, as in the Maritimes, to the organization of banking institutions. In early days prominent merchants issued their own notes, called *bons*, which they undertook to repay on demand, loaned out money on a small scale and occasionally accepted deposits for safe-keeping. In particular, the more important merchants transferred funds to and from other countries and dealt in the great variety of coins which then circulated in Canada. In addition to the confusion of many types of coinage, almost as varied as those in the Maritimes, the scheme of New York currency, eight shillings or "bits" to the dollar, was used in some places in Upper Canada in place of the five shillings equals one dollar of Halifax and Lower Canada. Accounts were kept in either Halifax currency or York shillings. Needless to say, the merchants found it difficult to carry on trade under these conditions.

In order to introduce some order into the currency and to carry on general banking functions, merchants in Montreal tried to get a charter for a bank but their proposal was vetoed by the British Government who feared that the new institution, like early banks in the United States, would extend credit too liberally, issue excessive amounts of paper money and generally commit the monetary heresies of pioneer communities. The need for a bank was so great, however, that in spite of rebuffs by the government in London, the merchants in Montreal persisted in their efforts to establish one. In 1817 they even went so far as to form an unincorporated association to carry on a banking business. Five years later the group obtained a charter from the province and the Bank of Montreal officially came into being.

Meanwhile, merchants in Kingston, Quebec and later in Toronto, had formed banks of their own and by 1836, there were thirty-six banks in British North America. A few of these failed during the depression of 1837, despite the fact that the Government of Canada permitted the banks to refuse to redeem their notes in gold. The prosperity of the 1850's led to the liberalization of the laws governing the establishment of banks. The result was a wave of new bank creations. In 1867, the four original provinces were served by a total of 29 banks, of which five are still operating, six have failed, and the rest merged with other banks. In the 1850's bank notes were often discounted in distant cities, that is, Bank of Montreal notes would be circulated in Kingston not at par but at a discount of one or two per cent. This discount and its accompanying inconvenience was slight compared with the jumble of coins, some of them clipped and even counterfeit, which had circulated before. Confusion in the monetary mechanism was reduced about 1858 by the adoption of the decimal system, with the dollar as the unit replacing the cumbersome pounds, shillings and pence. A completely satisfactory monetary system was not evolved until after Confederation but meanwhile, the chartered banks performed a valuable service to the business community and the public generally.

The economic development of the St. Lawrence Valley from the establishment of British rule to Confederation was one of steady progress. The main economic problems were those of immigration and settlement, trade relationships with Britain and the United States, the provision of canals and railways, and banking and currency. Economic life was concerned with three staples, potash, lumber and wheat, but the emphasis on self-sufficiency was still very great. The economy occasionally suffered from depression, and growth at best was slow. Nevertheless, progress was sound and a basis was laid for the more spectacular prosperity of later years.

SELECTED READINGS

BROWN, G. W., *Readings in Canadian History*, Toronto, 1940, pp. 263-286.

COWAN, HELEN I., *British Emigration to British North America*, Toronto, 1928.

CREIGHTON, D. G., *The Commercial Empire of the St. Lawrence, 1760-1850*, Toronto, 1937.

CLARK, S. D., *The Social Development of Canada*, Toronto, 1942, pp. 204-307.

CRUIKSHANK, E. A., "A country merchant in Upper Canada, 1800-12", Ontario Historical Association, *Papers and Records, 1929*, pp. 145-190.

EASTERBROOK, W. T. and AITKEN, H. G. J., *Canadian Economic History*, Toronto, 1956, pp. 253-72.

GUILLET, E. C., *Early Life in Upper Canada*, Toronto, 1933.
    The Great Migration, Toronto, 1937.

HAYDEN, ANDREW, *Pioneer Sketches in the District of Bathurst*, Toronto, 1925.

HEATON, H., *The Story of Trade and Commerce, with special reference to Canada*, Toronto, 1955 (rev. ed.), pp. 202-25.

INNIS, H. A., and LOWER, A. R. M., ed., *Select Documents*, Toronto, 1933, pp. 9-132, 217-309, 360-85.

INNIS, M. Q., *An Economic History of Canada*, Toronto, 1954, pp. 89-111, 129-64.

JONES, R. L., *History of Agriculture in Ontario 1663-1880*, Toronto, 1946.

LOWER, A. R. M., *The Square Timber Trade of Canada*, Toronto, 1932.
    "Immigration and settlement in Upper Canada, 1812-20", *Canadian Historical Review*, March 1922, pp. 37-47.

MOREHOUSE, F., "Canadian migration in the forties", *Canadian Historical Review*, December, 1928, pp. 309-29.

PATERSON, GILBERT, "Land Settlement in Upper Canada", Department of Archives, Ontario, *Report, 1920*, Toronto, 1921.

SKELTON, O. D., *Life and Times of Sir A. T. Galt*, Toronto, 1920.

5

Trade Relationships
to Confederation

ONE of the most important factors in the economic
history of Canada has been her trading relationships with other countries, especially with Great
Britain and the United States. Under the principles of
mercantilism, trade between the Canadian Provinces and
the American Republic was forbidden but smuggling was
wide-spread until, in 1822, the old regulations prohibiting
direct trade between British colonies and foreign countries
were, for all practical purposes, repealed. Nevertheless,
the volume of such trade remained small, at least until
after 1835, because of the similarity in the chief products
of the two areas. In the early period, therefore, Canada's
most important trade relationship was with Great Britain.

The significant factor in Anglo-Canadian trade was the
tariff preference which Britain gave colonial products, of
which the two most important for Canada were lumber
and wheat. On the former product the tariff preference
was as much as eighty or ninety per cent, that is, the
duty on timber from Canada was only one-fifth or even
one-twelfth the duty on Baltic and other foreign timber.
On wheat, the preference also varied but, from 1825 to
1843, the rate on Canadian grain was about one-quarter
of that paid on the foreign product. In 1836 the legislature of Upper Canada requested the abolition of the tariff
against Canadian grain. This request was ostensibly
granted in 1843 when Britain began to admit Canadian
grain at a nominal duty while retaining the existing rates

on foreign grain. Moreover, it was decided that flour
made in Canada from grain grown in the United States
would be admitted at the colonial preferential rate.
Apparently the preference on Canadian grain had been
extended by the Imperial Government.

The effect on Canada of these preferences was to expand
output of the articles, especially wheat. New agricultural
areas were opened up, particularly in Upper Canada, and
previously settled regions tended to shift rapidly from
self-sufficiency to staple production. Reasonably good
times in Canada coupled with poor crops throughout most
of Europe and a failure of the potato crop in Ireland
in both 1845 and 1846, encouraged immigration. Most
important of all, flour milling was stimulated especially
along the St. Lawrence River just above Montreal where
water-power was readily available, and American grain
could be easily secured for milling in Canada and exportation under the preference.

Finally, the preference and the accompanying prosperity encouraged canalization of the St. Lawrence River.
The stimulus toward improvement of the River came
largely from the outstanding success of the Erie Canal,
the construction of which, in 1825, from Albany to
Buffalo and Rochester, had provided a water route between New York and Lakes Erie and Ontario. The canal
had completely paid for itself within nine years, had
brought prosperity to the cities along its banks, and
had drawn to New York the enormous and rapidly expanding traffic of the Lower Lakes region. Montreal was
anxious to emulate New York. It considered that along
the St. Lawrence was a route superior to the Erie Canal.
The former was more direct, provided a shorter voyage
from the Lakes region to Europe, and, except for a few

rapids, had a channel that was deep enough for ships, whereas the Erie could handle only barges of a draught of not more than four feet. All that seemed to be required along the St. Lawrence in order to duplicate, if not to exceed, the prosperity brought by the Erie Canal was the construction of a series of relatively short canals around the rapids. These canals had been started earlier, but the prosperity of the 1840's speeded up the programme, and encouraged the government of the colony to borrow large sums of money to complete the entire scheme. In short, as far as Canada was concerned, the existence of the preference by Britain, and particularly its apparent extension in 1843, was regarded as an effort to help the colonists, encourage immigration and bring traffic to the new canals.

In Britain, on the other hand, the modifications in the preference were looked at in a different light. They were considered as a step in the direction of free trade. The mercantilism of the previous centuries was being abandoned in the face of new economic theories and new industrial conditions. Adam Smith, in his famous "Wealth of Nations" (1776), had set forth the theoretical shortcomings of mercantilism. The vital matter for a nation is not its stock of gold and silver, but the volume of goods and services available for distribution among its people. A country is prosperous when goods are plentiful and cheap. If it can get goods more cheaply by importing them than by producing them at home, it should do so. To follow the contrary policy, that is to stimulate production at home by means of tariffs or subsidies, increases costs and lowers the standard of living. Then too, the so-called "favourable" balance of trade is illogical, for it considers only the values of physical goods and ignores the value of services such as those rendered by the merchant marine and by investors. At all events it is impossible for all countries to have favourable balances at the same time.

These theoretical considerations regarding mercantilism were supplemented by practical factors. As it had developed through the centuries, mercantilism had come to mean a maze of petty restrictions on trade. These regulations were annoying to the new, ambitious business men, and their enforcement required a group of inspectors and other officials whose salaries were a burdensome expense to private enterprise. Commercial leaders wished to discard these outmoded and expensive restraints. Also, by the 1840's, the full force of the Industrial Revolution was being felt in England where it had started a century before. The commercial and industrial leaders in Britain were confident that they were now so far in advance of other countries that even if tariffs were abolished, they could meet any competition from abroad. But they could do so only if they had low-priced raw materials and if their workmen could obtain cheap food and low living costs. This involved abolishing the customs duties on lumber and other basic materials, and particularly on wheat, or corn as it is known in England. Business leaders hoped too, that by abolishing her own tariffs Britain would encourage other countries to do the same, and thus goods manufactured in Britain could be more easily sold abroad. Accordingly, British industrialists, anxious to get rid of petty restrictions and officials, confident of their own ability and hopeful of the future, supported the agitation for the abolition of the Corn Laws and the repeal of other mercantilistic legislation. Theory and practice worked together to modify the tariff on grain in 1843, to repeal the Corn Laws by 1849, and to whittle away and finally to abolish entirely the tariffs on timber and on all other commodities whatsoever.

Of course it was realized that the adoption of free trade might work to the detriment of the colonies, but this was not much of a deterrent. The prevailing idea was that "colonies have, without exception, been a cause rather of weakness than of strength to their respective Mother Countries". In any event, as soon as they became sufficiently strong they would revolt and become independent as the Thirteen Colonies along the Atlantic coast had done. Such a separation would not be particularly regretted in the home land, for the latter would be relieved of the very considerable expense of defending the colonies. In addition, trade between colony and parent might increase with political separation, as had happened with the United States. There were, indeed, some in Britain who felt that a special effort should be made to retain the political allegiance of the overseas Empire, but the common attitude was that national policies should be determined without too much regard to colonial aspirations. If the colonies were going to break away, the sooner the better.

To sum up, the underlying attitudes toward the tariff reduction of 1843 were entirely different in Canada and in Britain. In the colony they were looked upon with great expectations; in the mother country they were considered as part of a movement toward eventual free trade. It was only in 1846, when tariffs against foreign grains began to be slowly abolished, that the British attitude came to be appreciated in Canada. The complete abolition of the preferences three years later brought consternation to the colony. The expansion of agriculture, the investment in flour mills, the expenditure on the canals—all these were rendered worthless by what appeared to be a purely arbitrary action on the part of people whom the colonists had regarded as friends.

The plain fact of the matter was that even before the abolition of the preference, the St. Lawrence canals were failing to realize the expectations of their promoters. Ocean freight rates to Liverpool were higher from Montreal than they were from New York because of narrow waters in the River, the presence of fog in the Gulf, and thus the longer sailing time involved in spite of the shorter distance. Also, in 1845-46 the American Government made it possible, without the payment of duty, to ship grain from Canada across the United States to New York for export, that is, they gave Canadian grain the "bonding privilege". Thus, instead of American grain going to Britain by way of the St. Lawrence as had been hoped, Canadian grain was going to Liverpool via the Erie Canal. This was true even with the British preference. After its abolition the movement increased rapidly. Montreal was unable to compete successfully with New York. The reasons for its failure were chiefly economic, but they became apparent only about the time the preference was abolished. Consequently the discontent was directed against the political change, and resulted in the strongest resentment by Montreal business interests against Great Britain. Incidentally, the animosity of the trading group, most of whom were English-speaking, against Britain was greatly aggravated by the passage of the Rebellion Losses Bill which appeared to many of the merchants to be a bonus to "rebels".

This discontent found expression in the Annexation Manifesto of 1849, a document signed by nearly 1000 merchants and other prominent citizens of Montreal. It declared that, "the reversal of the ancient policy of Great

Britain, whereby she withdrew from the colonies their wonted protection in her markets, has produced the most disastrous effects upon Canada—unprosperous agriculture, real estate scarcely saleable upon any terms, rivers and canals unused, no manufacturing, few railways and so on. Our country stands before the world in humiliating contrast with its immediate neighbour, exhibiting every symptom of a nation fast sinking to decay". Accordingly it advocated "friendly and peaceful separation from the British connection and a union upon equitable terms with the great North American confederacy of sovereign states". The Manifesto went on to point a glowing picture of the prosperity which would result from such a union.

The Manifesto fell like a bomb-shell on political thought in Canada but failed to find any significant support outside Montreal where the depression was most severe. Almost all the English-speaking people in other parts of the country refused to sever the British connection. The French-speaking citizens generally held aloof. The church in Quebec opposed. Britain refused to give her consent to peaceful separation. A few Americans appeared so greedy to gobble up Canada that even some of the Annexationists appeared frightened of their own audacity. The remainder of the Annexationists changed their views when business revived, as it did in the early 'fifties with the construction of railways. In other words, business was good again when capital investment recovered, after having temporarily declined due to the cessation of constructing canals and flour mills. Another cause of business recovery was that the great length and durability of Canadian white pine enabled timber to retain a good share of the British market even without the preference. As one commentator has stated, "The movement had derived its vitality to a great extent from economic distress and did not long survive the return of prosperity".

Although the Manifesto was a fiasco in so far as it related to political union with the United States, it did have an effect on the economic relationships between the two countries. As already pointed out, trade, especially in grain and lumber, had developed across the border after 1835. In 1848 the United States imposed a duty on Canadian wheat and raised the tariff on lumber. These increases were serious to a country which was losing its preferences in Britain, and naturally the Canadian farmer and lumberman wanted them removed. In addition, Montreal merchants desired to bring more traffic down the St. Lawrence and the Colonial Government supported them in this attitude, for more traffic through the canals meant more government revenue from tolls. For these reasons Canada was exceedingly anxious to enter into a trade agreement with the United States.

Unfortunately, the Republic was uninterested. Canada could offer the United States several privileges namely, ready access to her markets, use of the St. Lawrence route on the same terms as Canadians, cheaper grain and lumber if the United States abolished her tariff on these articles, and the right to fish in Canadian, or more accurately, Maritime territorial waters. On the other hand, the United States was still chiefly an agricultural country and saw little to be gained from the small Canadian market. Few Americans were concerned with the St. Lawrence route because the Erie Canal and the expanding railways provided cheaper channels for trade. Only the South which grew cotton and imported food and feed was attracted by the prospect of cheaper farm products, a feature to which Northern farmers were definitely opposed. Americans were greatly interested in securing fishing rights in Canadian territorial waters for, by 1850, their own coasts had been fairly well "fished out". Nevertheless, on the whole, Americans felt that their gains from any agreement would be small in comparison with what Canadians would secure. On the general principle of protection versus free trade, the Northern States had been trying intermittently for at least thirty years to secure higher tariffs. To be sure the South, being dependent on foreign markets for its single staple and on the importation of manufactured goods from Britain, was fundamentally sympathetic to free trade. However, as the number of representatives of each section almost exactly balanced each other in Congress, it was tacitly agreed not to introduce any important tariff changes.

In view of specific objection in the United States to a treaty with the British North American colonies and the general hesitancy to adopt anything which might disturb the delicate compromise between the States, it is not surprising that Canadian efforts to arrive at a trade treaty proved unavailing. British statesmen, especially the Ambassador to Washington and the Governor-in-chief, Lord Elgin (1847-54), made several attempts to arrive at an agreement. At last in 1854 Lord Elgin, ably assisted by his secretary, Lawrence Oliphant, and by paid lobbyists, successfully negotiated a treaty largely through his own personal charm. As he himself said "The treaty was floated in on champagne".

The terms of the treaty were simple. A large number of goods including nearly all the products of the farm, forest, mine and sea, that is, the so-called natural products, could be sent by either country to the other duty free. United States fishermen could use Maritime coastal waters and come ashore to dry their nets or cure their catch. American vessels could use the St. Lawrence canals on payment of precisely the same fees as Canadian vessels, and in return Canadian ships were free to use Lake Michigan which is the only one of the Great Lakes wholly within the United States. The Treaty applied between the United States and all the eastern British colonies in North America, that is, to New Brunswick, Nova Scotia, Prince Edward Island and Newfoundland, as well as to Upper and Lower Canada but not to Vancouver Island, probably because it was too far away and unimportant. The Treaty was to remain in force for ten years and thereafter could be terminated by either party after one year's notice to the other.

Reciprocity came; so did prosperity. To some extent the first was the cause of the second. Although a few American farm products, especially tobacco which had previously been "home-grown" in Ontario, came to Canada most of the basic commodities moved southward—wheat, barley, wool and timber from the St. Lawrence Valley and coal, lumber and fish from the Maritimes to New England. This new market was of great value to farming, lumbering and fishing interests. The effort to bring traffic along the St. Lawrence canals almost completely failed although the Welland canal was used a good deal by American vessels. Even the virtual abolition of canal tolls on both American and Canadian vessels using the St. Lawrence failed to offset the advantages of New York over Montreal. Maritime territorial waters were used to a considerable extent by American fishermen.

But prosperity after 1854 was due to other factors besides reciprocity. The Crimean War (1854-56) kept Russian grain and timber out of Western Europe and helped Canadian producers of these articles. Later, the Civil War (1863-66) in the United States also enlarged the market. Both Canada and the United States were busy building railways during the 1850's and 1860's and their construction created a demand for food, horses, lumber and a few manufactured goods which Canada could supply. Also, after the discoveries of gold in California and in Australia, prices began to rise and rising commodity prices always create a feeling of prosperity. In short, a number of elements in addition to the Treaty itself caused prosperous conditions after 1854.

In 1866 the Reciprocity Treaty was abrogated by the United States, after notice had been given in the previous year. Most Americans felt that Canada was getting more benefits than they were, and a few doubtless hoped that Canada might ask to be annexed if reciprocity were suddenly withdrawn. From both sides there were charges of bad faith. When Canada increased her tariff on manufactured goods in 1858-59, the United States contended that this was contrary to the spirit of the Treaty which had assumed that rates on manufactured goods would remain unchanged. Canada replied that the Treaty applied only to natural products and that she was free to vary the tariff on manufactured goods if she wished. The United States protested when Canada partially removed canal tolls along the St. Lawrence, contending that this removal favoured the St. Lawrence route over the Erie Canal, whereas the Treaty required similar position to Canadian and American vessels. Canada's position was that the proper interpretation was equality of treatment along any one route not necessarily between routes. On her part, Canada charged that the United States defined natural products too narrowly and that she was levying duties on articles, timber for example, on the ground that they were manufactured when in reality they were not and should have been admitted free. The vagueness of some of the terms of the Treaty was a cause of friction between the two countries.

A final cause of abrogation was the apparent sympathy of Great Britain for the Southern States during the American Civil War. As a matter of fact, British feeling originally strongly favoured the North and several thousand Canadians had fought in the Northern armies. Toward the end of the war, however, there was a reversal of sentiment, for it appeared to many people in Britain that the war was being fought not on the high moral principle of anti-slavery, but on the basis of annihilation of the noble and cultured whites of the South. On the other hand, the Americans accused Canada of allowing Quebec to be used as a basis of attack on Vermont by Southern sympathizers. In any event the industrial and commercial Northern States were now in control of the American Government. They completely submerged the South whose political influence for years previously had almost exactly balanced that of the North in Washington, and which had supported the adoption of the Treaty. The North had little to gain from this particular treaty and was opposed to free trade on general principles. For numerous reasons, therefore, the United States abrogated the Treaty. Canada made repeated efforts to have the decision re-considered, for the loss of the American market was serious. All attempts being in vain, the provinces were compelled to adopt an entirely different approach to their problems,—the building up of a market within Canada itself.

Meanwhile the provinces of Upper and Lower Canada were considering their tariff policy on manufactured goods. Up until 1846, tariffs for the colonies had been framed in Britain in accordance with the principles of mercantilism. With the wiping away of the mercantilistic system and the granting of responsible government to the Canadian colonies, the provincial legislatures were given the power to make their own tariffs. The tariff adopted by Canada was a low one designed mainly to yield revenue to carry on the government. There was almost no protection, that is, no tariffs aimed at keeping out foreign goods and encouraging manufacture in Canada. In 1858 William Cayley, who was the cabinet minister in charge of finance, raised the rates and in 1859 his successor, Sir Alexander T. Galt, increased them still further. Galt denied any intention of adopting a high protective tariff like the United States. His hope was to encourage Canadian production by providing manufacturers with cheap raw materials and machinery. "The policy of the present Government in readjusting the tariff has been to obtain sufficient revenue for public need . . . [but] it will undoubtedly be a subject of gratification to the Government if they find that the duties, absolutely required to meet their engagements, should incidentally benefit and encourage the production in this country of many of those article which we now import". Notwithstanding Galt's protestations of a revenue tariff only, the tariff was distinctly protectionist in intent, though the rates were still low and the number of articles protected was small. Limited protection was adopted in order to aid the slowly developing Canadian factories and protect them against the larger, lower-cost establishments in the United States. The term "incidental protection" was adopted partly to mollify Canadian free trade sentiment, and mainly to placate feeling in Great Britain.

It will be recalled that by this time Britain was a

free trade country. Indeed free trade was a kind of gospel. Yet here was one of Britain's own colonies not merely adopting a tariff, but applying it against the goods of Britain herself. Hence it is not surprising that British manufacturers protested to the Colonial Government. Galt's reply was to affirm in unmistakable terms the right of a colonial government to formulate a tariff policy to suit its own needs even though this might, unfortunately, not meet with the approval of British manufacturers, nor even of the Imperial Government. Galt argued that unless a tariff with fairly high rates was adopted, Canada would lack the revenue to pay the interest on the money borrowed from Great Britain and invested in canals. Britain, therefore, had to choose between a tariff against her goods and no interest payments on her loans. Since Galt's famous reply Canada has been free to adopt her own tariff without official interference by the Imperial Government.

In 1866, in order to facilitate the adoption of Confederation, Upper and Lower Canada reduced their tariff slightly in order to bring it into line with the lower rates of New Brunswick and Nova Scotia. The position in 1867, then, was a low tariff mainly for revenue purposes but with some moderate protective features. In spite of their importance in previous years, there were no tariff preferences on Canadian goods by either Great Britain or the United States.

SELECTED READINGS

CREIGHTON, D. G., *The Commercial Empire of the St. Lawrence, 1760-1850*, Toronto, 1937.

INNIS, H. A. and LOWER, A. R. M., ed., *Select Documents*, Toronto, 1933, pp. 315-59.

INNIS, M. Q., *An Economic History of Canada*, pp. 109-112, 155-160.

HEATON, H., *The Story of Trade and Commerce, with special reference to Canada*, Toronto, 1955 (rev.) pp. 219-25.

MASTERS, D. C., *The Reciprocity Treaty of 1854*, Toronto, 1937.

MCDIARMID, O. J., *Commercial Policy in the Canadian Economy*, Cambridge, Mass., 1946.

TUCKER, G. N., *The Canadian Commercial Revolution, 1845-51*, New Haven, 1936.

6

Transportation
to Confederation

GOOD transportation is a prime necessity to all
pioneer communities. It is essential in order that
settlers and manufactured goods be brought in,
and that staple products be sent out, and in order that
contact generally be maintained with the mother country.
Within the colony itself good transportation is required so
that business, political and cultural ties may be sustained
between the various regions.

The early contacts with Britain were made, of course,
by sailing vessels. Because wind was an uncertain form
of motive power, the trip was slow and arduous under
the best of conditions but the ice, fog and narrow con-
strictions of the St. Lawrence made it exceptionally so.
Dependence on the vagaries of wind and current as far as
lake, river and coastal traffic were concerned, was relieved
by the invention of the steamship in 1807 by Robert Fulton, an American. It was impractical, however, to use
steam across the Atlantic, because the early engines were
so wasteful of fuel that the small ships of the time could
not carry enough fuel for the voyage and still have much
room left for paying cargo. Moreover, the paddle wheels
which the engine operated were easily damaged and were
almost useless in heavy seas. Accordingly steam was used
only when the winds failed, although in 1833 the *Royal
William*, a vessel built at Quebec for a group of Halifax
and Quebec merchants, crossed the Atlantic using steam
as well as sails for the entire distance.

One of the owners of the *Royal William* was Samuel Cunard, a Quaker of Loyalist descent, an alert merchant who had an exceptional capacity for getting other people to work with him. In 1839, with the help of Scottish capitalists, he organized a company to operate steamships across the Atlantic and was able to get an annual subsidy of 60,000 pounds sterling from the British Government to carry mail from Liverpool to Halifax, and thence to Boston. Cunard's vessels cut the time for the crossing from about seven weeks to a little over two and provided weekly service. Because they were expensive to operate, the ships of the Cunard line carried only the traffic which could afford to pay high rates, such as mail, package freight and first-class passengers. Meanwhile sailing vessels continued to handle almost all the ordinary freight both import and export, and the immigrants. The use of iron hulls, screw propellers, and other improvements in steamships reduced their operating costs and after 1860, they rapidly displaced sailing vessels in the trans-Atlantic service. Steamships brought the Canadian provinces nearer to the mother country both in point of time and money, but an important Canadian industry, shipbuilding in the Maritimes, was virtually destroyed.

Within the colony itself almost all the early transportation was by canoe, except in the Maritimes where sailing vessels connected the settlements along the coast. The canoe had the advantage of being made out of local raw materials and of being easily repaired in case of damage. It was a satisfactory means for carrying furs and other articles which could be fairly easily portaged around falls and rapids. On the other hand, it was not so advantageous for handling wheat and other bulk produce. This difficulty was partially overcome by the long, narrow bateau made of pine or cedar, and after about 1810, by

the Durham boat, which was of the same general type
but which had a capacity of about 35 tons of merchandise,
over seven times that of the bateau.

On the lakes, sailing vessels were used even as early as
La Salle's *Griffin* in 1679. Long before the War of 1812,
British sailing ships were operating along Lakes Ontario
and Erie, connecting the scattered settlements and handling supplies. They were also, of course, used on the
St. Lawrence from Montreal to Quebec where connections
were made with the trans-Atlantic vessels. Sailing vessels could not use the St. Lawrence from Prescott to
Montreal because of the existence of rapids and hence,
bateaux or canoes were the common means of transportation there. For the same reason the Ottawa remained a
canoe river. It provided a short route for the fur trade
with the Upper Lakes until, with the amalgamation of
the North-West Company and the Hudson's Bay Company,
all the fur traffic was transferred to the route through
Hudson Bay, and the Ottawa was left for lumber alone.

The development of steamships opened up new possibilities for transportation along the inland water-ways. In
1809, only two years after Fulton's successful trip, Montreal merchants built the *Accomodation*, a ship whose six
horse-power steam engine carried it from Montreal to
Quebec, 180 miles, in three days instead of the fifteen
or sixteen commonly taken by sailing vessels. The quick-
ness with which the new transportation medium was
seized upon by the colonists was indicative not merely of
the urgent need for better transport, but also of the alert-
ness of Canadians to developments in the rest of the
world. As it happened, the new steamship was not financially profitable so was replaced by the *Swiftsure* which
had a twenty-eight horse-power Boulton and Watt engine.
The success of the latter vessel led to a rapid increase

in the number of steamships on the lower St. Lawrence. Quebec City remained the chief terminus of trans-Atlantic trade which was still handled almost entirely by sail. In order to offset the disadvantages of their location, Montreal business men built tug boats to bring sailing vessels up the river instead of having them wait for favourable winds. The first steamship on the Great Lakes was constructed in 1816, and operated along Lake Ontario and sixty miles down the river to Prescott where its progress was stopped by rapids. Steamships also plied on Lake Erie.

The operation of steamships in the St. Lawrence Valley region was hampered by ice (which could not be overcome), by the falls of Niagara, by rapids along the St. Lawrence River between Prescott and Montreal, and by various obstructions on the Ottawa River and the lower St. Lawrence between Montreal and Quebec. The colonists were exceedingly anxious that these handicaps be overcome, for they wished easier and cheaper means to get out their products and bring in supplies and new settlers. Also merchants in Montreal, ambitious for their own prosperity, wanted to draw through their city all the traffic of the Lake region in both Canada and the United States. In addition, their future had been challenged and their envy stirred by the great success of the Erie Canal from Buffalo, on Lake Erie, to Albany, at the head of navigation on the Hudson River north of New York city. Furthermore, the governing classes were concerned with better transport as the War of 1812, and later the Rebellion of 1837, had emphasized the need of better communication from the standpoint of defence. Finally the mania for constructing canals in England stimulated development in Canada.

The construction of canals to get around the numerous

rapids along the St. Lawrence had begun on a small scale under the French regime, but had been neglected under British rule. The early plans were revived in the 1820's and entirely new proposals were made. The most ambitious of these was that of William Hamilton Merritt, for constructing the Welland Canal to connect Lake Erie and Lake Ontario, thus avoiding the falls of Niagara. Merritt was public-spirited, energetic, optimistic and so resolute that, in spite of continued financial reverses, the Welland was dug to a depth of eight feet in 1833. Meanwhile the Rideau Canal connecting Kingston with Ottawa (then called Bytown) was completed by the Royal Engineers. This canal, which enabled vessels to go from Montreal through Bytown to Kingston, was built at the expense of the British Government in order to provide a safer route than the St. Lawrence in case of war. Though constructed for military purposes, it opened up important areas in Lanark and Carleton counties to settlement and gave a useful outlet for trade. While these two canals were being built, several more along the St. Lawrence between Prescott and Montreal were also started though they were not finished until later.

A description of the individual canals would be tedious and, in fact, misleading because the development must be viewed as a unit. The fundamental objective of the entire project was to draw traffic from the west down the St. Lawrence and away from New York. The financing of construction was undertaken by the Government because the attempt to complete one canal, the Welland, under private auspices had failed. Also, the investors in England, though skeptical of the safety of investment in the colonies, were more prepared to loan to governments than to individuals. The unit, the entire project for the improvement of navigation in the St. Lawrence Valley, was completed in 1848 so that a boat drawing not more than eight feet of water could avoid the rapids on the St. Lawrence and the falls of Niagara. After 1855, by the use of an American canal at Sault Ste. Marie, the falls of St. Mary's River could be circumnavigated as well. In other words, traffic could go by way of lakes, rivers and canals from Chicago and Fort William to Montreal.

Unfortunately, this new navigation system was not a success. As already pointed out, its failure, coupled with the loss of the British preference, led to the Annexation Manifesto in 1849. Even when business prosperity revived in the early 1850's, the St. Lawrence canals still failed to draw the expected amount of traffic to Montreal. This situation continued in spite of the deepening of the Welland canal to ten feet, and the reduction of canal tolls in 1860. To be sure the total volume of traffic increased greatly over what it had been in previous years but, in comparison with the great increase in settlement in Ontario and in the United States south of the Great Lakes, the St. Lawrence canals failed to justify the expenditure made on them. The pull of the Erie Canal and of New York City was still too powerful for Montreal. Furthermore, the increasing use of steamships which had deeper draughts than sailing vessels reduced traffic through both canal systems, and involved the transshipment of cargo at Buffalo and Kingston from lake steamships to shallow canal vessels or barges. Finally the advent of steam railways caused a relative decline in the volume of traffic borne through the canals.

As far as land transportation was concerned, the necessity for good transportation confined early settlement to the shores of the rivers and lakes along which communication was alone possible. This was true under both French and British rule. Of course as soon as population

108 Canadian Economic Development

increased so that it could not readily be accommodated along the rivers, settlement was pushed back from the water front and roads were needed. Under the French regime these were supposed to be provided by the seignior. Similarly in Upper Canada under British rule each landowner was responsible for the road in front of his land. Due to laziness or carelessness, many settlers neglected their responsibilities. Also the existence of the Clergy Reserves and of land held by speculators made it almost impossible to maintain a continuous road of even fair quality.

Since the ordinary roads were so poor, the Government itself had to build roads with the object of facilitating the administration of justice and defending the country against attack. The more important of these roads were those north from Toronto (Yonge Street), across Upper Canada from west to east (Dundas Street and Kingston Road), in the Eastern Townships (Craig's Road), while the existing route from Montreal to Quebec was improved. Some leaders of settlement, notably Colonel Talbot, also built roads. In later years municipalities, formed on an extensive scale only after 1841, began to assume responsibilities for what passed for highways. A few turnpikes, that is roads built by private individuals who hoped to make a profit out of the tolls they collected for their use, were also constructed. The public disliked the toll roads very much and eventually they were bought out by the municipalities. At all events, facilities for overland transportation were slowly provided.

The roads—they can scarcely be called highways— were thoroughly poor, judged by modern standards. They were built by throwing earth from the sides in toward the centre. Over swampy ground, the road was built by laying logs or tree tops close together and covering them with a thin layer of earth. In wet weather such roads were quagmires, and in dry weather they were dusty and incredibly rough, especially since the heavy waggons and carriages lacked springs. In time the use of stone and gravel and the adoption of proper drainage improved the roads, but long after Confederation they remained "some poor, others worse". Nevertheless, they performed an essential function, for they provided the only means by which people and goods could reach the real highways which were the rivers and lakes or, later on, the railways.

In addition to water-ways and roads, after 1850 transportation was provided by railways. The news of the successful application of steam to land transportation was received with great enthusiasm in Canada. Many lines were projected, but by 1850 there were only sixty-six miles of completed railway in Canada compared with over 10,000 miles in the United States. The main reason for the backwardness of Canada was lack of money. Private interests found it difficult to raise funds in England for investment in a pioneer community. The Government was already heavily obligated to build canals and, in any case, Lower Canada would have objected to further increases in the public debt since the new railways were planned mainly in the Upper Province. The few lines which were completed were designed either to shorten the distance between water-ways or circumvent rapids. The railways were purely ancillary to the water routes.

After 1850 there was a rapid increase in construction. In 1854 the Great Western was completed between the Niagara and Detroit river frontiers, giving a direct connection between Michigan and the lines to New York City. The most ambitious project was the Grand Trunk. Started in 1852, it reached from Portland, Maine, through Montreal and Toronto to Sarnia by 1859 and to Chicago by 1879. In the meantime a number of other lines were constructed in both Upper and Lower Canada. The purpose of these lines was different from those finished before 1850. They were built partly to tap farming and lumbering communities in Canada, and mainly for the same reason as the St. Lawrence canals, namely, to draw traffic of the Western States through Montreal. The change in motive indicated a shift of emphasis from water-ways to railways as the fundamental transportation medium of the country.

The new railways were built by private investors in England whose earlier attitude towards Canada had reversed itself. The investor was converted on account of the general feeling of optimism at this time, the financial success of railways in England, and the extravagant promises of profits in Canada. These railways got some assistance from the Provincial Government and from the municipalities. Some of the latter were so anxious to get transportation facilities that they gave bonuses beyond all reasonable limits. For example, one town of 9000 people borrowed one and one-quarter million dollars to assist a railway and soon it was $625,000 in arrears on interest alone. Eventually, these municipal debts had to be taken over by the Province. Notwithstanding a few instances of extravagant aid, most of the capital was supplied by private investors.

Unfortunately, the Grand Trunk and the other railways built during this period were financial failures. The systems were constructed by English engineers unacquainted with traffic and climatic conditions in Canada. Railway practice in the United States was to build lines economically, throw them down in the cheapest possible manner and then improve them by re-investing the profits of an increasing volume of traffic. British practice, on the other hand, was to construct thoroughly. In comparison with the American scheme, this method involved low operating costs and high total payments for interest. This interest could be carried only if the traffic volume were large, thus making the amount of interest borne by any one unit of traffic small. If the estimate of traffic volume failed to materialize, as was the case with the Grand Trunk, interest on the bonds and dividends on the stock could not be paid and the investor lost heavily.

Even had the theory been suitable to Canadian conditions, its application was faulty. From an engineering standpoint the Grand Trunk was poorly built. The curves were sharp, the ballast inadequate and the rails cracked under the frost. The line was improperly located because it missed most of the towns, and spur lines had to be constructed to them. The gauge was wider than the standard American one and hence, inter-change traffic with American lines had to be moved from one type of car to another until in 1872-74, at huge expense, the Grand Trunk narrowed its gauge.

In view of all these factors it is not surprising that the road lost money. The Provincial Government advanced funds in 1856 to enable construction to be completed, but refused to lend to meet operating deficits. When bond interest was defaulted, the road was reorganized in 1862 with the original bonds becoming preferred stock and new bonds being sold. In the next few years the Grand Trunk had to struggle hard to prevent a second reorganization. Thus in the period just before Confederation, Canada experienced her first railway problem. It is to be noted, too, that the attempt to capture traffic from the American Middle West was, on the whole, a failure with railways as it had been with canals. To realize that transportation systems must rely mainly on local traffic within Canada was a hard lesson to learn.

Meanwhile the Maritimes were trying to construct railways, though the need for them was less great because of year-round water communication. The leading project was a line from St. Andrew's, then a busy seaport, to Quebec with the double object of serving the needs of defence and trade. The scheme failed mainly because the award to the United States of disputed territory between Maine and New Brunswick interfered with the proposed route. An effort was made in the early 1850's to build a line through New Brunswick to Portland, Maine, where it was planned to connect with Canadian and American systems. This scheme failed due to lack of capital. By 1867 New Brunswick and Nova Scotia together had less than 350 miles of railway, all of it serving local regions.

The construction of canals and railways had a significant effect on the future development of Canada. Most of the canals were built by the Government with funds borrowed in Britain. In the early 'fifties the Government added to its liabilities by guaranteeing the bond issues of railways, thus making it possible for the railway companies to borrow on favourable terms. In addition, it loaned to municipalities, most of whom borrowed to assist railways. Altogether, by 1861 the Province of Canada had an outstanding debt of sixty-six million dollars, a heavy burden for a population of about two and a half million, with a tax base much smaller than it is today.

In order to meet the interest on this debt more revenue was necessary. Every pioneer objects to direct taxation. He feels that life is hard enough without having to pay taxes to the government. Hence taxes have to be indirect, hidden so that the settler pays them without realizing it. The customs tariff is such a tax. Moreover, improvements in navigation, undertaken largely at Government expense, had reduced transportation costs, lowered the price of imported goods and thus saved Canadian consumers money. Since it was investment by the Government that had made the saving possible, it was only proper that part of this saving should be appropriated by the Government in the shape of higher custom duties. Thus expenditures on canals were one of the factors leading to higher tariffs, as Galt pointed out in introducing "incidental protection" into the Legislative Assembly.

In spite of the increases in customs duties, Government expenditures on canals and railways grew at a faster rate than did revenue even in good years. The result was that more money had to be borrowed until, by 1866, the debt of the Province of Canada had risen to seventy-seven million dollars. In the same year the taxing capacity of the Government declined, due to the contraction of business following the abrogation of the Reciprocity Treaty. The financial pressure upon the Province was very great and was temporarily relieved by Confederation.

Improvements in transportation had other important effects besides those on tariff policy and public finance. They reduced transportation costs, and enabled Canadian producers to sell wheat and other agricultural products in Britain in competition with other countries. They broke down the local self-sufficiency, and brought more and more communities from the use of barter to the use of money as a means of carrying on business. Because people became more dependent on export markets, they became more subject to the fluctuations of the business cycle. Railway and canal construction proceeded irregularly, and the alternate building and cessation of build-

ing created waves of prosperity and depression. Despite
the fact that railways accentuated business fluctuations,
the need for railways, particularly for a railway between
the St. Lawrence Valley and the Atlantic coast, remained
great. The inability of the provinces individually to
finance new roads or pay the debts on the old, was a
strong incentive for Confederation. Finally, better and
cheaper travel and communication tended to break down
parochialism in thought and to lay the basis for a
national instead of a provincial point of view.

SELECTED READINGS

AITKEN, H. G. J., *The Welland Canal Company: A study in Canadian Enterprise*, Cambridge, Mass., 1954.

CURRIE, A. W., *The Grand Trunk Railway of Canada*, Toronto, 1957.

GLAZEBROOK, G. de T., *A History of Transportation in Canada*, Toronto, 1938, pp. 1-187.

INNIS, H. A. and LOWER, A. R. M., ed., *Select Documents*, Toronto, 1933, pp. 133-216.

INNIS, M. Q., *An Economic History of Canada*, Toronto, 1954, pp. 100-08, 148-50.

McLEAN, S. J., "National highways overland", in Shortt, Adam and Doughty, A. G., ed., *Canada and its Provinces*, vol. X., pp. 359-472.

SKELTON, O. D., "The railway builders", in Wrong, G. M. and Langton, H. H., ed., *Chronicles of Canada*, Toronto, 1916, vol. IX.

7

Economic Aspects
of Confederation

THE preceding pages have dealt with Canadian economic history up to Confederation. That date was selected as a dividing point because of its political importance and because the 'sixties mark a turning point in economic development also. Heretofore each colony had existed as a distinct unit having relatively little contact with its neighbours. Now, for almost the first time, the colonies became conscious of certain features which they had in common, of certain forces which operated on all of them alike. Realizing their economic coherence, they saw the need for political union, for a central government which could satisfactorily deal with their common problems.

What were the common problems? First, the colonies had lost their special rights in both the British and the American markets. The abolition of the preference had cut out the first; the abrogation of reciprocity had shattered the second. Since markets abroad had disappeared, it was necessary to develop them at home by constructing railways between the colonies, by opening up the West and, perhaps, by reserving the Canadian market to domestic manufacturers.

Second, the colonies would have to erect military and economic defences against the United States. The army of that country, flushed with success in the Civil War, might be turned northward. The Fenians, a group of fiery Irish nationalists who conceived the strange idea of annoying England by attacking Canada, were using the United States as a base and the American Government was making little real effort to prevent them. Economically, the United States was slowly pulling the prairie region of the Hudson's Bay Company into its orbit. Instead of Canadian canals and railways capturing the traffic of the American mid-west as had been expected, the United States held on to this business and even drew traffic from Upper Canada along the Erie Canal. Finally, American farms and cities were attracting across the border new immigrants and native sons from all parts of Canada. Against the danger of military and economic absorption, the colonies would have to unite to protect themselves.

Third, more railways were required. A line was needed to connect the Maritimes and the St. Lawrence Valley, thus giving one region a larger market for its fish, and the other an ice-free seaport in British territory. A railway would eventually be needed also to connect both these regions with the struggling settlements on the Plains and on the far distant Pacific. Efforts to build the former line had failed and even the railways and canals already constructed were failures financially. In transportation, the colonies faced a common problem and only common action could solve it.

Next, the scattered colonies felt a common, and indeed an inevitable destiny, to develop the western plains. This region was still mainly in the hands of the fur trading Hudson's Bay Company. Its agricultural possibilities were largely neglected. It was in danger of being economically and eventually politically absorbed by the United States. To develop the region and preserve it within the British connection, the colonies must unite, because individually their resources were inadequate for the task.

Fifth, the provinces were going through industrial changes. The iron steamship was destroying the wooden ship-building industry of the Maritimes. The railways in the St. Lawrence Valley were robbing the river and lake boats of their traffic and rendering the investment in canals obsolete. In manufacturing, new methods of production, methods associated with the term Industrial Revolution, were being introduced displacing the old domestic industries. The self-sufficiency of agricultural communities was disappearing, and a new market for manufactured goods was available to Canadians provided they would take advantage of it. Decaying industries looked for succour in political change, and new industries looked forward to the prosperity which an inter-provincial market would bring.

Furthermore, the resources of the colonies were complementary. The advocates of union felt that the open seaports and fish of the Maritimes, the timber and manufactures of Upper and Lower Canada supplemented each other and that the products of the existing colonies would eventually find a ready market in the West. The idea was much criticized at the time but it was, nevertheless, an economic factor inducing union.

Finally, the colonies faced a common problem in finance. Upper and Lower Canada had virtually exhausted their financial capacity in constructing canals and aiding railways. Just before Confederation they had found it difficult to float a loan of moderate size even though they offered eight per cent interest. The fiscal position of New Brunswick and Nova Scotia was much healthier, though even there resources were inadequate to build railways on the scale desired. Incidentally, the colonies of British Columbia and Prince Edward Island which joined Confederation later, did so almost entirely because of their straitened financial positions. A larger union offered hope of relief from existing financial stringencies because it would give a larger base for taxation, and would be more likely to get assistance from the British Government and secure loans from the private British investor for the construction of railways and other public works.

Loss of markets, fear of the United States, railways, the West, industrial change, complementary resources, finance—all the colonies faced these problems. Gradually they realized that common action, a common central government was necessary to deal with them effectively. The problems were not those of governments alone. They were problems also of business men in both Canada and Britain—of farmers, lumbermen, fishermen, merchants, of the new factory owners in the one country—of owners of railway securities and government bonds in the other. One of this latter group, Sir Edward Watkin, president of the Grand Trunk, sought salvation for his road in a larger union and extension of his line westward into the Prairies and eastward to the Maritimes. He used his extensive influence behind the scenes, and was able to pave the way for the rapid passage of the British North America Act through the Parliament at Westminster. Colonial Governments were supported by business interests in their efforts to bring about Confederation.

To enumerate the economic motives lying back of Confederation does not mean that the movement was purely economic in nature. Over all was a spirit of loyalty, a determination to maintain British supremacy, a vision of a larger, more prosperous country. Back of it, too, was political deadlock, the impossibility of carrying on the government in the St. Lawrence region when a majority of both Upper and Lower Canadian representatives was ordinarily required. These political factors were probably the dominant ones but economic forces cannot be neglected.

In any event, in the division of legislative powers between the Dominion and the Provinces, the central government was given jurisdiction over almost all the important matters directly affecting business. These matters included trade and commerce, currency and banking, bankruptcy, the tariff, navigation, railways, canals, other works for the public advantage of Canada, the post-office, weights and measures, patents, bills of exchange and interest. The Provinces, in so far as industry and commerce were concerned, had authority to incorporate companies with provincial objects, to license shops, etc., and to control property and civil rights within the Province, an expression which the Fathers of Confederation apparently intended to include only the law of contract and some minor matters. Jurisdiction over agriculture and immigration was shared. In later years law courts interpreted the Act in such a way as to broaden the powers of the Provinces and weaken that of the Federal Government so that by the 1930's, the latter found itself incapable of handling the new economic and social problems which had arisen. Nevertheless, in the beginning, economic motives leading to Confederation were sufficiently strong to place legislative control over most economic affairs in the hands of the Federal Government.

In brief, Confederation took place from a variety of motives among which was the fact that the previously isolated colonies faced common economic problems. Confederation having been formed, one of the tasks of the new government was to deal with these problems. This involved the immediate and tangible job of acquiring the West from the Hudson's Bay Company, and of providing railways between the various regions. It involved also the long run and less tractible task of integrating the different colonies into a unified economy. Future pages will show what efforts were made to accomplish these objectives.

SELECTED READINGS

CREIGHTON, D. G., "British North America at Confederation", a study prepared for the *Royal Commission on Dominion-Provincial Relations*, Ottawa, 1940.

MARTIN, C., *Foundations of Canadian Nationhood*, Toronto, 1955.

TROTTER, R. G., *Canadian Federation: Its Origin and Achievements*, Toronto, 1924.

8

The Maritime Provinces
since Confederation

SINCE 1867 the Maritime Provinces have gone through a series of painful adjustments as a result of technological and market changes. In the process of adjustment strains have developed within the Maritimes themselves, and between these Provinces and the rest of the Dominion. Before considering these strains, it is necessary to examine the chief lines of economic activity in the region.

Originally the main business of the Maritimes was fishing, and salt cod was the staple. With the construction of the Intercolonial Railway and the development of refrigeration, the market for fresh fish—cod, haddock, halibut—in central Canada was opened up. Most of these fish are caught inshore by means of small boats with two or three men. The boats are rowed by hand or are operated by gasoline or Diesel engines. The men use gill nets and trawls and the catch is brought in daily to be salted, smoked (for finnan haddie), or dispatched immediately in a fresh condition. Since Confederation the trapping of lobsters, the production and later the culture of oysters, the canning of "sardines", and until they were nearly fished out, the catching of salmon have become important.

Despite these changes, salt codfish has retained the key position and foreign markets remain vital. After 1875, cod fishing inshore relatively declined and soon the bulk of the salt cod was caught from trawlers on the Banks. The trawlers sailed to the Banks and from each, from six to ten small rowboats or dories, each with two men, went out daily and caught fish by means of nets and sometimes by hook and line. Before about 1910, steamers owned or chartered by fish merchants went out to the fishing grounds, relieved the trawlers of their catch and then steamed back to the ports. The actual fisherman was unduly dependent, in fact often at the mercy of, the merchant from whom he bought supplies and to whom he sold his fish. The use of internal combustion and, later, of Diesel engines gave some relief from this dependence by enabling the fishermen to bring their own catch to the market ports more frequently, and to choose the merchant who offered the best price. Typically, the trawlers did not return until their holds were filled with fish which might be a matter of weeks. The most far-reaching change in fishing methods has been the use, since about 1925, of specially designed "draggers" in fishing. These vessels catch from two to four times as many fish per man as do the smaller, older sailing ships and they can afford to sell fish at lower prices. Operating with fewer men, the new vessels threw many fishermen out of work, reduced standards of living and made older equipment worthless. For a time Parliament limited the use of draggers but expensive dory-caught salt fish were hard to sell in competitive overseas markets. Dieselized draggers with mechanical aids for catching and freezing fish now dominate the industry on the Banks. Fishing from dories is still practised in-shore, chiefly for the trade in fresh fish.

Markets abroad were unsatisfactory between about 1925 and 1940. The collapse of sugar prices in the West Indies, and war in Spain reduced demand. Prices of fish declined drastically in the 1930's but recovered during World War II. Generally speaking, long before 1930 the industry had ceased to expand. The value of the Maritimes fish catch, after increasing steadily to fifteen million dollars in 1885, remained at substantially the same level to approximately 1930. The problem of markets would be quickly solved if Canadians would eat more fish. On a per capita basis we consume less than half the amount of fish used in Britain. One of the difficulties of increasing consumption is that of getting the fish quickly and, at the same time, inexpensively into the St. Lawrence Valley. The process of quick freezing and "fish sticks" have helped solve the problem. Higher prices for fish after 1945 have materially aided the industry but a good many of the 50,000 people directly engaged in Maritime fisheries in the 1930's have had to shift to other occupations, such as lumbering and subsistence farming, or have moved into Halifax and Saint John. Co-operation in the purchase of supplies, the encouragement of household industries, and the local production of farm goods have opened up new possibilities and given new hope to numerous communities. Indeed, many people regard the cooperative ventures organized by St. Francis Xavier University as a development of great significance both to the Maritimes and to the rest of Canada.

In agriculture the significant change has been decline over the area as a whole and, at the same time, progress in certain specially favoured regions. Much of the soil of Nova Scotia and New Brunswick is infertile, yields are low and costs are high. The railway enabled farm products to be brought in from lower cost regions in Ontario and the West. In the face of this competition many grain and live-stock farms were abandoned. Agriculturists then turned to specialized products such as apples, potatoes, dairy products and foxes. In the Annapolis-Cornwallis valley apples were grown for export as early as 1880. By the late 1920's the industry had steadily expanded until roughly two million barrels were exported each year, almost entirely to Great Britain. The problems of orchard location with respect to local variations in soil and climate, of pest control, of packing and of advertising—all of which are too complicated to be considered here—had received careful attention. During World War II the industry could not obtain space for shipping such a bulky product to Britain. After the War it found that Britain was raising many of its own supplies. Consequently the Annapolis growers have been forced to turn to dairying, poultry, berries, and vegetables.

In Victoria and Carleton counties in New Brunswick and in Prince Edward Island where the conditions of soil and climate are peculiarly favourable, the specialized agricultural product is potatoes. At first this industry was handicapped by the lack of cheap transport for a bulky product, and hence starch factories were set up to concentrate the product. Soon markets for potatoes were opened up in tropical America. Unfortunately, in 1927 prosperity in Cuba and the West Indies collapsed with the drastic fall in sugar prices. The increased production of beet sugar in Europe and of cane sugar in Java prevented the recovery of these areas. Also, by means of a tariff, Cuba encouraged the growing of potatoes at home and, although Cuba must still import the more virile northern potatoes for seed, a large market for Maritime potatoes disappeared during the 1930's. As a result, prices were unsatisfactory for several years. Despite objections from Ontario and Quebec farmers, a good market for fine quality Maritime potatoes has been opened in Central Canada. They are also sold extensively in New England and the West Indies.

The specialized product of the Maritimes which has attracted the most attention is undoubtedly fox furs. Early in the present century wild foxes were captured and raised in pens on farms in Prince Edward Island. The problems of diet, housing, disease, insect control, even the difficulty of getting foxes with a white tip at the end of the tail, were gradually solved and after several years of experimentation the industry enjoyed a violent boom, as much as $35,000 being paid for a single pair of silver foxes for breeding purposes. Since that time the industry has settled down to the production and sale of pelts and in spite of dependence on style changes, it still enjoys considerable prosperity. Fox farming is now an established business in every province in Canada and in foreign countries. The domestication of foxes has led to attempts at raising in captivity other fur-bearing animals, especially mink and to some extent raccoon, beaver and muskrats.

In addition to the production of apples, potatoes and furs, Prince Edward Island and parts of both Nova Scotia and New Brunswick raise a considerable volume of dairy products but normally not enough to satisfy the demands of the Maritimes as a whole. Hence some butter and cheese must be brought in. In many areas agriculture is of the self-sufficient type—the farmer grows about enough for himself and his family and little more—or it is supplementary to fishing or lumbering. In the latter case the farming methods are crude, yields are low and the quality relatively poor.

Mining in the Maritimes is concerned with gypsum and building stone, some gold, and principally coal. The coal resources are located chiefly in Cape Breton Island around Sydney, in Pictou county, about Joggins, with minor amounts in New Brunswick. The growing industrialization of Canada in the 1880's opened up new market possibilities for coal, but the Maritimes were slow to take advantage of them until 1893 when financial interests from Boston came in. This group consolidated several mining companies, provided better loading facilities, acquired specialized coal carrying ships, introduced better machinery in the mines, and set up a steel plant to provide an additional market for the coal. The gains from unified management and superior capital equipment soon became apparent in the figures of production which increased steadily to about 1920. Since that time coal output has fluctuated with general business but has declined relative to the economy as a whole.

Normally Canada supplies from her own mines only about one-half of her coal requirements, the remainder being imported from Pennsylvania or West Virginia and, in the 'thirties, from Scotland, Wales, Belgium and even from Russia. This relatively large importation occurs in spite of the fact that parts of Canada are fairly well industrialized, and the country as a whole contains about one-sixth of the world's known coal reserves. The reasons for this anomalous situation are numerous. A good deal of the Canadian coal is of rather poor quality. Maritime coal, however, is good for general steam purposes and fair for domestic use, although only the coal from the Sydney area is suitable for coking and gassing. Canadian coal resources as a whole are poorly located with reference to markets, for Ontario and Quebec, the most highly industrialized provinces, have none. Toronto is approximately 1000 miles from Nova Scotia, 2000 from Alberta and only 400 from Pennsylvania. It is natural that Ontario should import from the nearest source in view of the cost of transportation and the fact that poorer grade coals tend rapidly to disintegrate, or degrade, in transit and through handling. In addition the use of fuel oil, gasoline and hydro-electric power, and increased efficiency in the use of coal itself have reduced coal consumption. Finally Nova Scotia mines are high cost operators. The seams are not thick enough to make it easy to use mechanical equipment. Near Sydney the reserves are deep in the earth and stretch out under the sea. This means heavy lifts and gradients, lengthy airways, a long haul underground and less working time, since men are paid from the time they enter the shaft until they leave it, and a long journey to the face of the coal greatly reduces the time spent in actual mining. In the Pictou field the seams are badly faulted and folded. There have been intermittent labour difficulties. These are partially the result of high costs in other respects which lead mine owners to try to cut wages.

It is apparent that Maritime coal mines operate under a considerable handicap. Since 1897 their nearest market, that in the New England States, has been steadily reduced by American tariffs and, more important, by the competition of easily mined, high grade coal from Virginia and West Virginia. The coal miners contend that they should have reserved for them a larger share of the Canadian market and that coal imports into Canada should be limited by means of tariffs. Since 1928 a subvention or subsidy, amounting to something less than one dollar a ton, has been granted Canadian coal by the Dominion Government. In the 'thirties a tariff was erected against American imports with the object partly of aiding the Maritimes, and partly of favouring imports from Britain. The tariff and subventions have proved of very considerable benefit to the Maritimes which now supply substantially all the requirements of the province of Quebec, and the most easterly parts of Ontario but the coal industry has lost markets to fuel oil and natural gas in homes and offices, to diesel fuel on railways, and to hydro-electricity in factories.

Closely associated with coal mining is the iron and steel industry centring in the Sydney area. Cape Breton Island has no iron ore, but large quantities of excellent grade ore are easily brought in from the Wabana mines on an island in Conception Bay, Newfoundland. A Dominion bounty on the production of pig iron was given in 1883. Later it was applied to steel also, but little was done until American capital reorganized the coal industry and established steel mills. The early mills were concerned almost entirely with supplying steel rails for use in the expanding West. The cessation of expansion in the railway network since 1925 has eliminated most of the original market. Consequently the industry has had to shift to structural steel, plates, wire rods and, in general, to secondary steel products. In the shift the Maritime industry finds itself at a disadvantage because most of the manufacturers of machinery, automobiles, hardware and secondary products generally, are located in Ontario. Any iron and steel industry, of course, fluctuates violently with the business cycle. The Canadian industry is also dependent on tariff action at home and in foreign countries, not only on the basic articles but on secondary lines as well.

Manufacturing in the Eastern Provinces since Confederation is the story of the rise and decline of many small enterprises. By the 1880's ship-building had almost entirely disappeared due to the competition of the iron and later the steel product. This was a grievous blow to Maritime industry. There remained, however, numerous small factories producing shoes, leather, lath, shingles, sashes and doors, cotton textiles, sugar and so on. Before the turn of the century many of these plants failed because they were not able to compete with larger, more efficiently managed plants. Small factories failed in Ontario for the same reason but they were replaced by larger enterprises. No such replacement took place in the Maritimes because large scale factories need big markets for their goods. The chief market was in the St. Lawrence Valley and plants there had a very considerable advantage over those in the Maritimes. Moreover, when new industries such as automobiles and electrical goods came into being, they were located in the most populous region from which they could, if necessary, send their products by cheap rail or water transportation to the outlying parts of the Dominion.

In only four or five instances were Maritime firms able to resist the general trend of manufacturing to the St. Lawrence Valley. These Maritime firms are able to sell their goods all across Canada partly because the articles they produce—tea, sardines, sugar, candy, textiles and steel products—are commonly of high value in proportion to bulk, and hence are able to bear the relatively high freight charges involved in shipping to distant markets. Also these articles are made either from raw materials, such as coal and iron which the Valley itself does not possess, or from others which are brought in by water from foreign countries and manufactured en route to market. Since 1925, the extensive forest resources and supplies of cheap electrical energy have led to the establishment of pulp and paper mills. Of course the Maritimes produce their own perishable goods such as bakery products and newspapers. The number of persons engaged in all types of manufacturing in the Maritimes is only

seven per cent of the number of factory workers in
Ontario and Quebec. In 1870 Maritime manufacturing
produced thirteen and one-half per cent of the gross
value of all Canadian manufactured goods but in 1935,
this proportion had declined to four and one-half per
cent and by 1955 to approximately three and one-half per
cent.

In addition to agriculture, mining and manufacturing,
the Eastern Provinces are interested in trade and shipping. Halifax and Saint John are the only important
eastern Canadian ports which are open all winter. Unfortunately, New York handles a very large percentage of
Canadian sea-borne commerce because it has the advantages of being nearer to the industrialized centres of
Canada, and of having lower shipping and insurance
charges, and a larger supply of available shipping space.
The Maritimes are constantly demanding that a substantial proportion of this traffic should be diverted through
their ports, and have induced the Dominion Government
to provide excellent handling facilities at both Halifax
and Saint John. Tho volume of traffic handled by these
ports is considerable and the necessary handling, ship
operating, banking and clerical facilities provide employment for large numbers of people. Nevertheless, the pull
of New York City remains strong, and the Maritimes are
fearful that the St. Lawrence Seaway will be another
blow to their trade with Europe and the West Indies.

Since 1920 the Eastern Provinces have been interested
in promoting the tourist trade. They are able to offer
the tourist sport, salt water beaches, the famous Revers-
ing Falls, the apple blossoms of the Annapolis valley, the
rural serenity of Prince Edward Island and a colourful
history. They are near the populous cities of New
England. On the other hand they have the competition

of Maine and are required, if they want to attract tourists, to provide good highways. The construction and maintenance of roads involves large provincial expenditures, and it is a question how far it is desirable for the Maritime Provinces to increase public debt in order to assist the tourist trade.

From the preceding analysis it should be apparent that economic conditions in the Maritimes are none too bright. There has been a series of difficult re-adjustments in particular industries and the general trend has been downward. The area has suffered from technological changes. The emphasis in industry has shifted from wood, wind, water to steel, steam and hydro-electric power. The nicely balanced economy based on a close integration of fishing, lumbering, ship-building and trade has been completely upset by changes in industrial technique and the movement westward of the Canadian economic centre of gravity. The region participated to a relatively minor extent in the boom associated with the opening up of the Prairies, and shared the good times in the late 1920's to only a slight degree. Emigration to Montreal, to the West, to British Columbia and to Boston has been considerable and population in the three Provinces has declined relative to the population of Canada, and in some parts has declined absolutely, that is, in some areas there are fewer people now than there were in 1867. Altogether, economic development in the Maritimes has failed to keep pace with that in the rest of the Dominion.

The reasons for this decline are partly geographic and partly political in nature. The area suffers from a paucity of natural resources and poor location with respect to the national market. It is not a richly endowed region and it juts far out from the edge of the continent. It is separated from the large market in Ontario and Quebec by a wide stretch of barren rock, and from the Prairie market by the barren country north of Lake Superior. In summer the St. Lawrence river provides cheap water transportation, but this is available to the manufactured goods and coal of the rest of the world as well as the Maritimes.

In addition to these geographic disabilities, the economic situation has been aggravated, so it is claimed, by national policies. The Intercolonial Railway, built as part of the Confederation pact in order to provide a low cost outlet for Maritime products into central Canada, and a winter route for overseas trade from the St. Lawrence valley, was poorly located as far as trade was concerned. In addition, the protective policy adopted in 1879 has forced Maritime consumers to purchase goods made in Canada when, in the absence of protection, these articles could be more cheaply imported into the Maritimes from abroad. Tariff protection, it is true, favoured the establishment of certain industries within Canada but these were located, for the most part, in Ontario and Quebec. While the Maritimes have been forced to buy in a protected market, they continue to sell their most important products—apples and potatoes particularly—in a world market where they often suffer from the tariff action of other countries. Before Confederation the Provinces were able to adopt a tariff policy designed to meet their own peculiar situation. Since 1867 tariff policy has been determined by the majority of the Canadian people who, of course, reside in the St. Lawrence Valley. Considerable intellectual ingenuity has been exercised to measure the cost of the tariff per capita to Maritime residents, in comparison with per capita benefits to people in Ontario and Quebec. The statistical basis for such estimates is not complete but Maritime citizens are convinced that, although the tariff may have operated to the benefit of Canada as a whole, it has worked to the detriment of their particular region. They are not unanimous in demanding reduction of the tariff, but they do insist that the Maritimes should receive from the rest of the Dominion some concessions which will offset the burden of the tariff on them.

In order to offset their economic and political disabilities, the Maritime Provinces began, early in the 1920's, to claim concessions in the form of larger provincial subsidies and reductions in freight rates and so on from the Dominion Government. It is to be noted that the platform for Maritime claims, or rights as they soon became known, is not political in the sense of being supported by one party. It has general approval throughout the Maritimes or to use their own language, the issue is "not partisan but national". The Provinces, especially Nova Scotia, entered Confederation unwillingly, and since 1867 have not been admitted to full partnership in Dominion prosperity. The contention is that in the interests of national unity the situation should be rectified.

In 1926 a Royal Commission under the chairmanship of Sir Andrew Rae Duncan, a British industrialist and politician, was appointed to consider the problem. As a result of its recommendations provincial subsidies were increased, ferry service to Prince Edward Island was improved, the Federal Government appointed a deputy minister of fisheries to deal with the problems of that industry, new grain elevators were erected at Halifax, subventions granted to coal and a subsidy given to by-product coke plants using Canadian coal. More especially, railway freight rates were reduced by twenty per cent on traffic between any two points in the Maritime Provinces, and on the Maritime portion of traffic being imported or exported from Canada through Maritime ports. The same reduction of twenty per cent (increased to thirty in 1957) also applied to the Maritime portion of traffic moving from the Maritimes to other parts of Canada. These reductions were made with the idea of materially aiding Maritime industry and the movement of overseas traffic through Canadian ports. The difference between the normal rates and the reduced ones is paid to the railways by the Federal Government, and has totalled from three to five million dollars a year. The Maritimes do not regard the reduction as a subsidy, but merely as a transfer of the cost of maintaining the circuitous Intercolonial Railway from the people of the Eastern Provinces to the people of Canada as a whole. The transfer is justified because the Intercolonial was located not on an economic basis but for defence, and the cost of national defence is an obligation of the Dominion.

In spite of these concessions to Maritime claims, business conditions failed to improve and in 1933-34 Nova Scotia appointed its own commission of enquiry. In general it re-iterated the views of the Duncan commission, with the exception that it was inclined to blame tariff policy for the decline of industry in the Maritimes and its concentration in the St. Lawrence Valley. One of the commissioners was careful to point out however, that the industrial trend to Ontario and Quebec was probably inevitable though the tariff may have facilitated the movement. In regard to freight rates, it was pointed out that the benefit of the 1927 reduction was being "whittled away" because truck competition forced down rates in central Canada and, when the railways reduced their rates to meet this competition without making a corresponding reduction in the Maritimes, farmers, manufacturers and other shippers in Ontario and Quebec had an advantage, so far as freight was concerned, over Maritime shippers in sending their goods to market. The provincial commission also made a number of recommendations for improving conditions in the fishing industry and for attracting tourists.

As explained later, during and after the second World War, Canada enjoyed a great boom in which the Maritimes shared. Some Maritimers felt, however, that other Canadians regarded them highly during the War when their ports and shipyards were essential to defence, and then ignored them after the War was over. Since 1945, this area has had a reasonable measure of prosperity in specialized agriculture, in the tourist industry and in trade but coal mining, manufacturing and fishing will undergo a further long period of re-adjustment and possible decline.

SELECTED READINGS

CLARK, S. D., *The Social Development of Canada*, Toronto, 1942, pp. 95-203.

DAWSON, R. M., Royal Commission, *Report*, Halifax, 1945.

FORSEY, EUGENE, *Economic and Social Aspects of the Nova Scotia Coal Industry*, Toronto, n.d.

INNIS, H. A., *The Cod Fisheries*, Toronto, 1940.

INNIS, M. Q., *An Economic History of Canada*, Toronto, 1954, pp. 168-82, 282-92.

KEIRSTEAD, BURTON S., *Economic Effects of the War on the Maritime Provinces*, Halifax, 1944.

NOVA SCOTIA, Royal Commission, Provincial Economic Inquiry, *Report*, Halifax, 1934.

CANADA, Royal Commission on Maritime Provinces Rights, *Report*, Ottawa, 1926.

SAUNDERS, S. E., *Studies in the Economics of the Maritime Provinces*, Toronto, 1939.
    "Economic History of the Maritime Provinces", a study prepared for the *Royal Commission on Dominion-Provincial Relations*, Ottawa, 1940.

9

The St. Lawrence Valley
since Confederation

AMONG the several causes of Confederation, the need for greater economic development was one of the most important. As the years after 1867 unfolded themselves, development took place in part by opening up new economic regions in the Prairies, the Pacific coast and, later, the Laurentian Shield. Expansion occurred also by enlarging the economies already established in the Maritimes and the St. Lawrence Valley. In the provinces by the Atlantic growth was stunted, but in the Valley development was remarkable and falls naturally into four main topics—agriculture, manufacturing, mining, and lumbering.

Farming, the first of these topics, has been characterized chiefly by a shift from wheat to diversified agriculture. In the earliest stages of settlement agriculture in the Valley had been largely self-sufficient. Later it was dependent on one cash crop, wheat, and then in the eighteen-sixties and especially in the 'eighties, it became dependent on a number of staples—cheese, cattle, hogs, and other goods, some of them requiring so much capital and skilled labour in their production that they can scarcely be classified as staples.

The causes of the shift to diversification were numerous and complex. The export of superior quality and cheaply grown grain from the Prairies to Britain and even to Ontario itself during the early twentieth century dealt the final blow to wheat as a staple in Ontario, but long before this time other factors were at work. The continuous growth of one product on the same land tends to exhaust the soil, and involves intensive work on the part of the farmer only at certain times of the year. In the early period of settlement neither of these features was important, because the soil still had its original fertility and the farmer had plenty of work to do clearing land, building fences and so on. When these conditions no longer held, the farmer started to grow other crops which would, at the same time, secure better crop rotation, fertilize the soil and even out his own working load. The shift from wheat to dairying was aided also, by the invention of the centrifugal cream separator replacing hand methods of skimming the cream. Coupled with this was the development of the cheese factory and later, the creamery. These did not simply remove manufacture from the home; they greatly improved the quality of the product and thus tended to enlarge the market for dairy products abroad. Also, a market for live cattle opened up in Great Britain. As England became more highly industrialized, her domestic agriculture declined in importance and the demands of her urban population relatively increased. The use of the steamship enabled Canada to satisfy part of the growing British needs and encouraged the shift to dairying.

Within Canada itself, the steady growth of towns and cities enlarged the market for agricultural products. Not only did the market grow—it altered the character of its requirements. The more sedentary life of most of the people and a greater appreciation of food values led to a relative decline in the consumption of bulky products, such as bread and meat, and a great increase in the use of dairy products and vegetables. The change in demand was met by breeding better cattle, erecting silos, and paying more attention to animal feeds so that milk production throughout the year was more regular. Better roads enabled the fresh milk or cream to be hauled to cities, cheese factories or creameries with greater regularity. The perfection of the cheap canning process expanded the market for fruits and vegetables, once the prejudice against "tinned goods" had been overcome.

Originating in these complicated factors, changes in agriculture after 1867 displayed certain definite trends over the years. Throughout all the region there was a change from wheat to other field crops and animal production. In addition, certain areas concentrated their efforts on one product such as fruit in Niagara, cheese in South Oxford, garden truck around the cities and, more recently, tobacco in Norfolk county. In large measure this regional specialization represented a more exact adaptation to markets, soils and climate, that is to say, to economic geography, and was made possible by the development of cheap transportation by railroad and highway, which permitted the easy exchange of products between regions. Another effect of the movement to new types of agriculture was to require more skill and knowledge on the part of the farmer. To meet this need the Government created agricultural colleges, promoted experimental farms, fostered agricultural fairs, made agriculture a subject of study in rural schools, published farm bulletins and generally educated the farmer to meet his new problems effectively. The changes in agriculture resulted, also, in an increasing use of natural and artificial fertilizers and of agricultural machinery such as cultivators, seeders, reapers, hay loaders, grain separators, milking machines and a host of others. Although these machines removed some of the drudgery from farm life, they meant that it was increasingly difficult for the man without capital to start farming. They meant, too, that the most economically sized farm for machinery was larger than the most suitable size for hand methods and hence, there would have to be consolidation of farms and the movement of unnecessary farmers to the towns. This movement involved sacrifices in wealth, security and happiness on the part of individuals.

In spite of this, the rural standard of living greatly improved over that of pioneer days. The frame, or wooden house, which had displaced the early log one, was in its turn replaced by a brick dwelling. Oxen gave way to horses, and horses to the tractor and the private automobile. Fences of stumps or wooden rails were replaced by wire and, more recently, by electric fences. Better barns, more and better machinery, washing machines, mechanical churns, rural mail delivery, telephone, electricity—all these spelled rural progress. To be sure the typical rural home still left much to be desired, and the typical farmer probably worked harder and got less than the member of any other class in the community. Nevertheless, the progress from one generation to the next was considerable. More diversified output, greater skill and the use of more machinery resulted in a higher standard of living over a period of years.

It could not be expected that in the short run these changes, directly affecting as they did the working lives of a considerable proportion of the population of the Valley, could be effected without friction. The attempt to categorize the causes and results of the shift is apt to create an impression of orderliness which was far from existing in practice, at least when looked at from the point of view of a decade or so at a time. From about 1870 to 1895 farming was generally depressed. This condition of economic paralysis was particularly serious from 1890, when the McKinley tariff in the United States cut off the export of Canadian barley, live-stock, butter and eggs, to the late 1890's when exports to Britain increased. In an effort to help the farmers, governments speeded up the process of experimentation and education at home and attempted, by means of inspection and grading and by the appointment of agricultural representatives in Europe, to enlarge the sale of Canadian produce abroad. As a protest against conditions and following a similar development in the United States, farmers formed their own political party, the Grange or Patrons of Husbandry. The return of prosperity in the late 'nineties and the fact that leaders of the Grange made promises which they could not fulfil cut the movement short.

From 1895 to the Great War farmers were reasonably prosperous, even though they still had to adjust themselves to numerous changes in markets and production methods. Prices generally were rising and it was easy to send goods to the expanding cities in Canada or to Britain. For two decades before the first War the most important single agricultural export was cheese. Exceeding wheat in value in all but a few years of this period, cheese was almost an ideal staple for obvious reasons. Other farm exports of significance before the War were wheat flour, cattle, meats, raw hides and skins, apples, seed grain, oats and butter. Any economic difficulty which an individual farmer faced was fairly readily solved by going either to the growing towns, or to the rapidly developing West. During and immediately after the War itself, farming thrived. Unfortunately, a new period of depression or, at least, of painfully slow progress was introduced by the decline of prices, the increase in supply of farm products, and the shutting off of export markets due to higher tariffs by European countries which wanted to build up local sources of supply in case of another war.

This relative retrogression which lasted from 1920 to 1940 showed up in statistics of real income per capita and in the readily observable fact that, even in good years, the income of the farmer has not risen as rapidly as that of the industrial classes in the cities. During the depression of the 1930's, the farmer in the St. Lawrence Valley could make at least a living from his land. He had his garden and orchard, his chickens, his cow and he could "get by", for in this favoured area there has never been a crop failure comparable to those in the West. Nevertheless the farmer had less of clothing, less of amusement, less of services such as telephones and medical attention. He had to let his farm buildings run down for lack of money to buy lumber, cement and paint; his implements went without repairs, his land without commercial fertilizer; in short, he lived off his capital. Here and there individuals more capable, more favourably located, or perhaps more lucky than the mass resisted the general trend, but for the group as a whole, living standards did not keep pace with those of city workmen. In the two decades after 1920, agricultural conditions improved but not nearly as rapidly as urban conditions.

There were many reasons for this trend. The same number of farmers today, can produce a much larger volume of farm products than was possible fifty or even twenty-five years ago, because of the general adoption of improved agricultural methods. The use of implements, better drainage, commercial and animal fertilizers, better seed, the breeding of better animals and poultry and the culling out of the less productive individuals—all these meant an increase in the supply of farm goods without a corresponding increase in the number of farmers needed to produce the supply. This increase in supply was offset to some extent by the increases in urban population. On the other hand, there was a relative decline in the number of horses and hence a reduction in the demand for hay and oats. Foreign markets were cut down by tariffs and quotas. In particular, the British market for live cattle was cut off by legislation directed against the foot and mouth disease. In 1922 the cattle market in the United States was eliminated by tariff action, although some Canadian cattle were admitted after 1935 under a quota system. Canadian farmers could not successfully send hogs to Britain because they did not produce the smooth bacon type which the British consumer demanded. The market for Canadian cheese in Great Britain during peace time was lost by a series of events which illustrates the complications of tariff action in the inter-war world. Producers of butter in New Zealand enjoy certain advantages in the way of fine climate and excellent breeds of cattle so that in the late 'twenties, they were able to sell their butter in Canada in competition with the domestic product. Naturally, Canadian farmers protested against the imports and after the election of 1930, a tariff was set up in Canada against them. Thereupon the New Zealand farmers, being cut off in one market, began to search for another. They sent cheese to Britain, virtually destroying the formerly large Canadian exports to the United Kingdom. What Canadian farmers gained in one direction they lost in another. To sum up, St. Lawrence Valley farmers were faced with an increasing supply of goods and a demand which did not increase proportionately. Farmers in other lands faced substantially the same difficulties and the result was unsatisfactory prices.

In an attempt to solve the problem the farmers tried both co-operation and political action. Co-operation was only a partial success. Producers might go together to ship a carload of cattle or hogs to market. Each farmer received the sales price of his animals, less his share of the cost of shipping and selling the carload. He was assured, therefore, of getting all there was to get. More important was the fact that the farmer saw clearly what his particular animals brought, and hence was made to understand the special types of animal the market demanded. Previously, when the animals had been bought outright by a middleman, this information about the market never reached the farmer at all or if it did, it never directly touched his pocketbook, nor appreciably affected his production methods. Now the pressure on the farmer was strong, forcing him to bring his products into line with market requirements. Unfortunately, it is not easy to get the Ontario or Quebec farmer to co-operate with his neighbours. He is naturally conservative. Also he produces several types of food-stuffs, and for the full adoption of producers' co-operation, he would have to belong to a number of organizations—obviously a more difficult matter than if the farmers' output is confined to one article as is the case in the West. Producers' co-operation is important in live-stock and, in certain areas, in fruit, eggs and dairy products, but the largest proportion of the farm output of the Valley is still sold through the older channels.

On the side of consumers' co-operation, it was easy enough to cry that the middleman ought to be eliminated but it was not always understood that it was still necessary to perform the middleman's functions such as purchasing, collecting and maintaining stock, breaking bulk, extending credit and so on. These functions were already being efficiently performed by independent retailers in the towns, while automobiles enabled farmers to buy in cities if they wished. Another handicap on consumers' co-operation was the fact that farm organizations were often unwilling to pay enough to secure first-class managers. Hence, except in the purchase by the carload of farmers' supplies like binder twine and fertilizer, farmers' co-operation in Ontario and Quebec has fallen far short of being the success hoped for immediately after World War I.

In the political field, the farmers' movement was a protest against a rural standard of living which, during and after the first War, did not rise as rapidly as that in the cities. It was a protest also, against the apparent neglect of their interests by the established political parties and the ridicule heaped upon farmers at this time by the city resident. For four years after 1919, the farmers' party formed the government in Ontario, but was thrown out of office because of their inexperience in administration and dissension within their own ranks. Some contended that the party should be essentially a farmer, that is, a class group. Others demanded that it combine with city workmen to create an organization not unlike the Liberal or Conservative parties, but with policies of lower tariffs, producers' and consumers' co-operation, direct taxation, and popular control of finance and banking. At all events the party lost power and after 1923, slowly disintegrated being absorbed mainly by the Liberals. In Quebec both the political and co-operative movements were less spectacular than in Ontario, in the one case because of the pre-occupation of the people with conscription rather than with economic matters and in the other, because of the greater conservatism of the **farmer.**

The effort to adjust matters by direct and conscious economic and political action failed. Accordingly, solution of the agricultural problems was left to the operation of natural forces. Unfortunately the process of rural adjustment is painfully slow. The farmer's entire investment is on the farm and whether it be large or small in amount, he feels that he cannot abandon it or sell when the prices of farm equipment and real estate are badly depressed. Moreover, large numbers of families are involved. Also if a middle-aged farmer moves to the city, he finds it difficult to learn a new job even though he is typically industrious. His previous experience does not fit him to compete with skilled factory labour. At the same time he is reluctant permanently to accept an unskilled, or semi-skilled job since it yields little more in income than farming, and nothing in satisfaction to a man who has become accustomed to being his own boss. Of course the position of the farmer's son or daughter in the city is likely to be different. He may do well in the professions or in industry and commerce. But the exodus of young people from the old homestead leaves the remaining farmers to regret "rural depopulation" and to grieve over the decline of the rural school and the country church. In the depression, moreover, city jobs were scarce and youth "backed up" on the farms.

The gist of the farm problem under normal conditions is that there are too many farmers, but the process of getting rid of the less efficient of them is painful. It is, of course, conceivable that markets for farm products may expand either because of the reduction of tariffs abroad, or because of new uses for agricultural products at home such as converting straw into paper, or potatoes into industrial alcohol. Both of these processes, and others as well, are chemically possible but so far do not pay commercially. Unless new markets suddenly open up, there will have to be a new balance between agriculture and industry, a new proportion between the number of people producing food and the numbers engaged in manufacturing goods, in carrying on trade and in professional work. This readjustment will inevitably take a long time to work out, and the process of farm recovery to a standard of living comparable with that in the cities will be prolonged.

The second main development in the St. Lawrence Valley since Confederation is manufacturing. It is difficult to give a brief yet accurate description of this phase of economic life because of incomplete data, the number of products involved and the complexity of forces operating on each individual industry. In general terms the trend has been away from domestic production or scattered plants using local raw materials. It has been towards better grades, concentration in a few areas, machine techniques, imported raw materials, and national or even international markets.

These trends can be illustrated by particular industries. For example, the production of leather and leather goods was carried on in many pioneer homes and in most pioneer communities. A tannery using locally produced hides and local supplies of oak or hemlock bark would be established. The process, soaking the hides between alternate layers of bark until the tannic acid from the bark converted the hides into leather, involved no expensive equipment nor skilled labour. When nearby resources of tanbark were exhausted, it was easy for the plant to be moved elsewhere, and for the labour to be quickly absorbed in farming or in some other occupation. The product was poor in quality. It was used for clothing and around the farms in places where iron or canvas is now used. Some of the output went to the local shoe-maker, saddler or harness maker who sold finished leather goods to nearby farmers, and who were commonly paid in farm produce for their work. The shoes, or rather boots, and other articles these craftsmen produced were heavy and uncomfortable and the better grades were imported.

After about 1860 the local shoe-maker disappeared or became a repairman only. The majority of shoes came to be made in factories with the use of sewing and other machines. The factory industry was aided by the incidental protection of 1859 and greatly assisted by the National Policy which was designed, in this case, to keep out cheap American machine-made goods. For the most part the factories were located in the Montreal area, where they were attracted by cheap labour. The bulk of the output was in the hands of a relatively few large companies. Even so, the trend to consolidation by areas and firms was not as evident in shoes as in other industries, because of the ease of leasing shoe-making machinery.

Paralleling the disappearance of the local shoe-maker, was the closing of the local tanneries. Leather production became centralized in a few towns and controlled by a few families who incorporated their enterprises. Production was put on a more scientific basis and eventually chrome tanning was introduced. In place of poor quality hides carelessly removed by the farmer or local butcher, the raw material came mainly from large meat-packing companies who had the hides skilfully removed and cared for. Better raw materials and better tanning methods greatly improved the quality of the leather.

The market for leather changed also. Fifty years ago all children and, earlier than that, some adults went barefoot every summer. A single pair of heavy work boots for the men, fairly heavy shoes buttoned far above the ankle for the women, perhaps a pair of Sunday shoes (rarely worn on any other day of the week), heavy boots for the children, and rough carpet slippers for use in the evenings completed the family's footwear. Boots were kept flexible and water resistant by treating them at home with tallow or goose-grease. They were always re-soled and heeled, worn until "there was no wear left in 'em". Now-a-days shoes are low and laced. There are special ones for golf, dancing and other occasions. Shoes are made of canvas, felt, rubber, calf skin and real or imitation chamois as well as the original cow-hide. People walk less than formerly and thus use up less leather. At the same time shoes are often thrown away before they are fully worn out because they get out of style. The market for shoe leather has been affected by these factors.

Other uses for leather have changed too. Travelling bags, something for which the pioneer had no need, provide a good market. In harness and saddlery, consumption has generally declined and has shifted to meet the demands of the upper social classes who go riding for exercise, pleasure or prestige. The market for leather belting increased with industrialization but now faces competition from rubberoid products, chain transmissions and direct drive by electric motors. In short, the development of the leather industry, both of its marketing and its production, is one of constant change, of infinite complexity that defies brief summation.

The complex, ever changing picture of the industries producing and using leather is duplicated in woollens. In pioneer days the women of the household did spinning and weaving, using home grown wool. Later, local mills took over production first in weaving, where the primitive

household machines were cumbersome and hard to operate, and then in spinning. These mills had machinery,
though judged by later standards it was still of a simple
type. It was driven by water-power or, preferably,
by steam. Frequently the mills were on a custom basis,
that is, nearby farmers would bring to the mills raw wool
or yarn already spun at home, and would pay the mill
operator in wool or finished cloth for completing the
production process. The better quality and cheapness of
machine-made blankets or cloth over homespun soon
displaced the domestic industry in spinning, weaving and
dyeing. Once begun, the decline in the domestic industry
was rapid because the younger generation neglected to
learn the methods and the art soon died out.

The woollen industry received the benefit of protection
in 1858, profited when this was extended by the National
Policy, and gained even more when protection was increased in 1930. Also, in the course of time the tariff
was differentiated among woollen goods, that is, instead
of there being a general rate on all articles made of wool,
by 1930 different rates were applied to balls and batting,
berets, blankets, gloves and mitts, knitted woollen clothing, socks and seventeen types of woollen fabrics. The
object is to encourage production of those types of goods
which can be made in Canada without unnecessarily raising prices on other articles.

By the turn of the century the local custom mills were
disappearing and large factories in such cities as Montreal
and Brantford had taken their place, though a few plants
continued to operate in the smaller towns, especially during the Great War when the demand was great, and after
1930. The larger plants accounted for most of the output
of the industry, employed considerable numbers of workers and used a great deal of machinery, which in turn

involved a large investment. These dominant concerns sold all across Canada. Because of declining wool production, they had to import a good deal of their raw material.

The history of the iron working industries is complicated also. Under the French regime excellent quality iron was produced, though at high cost and by inefficient methods, at Les Forges on the St. Maurice, north of Three Rivers. The plant was continued after 1763 and its experiences duplicated early in the nineteenth century by a plant at Marmora, north of Lake Ontario, and another at Normandale in Norfolk County. In the course of time secondary iron products for which there was a large local demand—stoves, axes, cut nails, tools and the like— were made in several small plants. The construction of railways created a large demand for new types of iron goods. The original rails and rolling stock for the Grand Trunk and for some other lines was brought from England but locomotive works, rolling mills and car foundries in Canada supplied the replacements on these systems and some of the equipment for the later roads.

Production of iron products was hampered by lack of cheap coal and by the exhaustion of high grade bog-iron ore. These disabilities were offset by a tariff in 1879, and by a system of bounties introduced in 1883 and extended later. Modifications in the tariff have been frequent, and tariff schedules and subsidy allowances for iron and steel products are even more involved than those for other industries. The theory apparently is to give rates adequate to keep out foreign goods as soon as the Canadian market for any article, say steel rails, dropt iron forgings, telephone transmitters, tinplate or pocket knives becomes sufficiently great to justify the erection or enlarging of a plant to make them. In other words, the extension of protection from the basic to more and more of the secondary iron and steel industries appears to be progressive. Application of the theory is often haphazard, reflecting the political influence of localities and even of individuals. Also, it has proceeded irregularly in point of time, the largest increases and extensions coming in depression years.

The effect of the protection has been, of course, to increase the value and variety of iron and steel articles made in Canada. With the railway boom in the West the production of pig-iron multiplied twenty times and that of steel, nearly thirty times between 1898 and 1911. A blast furnace was opened at Hamilton in 1895, and at Sault Ste. Marie a few years later. Both these plants began by using Ontario ores from the Michipicoten district at the northeast corner of Lake Superior but shifted later to the American ore from south of that lake. In 1939, with the aid of a bounty from the Ontario Government, production of Michipicoten iron ore was resumed. The discovery in 1937, of a hitherto unknown deposit of high grade ore west of Port Arthur made another large resource available. Meanwhile the blast furnaces have been continuing to use United States ores. In the early years of the century they added steel rail plants to their facilities. Since 1920, the trend has been strong towards diversification—everything in steel from a carpet tack to the material for a huge bridge being turned out of the same big establishment. The automobile, the modern steamship, machinery for use in factories and mines and building roads, steel girders for buildings—all the complicated mechanism of modern industrial and commercial life requires steel. These demands are satisfied by a relatively few large plants, each with a huge investment and working behind a protective tariff. Agricultural prosperity and diversification in the East and expansion in the West created a great demand for farm implements, also supplied by a few large firms.

A description of other important manufacturing industries would tell a similar story—primitive beginnings and then change, complexity and consolidation. Generally speaking, before 1867, in fact before the 1880's, manufacturing was unimportant, for the chief interests of the country were in staples. Manufacturing, such as it was, used local raw materials (chiefly hides, wool, grain and wood) produced by relatively simple processes, and sold its output in the immediate vicinity of the plant. Imported raw materials were used in only a few cases, notably cotton and sugar, where there was a large domestic market and the technique of production was fairly simple. In order to facilitate the exportation of goods, railway equipment was made. In the main, manufacturing was linked closely to the staple products of the country and to supplying the more pressing needs of consumers.

Although stimulated considerably by the tariff of 1879, the growth of Canadian manufacturing was not particularly rapid throughout the 'eighties and 'nineties. The range of articles manufactured was impressive—glass, marine engines, sewing machines, rubber shoes, in addition to commodities like flour, beer, woollens and leather based on local raw materials. The total value, however, remained small relative to the output of farm, forest and sea. The number of male wage earners in agriculture alone, was over four times the number working in manufacture. Development was handicapped by relatively poor general business conditions, lack of conveniently located coal, shortage of capital, and difficulties of marketing in a country whose population was small, linguistically divided and geographically dispersed. Only in the late 1890's did manufacturing break away from the apron strings of staples and come of its own right to occupy an important position in the Canadian economy. Since then, it has shown three broad tendencies—expansion, concentration and the use of hydro-electric power.

The rapid expansion of manufacturing after about 1895 was caused by a number of factors. First, and probably most important, was the settlement of the West. The rapid influx of people and the extension of railways created a great demand for clothing, hardware, agricultural implements and other farm equipment, and for rails and rolling stock. Similarly, the exploitation on a more rapid scale than before of mineral and forest resources stimulated manufacturing. Moreover, a great many tasks which at one time were undertaken in homes or in local plants were being performed to an increasing extent in factories. Meat packing, butter and cheese making, biscuit and bread making, fruit and vegetable canning, tobacco curing, dress-making and the manufacture of men's clothing, laundry work, furniture and even casket making—these are examples of industries transferred, in whole or in part, to factories. In addition, new industries, new in the sense of novel, began in Canada as elsewhere. Automobiles, electrical goods, cement, chemicals, aluminum are examples of their products.

Manufacturing development was stimulated also by the protectionist tariff, which was continued without much modification after 1879. Also, as more parts of the Empire adopted the principle of British preference, and later as more foreign countries arranged with Canada to take advantage of her intermediate tariff, more goods were made in Canada for export. In particular American manufacturers, barred from foreign markets by high rates against American goods, found it advantageous to establish branch plants north of the border in order to sell abroad. This influx of American factories in a physical sense was accompanied by the borrowing of money and by the adoption of American production and managerial techniques. The Americans had developed methods of dealing with manufacturing problems arising under conditions similar to our own and it was natural that we should appropriate their ideas. The value to Canada of the importation of methods from more mature economies was as intangible as it was great.

As a result of these factors, expansion in manufacturing was rapid. From 1900 to 1910 the total value of goods manufactured in Canada multiplied nearly three times, and the number of persons gainfully employed in factories increased by 100,000 to a total of more than 400,000, or about 40 per cent of the number in agriculture. None of the statistical measures of growth in manufacturing is wholly satisfactory. Values of output are affected by changes in general price levels. The number of wage earners in factories does not keep pace with growth in other respects because, with more machinery, workers produce more goods per man. Similarly the number of establishments, especially in recent years, has increased very slowly but each plant is much larger than before. In contrast, the capital invested grows much more rapidly than the value of output because modern production involves the use of more and more machinery. The only really accurate measure of manufacturing development is physical volume, that is, the number of units irrespective of their value or the number of workers or plants involved. Unfortunately, such measurements have not been calculated before 1917. It is to be noted too, that any figures given here apply to the entire Dominion but the increases in the St. Lawrence Valley (Ontario and Quebec excluding the Laurentian Shield) are probably as great, and in early years greater, than for the country as a whole. In short, the data are subject to numerous qualifications, but speaking in general terms manufacturing in the Valley increased about threefold from 1895 to 1913.

During the first Great War the enormous demand for munitions, clothing and other war supplies caused a great boom in manufacturing. At the same time, the importation of certain types of manufactured goods from Europe was practically suspended and enterprising Canadian manufacturers took up the production of new lines. To some extent the spurt in manufacturing was an unhealthy expansion, for some of the factories built at that time could not be converted readily to peace time needs. Also when European producers began to export again after the War, Canadian manufacturers were loath to sacrifice the market they had secured. They demanded higher protection, particularly in the immediate post-war depression. Thus the consumer was asked to pay high prices for articles which could have been imported cheaply from abroad. On the other hand, the War accelerated the development of Canadian manufacturing and gave it a diversity which it would have taken years to attain under peace time conditions.

During the 1920's, all the factors operative after 1895 except the rapid expansion of the West, continued their influence. The establishment of American branch plants and the shift from home to factory production were specially pronounced. The great prosperity both at home and abroad and the steadily rising standard of living created a large market for manufactured goods. The net value of products manufactured, that is, the selling prices less the cost of raw materials, fuel and electricity amounted to nearly two billion dollars and the number of employees approached 700,000. On the basis of physical volume, manufacturing increased 50 per cent between 1923 and 1929.

The depression of the 1930's, accompanied as it was by the drought in the Prairies, led to a great reduction in output, especially in the capital goods industries. At the depth of the depression, (1933 as far as manufactures are concerned) net value was just over half the 1929 peak and the number of employees was less than half a million. The index of physical production was only a little more than the 1923 level. A marked increase in tariff schedules failed to counteract the downward trend, for Canadian prosperity is fundamentally dependent on the sale of staples abroad and high domestic tariffs cannot assist and may, in fact, retard the export of Canadian goods. During and after the second War expansion was amazing. Though interrupted by periods of cyclical contraction, expansion has been typical since 1895.

The second important trend after 1895, that towards concentration, had three aspects. One of these was the growth of large factories. These establishments could raise funds more easily than small plants because they were better known to the investing public. They could buy specialized machinery and use it continuously whereas in smaller factories the machines would have been idle part of the time, producing nothing while the interest on their cost kept up. Similarly, the big factories could engage highly skilled, specialized labour in shop and office. They could undertake research in production methods, and devise new uses for their product. They could also make use of by-products which in the small plant would go to waste. By producing many articles they could spread the cost of advertising and selling thinly over each unit of output. Sometimes they could secure favourable transportation rates. In short, they were able to secure the economies of large scale production.

Another aspect of consolidation was the tendency to concentrate in the larger cities. The mere fact of concentration of course, tended to create the big centres of population and as the cities grew they attracted still more industries. Usually, too, the cities got better transportation services. They drew the smaller towns into their economic orbit and, because it is easier to do business from the hub than from the rim, they grew still larger. The shift toward large urban centres started in the 1890's, but was accelerated after 1900 by the changes in production from home to factory, and especially by the establishment of entirely new or novel industries.

Not all cities profited equally by the movement as can be seen by considering the present distribution of urban population in the St. Lawrence Valley. At the top are Greater Montreal and Greater Toronto, with populations (in 1956) of 1,621,000 and 1,358,000 respectively. Together, they produce a wide variety of manufactures and accounted for 30 per cent of all manufacturing in Canada in the late 1930's and for 20 per cent in 1955. The relative decline has been brought about by the very rapid growth of industries, such as aluminum, steel and automobiles, located outside the big cities. Greater Ottawa, Quebec, and Hamilton had over 300,000 people in 1956: Windsor and London had more than 150,000 each, while Three Rivers, Kitchener, Sherbrooke, Kingston, Oshawa and Peterborough are in what might be called the 50,000 class. The succeeding class ranges downward fairly steadily from cities and towns with populations of a little over 15,000 to those with a few hundred.

This structure of the urban population is significant. Montreal and Toronto are the financial, industrial and trading headquarters of a considerable area. They are metropolitan centres exercising a kind of economic suzerainty over the surrounding cities. Some of the cities in the second category are not willing to admit that Montreal or Toronto are economically superior to them, and will contend that they are only numerically larger. Nevertheless they look to the metropolitan centres for leadership in business affairs. In their turn the secondary centres are surrounded by their own satellite cities in the lower brackets. In other words, the concentration of manufacturing in cities did not result simply in the growth of a larger centre of population than before; it resulted in a re-alignment of industrial, financial and commercial control.

Of course this concentration and re-alignment led to the decline of the typical small town of earlier days and a change in its functions. At one time it was the manufacturing centre for the surrounding community. But in the depression of the early 'nineties, many of its factories closed their doors. When business picked up after 1895, they did not fully recover for the newer, larger factories in the cities undersold them. Often the small-town plants, invariably wooden structures, burned down and were not replaced. Occasionally a local factory would survive either because of exceptionally able management or a well established trade name or, perhaps, because it converted itself to new requirements, as did the carriage factory at Oshawa when it became one of the important centres of the automobile industry. But for the most part, the factories in the small towns disappeared and the towns themselves became distributing points for goods made elsewhere. Even here their importance is waning, for the population on the surrounding farms is declining and people go over good highways to shop in nearby cities.

One of these towns used to have a population of three thousand, three saw-mills, a sash and door factory, two carriage shops, a furniture factory, a woollen mill, a tannery, two grist mills, a foundry, a salt works; also it had two grain elevators, three hotels and was served by eight passenger trains a day. At the present time its population is not one-third as large as before. All its industries have disappeared except the foundry which employs only three or four men, a grist mill and a brick plant. However, there is an excellent creamery. All the hotels are closed, though for a time one kept open by catering to tourists on their way to a summer resort a few miles away. No passenger trains serve the town for buses run to two nearby cities. Among the retail establishments are a farmers' co-operative store and several automobile service stations. The history of the town epitomizes manufacturing and general economic development in Ontario over the last fifty years.

The decline of the small town and the concentration of manufacturing in large factories and cities involved the growth of huge corporations. Bigger plants in the older type industries required good sized companies to own and manage them, and firms in the new industries like electrical goods and automobiles grew quickly to gigantic size. Moreover, one corporation would control a number of plants scattered in different places. Aggressive manufacturers would purchase a number of individual factories, close some of them, especially those in the small towns, and weld the remainder into one big organization. In the three years following the depression of 1907-08 there were 41 such industrial consolidations, absorbing 196 previously independent companies. Consolidations occurred in steel, cement, canned goods, paint, textiles, electric light and power, railways and banking. The movement toward organic union was revived in the 1920's, when investment bankers carried through the negotiations and sold the stock to a public that was greedy to buy. Almost all the consolidations made less money than their promoters promised. A few of them became bankrupt.

More significant for our purposes than financial loss to investors are the social problems involved. The public is disturbed because the consolidation of the manufacturing and other concerns may lead to agreements between them to hold up retail prices. It is concerned also, lest "big business" exercise a sinister influence on politics. It is afraid that control of the economic life of the country will become centred in the hands of a few financial magnates who will manipulate affairs to their own ends. Finally, the public fears that small businesses will be stifled by a few large concerns.

Public fears were shown to be at least partially justified as early as 1888, when a parliamentary committee revealed combines operating against the public interest in a number of different commodities. The effort to destroy these combines failed chiefly because no member of the public cared to go to the trouble and expense of prosecution, particularly since his efforts might be challenged in court by a wealthy corporation. Subsequent efforts to destroy other combines failed for substantially the same reason. In 1923, however, the Combines Investigation Act removed the chief difficulty by providing that facts pertaining to the existence of an alleged combine would be gathered at government expense. It is to be noted that the Act itself provides merely for the collection of data. It is anticipated that once the situation is revealed public opinion will be sufficiently strong to lead to the voluntary dissolution of the combine. If it fails to do so, prosecution may be undertaken under the Criminal Code.

On the whole, the Combines Investigation Act has been a successful piece of legislation. Combines have been revealed in the sale of coal, fruit and vegetables, proprietary articles, builders' supplies and corrugated paper boxes. Heavy fines have been levied in these cases. In one or two instances it was shown that, although a combine did exist, it did not work to the detriment of the public and therefore could not be penalized. On the other hand, operation of the legislation has been hampered by conflicts of jurisdiction between the Provincial and the Dominion Governments. The Act does not deal effectively with cases, as in aluminum, where one producer controls the entire output in Canada nor with cases, as in gasoline, where there is no collusion between sellers but merely a tendency for all of them, acting independently of each other, to follow the prices set by one of their number. The problem of the relationship between public interest and private business, especially large-scale private business, is exceedingly difficult and has not yet been worked out. In 1935 a parliamentary committee, later converted into the Royal Commission on Price Spreads and Mass Buying, revealed that large retail and manufacturing concerns were apparently beating down the prices of goods sold to them by cattle raisers and tobacco growers, and were using unfair tactics against their smaller competitors. In effect, the Commission dealt with the effect of the depression and of modern industrial organizations on poorly organized economic groups. The work of the

Commission received wide-spread publicity, but its legislative programme to license processors and set "fair" prices was considered by the courts to be within the jurisdiction of the provinces, and hence, beyond the legal control of federal authorities. During the second World War manufacturers consulted with each other, under government supervision, in order to maximize output, keep down costs, and "hold the line" on prices. After 1945 the Combines Act was again vigorously enforced.

To recapitulate, the consolidation of manufacturing since the 1890's has had three aspects—in large factories, in large cities and in large corporations. The movement has created sociological problems of urbanization and small town depopulation. It has involved also the economic problem of public control of private enterprise.

The final aspect of manufacturing change since 1896 is the production and use of hydro-electric power, an important industry in itself and one with a significant effect on other types of manufacturing. Ontario and Quebec have no coal and their local resources of petroleum are inadequate. The use of wood for industrial purposes is unsatisfactory from both business and public standpoints. The only power resource which the St. Lawrence Valley and neighbouring parts of the Shield have in abundance is water.

In pioneer days, water running through mill-races alongside natural obstacles or artificial dams provided sufficient power for grist mills, woollen factories and other local plants. The new large factories, however, required more power than water-wheels could conveniently supply. Hence steam engines were used and coal was imported from Pennsylvania. But when a strike in 1902 cut off the supply of coal and seriously dislocated trade, the attention of manufacturers and other business men turned back to water as a source of industrial power. At the same time leaders in municipal life became interested, partly because they wished to see the industries in their cities prosperous, and partly because they felt the need of a cheap means of household lighting.

Accordingly, in 1903, representatives from seven municipalities, including (Sir) Adam Beck, a manufacturer of wooden boxes in London, Ontario, formed an association to consider the problem. Beck was an enthusiast, a tireless advocate for the proposition that the water-power resources of Ontario should be developed at once. He insisted, too, that development should be under public control in order to prevent monopoly profits by private companies which had already begun to manufacture electricity at Niagara, and who owned the local power and light companies generating electricity by steam in other parts of the Province. Elected to the Ontario legislature, Beck was able to influence the Provincial Government to create, in 1906, the Hydro-Electric Power Commission. Beck's original intention apparently was that the Commission would act for the municipalities collectively and would become their legal agent in the purchase of electricity. When the Commission began to manufacture electricity, however, it needed more funds than the municipalities were willing to supply. The necessity of going to the Province for bond guarantees gradually erased the distinction between the Commission and the Government until, at the present time, the Commission functions very much like any other department of the Government.

At the same time the Commission has assumed more and more control over the municipalities. The need for setting rates high enough to pay the wholesale cost of electricity supplied by the Commission to each municipality, forced the central body to determine rates. Likewise the technical problems of distribution compelled the Commission gradually to assume other functions for the local units. The present situation is that each municipality raises its own capital and performs the routine tasks, but all really important decisions are rendered for the municipality by the Commission. In other words Government, Commission, and municipalities have integrated and the original distinctions between them, in so far as electricity is concerned, have become vague.

Although given authority in the original legislation to generate electricity, the Commission at first purchased it from private concerns. Within a few years it began to acquire existing plants or build new ones along several rivers, particularly, of course, on the Niagara. By the late 1920's the Commission had harnessed most of the resources in the more settled parts of Ontario itself. Fearing that the rapid industrial expansion of the time would soon create a shortage of power, the Commission entered into a series of contracts with private corporations in Quebec for the purchase of large blocks of power. By the time the power was to be delivered, the depression had reduced the need for it. In order to relieve itself of the obligation to pay for power which it could not use, the Commission, acting at the instigation of the Ontario Government, cancelled the contracts on technical grounds. Later it renewed most of them on terms more favourable to itself. The making and cancellation of these contracts was the occasion of a good deal of political wrangling within and without the Province. The Commission has been fairly free from politics of the disreputable sort, but the synthesis of Commission and Government is not without the danger that "Hydro" will be operated on political rather than on a strictly business basis.

Nevertheless, public ownership of hydro-electricity in Ontario has been a conspicuous success. The only serious mistake was the purchase and construction of radials, that is, electric railway lines between cities and suburban towns or other cities. This investment was a complete loss on account of the increasing use of automobiles. The chief benefits of public ownership have gone to domestic users whose rates are lower than in adjacent areas having privately owned systems. Low rates are available also to industrial and commercial users and have tended to keep down the cost of production, thus aiding Ontario manufacturing and mining. In addition, the wide distribution of hydro-electric power has served to keep industry in the smaller towns and, though it could not forestall concentration in certain large cities, it has prevented it from taking place to the same undesirable extent as elsewhere. Similarly, public ownership has extended its service to villages and small towns where private companies would be unwilling to assume the risk of loss. In short, "Hydro" has promoted both industrial and social welfare.

The causes of this success are several. The combination of centralized management and advice on technical matters with local control of routine functions is worthwhile. Criticism of the local board by hydro-users and municipal councils quickly finds its way back to the Commission, which is thus kept in close touch with its customers. The project was started at an opportune time. The technical problems of the generation, transmission and use of hydro-electricity had been fairly well solved. The market was growing rapidly because of a rising standard of living and expanding industrial development. In part, too, cheap hydro-electric power created its own market because factories producing chemicals and aluminum, which require enormous amounts of power, were established in Ontario in order to secure these low costs. Cheap power has also permitted the use of low grade ores, and thus has made another market for itself besides extending the life of mines in Northern Ontario. In brief, the reasons for the success of the Ontario hydro-electric system are complex and cannot be attributed solely to the virtues of public over private ownership.

The truth of the last statement is substantiated by the history of hydro-electric development in Quebec. In that province progress was slow until 1922, but extra-ordinarily rapid thereafter. Quebec has nearly twice as large reserves of power as Ontario. Most of its potential resources lie along the St. Maurice, Gatineau, St. Law-rence, Saguenay and Ottawa Rivers and hence, except the last-named, are entirely under provincial control, whereas Ontario's reserves are in boundary waters and can be developed only after agreement with other provinces, states or national governments. Unlike Ontario, Quebec had no public ownership until 1942, the resources being developed by privately owned corporations with a small amount of government regulation. The radical difference in methods of ownership in the two provinces was accounted for mainly by the social philosophy of the people of Quebec who favoured governments confining themselves to traditional functions. Other reasons for the dissimilarity were the strength of Montreal financial interests, the relative absence of ambitious medium sized cities which backed the early movement in Ontario, and the lack of an enthusiast like Sir Adam Beck. Under private ownership hydro-electric rates in Quebec, though not as low as in the neighbouring province, were cheap nevertheless, and have stimulated industrial and mining development. In the early 1940's Quebec launched a scheme of public ownership mainly because it feared the 'power barons'. The total developed water-power in Quebec and Ontario, including the very large amount produced and used in the Laurentian Shield, amounted to roughly seven million horse power in 1940, the equivalent of fifteen million tons of coal. By 1958 installed capacity in Ontario and Quebec was more than twice that of 1940.

Canadians continued to demand more and more electric power to run mines, mills and factories, to supply home and farm appliances, and to light dwellings, offices, and streets. In 1949 electricity was so scarce in Toronto that dim-out restrictions were imposed, i.e., power was cut off in homes and offices for an hour or two each day. The shortage was relieved by heavy rains which, in effect, added to existing capacity. Eventually, it was corrected by new hydro-electric generating stations and by the use of natural gas for domestic cooking and hot-water heating. Even so, stand-by plants using coal had to be built to meet seasonal peaks in the demand for electricity.

The latest resource of hydro-electric power to be used in the Lowlands was the St. Lawrence River between Cornwall and Montreal. Properly harnessed, it can generate roughly five million horse-power which will be divided between Quebec, Ontario, and the State of New York. For years before 1950 progress was hampered by the enormous cost, by doubts regarding the possibility of finding a steady market for so large an amount of power, and by political bickerings. The power project is tied up with a navigation scheme which is designed to permit ocean going ships to penetrate the basin of the Great Lakes, to allow Upper Lake carriers to reach Montreal, and to bring iron ore from the Labrador deposits to mills south of Lake Erie. Obviously the St. Lawrence Seaway and Power Project is of tremendous advantage to Canada.

To sum up, manufacturing development in the St. Lawrence Valley since 1867 has been one of slow progress for thirty years, and then rapid expansion accompanied by consolidation into fewer areas and larger business organizations, and by the use of electricity. It must be understood, of course, that manufacturing in Canada is by no means confined to the Laurentian Valley, and that the Valley is not co-terminus with Ontario and Quebec which also contain large parts of the Shield. Nevertheless, the Valley as such produces probably close to seventy per cent of all the manufactured goods of Canada. As far as individual articles are concerned, the region is responsible for all Canada's production of automobiles, and substantially all the electrical and rubber goods, farm implements, tanned leather, hosiery, carpets, medicinal preparations, toilet goods, cordage and most of the boots and shoes, canned fruits and vegetables, prepared breakfast foods, cigars and cigarettes and textiles of all kinds. In addition, the area produces a wide range of miscellaneous products from steam boilers to jewel cases, from abrasives to musical instruments, from leather belting to umbrellas, regalia and sporting goods. For the volume and diversity of its manufactured goods, the St. Lawrence Valley exceeds all the rest of Canada.

The reasons for this pre-eminence are fairly clear. It has the advantage of a large population, excellent transportation services by rail and along the rivers and the Great Lakes, a central location with respect to the rest of Canada, easy access to the techniques of the most industrialized section of the United States and, though it lacks coal, it has adequate resources of lumber, nickel, copper, salt, agricultural raw materials and water-power. In view of these advantages it is not likely to forfeit its industrial superiority to any other region of Canada and indeed concentration has become even greater since 1940.

Mining, the next main phase of economic development in the St. Lawrence Valley, is a relatively late feature in its history. Doubtless the early explorers hoped to find gold and silver in this area as the Spanish had done far to the south. In this they were disappointed, for whatever precious metals existed were remotely located and hard to extract. The first mineral resources to be exploited were not precious metals but humble iron at Marmora, and petroleum, "flowing gold", at Oil Springs and Petrolia. For years the world had been searching for a cheap substitute for whale oil. To be sure coal oil was secured by the distillation of coal shales, in New Brunswick among many other places, but its price was relatively high and the quantity small. The discovery of natural petroleum on the surface of certain streams in Pennsylvania a few years before, and the digging of the world's first oil well in 1859, heightened interest in the Oil Springs region. A great boom occurred in Western Ontario in the early 1860's, but within twenty years the days of spectacular flows were over. Oil wells had to be drilled instead of dug. Pumping was begun and the area settled down to a fairly regular, though generally declining production. The quantity of crude oil now produced is of negligible importance in supplying the total Canadian demand for petroleum products. Incidentally, in the early period coal oil, or kerosene, for lighting purposes and heavy oils for lubricants were the valuable articles and the gasoline a more or less useless by-product. The output of natural gas for heating purposes is important for a number of cities in Western Ontario.

The discovery of petroleum led to a search for it elsewhere in Western Ontario, and it was while drilling a prospective oil well near Goderich in 1866, that a bed of salt was discovered. Within twenty years salt wells had been drilled at various points, none of them far inland from Lake Huron and the Detroit River. The process of production was to run boiling water down the well where it would dissolve the salt, then pump up the brine and evaporate it in huge iron pans heated by wood fires. Competition among the scattered plants was keen and profits small. Hence they were gradually taken over by one or two large corporations which closed most of the smaller unprofitable works, prevented price-cutting and improved the quality of the product. The enormous available resources of salt are now being used in the manufacture of caustic soda, chlorine and other chemicals.

In the Eastern Townships of Quebec another mineral, asbestos, was being exploited after 1877, when its existence was disclosed during the construction of a railway. The early uses for asbestos were purely industrial and only recently, with the insulation of houses against heat and cold, has a domestic market been opened up. Production has fluctuated widely from year to year and the industry has, at times, been in financial difficulties. Canada produces a little more than half of the world's output of asbestos. In the St. Lawrence Valley there is also a large production of brick and tile, and cement.

In spite of the fact that gold and silver were not the first minerals to be first exploited in the Valley, they soon became the most valuable. In 1863 there was a gold rush to the Chaudière River area and, before the mines were exhausted twenty years later, about three million dollars' worth had been extracted. Other "strikes" and consequent rushes to Madoc, north of Lake Ontario in 1866, and to the vicinity of the Lake of the Woods in 1897, were more spectacular than they were productive of gold. It was only while the Temiskaming and Northern Ontario Railway was being constructed that new precious metal resources of great value were discovered. After 1903 the silver mines of Cobalt attracted miners from all over the world, a situation duplicated six years later with the gold of Porcupine, nearly ninety miles north-west. These new mines properly lie within the economic region of the Laurentian Shield and will be discussed in that connection.

As in mining, the history of the forest industry in Ontario and Quebec shows a decline in the Valley itself, and expansion in the Shield. By 1900 the square timber trade with Britain had completely disappeared and the export of deals was declining. The increase in population in the north-east quadrant of the United States and the denuding of most of this area, opened up a large market for Eastern Canadian lumber in the last quarter of the nineteenth century. After 1900, and particularly after 1920, this market was reduced due to tariff action and the competition of timber from British Columbia and Washington. Although the opening up of the West counteracted these declines to some extent, the lumber industry as a whole was of diminishing importance. Most of the huge trees of the Ottawa Valley had been cut down, and the virtual completion of land clearing in farming communities reduced the output there. Brick, iron and coal were forcing wood out of many of its uses in construction and heating. Lumbering still employs large numbers of men in the huge Ottawa Valley and north of Georgian Bay, but it is a mere shadow of its former self. Aside from pulpwood, the centre of Canadian lumbering has shifted to the Pacific coast.

The woodworking industries have also changed. Furniture making disappeared from the smaller towns and concentrated in Guelph, Kitchener, Stratford and a few other places. In recent years it has had to search rather widely for supplies of good quality domestic hardwoods, and is protected by a substantial tariff. The production of baskets, barrels, boxes and shooks almost collapsed in the 1920's, with competition from other types of containers. The output of carriages and wagons, made chiefly of wood, has been destroyed by the increased use of automobiles and trucks.

In spite of contraction in certain phases of the industry, the economic value of forests has by no means disappeared. Paper manufacturing is a forest using industry of great proportions. It began in 1803 in Lower Canada using, at first, rags and after 1860, wood as the basic raw material. Paper making progressed leisurely to 1900, then increased more rapidly to 1920 and boomed in the following decade. Speaking in very general terms, the mills established during the twentieth century concentrated on the production of newsprint and were located either in the Laurentian Shield or along its edges, and will be discussed in connection with that economic region. Mills in the St. Lawrence Valley proper are still important and, in the main, produce kraft paper for bags and corrugated paper boxes, and the higher grades of paper for books, ledgers, office and social purposes generally. The mills are located at Brompton, Montreal, Cornwall, Trenton, Georgetown, Thorold and other places. Due to the nature of their market their financial position is not as unstable as that of the newsprint mills.

In order to sum up the economic development of the St. Lawrence Valley since 1867, it is necessary only to recall the four phases: in agriculture, the shift to diversity; in manufacture, expansion, concentration and the use of hydro-electric power; in mining, a comparative decline in the Valley and a transfer to the Shield; in lumbering, a trend similar to that in mining. Each one of these phases is important in itself; combined and with the necessary financial, trading and transportation activities, they give employment to half the people of Canada, indeed, to three-fifths if the population in the adjacent parts of the Shield is included. The prosperity of the Valley is bound up with that of other parts of Canada but it is not dependent on one or a very few staples to anything like the extent that the other economic regions of the country are. In a word, it is approaching the stage of economic maturity. The trend toward maturity was especially noticeable after 1940.

SELECTED READINGS

BRADY, A., *Canada*, London, 1932, *passim*.

CANADA, *Report of the Royal Commission on Price Spreads*, Ottawa, 1935.

CHEVRIER, L., *The St. Lawrence Seaway*, Toronto, 1959.

DALES, J. H., *Hydroelectricity and Industrial Development in Quebec, 1898-1940*, Cambridge, Mass., 1957.

DONALD, W. J. A., *The Canadian Iron and Steel Industry*, Boston, 1915.

HEATON, H., *The Story of Trade and Commerce, with special reference to Canada*, Toronto, 1955 (rev. ed.), pp. 237-9, 257-67.

INNIS, H. A., ed., *The Dairy Industry in Canada*, Toronto, 1937.

INNIS, M. Q., *An Economic History in Canada*, Toronto, 1954, pp. 182-217, 266-82.

LOWER, A. R. M., *The North American Assault on the Canadian Forest*, Toronto, 1938.

MINVILLE, E., ed., *Nôtre Milieu—Aperçu Général sur la Province de Québec*, Montreal, 1942.

MOULTON, H. G., and others, *The St. Lawrence Navigation and Power Project*, Washington, 1929.

REYNOLDS, L. G., *The Control of Competition in Canada*, Cambridge, 1940.

WOOD, L. A., *Farmers' Movements in Canada*, Toronto, 1924.

10

The Prairie Provinces

THE early economic history of the Prairie Provinces is bound up with that of the fur trade which has already been examined. The first agricultural settlement was started in 1812, by Lord Selkirk in the Red River Valley, but for many years the colony hovered on the verge of extinction. The essential difficulty was that of every pioneer community, namely, securing a suitable staple. An attempt was made to raise sheep whose wool would find a ready market among the factories which the Industrial Revolution was creating in England. For some reason the sheep did not thrive in the Red River area. Then an effort was made to manufacture shawls from the "wool" of the buffalo which roamed the Plains. This effort failed due to the fact that the shawls never became popular, probably because the wool could not be easily dyed in different colours. Of course wheat could be grown, but the lack of cheap transportation facilities made it impossible to send such a bulky product to the outside world. Failing to find a suitable staple, the farmers had to content themselves with supplying their own needs and the food requirements of the fur-traders. The latter market was small and, therefore, the colony was forced back to a condition of self-sufficiency. The settlers were clothed in homespun and subsisted on dried buffalo meat and on flour ground by hand.

For sixty years after 1812 the colony grew slowly having, in 1849, only 5,000 persons and in 1871, only 25,000 not including about 48,000 in the present provinces of Alberta and Saskatchewan. For many years the settlement consisted of the Selkirk pioneers and their descendants, retired employees of the Hudson's Bay Company and half-breeds. There was no great inrush of settlers such as occurred in the United States during this period when, for example, 200,000 persons went to Minnesota alone in the years 1850 to 1860. After 1860, however, there were trickles of settlement into the Canadian West from Eastern Canada and the United States. At one time it was believed that the main reason for this situation was the opposition of the Hudson's Bay Company which feared that the expansion of agriculture would destroy the fur trade. Doubtless this opposition was significant especially in the early years, but more recently it has been suggested that during a good part of this early period the West was experiencing a drought similar to that of the 1930's. In any event the settlers did not understand the farming methods which are appropriate to a region of low rainfall. They tried to apply the agricultural practices to which they were accustomed in Europe or in Eastern Canada. Naturally these techniques failed under quite different climatic conditions.

Equally important as a reason for the slow progress, was the lack of a grain which would mature in a short growing season. The types of wheat then being commonly grown took over 130 days to mature, whereas in the average year the Prairie farmer could not be sure of more than 120 frostless days, and in many years the growing season was much shorter. Finally, the West lacked low cost transportation. The only access to the area was by boat and canoe from Hudson Bay or from Montreal (little used after 1821), or by huge Red River carts drawn by oxen to boats on the Mississippi, after 1844. All these routes were expensive. Cheap transportation was essential in order to put a bulky commodity of relatively low value in the markets of Europe at a price no higher than the cost of producing wheat in Europe itself. Before 1880, the cost of carrying wheat from Manitoba to market in Europe was literally more than the selling price in the market.

The restraints on Western development were very gradually broken. David Fife, a farmer living near Peterborough, Ontario, cross-pollenized different types of wheat and eventually evolved a variety which matured in from 115 to 125 days. By 1885 the production of this species, Red Fife, had become general in the Western farming community. Transportation difficulties were partially overcome in 1872 by a steamboat on the Red River. This steamer was a common carrier, that is, it would carry freight for any person on payment of a reasonable rate, whereas the earlier Hudson's Bay Company steamer had carried goods of that Company alone. By means of a portage and another steamer on the Mississippi, the Red River steamboat connected with United States railways at St. Paul. Later, direct rail connection was made with St. Paul. The Laurentian Shield constituted a formidable barrier to rail communication with Montreal, and it was not until the completion of the Canadian Pacific in 1885 that the Prairies had a direct route by rail to Eastern Canada and thence, by steamship, to Europe.

In spite of the acquisition of more suitable types of wheat and better transportation facilities, and notwithstanding a short boom in 1880-81, development proceeded slowly—the population in the agricultural areas of the Plains being only about 200,000 in 1891. The price of wheat declined from 1873 to 1895. Freight rates on the Canadian Pacific, though lower than for corresponding distances on United States lines, were too high to encourage settlement. In order to pay its operating and construction costs, the railway seems to have followed the policy of trying to sell at high prices the land it had been granted rather than dispose of the land cheaply, keep down freight rates, bring in settlers, and thus increase the volume of traffic and thus enlarge railway revenue so as to cover the railway's costs and yield a profit besides. An additional reason for slow progress was that most of the agricultural immigrants to North America were attracted to the United States. They were drawn to that region by the offer of free land, the expectation of quick profits, by intensive advertising and, down-trodden as many of them were by their home governments, they were charmed by the hope of freedom conjured up in the word "republic". Of course, in Canada, liberty was just as real and our homestead laws were even more liberal than those in the United States, but we were less aggressive in displaying our attractions and our development languished on that account.

After 1895 this situation entirely changed and the West enjoyed a boom of proportions unprecedented in Canada and rarely equalled elsewhere, a boom which lasted without a serious break until 1913. There were several reasons for this sudden expansion. Canadian settlers quickly borrowed the agricultural techniques, the methods of farming under relatively dry circumstances, which had been developed under similar conditions in the United States, or adopted the methods of the Mennonites who came to Manitoba in 1876 from the dry belt of southern Russia. Speaking in general terms, these techniques were summer fallowing in alternate years and the use of machinery. The former conserved moisture so that, in effect, two years' rainfall was used for one season's crop. The latter enabled a farmer to plow, reap and thresh the crop from a large number of acres so that even though the yield per acre were low—on the average about one-half the acreage yield in England, and one-third that in Denmark—the farmer normally had enough to cover all his expenses and still leave a reasonable profit.

A further reason for expansion was that all the really good farm land in the United States had been settled and the farming prospects of Canada were able to get some attention. The settlement of the Prairies can be regarded as part of a great movement of people from the Atlantic seaboard westward, a movement occupying nearly three centuries of time and occurring without much regard to national boundaries. Having established bases on the seaboard, the settlers infiltrated beyond the Appalachians and then, in the 1790's or earlier, thoroughly settled the upper part of New York State. In the next few decades settlers occupied most of Ontario and Ohio and, by about 1865, had swept as far west as Chicago. Westward across the treeless plains of the United States and northward into the forested regions of Minnesota, the broad sweep continued until, by about 1890, the agricultural land of the entire United States had been fairly well occupied. The American frontier had largely disappeared. The wave of settlement then rushed on into the Canadian plains.

Settlement of the West was facilitated also by the rise in the general level of prices after 1896. In 1897 a Canadian bank reported that "wheat, which within a year, touched the lowest recorded price in 250 years is again comforting the farmer with the old charm of one dollar a bushel". Rapid industrialization and urbanization in Europe created a great demand for food-stuffs and there were no high agricultural tariffs to keep out Canadian goods.

In addition, transportation charges were reduced. By September, 1899, the Canadian Pacific had cut its rates on grain to Fort William for export by the amount of three cents a bushel below the rates then existing. This reduction amounted to nearly twenty per cent from a typical wheat producing centre to the Head of the Lakes. Coupled with this benefit to the staple, the rates on certain settlers' requirements brought from Eastern Canada, namely, coal oil, cordage, implements, building materials and furniture, were decreased by as much as fifteen or twenty per cent. Further substantial reductions in railway rates were made in 1902. During the next few years freight rates by ship along the Great Lakes, by rail from Georgian Bay ports to Montreal, and by water across the Atlantic to Europe also came down. The development of very efficient elevators, of economical loading and unloading facilities and of low cost grain carriers on the Lakes, still further reduced the costs of handling the grain from the Prairie farm to the European market. The conjuncture of higher prices, lower production costs on the farm and lower transportation charges created a condition of prosperity for Western farmers.

The favourable circumstances were quickly taken advantage of by Dominion officials concerned with immigration. Carefully planned advertising was carried on in parts of the United States, such as Illinois, where land was high priced. Special efforts were made to repatriate Canadian farmers who had gone to the States earlier. From Ontario, the advertising brought farmers and farmers' sons. Many of them came on the harvesters' excursions, which the railway ran every fall to bring in large numbers of men to harvest the grain. Numbers of harvesters having come to work for a season decided to settle permanently. After 1900 the publicity was ex-

tended to Great Britain and later to the Continent.
Appeals were made, successfully, to religious groups such
as the Doukhobors and the Mennonites and to races like
the Icelanders or Galicians. Not all the people who
migrated could be assimilated into Canadian national life.
Many of them preferred to retain their own religion,
their own customs and to some extent their own language.
On the other hand, the second generation commonly
proved itself more ready to adopt Canadian habits, and
throughout most of the West there were sufficient numbers of settlers from Eastern Canada to preserve an
essentially British character to the institutions. Nevertheless the sudden inflow raised racial, religious and
educational problems of an acute character.

However much opinion may differ regarding the advisability of admitting immigrants of such diverse strains,
there can be no doubt that the result of all these efforts
carried on, as they were, under highly favourable general
conditions was a spectacular increase in numbers. In
1903 alone, more immigrants arrived in Canada than in
the SIX years, 1892 to 1897 inclusive. The peak was
reached in 1913 when over 400,000 were admitted, but the
collapse of the prices of land in that year, and the outbreak of the Great War in 1914, stopped the flow. Altogether, from 1895 to 1914, more than three million prospective settlers came to Canada. Not all these immigrants, of course, settled in the West, some of them being
absorbed in the growing industries in the East. Moreover at least one-third of the total immigrants were lost
to Canada, partly because of the return to Europe of labour
temporarily attracted here by railway and other developments then in progress, and partly because of the pull to
industrial cities in the United States. Nevertheless, the
number of immigrants from other countries plus the

natural increase of the population already there, plus the influx from Ontario, Quebec and the Maritimes, accounted for a net increase in population during the decade, 1901 to 1911, of 80 per cent in Manitoba and over 400 per cent in both Saskatchewan and Alberta. Three provinces with a combined population of perhaps 50,000 in 1871 had 420,000 in 1901, and 1,328,000 in 1911.

Coupled with the influx of people, there was an enormous inflow of capital, estimated at about one and one-half billion dollars, between 1900 and 1912. In part this capital was provided by the immigrants themselves. Americans brought their animals, farm and household equipment with them across the border. Canadians partially dismantled the farm back East to start up again on the Plains. Europeans, after they had arrived in Canada, had to buy what they needed to get their farms going. In every case the actual prosperity was so considerable, and the prospective prosperity in the imagination of the people was so unlimited that agricultural implements, fences, hardware, building supplies, kitchenware and furniture were soon purchased either for cash, or on promissory notes, or farm or chattel mortgages. In addition, capital equipment had to be provided in railways, elevators, retail and wholesale establishments, educational and government buildings. The railway network alone, expanded at an average rate of over two miles every single day for eighteen years. The newly-created province of Saskatchewan constructed, on the average, one school every school-day for the thirteen years before 1914. The provision of this equipment gave employment to thousands of people throughout the West and in Eastern Canada and, together with the expansion of farm acreage, enabled the West to enjoy unexampled prosperity.

The basis of this prosperity was wheat—one of the most important staples in our economic history. The first shipment of wheat out of the region was about 860 bushels sent to Toronto via St. Paul in 1876, when the Ontario crop was poor. In 1891, the total output of wheat was forty-two million bushels, multiplying to ten times this figure in 1915. At first the grain was handled in sacks but the adoption of the elevator system of the United States permitted handling in bulk, saved time and cut expenses. The Canadian Pacific did not have sufficient funds available to construct elevators itself. Consequently it encouraged independent financial interests to build elevators by providing them with free sites and by undertaking not to allow farmers to load their own cars. Needless to say, farmers objected to being compelled to ship all their grain through the elevators and they complained too, regarding the grades which they received for their product. To rectify the situation the Dominion Government set up certain standards of quality for grain, required that the railway erect loading platforms which farmers could use to fill their own cars, and stipulated that cars should be provided to all applicants without discrimination.

Meanwhile farmers in several communities had organized for their mutual protection. One of these groups, the Territorial Grain Growers' Association, brought the Canadian Pacific before the courts for contravening the Grain Act by failing to supply a car to farmers who wished to load their grain independently. The railway was fined the paltry sum of ten dollars but the moral victory was great. Farmers' organizations were so encouraged that they began seriously to consider entering the grain business themselves. After much discussion the Territorial Grain Growers turned down a proposal to enter the trade, but a group of farmers around Indian Head, Saskatchewan, formed the Grain Growers' Grain Company in which they purchased shares for two dollars each. The Company acquired a seat on the Winnipeg Grain Exchange and began to handle farmers' grain on commission. In this way, farmers who had loaded their own cars at the platform could send their grain to the Grain Growers' Grain Company who, in turn, sold it to agents of Eastern Canadian millers or European importers, and remitted the proceeds, less a commission of one cent a bushel, to the farmer or group of farmers concerned. The grain dealers already in the trade tried to force the farmers' company out of business by denying it trading privileges on the Exchange, and even by threatening to disband the Exchange or remove it to the Head of the Lakes. The Grain Growers' Grain Company thrived on opposition, for the actions of the Exchange merely served to substantiate the farmer's belief that the previously established trading organizations were operated to his detriment. An increasing number of farmers loaded cars by hand and sent their grain through the co-operative association instead of through the elevator companies. The farmers' company was a great success financially and, what was more, it used part of its profits to establish a magazine, a powerful influence for the education of farmers in the practices of the grain trade and the principles of co-operation.

Since the Grain Growers' Grain Company was solely in the commission end of the business, the farmer still had to ship his grain through a privately owned elevator or load a car from a loading platform. The farmer disliked the former method and he found the latter inconvenient and expensive because, in order to secure complete use of every car, the railway levied a charge (demurrage) if the car were not loaded promptly. To a farmer hauling grain by team perhaps ten miles to the nearest town, the demurrage charge raised difficulties. Groups of farmers in a few communities had already erected elevators of their own. Few of these had been profitable. The real cause of failure in most cases was poor management, but farmers believed that the trouble was excessive and unfair competition by the independent companies. They felt, also, that they lacked the funds necessary to establish an elevator in every important town and that a line or chain of elevators was necessary for success. Consequently, they brought pressure to bear on the various provincial governments to purchase or erect elevators to be owned and operated by the Government.

The agitation was particularly strong in Manitoba and here, in 1909, the Government acquired a number of elevators, paying extravagant prices for some of them. By 1912 the whole scheme collapsed because of the poor location of some elevators and continuous mis-management of all. The more favourably situated elevators were then leased, later sold, to the Grain Growers' Grain Company. Meanwhile, in Saskatchewan, a Royal Commission had recommended that the Government avoid entering the elevator business itself, but that it loan on a twenty year mortgage, up to 85 per cent of the cost of any elevator erected by a farmers' co-operative company. The local elevators erected under this scheme were to associate with each other to form the Saskatchewan Co-operative Elevator Company, Ltd. In spite of objections by some farmers that the Government had not gone far enough with its assistance, the scheme was proceeded with and in 1913, was adopted in Alberta also. Later the Grain Growers' and Alberta companies amalgamated into the United Grain Growers which continued to publish the

magazine, acquired a grain export concern and formed
live-stock and farmers' supply departments. The Saskatchewan Co-operative remained independent of the
merger because it wanted to confine its activities to grain
alone. These co-operatives were extraordinary, and indeed, spectacular successes. By 1920 they had about
60,000 members scattered throughout the West; from
their profits they paid good dividends to their shareholders, and from the same source they obtained funds
to erect new elevators and equip the old ones with the
most efficient machinery.

/ During the Great War enormous quantities of wheat
were required to supply the Allied armies and the civilian
population of Britain and France. In these two countries
domestic agriculture was neglected in favour of the production of munitions and implements of war, and one of
their former important sources of supply of wheat, Russia,
was cut off. The result of heavily increased demands and
reduced supply in Europe was exceptionally high prices.
Under their stimulus and the "Win the War through
Production" campaigns of the Canadian Government,
acreage greatly increased. Unfortunately for the war
effort, production did not increase proportionately because
during the War years weather in Western Canada, generally speaking, was not favourable to large crops. In
order to prevent prices rising too high or fluctuating too
rapidly under the stresses of war-time conditions, the
Government purchased all the wheat grown at a fixed
price which in the crop year, 1919-20, was $2.63 a bushel.
At this price, even though the cost of implements, farm
supplies and household needs had increased, the farmer
made money. In 1920, the Government felt that the war
emergency had passed and refused to continue the Wheat
Board. Shortly after the Government withdrew from

the market, the price of wheat began to fall and in September, 1921, averaged $1.51, and a year later, was a little less than one dollar a bushel at Winnipeg. This decline was disastrous to the farmer for he still owed for equipment purchased at inflated war-time prices, and the prices of clothing and other manufactured goods which he required fell much more slowly than prices of wheat. Since the Wheat Board and good prices had previously existed at the same time, it was easy to argue that if the Wheat Board had been continued the price would not have fallen. In spite of agrarian pressure the Government refused to re-establish the Board. To combat their disabilities the farmers in the West, like those in Ontario with whom they co-operated, formed their own political party, the Progressives. This group was not successful in getting much relief by means of political measures, even though it had control of the Governments of Alberta and Manitoba and, from 1921 to 1926, held the balance of power at Ottawa. The failure to secure favourable legislation forced the farmers to take matters in their own hands and create an agency of their own to handle all their wheat.

In attempting to find a solution to the problem of marketing their grain, Western farmers became interested in the experiences of the Citrus Fruit Co-operatives of California. The essential idea of the California organization was that each grower delivered his fruit to a branch of the Co-operative for grading, and received at once an initial payment in cash. The amount of the initial payment was determined by the executive of the association who estimated the average, or so-called basic, price at which the crop would sell and paid the grower perhaps 75 per cent of this, adjustments being made for different grades. As the crop was sold, the farmer re-

ceived two or three additional cash payments. The total
of all payments made to all growers was equal to the
total proceeds from the sale of all the fruit, less the cost
of operating the organization. The co-operative itself
operated on a non-profit basis, that is, it merely paid its
expenses and remitted all the remaining revenue to the
farmers whose fruit it handled. To put the matter in
different terms, all the fruit was put together in a vast
bin, or pool, and sold. After operating expenses had been
paid, each grower received from the co-operative a sum
which bore the same relation to the money received from
the sale of all the pooled fruit, as the quantity of his fruit
bore to the total amount of the fruit in the pool.

The Citrus Co-operatives had been outstanding successes but factors other than pooling may have been
responsible. By skilful advertising the Co-operatives had
greatly increased the demand for oranges, grapefruit and
lemons. Also, with a perishable product, it is important
to avoid gluts for these lead to loss through rotting or
price declines or both. The Co-operatives prevented glut-
ting by orderly marketing, that is, by diverting cars
which were on their way to Eastern markets away
from cities where gluts were likely to occur to places
where a relative scarcity existed. In the case of wheat,
however, there is little possibility of increasing consumption by advertising, and in a trade already highly organized and with a comparatively imperishable article, there
is little chance of further economies by orderly marketing.
Nevertheless, the example of the California Co-operatives,
together with that of the Wheat Board, was instrumental
in stirring up enthusiasm for a new type of farmers'
organization in the grain trade.

The new organization was based on pooling and the sale
of a very considerable proportion, and perhaps all, West-

ern grain by a single agency. In 1923 a wheat pool began to operate in Alberta and in the following year, in the other two provinces. Over these provincial pools was a co-ordinating body, the Canadian Co-operative Wheat Producers, Ltd., commonly known as the Wheat Pool. The original intention, apparently, was to have every farmer sell his grain through the one agency, that is, a one hundred per cent pool, but farmers were hesitant about tying themselves up with one organization for a term of years, and thus foregoing the right to sell by alternative methods, such as independent grain operators. Commonly the Pool handled only a little more than forty per cent of the crop.

Originally some of the Pool members seemed to have had the idea that the new organization, by refraining from selling when the price was low, could arbitrarily raise the world price of wheat. This was impossible because, although Canada ordinarily supplies over forty per cent of the world's export wheat, she provides less than fifteen per cent of the world's total wheat. Therefore, if Canadians tried to hold up the prices of their wheat above the world level, grain from other regions would come into the world market. The Pool soon discovered its limitations and decided that it had to do precisely what the individual trader does—sell when the price is considered to be a good one and refuse to sell when the price is too low. What is a "good" price is a matter of knowing the conditions of demand and supply and interpreting this information in terms of cents per bushel. Trading in wheat is basically a matter of shrewdness. Of course the Pool is such a big operator that its actions may in themselves affect the price temporarily but fundamentally, price is set by demand in various countries of the world and by rainfall, frost, hail, excessive heat and generally by climatic conditions affecting supply in every region in the world where wheat is grown. The Pool could make exceptional gains only if its managers had more information, or were more shrewd in interpreting it, than other men in the trade.

The Pool soon saw that the rewards of pure selling were not very great for the wheat trade is highly organized. Hence the Pool decided to go back to the co-operative elevator system by purchasing, in 1926, the Saskatchewan Co-operative Elevator Company. The Pool also arranged to work closely with the United Grain Growers' Company. The latter refused to sell out to the Pool because it would not divorce its elevator business from its operations in live-stock, farm supplies, publishing and insurance, but it agreed to handle Pool grain on a cost-plus basis. The Pool elevators have been very profitable because most of them use the latest machinery and are designed to give low costs. They handle a large volume and since the cost of operating an elevator is largely fixed, the greater the volume of grain handled, the lower the cost per bushel. The Pool also controls elevators at the Head of the Lakes and at Vancouver.

For the first few years of its existence the Pool handled grain in the same general manner as the independent traders. It is difficult to determine whether the Pool paid more to the farmer than the independents did. Probably the difference, if any, was not great. The Pool attempted to sell directly to the European miller and by so doing stirred up a good deal of ill-will from the commission merchants and importers in Europe. Each year the Pool sold the previous season's crop before the new year's crop came on the market.

Meanwhile the general wheat situation was reasonably good. After the immediate post-war deflation of 1920, the wheat market had more or less stabilized, with the world's average production for the years 1921-25 substantially the same as for the pre-war years, 1909-13. Of course between the two periods production in Canada had nearly doubled, and in Argentina and Australia had increased by fifty per cent, whereas European output had declined. After 1925, however, Europe, including Russia which was before the war a huge producer, gradually came back into the wheat picture. In 1928, world production of wheat was nearly thirty per cent above 1909-13 or 1921-25 averages. This was followed in the very next year by a crop fifteen per cent above average. In the face of this situation stocks of wheat rose and prices fell from an average in Winnipeg of $1.60 in 1929, to 42 cents in 1932, the prices quoted being for Number 1 grade wheat delivered at the Head of the Lakes. Because the Western farmer had to pay transportation charges to Lakehead and because his wheat was often poorer than Number 1 quality, his net returns per bushel were less than the figures quoted by anything up to fifteen or twenty cents.

As already pointed out, up to the crop year of 1928-29, the Pool had, each season, balanced sales and receipts. By the end of each crop year they had substantially no grain in stock and had paid to farmers all the net proceeds of the sale of the pooled wheat. On August 1, 1929, that is at the end of the crop year 1928-29, the Pool was holding 77,000,000 bushels of wheat on which it had advanced $1.18½ a bushel for the best grade, and proportionately less for poorer grades. The Pool felt that the price was too low and that it would be higher in the following year because the prospects for the Canadian crop were poor. For a time the price did increase and this seemed to confirm the Pool's action. Independent operators on the Grain Exchange were following the same policy. But before the end of the calendar year it had become clear that, although the Canadian crop was poor, the world crop was larger than normal. In February the price of wheat was $1.17 a bushel—less than the advances on the 1928-29 crop, and not a great deal more than the initial payment of $1 on the 1929-30 crop. Now the Pool had obtained most of the cash to make the advances by borrowing from the chartered banks with the grain as security. As the price was falling rapidly there was fear that, in order to get back their money, the banks would have to sell the grain, "close out" the Pool. The sudden sale of the enormous holdings of the Pool would lead to a disastrous break in the price. Consequently, the three Provincial Governments felt obligated to guarantee the banks against loss on the advances they had made to the Pool. Eventually the Provinces, aided by the Dominion, had to advance $22,000,000 under this guarantee but were repaid from the profits of operating the Pool elevators.

After this experience the Pool undertook to finance the 1930-31 crop alone. To avoid being "caught" it made the initial payment much smaller than the going price of wheat but so rapidly did the price fall that, in November 1930, the Pool was compelled to appeal again to the Government. In some instances it had already advanced more than the then market price and in other cases, the initial payment was so close to the market price that the Pool feared the banks might again threaten to close it out. Since the Provincial Governments were not in a sufficiently strong financial position to guarantee the advances, the Dominion did so, and to protect itself against heavy possible loss, it began to take an active part itself in selling wheat. The history of Pool operations has been sketched in some detail in order to show how, in spite of what appeared at the time to be careful management, inexorable forces pulled the Government into the wheat business.

After 1930 the Dominion Government dominated the market. Pooling was abandoned with the 1931-32 crop. The provincial pools were dissolved and the Canadian Co-operative Wheat Producers reverted to operating the large number of elevators which it owned. Government wheat policy was commonly referred to as Pool policy but this was really incorrect. In 1932, a direct cash subsidy or bonus of five cents a bushel was paid to the grower but this plan was abandoned because it was too expensive. In 1933, an international agreement among producers attempted to limit production, but the lack of storage capacity in the Argentine compelled that country to throw its grain on the market and this action was used as a reason, or an excuse, for non-adherence by Canada and other producers. During the years 1931-35 the Pool, virtually the Government, by a series of transactions too complicated to be outlined here, tried to keep up the price of Canadian wheat. It is difficult to say how much the Government's action helped the price of wheat. The natural forces in the world market moving prices up and down are undoubtedly more powerful in the long run than the influences of any individual agency or government. At the same time, conditions would have been more serious had the Government not intervened. In any event Canada found herself holding a larger and larger percentage of the world's annual carryover. Moreover, her policy stirred up much ill-will on the part of importers and millers in Europe.

The position of the Government in the grain business was regularized in 1935 by the appointment of a Wheat Board, replacing the unsatisfactory arrangement of operating through the Pool trading organization. A change in the Dominion Government resulted in a change in the personnel of the Board as well as a change of policy. Government holdings were not to be held at exorbitant premiums over the wheat of other countries, but were to be disposed of as soon as conditions warranted. The Board was empowered to buy wheat from farmers at a fixed price, and issue participation certificates entitling the producer who sold to the Board to receive a share of any amounts which the Board may receive above the minimum price when the grain is actually sold. Fundamentally the Board operated on a pooling principle but, since it worked under government guarantee, it was able to make a higher initial payment than the farmers' co-operative could safely undertake to pay. Most grain was handled through independent agencies and the Board acted from 1935 to 1940 mainly as "a buffer between chaotic conditions in the international market and farmers on the land in Western Canada".

The Pool is the outstanding example of agricultural co-operation in Canada. Without its operations and the government intervention which superseded it, conditions in Western Canada, during the 1930's, might have been much worse than they actually were. On the other hand active participation by governments in business operations has dangerous implications. It was only a long series of poor world crops which enabled the Dominion to escape without very heavy losses. Moreover the problem of drought in the Prairies in the 1930's, and the general problem of a highly variable regional income were both so unusually complicated that the Government had more than enough to do dealing with these challenging situations, without embarking on a strictly business venture of enormous magnitude.

The economy of the West is dependent on wheat, but the problems involved in this dependence are more far-reaching than those connected simply with the sale of the staple. Fundamentally the problem of the Prairie Provinces is one of variable income and heavy overhead charges. Income varies because of rapid changes in the world price, in the yield due to climatic conditions, and in grade. These factors do not necessarily tend to offset each other. Low yields in Canada do not always mean high world prices, and vice versa. If they did, the farmer's income in poor crop years would be about equal to his income in years with a high yield, low-priced crop. Furthermore what the farmer actually receives for his crop is the world price (that is, the price of wheat at Liverpool, the centre of the world market) less the cost of handling the grain from the country elevator to Liverpool. Usually the costs of handling amount to between thirty and thirty-five cents a bushel. These costs are fairly rigid, i.e. they decline only very slightly, if at all, with a decline in the price of wheat. If the price in Liverpool falls from $1.50 to 75 cents, the net price on the farm would decline from $1.15 to 40 cents a bushel. A reduction of fifty per cent in Liverpool means a fall of sixty-five per cent in the net to the farmer. When prices rise, the farmer's net income rises disproportionately.

In addition to rigid transportation charges, the farmer typically has to pay interest on his mortgage, and taxes on his farm. Also he ought to provide for depreciation on his buildings and machinery. Neither interest, taxes nor depreciation vary with crop prices, yields or grades. Furthermore, the costs of raising wheat are largely costs per acre and are pre-determined. The total expenses for plowing, cultivating, seeding, harvesting and threshing are practically the same whether the crop is large or small. If the crop is small or prices are poor, the farmer cannot go back and reduce his expenses for these were largely set once and for all when the crop was planted. On the other hand, with a large crop the cost per bushel is low and, given reasonable prices, the farmer makes money. In short, farming has some of the characteristics of a gamble. Prosperity varies with all the factors which determine world prices, with individual farm yield, and individual quality; this is aggravated by rigid transport expenses which accentuate the fluctuations in farm net; it is further complicated by the rigidity of most farm expenses.

These conditions are normal and inevitable and in the long run, the farmer must receive an income adequate to pay him at least as much as he could earn elsewhere. In the 1930's, however, there was a long series of years in which there was a coincidence of low prices and poor yields. Many farmers had no crops for five or six years on end. In the southern half of Saskatchewan and in adjacent parts of Manitoba and Alberta, there was almost a complete drought. In fact, drought is scarcely the word —had the same conditions occurred in Asia there would have been a famine, and only the assistance of the Government and of private individuals prevented famine here. In other parts of the West crops were also poor but nothing comparable to conditions in this belt. Everywhere the situation was grave; in the south, it was acute.

In view of the wide-spread distress one would have expected farmers to cease growing wheat or probably move elsewhere. As a matter of fact there was some migration to British Columbia, to Ontario and to the more favoured farming and mining regions in the north-central parts of the West. Nevertheless most of the people remained at home and continued to grow wheat, for there was no water for cattle and mixed farming. The people stayed, pulled in their belts, lived off government relief or cars of food given by other farming communities in Canada and hauled in without charge by the railways. The people let their store bills run if they could. They could not pay taxes to support their schools and telephone systems. Their buildings and implements went without repairs. They lived off their capital.

In many respects the problem of the 1930's was not simply one of the depression, but an accumulation of difficulties which had been latent for many years. The wave of settlement before the war resulted in a great increase in the birth rate. As these children grew they overflowed the public and then the high schools, creating problems of accommodation and teacher training. In the 1930's the number of young persons seeking employment on farms or in industry and trade in Western Canada was larger, relative to the total population, than elsewhere in Canada. Moreover, because of the great rush of settlers, the influence of patriotism during the war, and especially because of high prices coinciding with years of good rainfall, areas had been settled which, over a long period of years, had inadequate moisture to grow wheat. A more careful settlement policy would have reserved these lands for grazing and would have concentrated wheat growing in the areas best suited to it. Such concentration would have reduced the road and telephone mileage, cut down the number of schools, and generally reduced the cost of providing government services in the West. Unfortunately the mistakes had already been made; during the 'thirties they became apparent and, at the same time, infinitely more difficult to solve.

In view of the wide-spread distress, relief had to be

provided. In September 1937, of the approximately 755,-000 people on relief in Canada more than 300,000 were on agricultural relief and ninety per cent of these were in Saskatchewan. The Provincial Governments found themselves financially incapable of handling such a burden, for their own income from taxation was reduced. Indeed, the expenditures on farm relief in Saskatchewan for the years 1929-38 greatly exceeded the total ordinary provincial revenue for the same period. Hence the Dominion Government had to assume this burden directly. In addition, it had to make other advances and guarantees to the Prairie Provinces to cover other expenses, chiefly for paying interest on the provincial debts.

In order to relieve the farmer from part of the burden of interest, Debt Adjustment Acts were passed providing a moratorium, that is, denying the creditor the right to have the court enforce his claims, and in effect postponing payment of the debt except on a voluntary basis. In addition there was some compulsory scaling down under the Farmers' Creditors Arrangement Act, whereby debtor and creditor agreed on a reduction in interest or principal or both. Failing mutual agreement an adjustment, obligatory to both parties, was made by a law court. Provisions for complete revision of all the mortgage debt, both urban and rural, held by mortgage, trust, and insurance companies were passed by Parliament, but deferred on the opening of the second Great War. These adjustments gave some help to the individual farmer but scarcely touched the broad problem of variable income and heavy fixed charges.

Another proposal for the solution of the problem was to move people from the dried-out area in the south up to the north where rainfall was slightly greater, and evaporation less on account of the lower temperature. Some families did move and successfully re-established them-selves but, as a solution to the general problem, the scheme had decided limitations. A family with very little income for years on end is not in a position to assume the cost of moving. Once it has arrived on land in the north, it lacks the capital, not to mention the skill and experience, required for mixed farming. In any case the problem of maintaining the schools, telephones and medical services in the vacated areas is made worse when people move out, for the services cannot be cut down proportionately.

The final possibility is the re-habilitation of Prairie farms. Retain moisture by summer fallow, prevent soil drifting by planting rows of trees or by cultivating the land in strips with the alternate areas in grass, develop even better drought-tolerant grains than at present, abandon some land entirely—this is the programme. All these things had been applied for years but the intensity of the drought demanded more aggressiveness in their application. Efforts are being made also to prevent the large spring run-off of water by constructing dugouts (artificial ponds) and dams. It is realized that irrigation on a large scale is impossible because of cost and a posi-tive lack of water. On the other hand, it is expected that the dugouts will provide water for a farm garden or, as a last reserve, for stock so that families and communities can at least subsist in poor years. In areas where grain growing is impracticable under normal conditions the Province would move the few people whose lands have not already been seized for taxes to another locality; the Federal Government would then establish community pas-tures there, regrassing if necessary, and would lease pasturage rights to farmers in good lands roundabout. On the whole the rehabilitation programme is excellent.

The schemes adopted will prevent a breakdown in the morale of the people in the drought area in any future depression and enable them to keep body and soul together. People farther north will be able to make ends meet because they are less dependent on wheat and less subject to drought. The chief criticism of the rehabilitation programme is that it was started much too late. Nevertheless, the essential problem of variable income and heavy overhead remains. Since 1935 the Canadian Wheat Board has supervised interprovincial and export sales of all wheat, oats, and barley produced in Western Canada. Fundamentally it is a pool operated by the federal government. During the War farmers were able to pay off debts. Afterwards they bought the latest machinery and consolidated farms into larger operating units. In some years the biggest problem was that of storing exceptionally heavy crops until they could be profitably sold.

The preceding discussion has been concerned mainly with wheat, since the Prairie Provinces get over half their farm income from wheat and the remainder from coarse grains and animals. As early as 1911, throughout the West and especially in Manitoba, there was a pronounced shift to coarse grains, i.e. oats, barley, rye, and flax. Land which had been devoted to growing wheat alone was becoming "farmed out", that is, yields of wheat were being reduced through continuous cropping of that one product. A rotation of crops was necessary to permit the soil to recoup itself. Also, as time went on, weeds became more prevalent and it became desirable to grow a crop like barley which matured more quickly than wheat, thus permitting the farmer to get on the land earlier in the fall to destroy the weeds. Also diversity of production lessened the dangerous dependence on one staple.

During the drought of the 1930's, the planting of grass for hay and pasture was encouraged in order to prevent soil drifting. Finally, the progress of settlement toward the northern part of the area where rainfall is slightly greater and evaporation less than in the south encouraged mixed farming. The movement northward was expedited by the filling in of the railway network during the 1920's, and by the propagation of more quickly maturing types of wheat, notably Marquis developed by Sir Charles Saunders in 1902, and the less successful Garnet and Reward developed in 1929. Despite these improvements in plant breeding which aided the production of wheat in areas with shorter growing seasons, coarse grains and dairy products are much more important in the north-central areas than farther south. The grassy foothills of the Rockies were important cattle ranching areas even before the railways came, but their output of cattle and also of sheep increased greatly after 1900.

Since coarse grains are much less valuable in proportion to bulk than wheat, they are not exported to the same extent, especially in view of the low prices after 1920. Instead they are fed to live-stock in the immediate vicinity of the place of production and, if necessary, the more valuable live-stock, dead stock, or dairy products can be sent out of the area. In the twenty-five years after 1911 the number of cattle more than doubled, the number of sheep multiplied nearly five times and, in spite of mechanization, the number of horses increased by fifty per cent. The output of butter and cheese in the three provinces has steadily increased and in the 1950's was about two-thirds that produced in Ontario. In Southern Alberta, an area of about 350,000 acres is irrigated and specializes in the production of sugar beets, alfalfa and hogs.

One sub-region in the Prairies required special attention, namely, the Peace River country of Alberta and British Columbia. Although some colonizers went in before the first War, settlement on an extensive scale occurred only during the early 1920's when the Peace was widely heralded as the "Last Great West". The region can produce wheat of excellent quality and with certainty of a fair crop. On the other hand, it is handicapped by its distance from markets. The area agitated for years for an outlet to the Pacific, and coastal cities supported this agitation with "On to the Peace" campaigns. In the 1950's a highway and the Pacific Great Eastern, a railway owned by the Province of British Columbia, were extended into the area. The economic soundness of the railway is doubtful but British Columbia did not want the northern part of the province, including the section along the Alaska Highway, to become economically tributary to Edmonton.

The Peace River country is hampered also by the lack of water. The rainfall is higher than in most of the West and evaporation is less, because of the generally cooler weather even in summer. The result is that moisture is always adequate for crops, but the depth of the surface soil is so great that it is impossible to dig, and difficult to drill wells. The rivers have dug their channels so deeply below the general level of the land that it is hard to draw water from them. Consequently, dairying can be carried on in the Peace itself only to a limited extent. Hogs are raised in many districts north of Edmonton, because they do not require as much water as cattle and are a means of concentrating oats which, in their raw state, are not sufficiently valuable in relation to their bulk to bear the high transportation charges out of the region. Since 1957 the movement of natural gas by pipe-line has added another resource to the economy of this sub-region. The Alaska Highway has, as yet, very limited commercial significance.

The manufacturing of the West is based either on its agricultural resources such as meat packing, flour milling and dairy factories, or on the needs of the resident population such as baking, printing and oil refining. Although manufacturing in the Prairies has shown a steady growth in recent years, their total output is only about fifteen per cent of that in Ontario.

The mineral resources of the West, exclusive of those in the Laurentian Shield, are chiefly coal and petroleum. The total coal output, largely secured from the Drumheller and Coleman districts of Alberta, roughly equals the output of Nova Scotia in terms of quantity but is of poorer quality. It was used mainly for domestic and railway purposes throughout the West and for smelting in British Columbia. Since 1945 it has been hurt by natural gas, fuel oil and diesel fuel. Petroleum was discovered in the Turner Valley not far from Calgary in 1914. The field enjoyed a great boom in the late 1920's but was eclipsed by the discovery of oil at Leduc just south of Edmonton in 1945. Later drilling revealed the existence in the West of one of the world's great reserves. The refining capacity on the Prairies has been enlarged and pipe-lines for crude oil built to Vancouver, Sarnia and Toronto. By 1960 pipe-lines will deliver natural gas from enormous reserves in Alberta and the Peace River area of British Columbia to almost every large urban centre between Vancouver and Montreal. Natural gas is also exported to the Pacific Northwest of the United States.

To sum up, the general economy of the Prairie Provinces has been based on one staple, wheat, and its fundamental economic problem arose out of a variable income from

wheat coupled with relatively fixed charges. The output
of coarse grains and animal products is becoming more
important, while manufacturing and especially mineral
resources are increasing in significance. Yet Saskatchewan is still almost exclusively "The Wheat Province",
and despite recent developments, its neighbours still rely
heavily on agriculture. Even so, the economy of the West
is changing rapidly. On the whole the West is the best,
or worst, example of a staple economy in Canadian history.

SELECTED READINGS

BLADEN, V. W., *An Introduction to Political Economy*, Toronto,
1956, Chapter V.

BRITNELL, G. E., *The Wheat Economy*, Toronto, 1939.

CARROTHERS, W. A., *Emigration from the British Isles*, London,
1929.

DAWSON, C. A., *The Settlement of the Peace River Country*,
Toronto, 1934.
Group Settlement: Ethnic Communities in Western Canada,
Toronto, 1936.

DAWSON, C. A. and YOUNG, EVA R., *Pioneering in the Prairie
Provinces*, Toronto, 1940.

EASTERBROOK, W. T. and AITKEN, H. G. J., *Canadian Economic
History*, Toronto, 1956, pp. 476-513.

FOWKE, V. C., *Canadian Agricultural Policy*, Toronto, 1946.
National Policy and the Wheat Economy, Toronto, 1957.

GRIFFIN, H. L., "Public policy in relation to the wheat market",
C.J.E.P.S., August, 1935, pp. 482-500.

HEATON, H., *The Story of Trade and Commerce, with special reference to Canada*, Toronto, 1955 (rev. ed.), pp. 229-36, 240-51.

HEDGES, J. B., *Building the Canadian West*, Toronto, 1939.

INNIS, H. A. and LOWER, A. R. M., ed., *Select Documents*, Toronto,
1933, pp. 730-70.

INNIS, M. Q., *An Economic History of Canada*, Toronto, 1954, pp.
217-225, 236-52.

MACKINTOSH, W. A., *Prairie Settlement, the Geographical Background*, Toronto, 1934.
Economic Problems of the Prairie Provinces, Toronto, 1935.

MACGIBBON, D. A., *The Canadian Grain Trade*, Toronto, 1932.
The Canadian Grain Trade, 1931-1951, Toronto, 1952.

MORTON, A. S., *A History of the Canadian West to 1870-71*, Toronto, 1939.

MORTON, A. S., and MARTIN, CHESTER, *History of Prairie Settlement and "Dominion Lands" Policy*, Toronto, 1938.

MURCHIE, R. W., *Agricultural Progress on the Prairie Frontier*, Toronto, 1936.

PATTON, H. S., *Grain Growers' Co-operation in Western Canada*, Cambridge, 1928.

11

The Pacific Region

BRITISH Columbia and the Yukon constitute a distinct economic region in Canada. The area is distinct because of its mountainous character, its generally mild climate (except in the far north) its outlook on the Pacific and the varied nature of its resources. It is distinct also because until 1885, it stood almost completely aloof from economic development elsewhere in Canada. The region's early economic history was concentrated on furs but its present development is dependent on five main industries, namely, mining, agriculture, forestry, fishing and manufacturing, along with oceanic trade through Vancouver.

Mining in this region began after the discovery of gold in California (1849) had led to a search for it elsewhere along the Pacific Coast. In 1851 the Queen Charlotte Islands yielded three hundred pounds sterling of the precious metal, but the field soon played out. Seven years later the news of the discovery of gold, first along the Thompson near Kamloops, and then along the Fraser River near Yale, reached California and precipitated a great rush of frenzied people, estimated by San Francisco papers at as high as 30,000. Although British territory, there was no formal government on the mainland and hence James Douglas, the Governor of Vancouver Island, issued a proclamation under his own authority, extending his jurisdiction to the area. This action, later approved by the British Government, was instrumental in preserving law and order among the miners.

The gold rush reached great proportions. Diggings were scattered from Langley to Hope, sixty-three miles, were particularly thick in the following thirteen miles to Yale, and continued here and there along almost the whole length of the Fraser and Thompson. Mining was by the placer method. Gravel was shovelled from a sand bar in the river into a wooden cradle which was rocked back and forth while water was run through. The water, which was commonly supplied by a flume, washed away the gravel leaving the heavier gold dust or nuggets to settle to the bottom where they were caught by cleats or riffles. The prospector's pan in which water and gravel was washed around and gradually allowed to escape, was used only to discover whether or not a bar contained "pay dirt". The rewards of the miners might run up to $150 a day if the "diggings" were good, $25 a day was not uncommon, but many earned less than $3. Perhaps a third of the miners did very well, another third made a reasonable income and the remainder would have been better off if they had stayed at home. Miners were convinced that since the gold had obviously been carried down by the river from its headwaters a "mother lode" must exist somewhere. Hence they searched the upper reaches of the Fraser and its tributaries. They were rewarded in 1860 at Cariboo Lake and in 1862, at Williams and Lightning Creeks—regions of spectacular production in the early 1860's, and whose total output in five years of boom and another fifteen years of slow decline was between thirty and forty million dollars. In comparison with this the lower Fraser discoveries were "a flash in the pan".

These gold booms had important effects on the development of British Columbia. They advertised the region in Britain and America. They forced the establishment

of a government on the mainland and the divorce, nomin-
ally at least, of the government from the trading monopoly
of the Hudson's Bay Company. The collapse of the interior
gold rush in the late 1860's left the colony on the mainland with inadequate resources and a heavy debt. This
situation led to the union of the mainland and Vancouver
Island colonies, and paved the way for the eventual union
with Canada. The rushes stimulated local agricultural
and timber production. They lead to the establishment
of banks and trading centres. They encouraged improvements in shipping along the Coast and the lower Fraser,
and compelled the construction of a wagon road into the
Cariboo. In brief the gold rushes laid the basis for much
of the later development of British Columbia.

Toward the end of the century a new gold rush occurred,
this time to the Yukon. The news of the discovery of
gold along the Klondike and other tributaries of the
Yukon River reached the outside world late in 1896, and
at once there was a great rush of men from all parts of
the world up the river, through Chilkoot Pass and even
overland from Edmonton. A great boom, what has been
described as an economic cyclone, created Dawson City
with a population at its peak of over 10,000. A few made
great fortunes but, as usual, many were disappointed.
The richest deposits were worked over first by the use
of the crude placer methods of the earlier British Columbia
fields. Then the underlying gravel was exploited, though
the fact that the sands with the best gold content were
close to the bed rock and were frozen throughout the year
necessitated a system of thawing by wood fires, or by
heated stones thrown down to the bottom of shallow
shafts, or by running cold water through the frozen
gravels. Then the bars and river beds with less 'pay dirt'
were robbed of their gold by means of dredges, long

flumes and sluices and mechanical cradles. The sandy hills along the river banks were worked by forcing against them streams of water under such pressure that the gravel was washed through a mechanical cradle which extracted the gold. Eventually heavy mining equipment was brought in to crush the underlying rock and gravel, and extract the mineral from it. Coal, produced at places not far distant from the gold mines, was used to raise steam to thaw the ground and operate the machinery. In 1913, electricity was being generated for mining purposes thus lowering mining costs. Unlike Southern British Columbia and parts of Northern Ontario, the application of these improved techniques was incapable of lending permanence to the economy of the region. It has steadily declined in importance, and population in 1941 was only 4,900 or fifteen per cent of its peak in 1901 but rose to 12,000 in 1956. The Yukon now subsists on fur farming, the tourist industry, and national defence expenditures, though mining of silver, lead and gold is also important.

After the early gold fever in British Columbia had subsided, the Province turned to the exploitation of its other mineral resources. Coal had been discovered on Vancouver Island in 1835, and in the late 1840's some began to be sent to California and later, along the Fraser. Even so, it was not until 1875 that production exceeded 100,000 tons a year. The development was slow on account of the decline of gold mining, the imposition of duties by the United States, and the competition of coal brought from England in ships returning in ballast from carrying wheat from California, then an important grain growing area. In the 1880's the industry began to thrive. The railways provided a market for the coal because they used large amounts themselves, and gave access to industrial and domestic consumers. A great many mines were opened up in the Nanaimo region. The industry was put on a more profitable basis when the mines were consolidated and re-equipped by James Dunsmuir. Elsewhere in the Province, coal is mined at Fernie, Princeton and Merritt. Coal mining suffered severely during the business depression of the 1930's. Since about 1925 consumption has been reduced because of the use of more efficient methods of combustion in heating plants and because of competition from fuel oil, diesel fuel, natural gas, and sawdust which is used in many households in Coastal cities for heating. Several years ago the American tariff cut off what was formerly a good market for Princeton and Fernie coals. Generally, coal mining is of declining importance.

Silver, gold, copper, lead and zinc have been mined since the late 1880's in the Boundary district. In 1896-97 a great boom was experienced in the area, and Eastern Canada papers carried long dispatches on mining conditions especially in the vicinity of Rossland. The excitement about the region was soon overshadowed by the Klondike gold rush but the area, nevertheless, made progress. The history of the region is too complex to be given in detail but a few general trends stand out. In the early 1890's, the district seemed in danger of becoming economically tributary to Spokane, since the existence of long narrow lakes permitted tapping the traffic of large areas by means of a few relatively short railway lines built in from the south to the outlets of the lakes. Accordingly the Dominion Government in 1897, subsidized the construction of a railway from Lethbridge, Alberta, to Nelson, British Columbia. The line was later extended, largely with Provincial aid, across the southern part of British Columbia. Another important trend has been toward consolidation. One large corporation now carries on the smelting and a good deal of the mining in the district. It is able to raise capital more cheaply than smaller units can. It installs the most modern machinery, engages highly skilled managers and specialized mining engineers, metallurgists and chemists. It has been able to solve the problem of extracting minerals from very complicated ore bodies. The company is controlled by the Canadian Pacific which is, naturally, anxious to have the prosperity of the region continued in order that its lines may have a large volume of traffic.

Perhaps the most important trend, however, has been the steady improvement in the methods of extracting the minerals from the ore. The perfection of chemical processes of extraction, especially since 1920, has permitted a steady reduction in the cost of operation. The use of hydro-electric power has tended to the same end. The result is that the industry can use poorer grade ores which it did not pay to use with the earlier, more primitive methods. Also the base metals, especially lead and zinc, have become more important than the precious metals, gold and silver. In this way the Boundary district has been able to attain fairly continuous prosperity, whereas most mining camps are compelled to close up in a comparatively few years due to the exhaustion of mineral reserves.

Resources of metals are not confined to the Boundary area. Copper along Howe Sound, discovered in 1865 but not important until after 1900, was sent to Tacoma, Washington, for smelting before high operating costs and low prices for base metals forced the mine to close in 1956. The resources at Anyox, which at one time had the world's second largest copper reduction works, are now exhausted but copper in considerable amounts is still available at several points along the coast. Iron has also been discovered, deposits of tungsten, molybdenum, bismuth, antimony and cadmium exist and resources of clay, building stone and mineral salts are known. Gold continues to be mined and, indeed, its output increased greatly in the 1930's. Gold is secured partly as a by-product of other metals and partly in specialized areas of which the two most important are Bridge River, and the Zeballos area on Vancouver Island. Placer mining has virtually disappeared. Expensive rock-crushing machinery, under the control of large corporations has been introduced, as in other parts of Canada.

The mineral resources of British Columbia and the Yukon are varied and many of them still await development. The mining industry has aided agriculture, encouraged the development of hydro-electric power, the manufacture of explosives and, as a by-product of the sulphur fumes from copper refining, the production of fertilizer. Mining is, of course, an extractive industry and once the reserves are exhausted, the camps fold up. In order to secure continued prosperity mining requires either the steady development of new low-cost techniques, or the discovery of new areas. The huge consolidated enterprise in the Boundary area has, so far at least, been able to solve the first. On the other hand, the rate of discovery of new mineral areas has slowed down in the last few years. Heavy taxes on the profits of mining corporations are alleged to discourage expenditures on prospecting. At all events prospecting is difficult because of the mountainous character of the country, and transportation to mines by rail or highway is expensive for the same reason. The industry is unstable also, because the prices of metals, except gold, are subject to great fluctuations in the world market. The complex nature of the ores in British Columbia sometimes enables a mine to carry on production since a decline in the price of, say silver, may be offset by a rise or, at least, by the maintenance of the price of zinc or lead which are often found in the same ore body. Nevertheless, mining is not a wholly satisfactory basis on which to depend for prosperity.

The first agricultural development in British Columbia took place around the fur trading posts of the Hudson's Bay Company. Although production was small, these farms and gardens provided the traders with a welcome change of diet from their customary dried salmon, and reduced the amount of freight to be hauled laboriously into the country. Even more important was the fact that these farms demonstrated the agricultural possibilities of the region. Yet substantial progress came only with the gold-rushes to the Fraser and into the Cariboo. The miners created a large local market and prices were high, due to the cost of transportation. On account of these conditions some of the early farmers made extraordinary profits. For example, in 1863 one farmer drove thirty dairy cows into the Cariboo and netted $15 a day for four months. These profits, of course, disappeared as the gold-rush subsided.

Meanwhile the Okanagan Valley had been opened up, first for beef cattle and after 1874, for fruit. The Canadian Pacific and its branches made possible the export of apples and other tree fruits and also berries to the Prairies, where the chief market still lies. Just before the turn of the century the region was quickly settled by people, mainly from England, whose limited knowledge of horticulture was corrected by a Dominion experimental farm established in the vicinity. Because the rainfall is very limited in amount, most parts of the valley have to be irrigated. In the case of some of the irrigation schemes the promoters did not have proper knowledge of the available water supply, or they underestimated the seasonal variations in flow and the need for storage. Also the promoters did not appreciate that as an orchard becomes more mature, it needs more water. In consequence many projects failed and the Government had to come to the aid of the farmers concerned. The experiences of the Okanagan have been duplicated in other smaller areas throughout the valleys of southern British Columbia.

After 1900 the rapid growth of Vancouver, New Westminster and Victoria, and a change in dietary habits, stimulated dairying and truck farming in the lower Fraser valley and the Saanich peninsula. In the same areas, the climate favours the production of poultry, and here eggs are produced on a specialized commercial scale; quite a contrast to the small, poorly cared for flocks on many farms elsewhere in Canada. Cattle and sheep range the grasslands of the interior plateau of the Cariboo. As a rule precipitation is too light for field crops but alfalfa for finishing cattle for market is grown under irrigation in favoured spots. In the Yukon, good crops, especially of hay and roots, can be grown. Unfortunately the cost of transportation is so high that it does not pay to export farm products. As a result farming is confined to supplying local needs.

With the exception of the Cariboo and the Peace River Block, agriculture in British Columbia is hampered because of the high cost of land. In some places the forest cover is heavy and the cost of clearing is high; in others, the land must be irrigated and in still other areas, it must be dyked. Because land is expensive it is used intensively, a large amount of labour and capital (machinery in the form of spraying equipment, milking machinery, etc., and artificial fertilizer) being applied to a comparatively small amount of land in order to get high returns per acre. In general terms, British Columbia agriculture is concerned either with perishable products for sale in nearby cities, or with goods which cannot be grown on the Prairies.

The magnificent stand of timber along the coast attracted the attention of early explorers and settlers. It quickly provided a staple for export. In 1828 a cargo of Douglas fir was shipped to China, but the total development remained small for some years. A few simple mills were constructed to supply the needs of the Hudson's Bay Company and, later, the requirements of the gold rush with its demand for lumber for shacks, flumes and sluice-boxes. The first mill erected to engage primarily in the export trade was built at Alberni in 1861, but by 1870, Burrard Inlet was the centre of the trade. Lumber was sent to the Orient, Australia and South America. The construction of railways opened up new markets since they used substantial quantities of timber themselves and permitted lumber to be sent to the rapidly growing West, and excellent cedar shingles to the Prairies and the East. Production was facilitated by the highly indented coast-line both on the mainland and on Vancouver and the Queen Charlotte Islands, and the ease of hauling timber rafts down the protected channel along the coast to Vancouver. On the other hand it was hampered by steep slopes. The Panama Canal helped the industry just at the time the market in the Canadian West was beginning to decline. The Canal, by cutting the freight charges by as much as sixty per cent, enabled British Columbia to sell its forest products in Britain, in the Maritimes and, when tariffs were favourable, along the eastern seaboard of the United States. At present the industry is very heavily dependent on foreign markets.

New production methods have been introduced, in part by borrowing techniques developed under similar conditions in Washington and Oregon. In the early period trees were felled, trimmed, and then hauled by oxen or horses to skid-roads (roads with cross timbers greased with fish oil or tallow) and then pulled along the skid-roads to tide-water. Before 1890, donkey engines had replaced horses. To prevent the log binding against rocks and stumps as it was hauled along the ground, the front end was elevated by attaching a cable from it to a pulley at the top of a large "spar" tree, and thence to the donkey engine. Logging railways came into use for getting out timber which was located back from tide-water. By 1914, under the so-called sky-line system, the cable was suspended between two spar trees three or four hundred yards apart and logs, perhaps six at a time, were hauled clear of the ground. Usually they were carelessly allowed to swing back and forth just above the level of the ground, thus destroying all the young growth. Still more improved methods were introduced for "yarding", or hauling the logs to one point, and for loading them on flat cars. In the last few years caterpillar tractors, "cats" in the parlance of the trade, are used to yard to roads which are built in rough fashion by the company's "bull-dozers", and along which the logs are hauled away by heavy trucks and trailers. This method of logging has the advantage of being less destructive of new tree growth and is a boon to the small operator, because it involves less capital expenditure than sky-lines and logging railways. It cannot, however, be used on steep slopes.

Once the logs reach tide-water they are taken to mills in booms hauled by powerful steam or oil-burning tugs, a great advance from the paddle-wheel *Sudden Jerk* of the 1860's, which had only one speed and a non-reversible engine. The saw mills are large, steam operated, and use cranes and automatic log-turners, first introduced about 1900. The treatment of labour in the woods and mills has greatly improved. As has been the case in other parts of Canada, several pulp and paper mills have been established.

At present the forestry industry of British Columbia faces two big problems—markets and depletion. The first of these relates chiefly to access to foreign countries. The outlet in Western Canada fluctuates with agricultural prosperity there and the market in the United States, which from 1919 to 1931 took about forty-five per cent of the total output, has been partially cut off by a tariff. Consequently the markets are distant, chiefly in Britain and to some extent in the Orient. When ocean freight rates are low, the British Columbia product can be sold in these markets in competition with lumber from nearer areas, in the one case Norway and the Baltic countries, and in the other, Manchuria. When rates are high, the industry is handicapped. Similarly, changes in tariffs by foreign countries will affect the market. In any case prices and demand vary with the business cycle, a factor to which lumber is very sensitive since it is used in construction. Thus, aside entirely from competition from other building materials, such as concrete, steel, stucco and rubberoid products, the lumber market is typically unstable.

The problem of depletion is partly the matter of the prevention of forest fires and mainly that of over cutting. At the present rate of cutting, the merchantable supplies of Douglas fir will be used up in from ten to fifteen years. It is possible that improved methods of logging or higher prices for lumber will make it profitable to get out this Douglas fir which it does not pay to cut under present cost-price conditions. At all events, growth of new timber is not taking place fast enough to replace that being cut. A good proportion, perhaps half, of the cutover area is not reforesting properly with young trees and, in any case, it takes from two to three hundred years for fir to grow to the size of that being cut at present. The situation in regard to Douglas fir, a very high quality timber normally commanding a good price in foreign markets, is definitely serious. So far as other species are concerned, the supply is adequate for many years to come, but whether a region so far removed from the chief lumber consuming regions of the world can maintain its present prosperity depends on freight rates, foreign competition, tariff policies of other countries, and the demand for lower grade woods like spruce and hemlock.

Fishing plays an important part in the economic life of the Pacific coast province. Despite the fact that some exports of salted fish were made in the early years of settlement, it was only after 1885 that fishing reached significant proportions. Although it had been known as early as 1809 that food could be preserved by hermetically sealing it, it was the invention of a container or canister of steel covered with a very thin layer of tin (the tin can) that made the process cheap and, at the same time, rendered the product less susceptible to damage than if glass jars had to be used. The commercial feasibility of canning overcame the chief drawback of salmon as a staple which was its perishable nature. The completion of the Canadian Pacific opened up the Eastern Canadian market. As a result the fishing industry expanded rapidly, spreading gradually northward from the Fraser to the Skeena and Nass.

At first the fish were caught chiefly by Indians and were cleaned and canned by Chinese working on a contract basis. Gradually Anglo-Saxons, and then the Japanese in competition with them, began to undertake fishing using more modern, that is to say, more destructive methods than their predecessors. Much of the new equipment was loaned to the fishermen by the canneries each one of which was anxious to increase its own pack. Competition was keen and there was danger that certain areas might be "fished out". All agreements to limit production having failed, several companies owning canneries amalgamated in 1902, to form the British Columbia Packers Association (enlarged 1927). This group purchased a number of small plants, dismantled the uneconomic ones, installed better equipment in the rest and generally tried to stabilize the industry.

Since 1900, a number of significant changes have occurred in the industry. The export market has grown steadily until at present it consumes about half the pack, with Great Britain and other European countries as the chief outlets. Fresh salmon is frozen and sent to Eastern Canada in refrigerator cars. Machinery, usually electrically operated, has been devised for cleaning and cutting the fish though the best grades are still hand-packed. The offal, previously wasted, is now used for fertilizer or valuable oil. Fishing boats are operated by gasoline instead of sails and oars. In 1927 the number of fishing licenses issued to Canadians of Japanese descent was limited to four hundred yearly. After being debarred entirely in World War II, a few have been re-admitted. The seasonal nature of the business presents difficulties. Also the problem of conservation is acute since some methods of catching, such as trap and purse seining, are highly destructive of fish life. Proper methods of conservation are hard to adopt because of the conflicting jurisdictions of Provincial and Dominion Governments, and the need for concurrent legislation by Canada and the United States. Unfortunately the operation of fish hatcheries seems to offer only a partial solution to the problem. In spite of considerable "over-fishing", the salmon remains by far the most important commercial fish in British Columbia.

Fresh cod is sent mainly through Prince Rupert to markets in the West and even to the Atlantic Coast. Halibut, herring and pilchard are caught and used partly for human consumption, partly for oil, since fish in the Pacific Ocean seem to have a higher oil content than those in the Atlantic. Though not biologically a fish, whales are a minor sea resource in British Columbia being caught by ships from two stations on the Queen Charlotte Islands. Sealing, though exceedingly important in the 1880's, has now disappeared as far as Canada is concerned for, in accordance with a treaty with the United States, seal-fishing is now restricted in the interests of conservation.

In manufacturing, British Columbia ranks after Ontario and Quebec among the Canadian provinces but it is a very poor third indeed. Most manufacturing is concerned with the production of lumber, and pulp and paper, or with fish packing. In addition, oil refining, meat packing, canning and manufacturing for a strictly local market, like commercial baking and printing, are carried on. The Province has huge water-power resources. The heavy rains along the coast and the mountains give high heads. A head is the volume of the flow of water multiplied by its fall. The chief drawback to hydro-electric development is that the cost of harnessing and distributing power is typically heavier than elsewhere in Canada. At Kitimat, a few miles south of Prince Rupert, an extraordinarily cheap resource of hydro-electricity is used to make aluminum on a large scale.

British Columbia suffered a short but spectacular boom

from 1910 to 1913, and between the First and Second World Wars enjoyed a greater and, at the same time, more solid expansion. In the decade of the 1920's, the provincial output of lumber doubled, that of copper more than doubled, while the output of silver multiplied three times, of zinc four times and of lead ten times. Moreover, the development of trade through Vancouver was extraordinarily rapid. In the early 1930's, tariff action by other countries and the great decline in base metal prices handicapped the Province during the depression. Also the sudden collapse of the construction industry created widespread unemployment. Nevertheless the decline of per capita income in British Columbia was no greater than that for the Dominion as a whole. Expansion after the Second War was unprecedented.

The Province's greatest economic problem is of a long-run character. Many of her resources, mining, forestry and fishing, are of a wasting nature though the last two are not necessarily so. Besides, the sparseness of the population over much of the area and the mountainous terrain make the cost of government high, and a substantial debt for the construction of railways and highways has been incurred. Should any of the three industries using wasting assets suddenly collapse the Province would be left in a serious condition. It is to be hoped that this danger will be indefinitely postponed by the expansion of trade through Pacific ports, the development of manufacturing with hydro-electricity as a source of power, and the careful use of the varied resources of the Province.

SELECTED READINGS

BRITISH COLUMBIA, *Manual of Provincial Information*, Victoria, 1930.

CARROTHERS, W. A., *The British Columbia Fisheries*, Toronto, 1941.

CLARK, S. D., *The Social Development of Canada*, Toronto, 1942, pp. 308-79.

HOWAY, F. W., *British Columbia, the Making of a Province*, Toronto, 1928.

HOWAY, F. W., SAGE, W. N., and ANGUS, H. F., *British Columbia and the United States*, Toronto, 1942.

INNIS, H. A., and LOWER, A. R. M., *Settlement in the Forest and Mining Frontiers*, Toronto, 1936.
Select Documents, Toronto, 1933, pp. 771-808.

INNIS, M. Q., *An Economic History of Canada*, Toronto, 1954, pp. 225-235, 252-66.

SAGE, W. N., *Sir James Douglas and British Columbia*, Toronto, 1930.

12

The Canadian or Laurentian Shield

FOR the first few centuries of its existence Canada was a land of length without breadth, a string with a few beads of settlement along it. Even after the pre-War boom and the construction of several lines of railway, Canadian settlement was still narrow. But following the First World War, more depth was added and Canadians began to look northward and not merely east and west. To the original four economic regions—the Maritimes, the St. Lawrence Valley, the Prairies and the Pacific Coast—there was added a fifth Canada, the Laurentian or Canadian Shield.

The boundaries of the new economic region are not clearly defined. Geologically, the Shield is that great horse-shoe of igneous rock around Hudson Bay with an offshoot into Minnesota and another toward New York State. It incorporates most of Quebec north of the St. Lawrence and all Ontario except the western peninsula, the area immediately north of Lake Ontario and the lower Ottawa Valley. The region also includes the area north of a line drawn diagonally from the south-east corner of Manitoba to the north-west corner of Saskatchewan and thence northerly, bisecting Great Slave and Great Bear Lakes. Though not geologically part of this region, the lowlands south of James and Hudson Bays and the valley of the Mackenzie are considered to be part of the area in an economic sense. The chief industries of this enormous region, whose area is more than one-half that of Canada, are mining, pulp and paper production and, to a much less extent, agriculture and furs.

The earliest economic approach to the Canadian Shield took place when furs were exported from the region. Indeed, the first settlement on Hudson Bay was established only sixty years after Quebec itself was founded. But furs are a kind of "grab and run" economy, not providing a basis for large scale permanent settlement. Another skirmish with the economic forces of the Shield took place in the 1880's when settlers spilled over, so to speak, into the agricultural lands along the north shore of Lake Ontario, into Haliburton and the north half of Frontenac and Hastings counties. The land here is too rocky and the covering of soil, where any exists at all, is too thin to permit a profitable agriculture. Consequently, the settlers were thrown back with heavy losses in their standard of living and their self-respect.

When the agricultural areas of the Plains were being opened up, the Shield was regarded as a very definite barrier to their development. To be sure, a few mineral resources were discovered north of Lake Superior but for the most part, settlers and business men plunged through the rocky wastes in an effort to reach the more easily acquired wealth that lay beyond. It was only in the early part of the twentieth century that a real effort was made to exploit the wealth of the Shield itself. In order to open up a large area of good clay soil believed to be excellent for agriculture, and to make sure that the potential trade of the north country would go through Toronto rather than via its rival Montreal, the Ontario Government built a railway, now called the Ontario Northland, northward from the existing lines at North Bay. During the process of construction silver was discovered in 1902, at Cobalt. A few years later gold was found at Porcupine, ninety miles to the north-west and in 1912, at Kirkland Lake. The railway was pushed on to these points and eventually, in 1932, to the foot of James Bay. After the first War pulp and paper mills were constructed along the line, notably at Iroquois Falls. Two hundred and fifty miles to the westward another railway, the Algoma Central, was built from Sault Ste. Marie by the iron and steel interests at that point. The purpose of the line was to give access to the iron ores in the Michipicoten district. It was later extended to tap gold and pulp wood resources farther north.

In Quebec the Shield was attacked first by a railway line to the farming area around Lake St. John. The extensive water-power resources of the region were later used at Arvida, for producing aluminum from bauxite imported chiefly from British Guiana. These north-south railway lines in Ontario and Quebec were like three fingers feeling out the resources of the area. The National Transcontinental, now part of the Canadian National, running directly from Quebec to Winnipeg, was a transverse line joining the tips. It was designed to open up the Clay Belt, an elliptical shaped area of fertile soil stretching from east of the Quebec-Ontario boundary to Kapuskasing. In 1920, however, ores containing copper and gold were discovered at Rouyn. Five years later a railway line was driven southward to this region from the old National Transcontinental and then another, northeastward from the Ontario Government road. Further gold discoveries resulted in lines easterly from Rouyn and through Chibougamau. Other lines built in the late 1950's bring iron ore to Sept Iles and Port Cartier.

While these events were taking place, Manitoba was also pushing northward. Even in the 1880's an effort had been made to build a railway to Hudson Bay which, by providing an alternative outlet for grain, would permit escape from the monopoly of the Canadian Pacific. This effort came to naught but in the first decade of the twentieth century the project was revived. Construction was abandoned during the War but the line was completed in 1929. The Hudson Bay Railway was expected, by the West, to provide a cheap outlet for their grain. The distance from the grain fields to Liverpool is about twenty per cent shorter by way of Hudson Bay than via Montreal. The route through the Straits had been used by the Hudson's Bay Company for over two centuries without undue loss of ships, and it was believed that navigation would be even safer now that airplanes, radar and radio stations can be used to detect ice-fields and warn shipping of their location. Unfortunately, navigation in Hudson Straits closes by the end of October so that it is not possible to get out much of one year's crop until the following spring. It is uneconomical to store the grain at a Bay port over the winter, and hence the route has not become important as a grain carrier. After the railway had been constructed nearly to Port Nelson, its terminus was changed, on the advice of a British expert, to Churchill in order to take advantage of a better natural harbour. The mileage by rail was slightly increased by this change, and the considerable investment which had already been incurred for port facilities at Port Nelson had to be largely abandoned. Mineral resources were discovered at Flin Flon on the Saskatchewan-Manitoba boundary. In 1928 a line was built into the town from the Hudson Bay Railway. In 1953 it was extended northward to another base metal mine at Lynn Lake. Hydro-electric power is produced near these towns. Traffic with

Europe along the Hudson Bay Railway is growing but the line is chiefly important in defence and in the development of nearby mines.

Just before and during the first War, Alberta too, became ambitious to penetrate the North. She built a railway from Edmonton to Waterways, near the junction of the Athabaska and Clearwater Rivers. Beyond this point flat bottomed, paddle-wheel steamers could carry goods during the summer along the broad, but shallow waters of the Mackenzie and its tributaries. The line was not profitable to the Province and has since been disposed of to the two transcontinental railways who operate it jointly. The Edmonton, Dunvegan and British Columbia toward the Peace River belt was built by private investors during and immediately after the Great War but, having failed, it was taken over by the Canadian National and the Canadian Pacific to be operated jointly.

These half dozen lines of railway, along with the transverse line in Ontario and Quebec, opened up the regions adjacent to them and provided the main bases of attack upon new areas of the Laurentian Shield. Beyond the railheads, exploration and development was carried on by canoe or steamer and, after 1925, by plane. Indeed, air transportation has wrought an economic revolution in the Shield, for it permits men and equipment to be carried in a few hours to places which would have taken weeks of painful toil to reach by the older methods. New regions can be quickly explored and new mines developed with great speed. In recent years tractor trains, i.e. caterpillar tractors pulling heavily laden sleighs, are used to haul in bulky goods during the winter, and gasoline propelled boats with shallow draught do similar work during the summer. Laying the steel tentacles and proving the existence of valuable resources occupied the first quarter of the century; extending economic activity beyond these limits by means of the internal combustion engine is the key to future development.

It is obvious that the attack on the Shield has been concerned primarily with minerals and, to a lesser degree, with agriculture. Copper was the first important mineral product of this economic region. It had been discovered in the eighteenth century at Bruce Mines, north of Lake Superior, but due to its remote location it was neglected until the late 1860's when the reserves were tapped and, though large, were quickly exhausted. A more important area, one with complex ores containing both copper and nickel, was discovered near Sudbury in 1883, during the construction of the Canadian Pacific railway. The output increased rapidly, especially during the Great War when copper was much in demand for munitions, and afterward when it was used in the growing electrical industry. After 1930 production fell off because prices went to extraordinarily low levels. In fact it was only because copper, which by this time was being smelted at Rouyn and Flinflon, in addition to Sudbury, is found in conjunction with precious metals or nickel that production could be maintained at all. In the late 1930's, prices improved and output reached new high levels.

Early development of the Sudbury area was associated mainly with copper, but during the War (1914-18) there was a great demand for nickel for use in the production of armour plate. After the War this market was sustained by the perfection and increasing use of alloy steels, that is, using nickel in combination with steel, copper, aluminum and other metals for purposes to which these metals alone are less well suited. From the start the development was under the control of a few companies, and since 1928 one company has controlled eighty per cent of the world production of nickel. This corporation has lowered the costs of production, expanded the market, and introduced pension and stock ownership plans for its employees. Its potential ore reserves are ten times the total production over the last fifty years and are valued at two and one-half billion dollars. The nickel and copper industries are both of a more permanent nature than gold mining, and hence have been able to escape much of the financial manipulation and the abandonment of plant associated with precious metals.

Silver is another important mineral of the North though over half of Canada's present output comes from southern British Columbia. Silver in the Laurentian Shield was discovered first at Cobalt, sometimes in "grass root" mines, i.e. those where the silver was concentrated in narrow veins coming to the surface, and containing ten, twenty-five, even as much as fifty per cent of the precious metal. All that was needed to put the mine on a paying basis was a hand drill and a few bags of powder. Quick profits fired the public imagination and prospectors and investors rushed in, especially in the year 1906. The money made and the mining experience gained in this area went far toward the development of mines elsewhere in the Shield, but nowhere could profits be made as rapidly and with as little capital expenditure as in the Cobalt silver camp. The silver produced in 1939 in the Shield, though less than half the quantity of 1912 when the Cobalt area was at its peak, comes from ores which also contain either copper, nickel, gold and radium. In the 1930's the price of silver fell but later Cobalt revived as a producer.

The Shield also produces the mineral cobalt, as well as platinum and palladium. The latter two are exploited mainly at Sudbury, making Canada the leading producing country of these very valuable minerals. One mineral of the Shield which attracted a good deal of attention for a few years was radium, discovered in 1930, at the east end of Great Bear Lake where a modern mine was established. One effect of the discovery was to reduce the price from $55 to about $22 a milligram. Uranium is found at many places in the Shield, notably at Uranium City, 32 miles south of the northern boundary of Saskatchewan, and at Elliot Lake, east of Sault Ste. Marie. Titanium, a light weight rust-resistant metal valuable as an alloy in steel, is found near Quebec City. Finally, petroleum has been refined at Norman on the Mackenzie near the Arctic Circle for use on river boats and in mines and airplanes. A huge supply of petroleum is locked up in the tar sands at McMurray. These oil resources belong to the Shield economically but not in a strict geological sense.

Despite the variety of minerals produced in the Shield, the premier place is held by gold. Beginning with its discovery at Porcupine in 1911, gold has been revealed at widely separated points. The three most important mining areas at the present time are the Chibougamau and Noranda regions of Western Quebec and the districts of Timmins and Porcupine in Ontario. Smaller camps are scattered across the rest of Northern Ontario and Eastern Manitoba. Important camps exist at Flin Flon and at Yellowknife just north of Great Slave Lake. The steady exploration and development of gold mining in the Shield was greatly accelerated in the 1930's, with output more than doubling in the decade. The use of airplanes, advances in geological knowledge, a reduction in the costs of production because of the low cost of wages and supplies, and a substantial rise in the price of gold were the causes of this increase.

In the course of its expansion, gold mining has displayed several trends. One of these is the rapid rise and then the equally fast decline of individual camps. The discovery of a small but fairly rich concentrate of gold is likely to promote a rush of men to prospect and stake the surrounding areas. Once the concentrate is exhausted, and it is realized that the area round about has only small quantities of gold in large amounts of rock and, therefore, will not pay to develop, interest in the region evaporates, usually within five years of the initial strike. Another reason for collapse is the inability of the developing corporation to raise sufficient capital to really "prove up" the mine. Enormous sums are now usually required to put a prospective mine on a paying basis. Up to the time the mine pays dividends the company can sell only hope in the future, "the possibility of growing rich beyond the dreams of avarice". If it cannot sell enough stock on the basis of promises, the corporation may have to abandon operations even though the expenditure of a relatively few more thousand dollars would result in a paying enterprise. In any case abandoned gold mines are typical of the earlier-explored parts of the Shield. It must, of course, not be forgotten that a few mines, notably Lake Shore and Hollinger, appear to have a long life ahead of them but the typical experience is the rapid rise and decline in prosperity at dozens of points over the Shield.

Another trend in gold mining is the use of machinery and the dominance of large corporations. After the "grass root" veins of the Cobalt area had been exploited, it was necessary to sink shafts, and as these became deeper and the side-tunnels or adits became longer, it was essential to introduce ventilating equipment and hoisting machinery. Gradually silver mining was put on a capitalistic basis. All the later precious and base metal mines were on such a basis from their beginning. Their minerals were not as highly concentrated and their ore-bodies, generally speaking, were located at greater depths below the surface. The most pronounced example of the need for capital is one mine at Flinflon where twenty-five million dollars were spent before production began. Obviously, only corporations in which at least some stock is sold to the public can finance such endeavours. Only very rarely is an individual prospector able to put his mine on a paying basis without financial aid from the outside. Usually if his claims show signs of being really valuable he sells them to a large corporation. The latter is anxious to get them partly because it wants paying properties, partly because, having its own mill for the treatment of ore, it needs a continuous supply of ore in order to keep the mill in operation. Thus some of the bigger companies have tended to become financial syndicates or holding companies, owning or controlling small subsidiary mining concerns. A few such holding companies have been organized independently, that is, by purchasing a large number of claims and not as an outgrowth of a concern with a producing mine of its own.

As the large corporations became dominant, more and more emphasis was put on finance. To some extent the profits derived from the development of one area were used to exploit the next. Sometimes those who had gained in the first venture lost all that they had in the second, but a few individuals seemed to have an uncanny ability to "pick a winner every time". In addition, the general public wanted to participate in the activity, not so much by rushing in to stake out claims as they had done in the earlier period of placer mining in British Columbia and the Yukon, or of the grass-root silver mines, but by purchasing stock in mining companies newly established or already operating. The public was lured by the extraordinary profits of a few men, by the names of the prominent individuals who promoted the various ventures, and by the naïve belief that properties near dividend-paying mines, must always in themselves be valuable. New companies were constantly being started and the public invited to subscribe cash for part of the stock, with the understanding that the "big names" were to purchase the bulk of it. Often the "names" received their stock for claims, promotional activities and other intangible assets of doubtful value. If the company earned dividends, which are of course paid on the basis of number of shares held, the bulk of the earnings went to the insiders; if the company failed, the promoters lost a little of their reputation and the public was out the only hard cash put into the enterprise. The episode was soon forgotten only to be repeated with a different company, another "sure thing" in a different part of Northern Ontario or Quebec, and with other members of a gullible public, or perhaps even the same ones.

The more barefaced of these and other methods were prevented by legislation passed by several provinces beginning in 1927, and by a series of prosecutions a few years later. Public confidence in mining stocks was thus restored and the rise in the price of gold in 1933, created a new flood of investments. Methods of mining finance are, from the nature of things, less conservative than those of other types of business. The task of legislation is to prevent fraud or positive abuse of privileges on the one hand, and yet not unduly delay the promotion of legitimate, albeit inevitably risky, enterprises on the other.

As already explained, the mining industry provides its own finances to a considerable extent, since individuals and mining corporations often use profits already secured from gold to undertake further prospecting and developing operations. At the same time, large amounts of money have been supplied by business men, labourers in the mines themselves, clerks, farmers, even the proverbial widow and orphan anxious to make a quick fortune. Over half the mining capital has been provided within Canada, but it is estimated that nearly forty per cent of the capital stock of dividend paying mines is owned in the United States. Such investment tends to raise the prices of stock of established mines and encourages Canadian mining men to sell out at a profit, and then reinvest in the shares of non-dividend-paying mines which have a good future. Thus, it is claimed, American investment is of considerable indirect value to Canadian mining. Ownership of Canadian mining stock by British investors does not exceed ten per cent. As previously indicated, the financing of nickel and other base metal mines is more conservative than financing gold.

Another trend in mining has been toward the use of low grade ore as a result of the reduction of costs. In part, costs were cut by the use of machinery and of chemical processes, in part by the construction of railways replacing roads as means of bringing in supplies for the workmen and the mine itself, and in part they were reduced by the use of hydro-electric power. Many of the technological methods and most of the early machinery were imported from the United States, although since 1925, an increasing proportion of the machinery has been made in Canada by branch plants of American firms. As costs were lowered, it sometimes became profitable to exploit previously discovered areas whose ores contained too small a percentage of precious or base metals to pay the costs of extraction under the old methods.

With dominance of machinery, labour as a whole needed

to be less skilful and with the growth of the size of the industry, larger numbers of workmen were required. The early rushes of Canadian and American prospectors were replaced, especially in the 1920's, by an influx of relatively unskilled men, chiefly Europeans—Hungarians, Poles and other Slavs—whose work is directed by a comparatively few highly competent English-speaking engineers and, more recently, by men of their own race born and educated in Canada. Labour leaders for many years found it difficult to organize these men into unions because of their differing nationalities and the determined opposition of the mine managements. Nevertheless, working conditions are reasonably good and wages are high, though the speculative nature of every mining development creates a certain recklessness on the part of the workers, and the fact that the population is predominately male raises social problems not easy to solve. In part, these social and racial difficulties are the result of the industrial immaturity of the region and will correct themselves in time.

The development of mining in the Laurentian Shield has been of the greatest significance to the Canadian economy as a whole. The amount of capital employed is difficult to estimate, because profitable mines write down the book value of their assets for the reason that after the ore body is exhausted, the mining plant will have no resale value. A further difficulty arises from the fact that statistics are compiled by provinces and not by economic areas. Probably over six hundred million dollars is invested, and at least 75,000 men are directly employed in mines in the Laurentian Shield. In addition, huge but undeterminable sums are spent for freight, electric power, fuel and lubricants, building materials, explosives, insurance and a wide variety of machinery, mine, railway and electrical equipment, motor vehicles, chemicals and so on. These purchases stimulate manufacturing and trade in the older regions of Canada. They were particularly important during the depression of the 1930's for mining, especially of gold, was the only important Canadian industry which expanded during that period. Mining, of course, is an extractive industry; it uses up resources and, unlike agriculture, does not replace them. Although a few of the existing mining areas, notably Sudbury, Porcupine, Rouyn and Flin Flon, seem to be more or less permanent, eventually workers in most mines will have to shift to new mines or get jobs in other industries. Since 1945 gold mining, squeezed between rising costs and the fixed price for gold, has been subsidized by the Dominion. Northern Ontario hopes to start secondary industries using Western natural gas brought by pipe-line.

The second important industry in the economic life of the Laurentian Shield is the production of pulp and paper. As already explained, the manufacture of paper in Canada began early in the nineteenth century, using rags as the chief raw material. After 1860 the industry used wood and the process of production was, simply, to dessicate the wood by holding it against rotating grindstones, then spread the ground wood mixed with water in a thin layer on a moving belt and dry it very rapidly. Later improvements consisted of chipping the wood mechanically, then boiling it in a bath containing certain chemicals and finally spreading and drying the mixture.

Paper production increased slowly until 1900, and moderately until 1920. Thereafter it literally grew like a mushroom and soon Canada was producing forty per cent of the world's supply of newsprint. Not all this rapid development occurred in the economic region which we have called the Laurentian Shield. Some of it took place at Powell River and Ocean Falls in British Columbia, some of it in the Maritimes with mills at Edmundston, Dalhousie and Bathurst, New Brunswick, and at Liverpool, Nova Scotia. Still other mills, especially those for the production of the better grade of writing and book paper, were located in the St. Lawrence Valley. Nevertheless the bulk of the mills are either scattered throughout the length of the Shield itself or along the southern edges of it, at such points as Pine Falls, Kenora, Fort Frances, Port Arthur, Kapuskasing, Iroquois Falls, Sturgeon Falls and Three Rivers.

The causes of the extraordinarily rapid development of paper manufacturing in the Shield are numerous. First of all, there was an enormous resource of coniferous trees, chiefly spruce and balsam, too small for sizable lumber but excellent for pulp wood. Not far away, in the United States was a very populous area whose paper needs were increasing because people were beginning to read more magazines and newspapers, and because the sizes of these publications were increasing greatly due to the large amount of advertising which they carried. Moreover, by 1920, the Eastern United States had virtually exhausted its own easily accessible forest resources. The Provincial Governments in Canada did not permit the export of pulp wood to American mills and consequently, many of the mills had either to close down or migrate to Canada. When they moved northward, the mills had the advantage of being nearer their most bulky raw material. Also they could have the logs floated directly to them along the rivers and lakes which cover a large part of the area of the Shield. Finally, mills in Canada had the advantage of almost unlimited potential sources of water-power. This power was needed in large amounts to operate the huge paper-making machines and, in an area devoid of coal, to generate steam for cooking and drying.

In view of all these factors it is not surprising that the pulp and paper industry developed in Ontario and Quebec on a huge scale and in Manitoba, to a smaller degree. Unfortunately, the industry was badly overbuilt in the sense that the industry as a whole could produce far more newsprint than could be sold at profitable prices. In the 1920's, however, profits in pulp and paper concerns were exceptionally good and due to favourable conditions in the stock market, new securities were easy to sell. The Governments of Ontario and Quebec rivalled each other in inducing new companies to construct plants. With the depression the demand for newsprint fell off about thirty per cent; companies bid against each other for the available business, and the price of newsprint was reduced by forty per cent between 1929 and 1933. Paper making companies found themselves in financial difficulties. Even though their income was falling they had to continue to pay interest on large amounts of bonds on their paper mills and hydro-electric plants or, if they bought their power from other corporations, they were obliged, under their long term contracts, to pay for power which they could not use. Seven of the largest producers representing about half the total Canadian capacity, became bankrupt and to prevent the financial collapse of the remainder of the firms, members of the industry attempted to maintain prices. A few companies refused to adhere to the agreements and newspapers, especially those in the United States, protested bitterly against the threat of artificially increasing prices. The Governments of Ontario and Quebec feared the loss of revenue from timber royalties and the human suffering which would result from the closing of plants. Hence they tried to introduce some order into a chaotic condition. All these efforts were only partially successful. It remained for an improvement in general business, a rise in the price of newsprint, and the reorganization of the capital structures of some of the larger corporations to put the industry back on its feet.

During and after the War, the production of newsprint increased rapidly. Newspapers grew in size because they carried more news and bigger advertisements. Newsprint manufacturers in Canada found that they could profitably meet the prices charged by Scandinavian suppliers along the Atlantic Coast of the United States. Potential competitors in the Southern States could not solve the technical difficulties of manufacturing good paper from the jack pine of Florida and Georgia on a commercial scale.

Canadian forestry has also gained from the expanding consumption of wood for packages, plywood, plastics, rayon, and cellophane. When used for these purposes, the wood may be from smaller trees, branches or sawdust, or from species formerly considered of little commercial value.

Federal and provincial governments, in conjunction with lumbermen and users, conduct research in wood chemistry, resins, paints and preservatives, techniques of logging and manufacturing, the elimination of waste, reforestation, and protection against fire, predatory insects, fungi, and other diseases. The danger that our forest resources will be completely depleted within the near future seems less acute than was feared in the 1920's.

Subsidiary to both mining and the pulp and paper industry is the production of hydro-electric power. The numerous lakes and rivers, with the latter frequently falling in rapids, the fairly regular rainfall throughout the year, the hard rocks providing excellent foundations for dams and other works—these are the physical bases of develop-

ment. The fact that the technical problems of generation
and transmission were fairly well solved by 1925, the ease
of obtaining capital and the possibility of flooding large
areas without the expense of removing settlers or buildings—these gave economic advantages. The result has
been that water-power plants with an installed capacity
of over seven million horse-power have already been constructed in the Shield. Such an enormous supply of
cheap power is an extraordinary advantage to both mining and paper manufacturing, particularly because the
area is far removed from sources of coal and oil. The
hydro-electricity of the Shield is increasingly being used
in the thickly settled St. Lawrence Lowlands.

The agricultural possibilities of the Laurentian Shield
are difficult to assess. There is plenty of fertile land, at
least thirty million acres, in the Clay Belt of Ontario and
Quebec, the district round Lake St. John and along the
edges of the Shield in Northern Saskatchewan. Elsewhere the soil cover is either non-existent or scanty. Even
where the soil is suitable, the winters are severe, the sum-
mers short and early frosts are not unknown. Nevertheless, heavy crops of hay and roots—the foundations of
dairying—can be grown. Also, agriculture in the Clay
Belt and in small areas elsewhere in the Shield is aided
by the fact that it can supply dairy products and fresh
vegetables to nearby mining and paper-making towns.
Potential farm land is heavily forested and hence expensive to clear. On the other hand the farmer has a chance
to sell pulpwood from his land, or to work during the
winter in mines or paper mills. He can thus make sure of
a cash income until he can establish himself agriculturally.
The danger is that once the farmer has sold all the pulpwood from his land, he may not be able to make a living
from the land alone.

The generally accepted conclusion is that although

prosperous farming has developed in the Lake St. John region and in a few parts of the Clay Belt, the agricultural outlook of the area as a whole is only moderately bright. Of course the situation would be completely changed if the prices of farm products were to rise, or if large numbers of immigrants were prepared to come to Canada and work on farms. When farm prices and costs are normal, the area can provide a livelihood superior to that of most of the farm population of Europe. But on the assumptions of relatively low agricultural prices, the greater attractiveness of jobs in cities, and the inexperience of settlers in "making land" in the bush, the Laurentian Shield has limited agricultural prospects.

Mining, pulp and paper making and, to a slight extent, agriculture are the important industries of the Shield but these are supplemented by the furs of what might be called the Far North. The most valuable fur-bearing animal of that area is the silver fox which is now ruthlessly hunted. Dominion, provincial and territorial governments are all trying to conserve fur-bearing animals and fish. They limit the size of the catch and the number of animals that may be shot by any hunter. They enforce closed seasons. They provide wild life sanctuaries to stop the extinction of some species and re-stock surrounding areas. Finally, they try to preserve and extend marshes for beaver, muskrat, and edible birds.

The natives of the Far North are becoming dependent on the white man's goods and are slowly tending to lose their traditional way of life. There is a break-down in native culture similar to that which occurred in Eastern Canada during the French regime.

The Laurentian Shield is the newest economic region in the Dominion. To be sure, a beginning was made in the seventeenth century with furs as a staple, but substantial development came only after 1920 with the staples of newsprint and minerals, especially gold. Of the five economic regions in Canada, the Shield is the only one which lacks a consciousness of its economic unity. In part this is a result of the recency of development. In part too, it is the effect of a relatively small, often migratory, population scattered in pockets of settlement over an immense territory. Also, with the exception of a few years when the newsprint industry was depressed, the economic development of the region has been in the process of constant expansion and has never experienced the strains which pull together brothers-in-need.

A further reason for the lack of consciousness of economic cohesion is the non-existence of a wide gap of barren territory, separating this economic region from its neighbours to the same extent as the Gaspé peninsula, or the Shield, or the Rocky Mountains segregated the older regions from one another in their formative periods, and gave each area an opportunity to develop local loyalties. Looking at the matter from another viewpoint, one might say that it was easy for economic life in the St. Lawrence Valley and the Prairies to spill over into another economic region. In fact, most Canadians regard the Shield as merely an extension of the older economies. This attitude is shown in the efforts of all the Western Provinces to have their boundaries extended to the Arctic Ocean. The fact of the matter is that the Shield is an economic area, distinct from the others, and it may in time develop its own corporate feeling in economic affairs.

As the Shield has developed it has had a significant influence on the other sections of the Canadian economy. It provides an important outlet for farm products and for other consumer's goods, especially luxury or semi-luxury articles which a get-rich-quick population likes to buy.

It also supplies a market for heavy machinery, electrical and other types of capital equipment. The pulp and paper mills, and especially the mines, are the basis for large financial transactions in Toronto and Montreal. Taxes on the mines are an important source of provincial revenue. In Ontario, the staples of the Shield and the back-haul of manufactured goods and food provide the bulk of the traffic for the provincially owned railway. Ores, pulpwood, machinery and food-stuffs create considerable traffic for the transcontinental lines. This traffic is important on account of its volume and the fact that on the whole, it can afford to pay high freight rates. Furthermore it fills in the "bridge", the mileage which connects the eastern and western areas which originate traffic, but which formerly gave rise to no more traffic itself than does a literal bridge across a river. Incidentally the mining of nickel, copper, and other base metals gives rise to a larger volume of freight than precious metal mining. In the former cases, the finished products are bulky, a smelter is required near the mine; thus relatively large quantities of supplies must be hauled in for use by the smelter and its workmen. In the case of most gold mines, however, comparatively small mills can be established even in areas with limited transportation facilities and the valuable concentrated ores can be carried or flown out to rail-head. On the other hand, in the case of the deeper, larger gold mines employing large numbers of men, the amount of machinery and supplies which have to be transported is considerable. In any event the traffic is of appreciable value to the railways.

The less tangible results of the northern development are also important. The newest economic region gives more breadth to the Canadian economy in the physical sense. Whether it has given more breadth in the sense of stability is debatable. Certainly it gave a better balance to the Dominion during the depression of the 1930's. It is true that gold mining was aided by the arbitrary revaluation of the American dollar, a fortuity which may not be repeated in another period of hard times. On the other hand, the other factors leading to a revival of gold mining when general conditions are bad may be expected to operate again, and the instability of the paper manufacturing companies was due more to lop-sidedness in their financial structure than to the inherent nature of the industry. In the long run, of course, the two chief business activities of the Shield are based on wasting assets, but at what date the resources will be exhausted and what will happen when they are, are imponderables which defy evaluation. At all events the Shield has been a factor of steadily increasing importance in the Canadian economy since 1920, and is likely to continue to be so for many years to come.

SELECTED READINGS

BLADEN, V. W., *An Introduction to Political Economy*, Toronto, 1956, Chap. VI.

FINNIE, R., *Canada Moves North*, Toronto, 1942.

GUTHRIE, J. A., *The Newsprint Paper Industry*, Cambridge, Mass., 1941.
The Economics of Pulp and Paper, Pullman, Wash., 1956.

HOFFMAN, A., *Free Gold: The Story of Canadian Mining*, New York, 1946.

INNIS, H. A. and LOWER, A. R. M., *Settlement in the Forest and Mining Frontiers*, Toronto, 1936.

LOWER, A. R. M., "The assault on the Laurentian barrier, 1850-70". *Canadian Historical Review*, December, 1929, pp. 294-307.

MAIN, O. W., *The Canadian Nickel Industry*, Toronto, 1955.

MOORE, E. S., *The Mineral Resources of Canada*, Toronto, 1933.
American Influence on Canadian Mining, Toronto, 1941.

WATSON, J. G., "Mining finance in Canada", in Parkinson, J. F. ed., *Canadian Investment and Foreign Exchange Problems*, Toronto, 1940, pp. 228-38.

13

Newfoundland

THE early history of Newfoundland is dominated by a single staple, cod, and by the doctrines of mercantilism. John Cabot who discovered the island in 1497 took back glowing accounts of the wealth of fish on the Grand Banks. By the first quarter of the sixteenth century fishing vessels from England, France, Spain and Portugal were coming to these waters year after year. By 1554 the main features of the coastline had been named. In 1583 Sir Humphrey Gilbert took possession of the island in the name of Queen Elizabeth.

During the first half of the seventeenth century several efforts to found permanent settlements were made, including one by Sir George Calvert (Lord Baltimore) who later established the present state of Maryland These efforts failed because of the climate, lack of capital, and especially the opposition of English Governments and merchants. Racks or 'flakes' were set up on shore to help cure the fish but men rarely stayed in the new land from one season to the next. Still English business men and officials appreciated the worth of the trade. It gave England a profitable export and provided a basis for large inflows of precious metals from other countries. In addition the fishery was a valuable nursery for sailors and hence essential to British naval supremacy.

If the Newfoundland fisheries were to occupy their proper place in mercantilist theory, they must not be allowed to get into the hands of foreigners or even of permanent settlers on the island. One way of carrying out this policy was to grant companies of merchants exclusive rights to trade. In 1634 a charter was conferred on certain merchants from the West Country, that is, from Bristol, Exeter, Teignmouth and other ports in Somerset, Cornwall and Devon. This charter, re-issued in 1661 and 1670, prohibited settlement in Newfoundland. Meanwhile in 1662 the French had a small colony in Placentia. On several occasions the French and at one time the Dutch attacked the English establishments. But by the Treaty of Utrecht (1713) the French recognized English sovereignty over Newfoundland and all its adjacent islands with the exception of St. Pierre and Miquelon which are still French possessions.

Although as many as 400 ships came annually to fish on the Grand Banks, for the most part fishermen continued to return to their native land each autumn. Permanent residents numbered only 120 in 1683, 3,000 in 1750, and 12,000 in 1775. The settlers came mainly from Ireland where the standard of living was generally so low that Newfoundland, isolated as it was, seemed attractive. During the Napoleonic wars the Newfoundland fisheries did not have to face competition from Spanish, French and Portuguese vessels while they enjoyed good markets in Britain, around the Mediterranean and, by running Napoleon's embargo, on the Continent itself. The seasonal shifting of workers between England and the fishing stations proved difficult. Accordingly large numbers of folk from the West Country came to settle in Newfoundland, more than 11,000 arriving in 1814-15 alone. The merchants of Bristol gradually lost control over the fishing industry and a new merchant class, a 'codfish aristocracy', grew up in St. John's.

Throughout the entire nineteenth century the export of cod stood up remarkably well, fluctuating only between

900,000 and 1,000,000 quintals of 112 pounds each. Though prices fell suddenly after the Napoleonic Wars they recovered quickly, remaining at satisfactory levels until 1860-68. Sealing was important for the revenue it produced, for the stimulus it gave to shipbuilding, and for the employment it provided in the two or three months before the summer codfishery began. Newfoundland seals are covered with rather coarse hair, not fur. Though the hides make good leather, the chief value of the Newfoundland seal lay in the two inches of fat or blubber just inside the pelt. After this fat was rendered down, it was used mainly for making soap and for lighting homes in the days before coal-oil lamps or electric lights. Whaling in the North Atlantic was mainly in the hands of New Englanders. In the mid-nineteenth century shipbuilding was relatively as important in Newfoundland as in nearby Nova Scotia. Agriculture lagged behind, however. As a rule the holdings were small and were worked by women and children or by men when they were not occupied in fishing. Most of the foodstuffs were brought in from New England.

In the 1860's codfish prices collapsed, largely because sales could not readily be made in the southern states during the American Civil War. After 1870 codfish commanded a satisfactory market and the island was undeniably prosperous. An economy based on a single staple is notoriously unsteady. This fact was recognized by officials even in the early part of the century. Unfortunately they had not been able to persuade people to turn from fishing to agriculture and so dependence on a single export had continued. In 1864, copper began to be mined on the shores of Notre Dame Bay and about ten years later even more valuable mines were opened up elsewhere. Coal and other minerals had been found on the west coast and a railway was projected to run from St. John's more or less paralleling the south shore to St. George's Bay. The British Colonial Office raised objections because it feared the line might interfere with the rather broad claims to territory made by France under the Treaty of Utrecht. Accordingly the route was changed to run northward. A company was generously subsidized by the Government of the colony and construction was begun. In the 1880's local industries were established to manufacture rope, fishing gear, and nets. A dry-dock was erected and foundries started. Altogether the years after 1870 were characterized by a broadening of the economic base, by local enterprise, and by general prosperity.

In the early 1890's, however, the Island was visited by two calamities: in 1892 three-quarters of St. John's was destroyed by fire with a total loss, after insurance, of over fifteen million dollars; two years later both leading commercial banks failed and the Government Savings Bank had to suspend payments. As the local currency was valueless, trade was at a standstill. Inability to pay interest on the public debt was avoided only by a loan from Britain. To provide a sound medium of exchange, Canadian banks opened in St. John's and elsewhere. The colony expressed its willingness to enter Confederation and the Dominion offered as favourable terms as had been given to any of the existing provinces. The Government at Ottawa contended that it could not reasonably be expected to go any further than this, but it was severely criticized both at the time and since for its niggardly attitude. Newfoundland felt that unless the Dominion took over virtually all its debt and granted large subsidies the local government would be unable to carry on, particularly since it would lose its chief source of revenue, the customs tariff. In any event, negotiations broke down. The local government was able to borrow in Montreal, New York and London. As business revived fairly quickly, the colony pulled itself out of its immediate difficulties.

The events of the 1890's effectively destroyed whatever hopes there may have been for a prosperous Newfoundland based on local capital and local control. Even before the financial smash, Sir Robert Reid, a Scots-Canadian from Montreal, had been active in promoting the trans-island railway. In 1899 the Government transferred to Reid and his associates practically all the island's railways, shipping lines, and telegraphs, as well as the St. John's drydock and extensive timber and mining rights. In return Reid undertook to operate the railway to Port-aux-Basques, which it had reached in 1897, and to run fast steamships between this point and Sydney, N.S. Such bitter objections were taken to the generosity of the Government and the monopoly features of the contract, that it had to be modified. Nevertheless, the Reid interests continued to have a powerful influence on the economy.

In 1895 the deposits of high-grade iron ore on Bell Island in Conception Bay were opened up. Since that date these Wabana ores have supplied the blast furnaces at Sydney and have been exported to Germany. Sydney also depends on Newfoundland for most of its limestone, another raw material used in smelting iron ore. Outcroppings of lead and zinc at Buchans on Red Indian Lake had been known for many years before exploitation began in 1927. The delay in development was caused by the complexity of the ores and the technical difficulties of separating one mineral from another and from the worthless rock or gangue. Although the original reserves have been almost depleted, nearby resources have been found.

Besides its minerals, Newfoundland is wealthy in timber, chiefly spruce and balsam. The wood is used for fuel and the lumber for ships, houses, furniture, and pit props which are sent to Britain. In 1905 Lord Northcliffe, the owner of a chain of newspapers in England, became interested in developing his own supplies of newsprint. In 1909 he opened a plant at Grand Falls where he had cheap hydro-electric power, adequate timber limits, and easy access to the port of Botwood. Later the Northcliffe family acquired another modern plant at nearby Bishop's Falls. Another mill at Corner Brook on the west coast has been operating since 1925, having been owned by American and then by British interests. In the newsprint towns and at Buchans the industries have laid out model towns with comfortable homes, schools, hospitals, and recreational centres for the use of their employees.

The influx of outside capital had a pronounced influence on the Island's economic and social life. It reduced the dependence of the people on codfish but not on foreign markets. Although Newfoundland's prosperity now hinged on more than one staple, it was still cyclically uncertain as staple economies are bound to be. The Island was obligated to pay interest and dividends to outside capitalists. In particular, the Government had borrowed substantial amounts of money to build the railway and for other public works. As the debt was chiefly held abroad, the Government now faced a foreign exchange problem. Workers in mills and mines became dependent on steady work at good wages whereas the fishing population had become inured to variable incomes. Increased industrialization led to the growth of class distinctions between management and men, to the unionization of labour, and to demands for better education, public health services, and old age pensions.

In 1923 the Reid interests ceased running the railway because of heavy losses. The Government was forced to take over the line and the steamships owned by it. Due to political pressure government-owned vessels began to call at almost every outport. Service became so slow and tedious that privately owned steamers and schooners captured most of the carrying trade between the larger outports, thus adding to the losses on the Government system. The railway itself ran through much unproductive territory, and it had a circuitous route between St. John's, Port-aux-Basques, and thence by steamer to the mainland. Shippers at Buchans, Grand Falls and Bishop's Falls mainly used their own railways to Botwood rather than the Government system to St. John's. The line was narrow gauge (three feet six inches between the inside of the rails) so that all freight to and from the mainland's standard gauge railways (four feet eight and a half inches) had to be transferred from one kind of freight car to the other. Finally, the line was sometimes weather-bound for days at a time because of deep snow in the vicinity of Topsails.

Due to losses on the railway and increased expenditure on education and other social services, the Government was unable to balance its budget. In the 1920's its annual deficit averaged two million dollars a year and the debt more than doubled. Newfoundland with fewer than 300,-000 persons had a national debt of over $98,000,000 in 1933 whereas Ontario with eleven times as many people and much larger resources had a provincial debt of $523,-000,000.

In the 1930's the almost simultaneous drop in the prices

of fish, newprint and minerals caused consternation. The
mines and mills reduced their staffs and cut wages. As
it happened, the catch of fish was low for three consecu-
tive years. In the winter of 1932-33 about one-quarter
of the population was on relief. Investment bankers refused to bid on a loan which the government proposed,
but Canadian banks and local interests advanced enough
cash to enable the Government to carry on its activities
for the time being. A Canadian oil company received a
monopoly of the import of petroleum products in return
for paying $300,000 annually to the government.

Notwithstanding stringent economies including the
slashing of grants to schools, the Government still had
deficits. In the fiscal year 1930-31 the deficit was about
four million dollars in a total budget of less than fourteen
millions. Rates of taxation were high but people did
without goods when their incomes were low. Since most
of the tax revenues came from customs duties, the Government's revenue slumped. It was hopeless to raise tax
rates when every industry was flat on its back. The
Government was morally obliged to provide subsistence
and a bare minimum of social services for the population
which was impoverished, scattered along 3,000 miles of
coast, and employed, if at all, in seasonal industries. The
Government was also legally bound to pay in New York,
London, and Montreal the interest on the capital outlays
and borrowings for current expenditure made in the
1920's. Hard-pressed on every side, Newfoundland was
in danger of having to default on its interest payments.

Newfoundland was also embarrassed by her huge mainland dependency, Labrador. The Island Government had
long-standing claims to this area, claims which were
based on treaties made between Britain and France prior
to the conquest of Canada in 1759-60. The Canadian

Government had always insisted that Newfoundland's rights extended to no more than a fringe of coast. The latter claimed all the land drained by the rivers entering the Atlantic between the Straits of Belle Isle and Cape Chidley. In 1927 Canada and Newfoundland submitted the question to the Judicial Committee of the Privy Council which ruled in favour of the Island.

The new boundaries of Labrador enclosed an area of 112,000 square miles, including perhaps 40,000 square miles of commercially valuable woodlands, vast water powers, and undiscovered mineral wealth. Unfortunately, Newfoundland lacked the resources to develop the potentialities of the territory. Ships came each summer to fish off the coast and to pick up the catch of the 'liveyeres' who stayed throughout the year, fishing in summer and hunting or getting out fuel in winter. The standard of living was often deplorably low. By his heroic work Sir Wilfred Grenfell brought medical assistance to the Europeans, Indians and Eskimos scattered along the coast. The Grenfell Association and the Moravian Brethren maintained schools and mission stations but the Government in St. John's could offer little by way of economic help or social services.

In 1933 the Governments of the United Kingdom and Canada made a temporary loan of $3,100,000 to the Newfoundland authorities. Then the United Kingdom appointed a Royal Commission consisting of one member from Britain, one from Newfoundland, and one from Canada. After examining the Island's history, financial position, and future prospects, the Commission attributed part of the difficulties to the weaknesses of the local legislative assembly and the evils of party politics. Accordingly it recommended that Responsible Government be temporarily suspended and public affairs put in the hands of a Commission of Government appointed by the United Kingdom which was to advance funds to prevent insolvency. This proposal was accepted by the Newfoundland legislature and the British Parliament.

Three of the Commission of Government, which took office in 1934, came from Britain and three from the Island, but the former had all the important departments. They headed Finance which included customs, the post office, broadcasting, the government-owned hotel in St. John's, and the civil service; Natural Resources such as fisheries, forestry, agriculture and land settlement; and Public Utilities and Supply which covered all public works, the railway, government steamships, civil aviation, highways, mines and labour. The three Commissioners from Newfoundland were in charge of the departments of Public Health and Welfare, Justice, and Home Affairs and Education.

Until 1939 the Commission had to contend with continued depression. The returns from the codfisheries, while fluctuating considerably, were generally poor. This was due to low prices, poor catches, political unrest in one market, Spain, and prostration in another market, Brazil. The export of paper products declined even after 1936 when business generally had passed the depth of the depression. The mining of iron ore steadily improved while Buchans had operated full time throughout the depression. But the economy was so heavily dependent on prosperity in the fisheries that large numbers were still on relief.

After the outbreak of war Newfoundland's economy benefited substantially from defence expenditures by the British and United States Governments, by rising prices and better markets for fish, and by the strong demand for base metals and newsprint. Employment was easy to obtain, though wages remained far below Canadian rates. Very gradually confidence in the Island's future revived.

Between 1934 and 1940 the Commission's annual deficits averaged about $1,500,000. Part of the deficits were accounted for by the increased scale of payments to relief recipients, old age pensioners, and schools. On the other hand expenditures were reduced by refunding the public debt. The old Newfoundland securities which paid interest of 5 to 6½ per cent or even higher were replaced by 3 per cent stock unconditionally guaranteed by the United Kingdom. During the War revenues were buoyant and for the first time since 1917 the Government had a surplus. By 1949 the net debt had been brought down to about $70 million and some $26 million set aside in reserves.

Since codfishing was the mainstay of the economy, the Commission of Government spent time and money on its restoration. It facilitated the building of schooners to restore fishing on the Grand Banks and so loosen dependence on the in-shore fisheries where the catch is less certain than off-shore. It created cold storage plants and bait depots along the coast. It tried to improve the quality of fish sold abroad by licensing exporters, scientifically studying the process of curing with salt, and giving practical advice to fishermen, many of whom were careless or ignorant of the best procedures. By reason of these efforts Newfoundland fish brought as good or better prices in foreign markets as the fish of Nova Scotia or Iceland who were Newfoundland's main competitors. In 1947 the Commission set up an organization which would have the exclusive right to sell Newfoundland salt codfish in overseas markets. Since the war domestic sales have been slowly declining.

Moreover the Government induced a large American corporation to erect a plant for quick-freezing fish. The Commission surveyed possible markets for haddock and herring which had been neglected due to the Island's concentration on cod. In short, the Commission tried, first, to improve the marketing of salt cod which is sold mainly to low income groups in Brazil, the Caribbean, and the Mediterranean, and second, to develop sales in North America of the more palatable frozen products. In addition the Commission encouraged the canning of lobsters and tried to improve the quality of cod liver oil, a valuable export used as medicine, for tanning leather, manufacturing soap, and making oil cloth. The canning of fish is a growing industry.

The Commission was more successful than any previous administration in advancing agriculture. In the winter of 1933-34 a group of St. John's citizens organized a scheme whereby farmers would co-operate in clearing land, erecting buildings, constructing roads, and carrying on farming generally. The group of farmers would collectively own bulldozers, stump pullers, ditchers, tractors and other equipment for clearing land as well as the ordinary implements for planting and harvesting crops. The first venture, at Markland on the Avalon Peninsula, was followed by other schemes elsewhere with the Government rather than a group of public-spirited individuals supplying the initial capital and giving expert advice. The communal idea became weaker in time but was helpful in getting the projects started. The Commission set up a demonstration farm to which is attached a school specializing in short courses in agriculture.

Over the years St. John's merchants with their offices in Water Street came effectively to control the political and economic life of the Island. At the beginning of the season, fishermen obtained gear and household supplies on credit from the local general store or the supply boat, i.e., a schooner trading in the outports. When the year's fishing ended, their catches were valued and any balance was paid in cash or goods. Should there be no surplus, the fishermen remained in debt to the local dealer who, in turn, was obligated to the Water Street wholesaler. Because of a poor catch or low prices, every fisherman became sooner or later dependant on credit from the large exporter. Once immersed in debt, the fishing folk found it nearly impossible to escape the coils of the system. Meanwhile the Water Street merchants took the risk of a decline in price until the salt fish could be sold in a distant market. The evils of this economic system had been recognized for decades. The Royal Commission of 1934 suggested that legislation be passed to require payment in cash of a fraction of the value of each year's catch. This proving unworkable, the Commission of Government did what it could to kindle interest in co-operatives for the purchase of supplies, the sale of fish, and self-help generally. These efforts, along with good markets for fish during and after the War, and the growing sales of fresh fish, give some hope of relief from the worst evils of the credit system.

The Commission made substantial advances in administration. Customs duties normally provided about three-quarters of the public revenue. In their efforts to forestall default in bond interest, previous Governments had raised the tariff so steeply that people could not afford to buy imported goods. The smaller volume of imports, even at the high rates of duty, yielded less revenue than the older, lower rates which had permitted goods to enter in reasonable volume. The Commission reduced some rates and, in addition, called upon customs

officials to enforce the regulations more strictly. By
agreement Newfoundland cut its duties on some foodstuffs and textiles from the United States which, in return, gave concessions on minerals and fish. Most of all,
the Commission improved the civil service by granting
security of tenure, sending Newfoundlanders to Britain
for special training, and eliminating the worst features
of political and religious influence in the making of ap-
pointments. By these means it was able to attract a
number of able young men into the public service.

Despite its apparent success the Commission of
Government was not popular. Many Newfoundlanders
felt keenly the loss of responsible government which they
had enjoyed since 1855. Water Street merchants resented
the loss of their political power. They disliked having
to pay income tax which fell mainly on them since the
incomes of fishermen and farmers were relatively low.
The merchants opposed the widening of social services
either because they felt dependence on the state would
sap the efforts of individuals to improve their lot or because they felt the local government was too poor to stand
the expense. In Water Street's opinion, the Commission
had paid too much attention to strengthening other economic groups, notably co-operatives and trade unions. In
the outports, the attitude toward the Commission was
often apathetic, the general feeling being that one government was about as bad as another.

After the War Britain decided not to continue financial
support to Newfoundland. Neither could she agree to
keep on buying Newfoundland's fish and newsprint since
the Island used the currency of Canadian banks and
Britain was short of Canadian dollars. Further, she was
anxious that the Island, formerly a self-governing dominion, should again have Responsible Government.

Hence the Commission, with the consent of the Government in London, called a National Convention in 1946. Delegates to the Convention must have been resident in their constituency for two years prior to the date of the election. This provision prevented dominance by Water Street. However, so great was the indifference of the public toward political affairs that only about 20 per cent of the electorate voted. The proceedings of the Convention, which were broadcast, helped educate the public in democratic processes.

The Commission recommended a plebiscite in which the electorate could vote in favour of either Responsible Government or continuing the Commission for a further period of five years. The British Government insisted that the question of confederation with Canada be added to the ballot. In the ensuing vote, 45 per cent favoured Responsible Government, 41 per cent confederation, and 14 per cent the Commission arrangement. None of the choices received a clear majority of the votes cast and, in accordance with the original plans, a second plebiscite had to be held with the choice receiving the smallest number of votes left off the ballot. In the second vote the majority for confederation was 7,000 out of 145,650 votes cast. In both plebiscites roughly 85 per cent, an extraordinarily high proportion, of the eligible voters went to the polls.

Several factors influenced the decision. Though its position was temporarily sound, it was questionable whether the local government could finance itself without support from a stronger, more diversified economy. Certainly, it could not provide for its own defence and, being a bastion of North America, defence could not be ignored. Further, it might face an insuperable problem of foreign exchange.

The Canadian Government would extend unemployment insurance, old age pensions, family allowances, and price supports for fish to the Island on the same basis as to the existing provinces. It undertook to operate the Newfoundland Railway (750 miles), the government-owned coastal steamships, the government hotel in St. John's, the telegraph system, and the main broadcasting stations. It also planned to construct a road across the Island as part of the Trans-Canada Highway. By taking over these public works, the Dominion relieved the Island of some of its most pressing burdens.

A great deal of the wartime prosperity was due to Canadian and American spending on the Island. Newfoundland drew more of its supplies from North America and was selling more of its goods on the mainland than ever before, and the results were apparently good. Memories of Newfoundland's fate when it had stood alone were vivid and unpleasant; apparently it would be a safer bet to follow up economic integration with Canada by political union.

The Island's customs tariff would, of course, be abolished. The Government would lose what had been its main source of revenue, but in return it would receive subsidies from the Dominion on an equitable basis with other provinces. Removing the duties would lower the retail prices of some goods and so tend to improve the standard of living. Lower freight rates, which were also agreed upon, would have the same effect. Since employees of the former Newfoundland Railway were to be paid at the same rates as the rest of the Canadian National System, some wages would rise immediately. Newfoundlanders hoped that wages in other industries would eventually approach the scales paid on the mainland.

Relations between Canada and Newfoundland had al-

ways been close. Both Dominions owed allegiance to the
same King and, until 1934, had enjoyed the parliamentary
system of government. In the first World War Newfoundlanders served in their own renowned regiment and
in the Royal Navy. In the second War they joined the
Canadian navy, army and air force. In 1941 some 26,000
natives of Newfoundland were living in Canada. A much
larger number had family connections in the Island
for during the years of depression emigration to both
Canada and the United States had been as high as 15,000
per annum. Church connections had been particularly
intimate and religious denominationalism is powerful in
Newfoundland's social and political life. Branches of
Canadian banks did all the banking business on the Island
and supplied it with all its currency except silver coins.
Canadian trust and insurance companies were established
in St. John's and elsewhere. An indigenous labour movement began as early as 1908. By 1934 trade unionists
numbered roughly 20,000 and were active among fishermen, miners, lumbermen, paper-makers, longshoremen,
and railway workers. Since then, membership has doubled
and the unions were, broadly speaking, part and parcel
of the Canadian labour movement. The most important
non-economic factor in the movement for confederation
was the enthusiasm and dynamic force of Mr. Joseph
R. Smallwood who was later the first provincial premier.
Without his efforts the verdict of the people might have
been quite different.

Opposition to Confederation centred in St. John's and
the Avalon Peninsula. Merchants felt their business
would be ruined by mail order houses in Halifax which
could send in their goods more cheaply than before. They
considered that Canadian firms would take the cash business and leave them with the less profitable, long-term

credit needed by fishermen. The larger merchants were simultaneously exporters, importers, wholesalers, and retailers with stores in St. John's. They acted as insurance brokers or agents for steamship companies and had money invested in fishing and sealing. They used their influence in all these lines of activity to oppose Confederation.

Local manufacturers thought their cordage, clothing, and castings would be driven off the market. Producers of oleomargarine (made from the oil of whales and fish), aerated waters, bread, and ice cream did not fear being displaced for their output is bulky, perishable, and suited to manufacture near the market. Still, they were sympathetic with other manufacturers and business men.

Newfoundland's traditions militated against Confederation. In 1867 it was understood she would become one of the provinces but the colonial legislature rejected the plan, partly because of local patriotism, partly because Ottawa was then no more accessible than London. In the negotiations in 1895 Newfoundland's pride was hurt by the rather supercilious attitude of the Dominion Government. Later she felt she would lose some of her self-respect if she entered with such a load of public debt. These psychological resistances to union were deep-seated. Finally, Newfoundland was impressed by the complaints of the Maritime Provinces that Confederation had not brought them the prosperity which had been promised.

Since March 31, 1949, when Newfoundland became Canada's tenth province, the advisability of Confederation has ceased to be an issue. The Island and Labrador have benefited from the social services provided by the Federal Government. Capital has flowed in for investment in mining and newsprint. The market for fish has been quite good. Whereas at least as late as 1925 almost all the population was directly or indirectly dependent on fish for its livelihood, in 1949 only 28,000 were so engaged. Roughly 18,000 worked in newsprint and sawmills, 4,000 in mining, 1,000 were full-time farmers, and the rest of the working population were occupied in transportation, trade, finance, manufacturing, and the public service.

The total population of the Province, mostly descendants of settlers from southern England and Ireland, is 330,000. About one-seventh of these live in St. John's which has its own municipal government. Other places like Buchans and Corner Brook began as company towns but later established their own elected councils. Most of the smaller communities or outports are administered by the Province, but in 1948 there were fourteen incorporated municipalities. The unwillingness of Newfoundlanders to pay direct taxes and, in some cases, the low taxable value of local property, has retarded the growth of municipal organizations. The schools are run by the Anglican, United, and Roman Catholic Churches which divide the religious loyalty of the people almost equally. A few schools are controlled by the Salvation Army, the Seventh Day Adventists, and non-denominational authorities. Memorial University in St. John's gives courses in teacher training, adult education, Arts and Engineering. It shares in the grants made by the Dominion to institutions for higher education.

Though nature has not been prodigal in her gifts to Newfoundland, the Province has considerable potential wealth. Fishing on the Grand Banks and in-shore has been carried on for well over three hundred years with no indication of depletion. On the other hand salt codfish is not especially appetizing and can be sold regularly only to people who are unable to afford better tasting foods. The existing newsprint mills can successfully

compete in either the British or the American markets.
One or two more mills might profitably be established.
Up to 1950 agriculture was confined to the Avalon Peninsula due to fair soils and proximity to the market in St.
John's. Better soils are located in the vicinity of Deer
Lake and around St. George's Bay. As the cost of transportation is lowered, these districts can be expected to
grow foodstuffs for sale in nearby newsprint, mining, and
fishing communities. Potatoes, roots, and hay do well.
The Island has 84,000 sheep, 23,000 cattle, as well as hogs,
goats, and poultry. Grain does not especially thrive because of late springs and moderate summer tempera-
tures. In any case it can be brought in cheaply from the
mainland. Some farming, or rather gardening, is part-time
work for fishermen and their wives. Most of the farms
are small, a farm with five acres under cultivation being
considered large. The meagreness of agricultural development is due to soil infertility, the high cost of clearing
land, unfavourable climate, and competition from the
favoured farm lands of the St. Lawrence Valley and the
Prairies.

Deposits of iron ore, base metals, and limestone have
already been mentioned. Geological surveys are being
made annually and new resources will doubtless be discovered. Coal measures are found near St. George's Bay
but they are less convenient to the main market in St.
John's than Sydney, Nova Scotia, and fuelwood is a
strong competitor. The enormous iron reserves on the
Labrador-Quebec boundary will unquestionably help Newfoundland's economy, especially since the mining companies are obliged to hire Newfoundlanders whenever
possible. A railway line from these resources to tide-
water on Hamilton Inlet would have been shorter and of
greater importance to Newfoundland than the one which

was constructed to Sept Iles on the north shore of the Gulf of St. Lawrence. But the southerly route is open for a longer period each year and less exposed to enemy attack.

The development of hydro-electric power on the Island is limited by the absence of high mountains and large waterfalls, though helped by reasonably heavy rainfall and by the presence of lakes which act as storage basins for water. Grand Falls on the Hamilton River in Labrador is more than twice as high as Niagara Falls. It is believed to be capable of generating four million horse-power of electrical energy. Yet, despite its potentialities, Newfoundland is still vulnerable to the hazards of a staple economy.

SELECTED READINGS

CURRIE, A. W., *Economic Geography of Canada*, Toronto, 1945, pp. 423-42.

DOMINION BUREAU OF STATISTICS, *Province of Newfoundland, Statistical Background*, Ottawa, 1949.

C. R. FAY, *Life and Labour in Newfoundland*, Toronto, 1956.

MACKAY, R. A., ed., *Newfoundland: Economic, Diplomatic, and Strategic Studies*, Toronto, 1946.

MAYO, H. B., "Newfoundland's Entry into the Dominion", *C.J.E.P.S.* November, 1949, pp. 505-22.

REPORT OF THE ROYAL COMMISSION ON NEWFOUNDLAND, 1933, (the Amulree Report).

14

Transportation and Communication
since Confederation

CONFEDERATION increased rather than diminished the demand for good transportation facilities. Up to 1867 the objectives, in so far as transportation within Canada itself was concerned, were to develop local regions and to draw traffic from the American Mid-West down the St. Lawrence Valley. The means adopted were numerous—canoes, Durham boats, sailing vessels, steamships and especially railways. In the period immediately after Confederation, there was but one objective, to unite the outlying colonies with the central provinces of the new Dominion, and there was but one means, railways.

The first railway built with the new purpose in mind was the Intercolonial. Construction of this road was required, under the British North America Act, in order to connect the Maritimes at Halifax and Saint John with the St. Lawrence Valley at Quebec and Montreal. Because it was to serve mainly as a political link and as a route for troops in case of attack, the railway was located along the Gulf of St. Lawrence, as far back from the American boundary as possible. Like the Grand Trunk, it was to be built according to English rather than American standards. When the Intercolonial was completed in 1876, it was operated under one of the departments of the Dominion Government even though a considerable body of opinion favoured leasing it to the Grand Trunk.

The Intercolonial was never a financial success. Through traffic was hard to secure in Montreal because the Grand Trunk had its own line to the Atlantic at Portland, Maine, and in later years the Canadian Pacific had its own direct route to Saint John. In any event the Intercolonial's route was circuitous, being at least two hundred miles longer from Montreal to Halifax than it would have been had it been built directly, that is, on economic rather than on military grounds. In addition, local traffic was small, for the route missed the fertile St. John River valley and was exposed to competition from coastal shipping. Also the road had been built at high cost and suffered from heavy interest charges. Operation by the Government led to considerable political interference and high expenses. Consequently the road invariably had a deficit which had to be borne by the Dominion Government. On the other hand the Intercolonial gave Maritime producers low rates and assisted them in selling in the St. Lawrence Valley. It brought the two regions together in a cultural and political sense, and helped slowly to destroy the original Maritime connotation of "Canada" meaning the old province of Canada (Ontario and Quebec), not the present Dominion. Finally because the Intercolonial was built as a political and military road, it should, perhaps, not be judged by ordinary commercial standards.

The other railway designed to bind the colonies on the edges to those in the centre was the road to the Pacific. Such a line had been envisioned in the 'thirties and seriously considered in the 'fifties, but it took events of the 'sixties and early 'seventies to make the line necessary and, at the same time, possible. The acquisition of Rupert's Land from the Hudson's Bay Company in 1869, the danger that American railways would invade the region

from the south, the need to connect the British colonies
in the eastern half with those in the Red River Valley
and on the Pacific coast, the greater financial strength
of the federated colonies were all factors encouraging
construction of a transcontinental road. But the matter
which ultimately forced its construction was the admission of British Columbia into Confederation in 1871.
Under the terms of union a railway was to be begun
within two years and completed within ten. A transcontinental road became a legal as well as an economic
and political necessity.

Building such a road had been contemplated by the
Grand Trunk for many years because it hoped that a
westward extension would relieve its financial position.
It proposed to build from its existing terminus at Chicago
north-westerly to Winnipeg, and thence across the Plains.
Alternatively, it would build from the head of navigation
on the Lakes to Winnipeg and then west. In any event
it planned to construct the line slowly. Its proposals
were unacceptable to the Government. The latter insisted
on an all-Canadian route even though this would involve
building across the barren country north of Lake Superior.
Neither the Government nor the Grand Trunk would
modify its position and the scheme fell through—indeed
it was perhaps never seriously considered by the Canadian
public as a whole.

The rejection of the Grand Trunk proposal left the field
open to new companies to be formed for the purpose of
building the line. One of these companies was organized
by a group of Montreal business men headed by Sir Hugh
Allan. This syndicate, after associating with them prominent individuals from other parts of the country, got a
charter from the Government of Sir John A. Macdonald
in 1872. They agreed to build a railway to the Pacific

in return for thirty million dollars in cash, and a land grant of fifty million acres. Immediately after obtaining the charter the company dispatched agents to London to raise the rest of the funds needed to finish building and equipping the road. Work on the line was already proceeding when, early in the parliamentary session of 1873, a Liberal member accused the Conservatives of receiving financial assistance from Sir Hugh Allan in the election of the previous year. Whether any aid was given and if so, whether it influenced the Government to favour the Company to the detriment of the public interest, are questions which need not concern us. The important matter is that this "Pacific Scandal" destroyed all possibility of raising funds in Britain. The Macdonald Government resigned and the project collapsed.

The policy of the succeeding administration was to proceed slowly. Mackenzie, the new Prime Minister, was a cautious man and anxious not to place any additional burdens on the taxpayer. Also, the business depression after 1873 limited the opportunity to raise money either by the Government or by private individuals. Nevertheless, surveys for the route were steadily pushed forward, short railway lines were built to connect western waterways and generally, the basis was laid for further construction when conditions were more favourable.

Meanwhile British Columbia was becoming thoroughly annoyed by the failure to construct the line which, according to the terms of union, was to be completed in 1881. In fact the Pacific Province threatened to secede from the union and only the tact of the Governor-General, who went to British Columbia via San Francisco, induced it to be patient. The election of 1878 returned the Conservatives to power on a platform of the National Policy and immediate completion of the transcontinental. In view of the continuing depression little could be done at once but in 1880, the Government formed a contract with a Montreal group, chief of whom were George Stephen, (later Lord Mountstephen), R. B. Angus and in the background, Donald Smith (later Lord Strathcona). These men had made a fortune in the purchase and operation of a short railway line out of Minneapolis and were now prepared to pledge their resources in a transcontinental, the Canadian Pacific.

The Company undertook to construct a road from Callander, Ontario, the westernmost extension of existing railways in the Ottawa Valley, to the Pacific coast within ten years. In return it was to receive from the Government twenty-five million dollars in cash and twenty-five million acres of land. It also got, without cost to itself, the 713 miles of railway already constructed or contracted for by the Government and extending from the Head of the Lakes to beyond Winnipeg, and from Port Moody up the Fraser Valley. Finally the Company received the use of the completed surveys, and a monopoly of the territory south of its main line for a period of twenty years.

These terms appeared exceptionally generous and were much critized at the time on the grounds of giving too much and receiving too little. On the other hand, it was argued that assistance of such proportions was essential if the railway were to be built at all. The Western Plains were largely uninhabited, the mountains in British Columbia and the rocky territory north of Lake Superior were formidable barriers, and the obligation to complete the road in its entirety within a short time instead of building gradually, using profits from completed sections to pay for further extensions—these were factors to daunt the faint-hearted. In addition, only extensive government aid could have induced investment in the road by Englishmen whose belief in the value of Canadian securities had been badly weakened by their experience with the Grand Trunk. Finally, the road to the Pacific was completed in slightly less than half the time agreed upon. On the whole the bargain was a good one.

The completion of the railway did not end its difficulties. In the largely unsettled Plains, traffic was almost impossible to secure. The attempt to capture intercoastal American and trans-Pacific traffic from transcontinental lines in the United States led to a slashing of rates. Business conditions were generally poor. Because there was little traffic to be had along the original system, the Canadian Pacific purchased a network of lines in the settled regions of the St. Lawrence Valley, and built a short line across the state of Maine to the winter port of Saint John. This policy led the Grand Trunk to make similar purchases of previously independent lines. Soon most of the lines in Eastern Canada, except the Intercolonial, were owned by either the Grand Trunk or the Canadian Pacific. Competition between the two was intense and rate cutting and loss of income was the result. The Canadian Pacific indeed "had a long and dreary season of unprofitableness" as the London *Economist* had predicted.

After 1897, however, the Canadian Pacific was able to put itself on a sound financial basis mainly on account of the rapid expansion of the West. Under the stimulus of this prosperity, the Railway extended its lines, improved the trans-Atlantic and trans-Pacific steamship services it had acquired, operated passenger and package freight vessels on the Great Lakes, built hotels, and developed irrigation systems; in short, it grew up with the country. And withal, it maintained a sound financial position and its securities, held mainly in Britain, were highly regarded. It had two great advantages. Its lines were built according to American practice—economically constructed, well located, cheap to operate. At the same time its financial structure followed the English model—a relatively small amount of bonds, and hence ability to ride through a depression without foregoing payment of bond interest and assuming the risks of reorganization.

While the Canadian Pacific was establishing itself in this way, two new transcontinental railway systems were coming into being. The first of these was the Canadian Northern, which began in 1897 as a local line running north to Dauphin from the Canadian Pacific at Gladstone, Manitoba. This half worn out line was managed with extraordinary skill by (Sir) William Mackenzie and (Sir) Donald Mann, two ambitious Canadians who had got their start as building contractors on the Canadian Pacific. These men soon began extending their line and, with the aid of the Manitoba Government, built a road to Port Arthur. By the same means they leased the lines within Canada of the Northern Pacific Railway, an American line, which had failed. As the West developed they built new lines, invariably constructing them economically and locating them in regions with good traffic possibilities. In addition they acquired existing lines in the Maritimes and built through Toronto, Ottawa and Montreal to Quebec. Mackenzie and Mann followed the policy of expanding first in areas where business was to be had and money to be made. Later they planned to complete their transcontinental line by building the links in less profitable regions, namely, through British Columbia, north of Lake Superior and diagonally across New Brunswick. By 1915 the line had been finished from sea to sea, but it had not yet had time to build up traffic throughout its length so as to become a paying proposition.

The most distinctive features about the Canadian Northern were the economy of its construction and operation, and the amount of government assistance it was able to secure. The line was operated cheaply, even frugally. It was said that the track was so poor that it was likely to jump up and hit the trains from behind; the rolling stock was often insufficient in amount and inadequately maintained. Nevertheless the road handled a good volume of business and did so profitably, until financial difficulties during the War hampered its further development. The other feature was the amazing amount of aid Mackenzie and Mann were able to extract from governments—federal, provincial and municipal. Some of this aid was in the form of land and cash subsidies. But most of it was in guarantees of bond interest, that is, the governments would guarantee that if the railway were unable to pay the interest on the bonds which it sold to the public, they would do so themselves. By means of these guarantees Mackenzie and Mann were able to raise money more easily and more cheaply than would otherwise have been possible. At the same time the public obtained new railways without cost to itself, for it was expected that the railway would make such large profits that the governments would never be called upon to make good their guarantees.

Besides the Canadian Pacific and the Canadian Northern, there was the Grand Trunk Pacific, still another transcontinental railway projected in the decade before the first Great War. In the last few years of the nineteenth century the unfortunate Grand Trunk had become revitalized under the energetic control of Charles M. Hays, an American with an almost uncanny ability for putting bankrupt railways back on their feet. After its re-organization of 1862, the Grand Trunk had always been able to pay its bond interest, and in a few good years it paid dividends on its preferred stock, but never in its history had it paid anything on its common or ordinary shares. Hays had increased earnings to relatively high figures, but he feared that the traffic from the rapidly developing West would be carried past his road by its competitors, and that the Grand Trunk would be encircled by its rivals. Accordingly he made plans to extend his system southward from Montreal to Providence, Rhode Island, where car ferry connections could be made with the huge traffic centre of New York, and he applied to the Dominion Government for assistance in building a line through Canada to the Pacific coast. It was Hays' intention to build only from North Bay, the point nearest the North-West which the existing Grand Trunk system reached, but the Government was afraid that with such a line, the Grand Trunk would send western traffic out through the American seaports of New York and Portland. Therefore, in order to keep the traffic within Canada, the Government insisted that the Pacific extension be built directly across Northern Ontario and Quebec, to the city of Quebec. Then, to satisfy the demands of the Maritimes, the party in power had the line extended further to Moncton, a point roughly equidistant between the rival ports of Saint John and Halifax. The Government itself was to construct the section, known as the National Transcontinental, east of Winnipeg and lease it to the Grand Trunk Pacific at a moderate rental based on the cost of the line. The Grand Trunk through its subsidiary was to build the part west of Winnipeg, with the assistance of Government bond guarantees.

The new system was to be built on the English model with low operating costs and high interest charges. Unfortunately the costs of construction greatly exceeded expectations, due to increases in wages and in the cost of fuel and supplies during the decade preceding the first War. Excessive cost was particularly apparent on the National Transcontinental. In fact, when this section was completed in 1915, it had cost so much that the Grand Trunk refused to take it over. As a result the Government had to operate it on its own account. Unfortunately the road could not even pay its operating expenses, that is, its wages, fuel and repairs, without including interest at all. It had been expected that this section would make great profits hauling grain by rail to eastern Canadian ports. This traffic did not materialize because steady improvements in elevators, and in ship operation and design enabled the lake boats to cut their rates to a point below what the railway could afford to make. The local traffic, that is, the amount of freight and the number of passengers originating along the National Transcontinental itself was small. On the western, or Grand Trunk Pacific section, local traffic was larger in amount, but was inadequate to carry the expense of operating the line including the unproductive sections in the mountains, and the heavy interest on the whole project. The sudden death of Mr. Hays was a great loss to the Company. Finally the financial stringency associated with the outbreak of the War choked off investment from abroad.

The situation in 1914 was that neither the Canadian Northern nor the Grand Trunk Pacific had been completely built; on the portions already finished the systems had not had time to develop the country and build up traffic volume; the cost of labour and construction materials was going up rapidly; and the financial markets of the world were concerned solely with financing the War. As the War progressed the last two factors became even more acute. Moreover, though railway operating costs increased, rates which are the basis of receipts remained relatively fixed. In consequence, both railways lacked the revenue to pay their bond interest. The Government had guaranteed some of the interest, and the rest it could not permit to be defaulted, for to do so would be to force the roads into receivership. Bankruptcy of two large railways would be a serious blow to Canada's credit at a time when the Government urgently needed to borrow enormous sums for war purposes. Accordingly the Government was compelled gradually to assume complete financial responsibility for these two lines, and also for the Grand Trunk whose remaining strength had been drawn from it by its Prairie extension.

In 1922 the various lines controlled by the Government, that is, the Grand Trunk, Grand Trunk Pacific, National Transcontinental and Canadian Northern, along with the Intercolonial and the uncompleted Hudson Bay line were put under one system, the Canadian National Railways, with a total of over 22,000 miles of main line track. As president and general manager of the system, the Government appointed Sir Henry Thornton, an American who had had extensive railway experience in Britain. Thornton faced a truly tremendous task. His system consisted of a patchwork of lines, some of them built to compete with each other, all of them bankrupt, heavily indebted, poorly equipped, poorly maintained and with a personnel whose lack of enthusiasm for their jobs reflected the mass of junk they were supposed to operate. But Thornton was a big man in physique, appetite, ability and courage. Before long he had welded the derelict lines into a unified, efficient, well equipped system and had fired it with a real *esprit de corps*. Unfortunately he went too far. He built hotels on a luxurious scale, constructed lines far in advance of requirements and into territories adequately served by the competing system, acquired steamship lines duplicating services already in existence and, generally, spared neither effort nor money to build up the road. For his extravagances the Government was partly at fault, since it made little effort to stem the pressure which came from both political parties in the various parts of the country for the unwise extensions. In further extenuation of Thornton's policies, it must be realized that the late 'twenties was a boom period and all other types of business were expanding at an unwise rate also.

The drastic decline of business in the depression following 1929 caused questioning of Thornton's methods. The National Railways had to borrow from the Government for a small part of its operating expenses and all of its interest. Deficits on the Canadian National ran, in some years, to sixty million dollars and all the Government's revenue from the income taxes was required to meet them. At the same time the privately owned system, the Canadian Pacific, had to forego payment of dividends on its preferred and common stock which it had paid for many years, though it was able to earn and pay the interest on its comparatively small debt.

To consider the entire railway problem in Canada, the Government in 1931 appointed a Royal Commission. In its report this body castigated the National Railways for their extravagance and emphasized that, faced with competition, the Canadian Pacific had also undertaken unwise expenditures and should not, therefore, be excused "from a share in the general competitive folly". The Commission suggested changes in the organization of the Canadian National so as to remove the management from regional political pressures. It also recommended that the two systems which together controlled most of the railway lines in the country, should co-operate with each other with a view to eliminating duplicate services, abandoning non-paying branch lines, consolidating trains and generally reducing costs. The result of the economy proposals was a comparatively small saving. This was due to objections by labour who feared loss of jobs, and by the public which wanted the old services retained. Chiefly, the scheme failed because neither road was ready to give up any traffic unless it received compensating advantages.

Although almost all the present railway network of Canada is included in either the Canadian National or the Canadian Pacific, separate companies serve coal mines near Sydney, N.S. Moreover, American railways reach Montreal, Winnipeg and Vancouver, and use the short-cut north of Lake Erie between Michigan and New York States. Other lines are essentially colonization roads like the Ontario Northland to Cochrane and Moosonee and the Pacific Great Eastern, both provincially owned, the latter being a financial incubus on British Columbia. There is also the Northern Alberta Railways, constructed by the Province, but now owned and operated jointly by the two transcontinental systems.

The physical provision of railways would serve the needs of Canadian business only if rates were set at a reasonable level. The early rates charged on railways in Eastern Canada were determined by the necessity of meeting the competition of American lines and of lake and river steamships. In the West, the first rates on the Canadian Pacific were so high as to stifle settlement but these were reduced, chiefly in 1897, by the Crow's Nest Pass Agreement. In return for a subsidy for the construction of a line through the Crow's Nest Pass into Southern British Columbia, the Canadian Pacific reduced its rates on grain eastbound to the Head of the Lakes for export, and on building materials and other settlers' supplies westbound. When the Canadian Northern received a subsidy from the Manitoba Government for the line to Port Arthur, it agreed to reduce grain rates still further. The low railway rates on grain for export were important in creating a great boom in the West after 1900.

During the 1914–18 War, rates in general were increased, though not fast enough to give much relief to the hard pressed lines now included in the Canadian National. In the 1920's rates were reduced partly by order of the Railway Commission, and partly by the Maritime Freight Rates Act, and by legislation which restored the Crow's Nest Pass Agreement rates on grain and flour but not on the other articles. Lower rates on grain for export were also given Vancouver. After 1947 many tolls had to be raised to cover higher operating costs. Other rates and fares were cut to meet competition from trucks, buses and cars. Since 1951 all rates except on Western grain for export and on other export, import and competitive traffic must be at the same rate mile for mile anywhere in Canada, except in the Maritimes and Newfoundland. The Dominion subsidizes railways to keep down rates on Western export grain.

To prevent abuses, the Federal Government set up, in 1903, the Board of Railway Commissioners with full control over railway rates, safety precautions and highway crossings, as well as the rates of telephone, telegraph and express companies. Though handicapped at times by political interference and inexperienced personnel, the Board on the whole has performed its functions well. In 1938 its powers were enlarged to include some inland water-lines and air-lines (later transferred to the Air Transport Board) and its name changed to the Board of Transport Commissioners. Incidentally the quality of railway service in speed, convenience and certainty has greatly improved over the years, especially since 1950.

The rapid expansion, and then the financial difficulties and control of the railways, is only part of the history of transportation since Confederation. Interest in canals which had been so strong in the 1840's, declined greatly with the construction of railways, though the older transportation agency continued to carry a substantial volume of traffic. Before the end of the nineteenth century the Government had, by building a new canal at Sault Ste. Marie and deepening the old Welland and St. Lawrence canals, created a fourteen foot channel between Montreal and the Head of the Lakes. The object now was not to draw traffic from the American mid-west, but to assist the development of the Canadian Prairies.

When the West began to boom, the demand for improved canals to get grain down to tide-water cheaply was renewed. Accordingly, in 1913, Canada began a new Welland Canal on a scale which far exceeded any of its predecessors. It was nearly twice as deep, had eight locks in place of twenty-six, and each lock was very much larger than before and could be operated much more rapidly. The new canal, completed in 1932, permitted the largest grain carriers on the Upper Lakes to come down to Kingston on Lake Ontario, and thence to Prescott. Even so, most of the grain continued to be trans-shipped to railways at Buffalo or to smaller boats at Port Colborne, for normally it does not pay to have the largest boats spend time in locks or narrow channels.

The St. Lawrence Seaway, opened in 1959 by Queen Elizabeth and President Eisenhower, provides a channel twenty-seven feet deep from Montreal to Lake Ontario. Ocean-going vessels may enter the Lakes, carry grain direct to Liverpool, and haul industrial products between ports on the Great Lakes and the markets of the World. Moreover, the Seaway allows large lake carriers to go all the way to Montreal, thus eliminating trans-shipment of grain at Prescott or ports on Georgian Bay. After many years of fruitless negotiations with the United States, in 1951 Canada decided to finance the Seaway herself. Later, the two nations agreed on joint construction of the Seaway and on means of developing the hydro-electric power of the upper St. Lawrence River. Tolls are levied on ships and their cargoes in order to meet the operating expenses of the Seaway and amortize its cost over fifty years. Users of electricity will pay for the power plants.

In spite of the fact that it lies far beyond our boundaries and is controlled by a foreign power, one of the important canals in Canadian development is the Panama. It has stimulated the rapid development of ports on the Pacific coast—Vancouver, Victoria and New Westminster. It permits grain from Alberta and lumber from British Columbia to be exported cheaply, and manufactured goods to be brought in readily. It has forced down transcontinental rates on the railways because of the possibility of shipping goods by water from the Maritimes, and even from Montreal and Toronto, to the Western coast. Altogether its influence is considerable though hard to assess exactly.

The early highways in Canada were thoroughly bad and were improved only with the increasing use of automobiles. As the need for better highways became greater, and especially when the need for trunk roads connecting the large cities developed, the municipalities which had previously been solely responsible for road construction and maintenance found the task beyond their financial ability or, perhaps, beyond their willingness to assume. Hence the Provincial Governments took over more and more mileage. They built excellent roads of asphalt or concrete in settled regions, constructed others of gravel and stone in less thickly populated areas, and projected cheaper roads into new agricultural communities and mining camps. The enormous cost of these developments greatly increased the amount of the provincial debts.

The Provinces try to recover their expenses for the maintenance and construction of highways by licensing vehicles, drivers and chauffeurs and chiefly, by taxing gasoline and diesel fuel. In most provinces highway users pay only part of the cost of through highways. The burden of taxation has to be equitably divided among private cars, motor buses, and commercial and farmers' trucks. The cost of city streets and ordinary country roads is chiefly met from municipal taxes on real estate. The Dominion builds roads in national parks and the Territories. It has also helped finance the trans-Canada highway, and roads to mineral and fishing resources.

The growing use of motor vehicles has taken traffic from railways and forced them to reduce many freight rates. Railways have tried to offset these losses by more efficient operation, dieselization, hump yards, and the consolidation of repair shops. By the late 1950's it was clear that these efforts were not enough to compensate for higher wages, dearer fuel, and continued erosion of traffic. So a Royal Commission recommended that railways be allowed to cut costs through a broad programme of eliminating non-paying branches and passenger trains. The Dominion will subsidize these services for a few years to protect communities against a too sudden withdrawal of branches and the cancellation of trains.

Pipe-lines, which for centuries had been used to convey water, were built in the 1860's for petroleum and natural gas in Western Ontario. The big expansion came after 1945 for the movement of oil and gas from Alberta.

Canadians are interested not merely in transportation services within the country itself and rail connections with the United States, but also in steamship connections with the rest of the world. The Canadian Pacific operates trans-Pacific and trans-Atlantic services, competing with British owned vessels operating on regular schedule and with tramps of every nationality. Improvements in ships such as steel hulls, reciprocating steam engines and better design of vessels steadily reduced ocean shipping charges to the great benefit of the staple industries in Canada. The first War created a great shortage of vessels and sky-rocketed rates. To assist Canadian export trade, the Government constructed vessels at high cost and continued this policy long after the time when shipping space was plentiful. Consequently the Canadian Government Merchant Marine, as it was called, could be operated only at a very substantial loss and eventually was disposed of at a great sacrifice. The Canada-West Indies service was continued until 1958, and was operated by the Canadian National Railways under government subsidy. In addition to trans-oceanic services by Canadian and other companies, ships operate on regular schedule along the Pacific and Atlantic coasts. To assist ocean traffic the Federal Government spends large sums for the construction and maintenance of harbour works and also for lighthouses, ice-breakers, dredging and other aids to navigation. During the Second World War the Government built and operated many merchant vessels. By selling them promptly after the end of the War, it avoided heavy losses. In 1960 it again started to subsidize ship-building.

While these developments were occurring in railways, canals, highways, pipe-lines, and shipping, another means of transport, the airplane, was being perfected. Pioneer attempts at flying were made before the first War, and the first flight in Canada took place off Cape Breton Island in 1909. Nevertheless, it was not until after the War that any important developments took place. Planes were used for locating forest fires, detecting smugglers and ships violating fishing regulations, surveying and, of course, for military purposes. They were used also, and to an increasing extent, for carrying men and supplies to mining camps which were inaccessible by other means of transport, except at great expense. During the 1930's, more freight was carried by air in Canada than in any other country in the world.

Meanwhile efforts were being made to establish lines to carry passengers, mail and valuable express on regular schedules between large cities. In the late 'twenties construction of landing fields and navigation aids for a transcontinental airway was begun. Abandoned in the early part of the depression, the scheme was revived and completed in the late 1930's. Trans-Canada Air Lines was incorporated under Government auspices to acquire planes and provide regular service by air from Victoria to Halifax. This service, started in 1938 over part of the route and extended by successive stages or "legs", was complete by 1940. Just before the outbreak of the second War, trans-Atlantic service from Montreal to Britain was inaugurated. Subsequently Trans-Canada Air Lines flew regular services from Canada to New York and other American cities, Bermuda and the British West Indies.

The so-called bush operators flying the north-south routes between rail-head and northern mining camps have been consolidated into Canadian Pacific Airlines, which is a wholly owned subsidiary of Canadian Pacific Railway. This company has provided responsible management for the northern routes and also flies to Europe, Japan, Australia and New Zealand. Several other airlines have regular flights along specified routes in Canada and under special contract will fly prospectors or sportsmen to any place where it is possible to land the plane.

In 1944 the Government set up the Air Transport Board which advises the Minister of Transport on the location of commercial airports, landing fees for aircraft, and so on. Subject to the Minister's approval, it authorizes passenger fares and charges for air freight and express. It issues licenses to commercial airlines upon proof that the public needs the service which is proposed and that the operators are both experienced and financially responsible. By allocating routes to particular companies, the Board is expected to avoid the wastes of competition and keep commercial aviation on a sound basis. Because of Canada's stake in world trade and her position on the direct air route between the most thickly settled portions of North America and Europe, she has taken an active part in international conferences dealing with civil aviation. The headquarters of the International Civil Aviation Organization is in Montreal.

Improvements in communication kept pace with those in transportation. In 1867, the existing postal services of the various Provinces were taken over by the Dominion and steadily co-ordinated and improved. Parcel post, a savings bank (much used by new European immigrants whose previous experience made them skeptical of other financial institutions), free rural and city mail delivery were introduced. Mail service was provided even in the most remote communities. In 1897, the Canadian Post-master-General was instrumental in securing an agreement for Imperial penny postage. Within Canada the mails were carried for a time by stage or courier, then by railway, steamship, dog-team, and more recently, by bus and airplane as well. The financial set-up of the post-office is complicated. For many years after 1915 a war tax of one cent on all letters went into general tax revenues. Also the post-office carries the mail for all Federal Government departments without charge and in return its buildings are provided for it free. It performs a vital service in binding the people of the country together, and in educating and entertaining them by giving exceptionally low rates on newspapers and magazines.

The telegraph was originally constructed and used by railways for the purpose of controlling train movements. Soon it was used also by the general public for social and business purposes. In order to provide communication with outlying, sparsely settled districts such as the Yukon, the Federal Government owns and operates a number of telegraph lines. As far as the telephone is concerned Canadians have a special interest in it. The early experiments on the earliest successful telephone were conducted in Brantford, Ontario, although it first became of practical value in the United States. Starting in Hamilton in 1878, telephones were rapidly installed in Canadian cities and were soon extended to rural communities as well. Because of the Laurentian Shield, a trunk-line across Canada wholly within the country was not completed until 1935. In almost all Eastern Canada and in British Columbia, the systems are operated by private capitalists while in the Prairies, they are under public ownership.

Still another means of communication is the radio. Successful wireless transmission of messages by code was accomplished before 1900, but it was not until 1920 that communication by telephony was perfected. The first Canadian radio broadcasting station was opened in that year at Montreal. Since then, there has been an astonishing advance in overcoming technical difficulties and reducing the prices of receiving sets. Later on in the 1940's high fidelity broadcasting was another notable advance. At first, broadcasting in Canada was solely under the control of private stations operating independently of each other and receiving revenue from advertising. In 1927, these stations were linked up temporarily in order to broadcast the ceremonies in connection with the celebration of the sixtieth anniversary of Confederation and the official opening of the new Welland Canal. The first permanent chain of stations was created by the Canadian National Railways. This chain was taken over in 1932 by a non-profit company, later called the Canadian Broadcasting Corporation, formed under Government control. This organization was to bring to Canadian listeners the best programmes from other countries, and also present programmes of a distinctly national character. The CBC broadcasts in both French and English, and gives opportunities for Canadian talent. It excels in its news, educational and cultural programmes but American stations have the advantage in variety shows and popular music which are sponsored by wealthy corporations. By 1960 the CBC's television network (started 1952) covered most of the settled parts of Canada. Early in its career the CBC had to depart from its original policy of not accepting advertising. For a time it got the revenue from an unpopular tax on radio sets. Television has proved so expensive that the Dominion has had to subsidize the CBC heavily. About 175 privately owned radio stations and 40 television stations operate throughout Canada. The Government owns wireless stations along the Great Lakes and the sea coasts to aid navigation, and in northern Canada to communicate with isolated police, military and trading posts.

The development of transportation and communication within Canada has been considered at some length because of their intrinsic importance to a country "of magnificent distances". Canada has sometimes been called a triumph over geography. Railways, canals, highways, airways, and the post-office, telegraph, telephone and radio have permitted that triumph to occur. They are the keys to the exploitation of Canada's scattered resources and to whatever cultural and political unity Canadians have achieved. The existence of an enormous government debt in railways, canals and harbour works is evidence of the necessity of providing means whereby the staples of the nation can be exported cheaply, at the same time as the various economic regions are linked closely together.

SELECTED READINGS

CURRIE, A. W., *Economics of Canadian Transportation*, Toronto, 1959.
    The Grand Trunk Railway of Canada, Toronto, 1957.
EASTERBROOK, W. T. and AITKEN, H. G. J., *Canadian Economic History*, Toronto, 1956, pp. 409-44.
FOURNIER, L. T., *Railway Nationalization in Canada*, Toronto, 1935.
GLAZEBROOK, G. P. deT., *A History of Transportation in Canada*, Toronto, 1938.
HEATON, H., *The Story of Trade and Commerce, with special reference to Canada*, Toronto, 1955 (rev. ed.), pp. 214-17, 227-9, 235-6, 251-5.
INNIS, H. A., *A History of the Canadian Pacific Railway*, London, 1923.
    "Canada and the Panama canal", in Innis, H. A., and Plumptre, A. F. W., *The Canadian Economy and Its Problems*, Toronto, 1939, pp. 331-50.
Royal Commission on Transportation, *Report*, Ottawa, 1951 (Turgeon Commission); also 1961 (MacPherson Commission).
STEVENS, G. R., *Canadian National Railways*, Toronto, 1960, 1961.
THOMSON, L. R., *The Canadian Railway Problem*, Toronto, 1938.

15

Trade Relationships since Confederation

T HE Canadian Provinces at the date of Confederation were considerably perturbed about their international trade relationships. They had been ignored by Great Britain in 1849 and spurned by the United States in 1866. Failing to retain preferences abroad, four provinces entered into Confederation in the hope, among other things, of increasing the volume of trade among themselves. At the same time, they wished to remain prepared to seize upon any favourable development for the renewal of trade concessions in the United States since Britain, having adopted a policy of no tariffs, could obviously not give lower duties to Canada.

Under these circumstances the low tariff which was designed mainly for revenue purposes was continued by the new Dominion Government. When government revenue fell off during the depression which began in 1873, the rates were increased, but the truly protective items remained few in number. The Liberal Government of the time was urged by some of its members to introduce more protective features. This proposal was not accepted due to opposition by Maritime Liberals, the extreme caution of Prime Minister Mackenzie and the uncertainty in the public mind. It was agreed on all sides that the most advantageous plan for Canada was reciprocity with the United States. Raising the Canadian tariff against American goods might be interpreted in the United States as closing the door on reciprocity. Consequently, most Canadians hesitated to increase tariff schedules but when the depression wore on more and more people realized, first, that the prospect of reaching a reciprocity agreement in the near future was becoming negligible and, second, that business conditions in Canada were such that aggressive action of some kind was required. Sentiment for protection gradually crystallized, beginning in Ontario cities such as Hamilton and Toronto which were ambitious to establish new industries.

In order to take advantage of this sentiment during the election campaign of 1878, the Conservative party came out strongly in favour of protection, the so-called National Policy. In their campaign they emphasized the reasonableness of having a tariff against goods from the United States if that country persisted in having a tariff against ours; they pointed to the prosperity of the Republic under its protective policy, and of Canada immediately after the Galt tariff was applied; they claimed that higher tariffs were required to provide revenue with which to construct the railway to the Pacific, and to stimulate traffic within Canada once the road was built; and in Quebec especially, they contended that factories must be set up in Canada to keep within the country the young men who were already beginning to flock to the industrial towns of New England. On the other hand, the Liberals held firmly to the ideal of reciprocity and pointed with pride to the record of their government on the basis of economy and cautious progress.

The victory of the Conservatives led immediately to the introduction of legislation increasing the tariff rates from seventeen and one-half to twenty per cent on manufactured goods not otherwise provided for, i.e., on manufactures generally. In addition schedules were differentiated, that is, instead of one rate which applied to almost all manufactured goods, different rates were applied to different articles, the rate being presumably determined by the amount of protection needed to encourage production of the article in Canada, instead of importing it from abroad. For example, the rate on cotton, silk, glass-ware, wall-paper and carriages was thirty per cent; on boots, buttons, woodenware, twenty-five per cent; on pig iron, formerly free, two dollars a ton and so on.

The application of these rates was followed, in the early 1880's, by an increase in manufacturing and in prosperity generally. How much of the prosperity was due to the tariff as such, and how much was due to other circumstances is a matter on which there was a considerable difference of opinion at the time. The Conservatives, of course, attributed the good times solely to the tariff. The Liberals pointed out that conditions were improving throughout the world. They also declared that manufacturing in Canada had begun before the National Policy and would have increased without it. Out of the plethora of political opinions, the conviction emerges that the National Policy after 1879 merely intensified trends toward manufacturing which were already evident.

During the long rule of the Conservative party from 1878 to 1896, there were no fundamental changes in the tariff except to extend protection more broadly to all iron and steel products, and to moderate the schedules on agricultural implements, textiles and sugar. Efforts to renew the Reciprocity Treaty of 1854-66 with the United States were made on several occasions but always without success. In the late 'eighties an agitation developed for Commercial Union with that nation, that is, complete free trade between the two countries, a common tariff against outsiders and the division of the total revenue on the basis of population. In spite of support by influential men and newspapers in both nations, the campaign collapsed through a combination of circumstances, chiefly the emergence of other political issues such as the Manitoba school question in Canada and monetary reform in the United States.

When the Liberals came into power in 1896, they made no effort to abolish the protective tariff in spite of the fact that they had denounced the National Policy while they had been in opposition. One of the reasons for this apparent inconsistency was that the United States had by now emerged as a strong industrial nation with a tariff, high since 1863 and only recently increased still further. It was illogical that Canada should lower or abolish her tariff to admit goods from the United States while that country, without regard to Canadian interests, raised her tariff to keep out our goods. Of course the Canadian tariff applied to goods from other countries of the world besides the United States but the volume of goods going across the border over the tariff wall on either side has been so great and the influence of the actions of our nearest neighbour on Canadian public opinion so pronounced that tariff policy in Ottawa has, at times, been almost entirely determined with reference to policies in Washington. Retaliation, or as we prefer to say, a brick for brick tariff, against the United States has been an important factor in maintaining a high tariff in Canada.

Although the Liberals made no serious breaches in the tariff wall, they did make some changes. Duties on some iron and steel articles were replaced by bounties, the benefit to the producer being the same in both cases. The duties were reduced on farm machinery, on binder twine and barbed wire and on some types of equipment used by manufacturers, that is, generally speaking, on the implements of production in the basic industries. The most distinctive feature of the Liberal tariff policy, however, was the "reciprocal" tariff. This meant a rate applicable only to Great Britain, although initially it applied also to other countries, Belgium, Germany and several more with which Britain had most favoured nation treaties. A most favoured nation treaty is one whereby two countries mutually agree that they will give each other, either generally or on specific commodities, rates which are as low as those given to any other country. When Britain originally made her trade treaties with Belgium and so on, Canada and other colonies had been included in the provisions. Therefore, when Canada gave the United Kingdom low rates, these rates were automatically extended to other countries. All trade treaties subsequently entered into by any part of the Empire provide that most favoured nation clauses exclude rates given by one part of the Empire to another. In other words the clause has been interpreted to mean most favoured *foreign* nation treatment. For example if, after 1898, the clause were included in a treaty with France, and in a still later treaty Canada gave Spain lower rates on Spanish wines than the original rate on French wines, the lower rate would automatically apply to France. On the other hand, it would not apply to France if Canada's later treaty had been with Australia. Before 1898, however, the clause was not interpreted in this way, and it was only by denouncing all her trade treaties with other countries that Britain was able to accept the concessions Canada offered without sharing them with Belgium and other countries.

The reciprocal tariff of 1897, which was originally one-eighth lower than the general rate, was soon changed to one-quarter and in 1900, to one-third less than the ordinary rate of duty. In 1904 this method of uniform reductions from the general rate was discarded and a separate schedule of British preferential rates, as they soon came to be known, was adopted. Following Canada's lead almost every part of the Commonwealth has adopted the British preferential feature in its tariff.

From a political standpoint the British preference was a shrewd move. It was a benefit freely granted to the Mother Country without asking for anything in return. Thus it took advantage of the strong imperialist sentiment of the time and allowed the Liberals, under a French-speaking leader, to demonstrate to ultra-imperialists that loyalty to the Crown was not a prerogative of the English-speaking Conservatives. From a purely economic standpoint the preference was equally shrewd. It appeared to give a positive reduction in tariffs and, therefore, to be a step in the direction of free trade. In many cases it really did reduce the protective wall. But by setting the preferential rate sufficiently high to give protection to Canadian industry and by placing the general rate still higher, protection could still be maintained for Canadian industry. In some cases this subterfuge was followed.

Frankly the Liberals were attempting to arrive at a compromise between their own members, of whom those from the West and the Maritimes wanted lower rates, and those from many districts in Ontario and Quebec desired the essentials of the protective system maintained. There is nothing discreditable in such an attitude, for in a democratic country one part must be prepared to make concessions to other regions. The important thing is that the programme of protection, first adopted by Conservatives in 1879, was continued by the Liberals without significant change. However much politicians might differ on the platform, in practice Canada had a stable tariff policy.

As part of their policy of compromise the Liberals, in 1904, introduced a dumping duty. Manufacturers contended that foreign combines were throwing, or dumping, goods on the Canadian market at prices so extraordinarily low that existing tariff rates gave no protection, and that Canadian factory workers were being thrown out of jobs by unfair competition from abroad. Hence it was provided that when goods are imported into Canada at less than their fair market value in the country of origin, a special duty equal to the difference between the actual price and the fair market value is to be assessed against them. The dumping duty is not properly applicable when foreign, say German, goods are sold in Canada for less than Canadian-made goods but only when they are sold here for less than they are sold in Germany, their country of origin. The dumping duty, first introduced by Canada, has been copied by other nations.

In 1907 a general revision of the tariff took place. After a lengthy enquiry by a committee of three cabinet ministers who toured the country, the entire schedule was overhauled. Goods were re-classified in accordance with new trading conditions which had arisen in the course of years. No radical change was made in the rates but the tariff rates were divided into three columns: the British preferential which was lowest; the intermediate, which applied to non-British countries with which Canada had, or expected to make special trade treaties; and the general rate, the highest of all, which applied to all other countries. The relationship between the three columns was not uniform but varied with different commodities. The columnar principle has been followed in subsequent tariff schedules.

The revision of 1907 was a disappointment to the West which had hoped for lower rates, especially on implements, clothing and other articles which they required. In the course of a tour of the Prairies in 1910, the Prime Minister, Sir Wilfrid Laurier, was much impressed by this attitude. In view of the support which he drew from industrial regions in the St. Lawrence Valley, he could not undertake greatly to lower the rates on manufactured goods. He could, however, try to enlarge the market for the goods which the West and other staple-producing regions of Canada had to sell. Accordingly emissaries were dispatched to Washington and early in the summer of 1911, it was announced that they had succeeded in negotiating an agreement for the free exchange of natural products between Canada and the United States. In essence, the agreement was a restoration of the Reciprocity Treaty of 1854. It was exactly the sort of thing which Canadian leaders, both Liberal and Conservative, had been trying to secure ever since 1866. What was more, it was actually accepted by the United States Senate, previously the stumbling block to all efforts. In Canada the agreement was greeted with jubilation.

As the summer went on, however, enthusiasm for the agreement cooled down. The railways opposed it; they claimed that they would become the "stub-ends of American lines", that all the magnificent transportation facilities, constructed at great sacrifice to carry traffic east and west across Canada, would become worthless while a few lines carried traffic north and south. Manufacturers opposed; although they were not mentioned in the agreement and there was nothing to prevent Canada keeping up her tariff on manufactured goods, they feared what *might* happen. These two groups combined to provide a well organized opposition, able to stir up and consolidate public sentiment against reciprocity. Members of the public opposed because of the uncertainty of the agreement; they felt that Canada, after decades of being scorned by the United States, was at last strong enough and prosperous enough to stand on her own feet; they feared that economic association with the United States would eventually lead to political annexation. Indiscreet statements by certain Americans lent colour to this latter fear, and stimulated in Canada a frenzied patriotism which was an important factor in swinging the election. All these factors, combined with suggestions of incompetency on the part of a government long in power, led to the defeat of the Reciprocity Agreement. The majority, in terms of total votes cast, was not large but the decision of the country was unmistakable.

After 1911 the tariff remained much the same as before though there was a good deal of altering of individual items, "tariff tinkering" it was called by opposition critics. During the war the rates were increased, partly to provide additional revenue to help prosecute the war and partly because specific duties, that is, rates in cents per unit, as per yard or per pound, yielded relatively less protection to Canadian manufacturers when prices rose. When the Liberals came into power in 1921 they made few immediate reductions because, even more than when they held office before, they were dependent for support on the industrial areas of Quebec and Ontario. Meanwhile the Progressives, a political party representing the agricultural interests, and strongly in favour of lower tariffs on the manufactured goods which they had to buy, had become a powerful force in Dominion politics. From 1921 to 1926 they held the balance of power in Parliament. In order to maintain themselves in office, the Liberals had to secure the support of this group. This they did by making moderate concessions on agricultural machinery, textiles and a host of minor items used by consumers. Nevertheless the general protective system was not impinged upon. Instead the Government, over the head of the Board of Railway Commissioners, restored the low rates on grain as set forth in the Crow's Nest Pass Agreement. The West was thereby assisted in selling its grain abroad more profitably. Relatively higher net returns for its staples reconciled the West to higher tariffs and higher prices for the machinery, clothing and equipment which it used.

In the succeeding years of their administration, the Liberals made few tariff changes although they did reduce the tariff on the cheaper types of automobiles in 1926. In 1929 they proposed, in the so-called Dunning budget, to revise the tariff in its entirety. Where there was little important Canadian production the tariff was abolished. In response to the demands of Nova Scotia the rates on iron and steel were raised. The preferences on Empire products were substantially increased. In view of the prosperity of the country and the apparently lessened need for government revenue, the rates on tea and other purely revenue items were reduced. Also there was considerable re-classification of items, without significant change in the rates. In other words, as in 1907, the tariff was brought into line with new circumstances.

The election of the Conservative Government in 1930 led to sweeping increases in customs duties "all along the line". The object was to reduce imports greatly, encourage production in Canada and thus provide jobs for Canadian workmen and prosperity for the country as a whole. The Canadian tariff which heretofore had been moderate, in comparison with countries like the United States or France, now became definitely high. In addition, the dumping duty was applied more frequently. Also in view of the chaotic conditions in the currencies of various countries, the Government refused to accept the invoiced price of the articles as the value for tariff purposes and applied arbitrary valuations. Thus the Canadian tariff became not merely high, but uncertain.

In 1932 tariff relations with Great Britain again became significant in Canadian economic history. For over eighty years Britain had been a free trade nation. Britain had had tariffs, but these were solely for revenue purposes and not designed to give protection to British industries. To this statement there was an apparent exception. The tariff on certain products, iron, steel and chemical or so-called "key" industries, was definitely protectionist, but it was introduced after the first War as a measure of national defence and not for economic reasons. Under the financial strains of the depression of the 1930's the Government, in 1932, repudiated the gospel of the nineteenth century and applied a low rate of duty to a wide range of commodities. Within a few months the rates were increased and differentiated. Goods from the five fully self-governing Dominions, from India and from Southern Rhodesia were exempt from the tariff until after a Conference had been held. Goods from the colonies, that is the remainder of the Empire, were exempt indefinitely.

At the Imperial Economic Conference which was held in Ottawa in 1932, it was found to be impossible to arrive at a general agreement between all parts of the Commonwealth. Instead a series of agreements was drawn up between the component parts, e.g., Canada and South Africa, New Zealand and Southern Rhodesia. The most important of these agreements as far as Canada was concerned, was the one with Great Britain. Under its terms the United Kingdom exempted Canada from the tariff of 1932 for a period of five years and in return Canada reduced her rates on a considerable number of articles imported from Britain. Generally speaking the attempt was made to shift Canadian trade to the United Kingdom from the United States, that is to say, we undertook to import more from a country which treated our exports on more favourable terms than those of most other nations, and to import relatively less from the nation which gave our exports no special concessions. The value of the trade so shifted was considerable in amount.

The Ottawa agreement had far-reaching implications. Foreign countries regarded the attempt of the Empire to form a mutual trading bloc with some apprehension. They felt that close economic association between the group of British nations and colonies, comprising one-quarter of the world's population, challenged their own economic position. To protect themselves they retaliated by raising their tariffs. Thus the increase in trade between parts of the Empire has to have set against it the decline in the volume of trade between the Empire and foreign countries. Moreover, there arises the difficulty of dealing with other countries like Denmark and the Argentine which stand outside the Empire in a political sense, but are within it economically in as much as they sell their produce almost entirely and buy their goods to a considerable extent in Great Britain. Finally, there is the possibility that the bond joining various parts of the Empire with each other and with the Crown may be weakened by wrangling over economic advantage, and might better be left on a purely sentimental basis.

In spite of the difficulties of negotiating an agreement satisfactory to both the mother country and the Dominion, a new arrangement was made in 1937. Moreover, in 1935 a trade agreement, the first accepted by both countries since 1854, was made with the United States. Canada also has agreements with many other countries —with all the other Dominions and the more important colonies in the Empire, with France, Japan, Brazil, Uruguay and so on. Speaking in general terms the aim of these treaties is to permit Canadian natural products such as wheat, and manufactured goods like farm machinery and autos, to enter other countries at favoured rates in return for favoured admission of articles not produced in Canada, like fine quality wine and tropical fruits. In part the intention is to extend the market for Canadian goods abroad at the expense of American goods now sold in Canada.

The tariff history of Canada since Confederation is not easy to summarize. Our most important trade relations have been with Great Britain and the United States which, together, account for about eighty per cent of our total external trade. Our tariff relations have been affected in the one instance by Imperial sentiment and in the other, by proximity to a country which is larger and more mature than our own. From 1879 to 1930, Canada had a reasonably moderate as well as a comparatively stable tariff; since 1930 our tariff has been high and at certain times unstable. Recent agreements have not modified the essentially protectionist nature of our tariff policy. Due to the multitude of interests affected and the great many tariff treaties, almost all of them with most favoured nation clauses, now in effect, the task of negotiating new agreements has become unbelievably complicated. Hence tariff-making has become a task for experts. It was partly for this reason that a Tariff Board was constituted in 1931, to inquire into such matters as the effect which an increase or decrease of the existing rate of duty upon a given commodity might have upon industry or trade and upon the consumer. The Board also acts as a court of appeal from the rulings of customs officers regarding the classification of goods, the fair market value of goods for duty purposes and so on. The Board advises the Minister of Finance.

In 1944 the trading nations of the free world, including Canada, signed a General Agreement on Tariffs and Trade, commonly called GATT. They undertook to work towards reduction of tariffs and removal of import restrictions. In 1948 Canada, the United States and eighteen European nations formed the Organization for Economic Co-operation and Development (OECD). Its main objectives are to strengthen the economies of member countries, help under-developed nations, and increase world trade. In essence, this is the economic arm of NATO, the North Atlantic Treaty Organization.

Meanwhile, in 1958 France, West Germany, Italy, the Netherlands, Belgium, and Luxembourg signed the Treaty of Rome and set up the European Economic Community (EEC) or Common Market. By early 1962 they had progressively cut their tariffs against each other by 40 per cent, except on agricultural products. They had formulated a common farm policy and were beginning to apply a common tariff on all imports from non-member countries. A second group, the European Free Trade Association (EFTA), formed in 1959, consists of the so-called outer seven—Britain, Norway, Sweden, Denmark, Austria, Switzerland, and Portugal. Each country has reduced its tariff with other members of EFTA, while retaining its own rates against the rest of the world.

In 1961 Britain applied for membership in the Common Market. The governments of Canada and some other members of the Commonwealth at once became perturbed because they feared loss of their preferences in the United Kingdom. Early in 1963 France rejected the British application and Canadian exporters began to breathe more easily. Any change in the tariff policy of either Britain or the United States is likely to have serious repercussions on Canadian trade and prosperity.

Leaving now the matter of tariffs and turning to foreign trade generally, we find that Canada occupies a very important position in the international trading world. With less than one per cent of the world's population we normally carry on between three and four per cent of the world's trade. As a trading nation we ranked fourth in the 1950's, being exceeded only by the United States, Britain and West Germany. By 1960 we had slipped to fifth place and behind France. In 1956 our per capita exports and imports were $328 and $389; in 1929 they were $136 and $126; and in 1867 about $15 and $21. The volume or quantity of goods traded has not grown nearly as much as values, since prices have risen over the years.

Despite cyclical declines, our trade grew rapidly up to 1913. We sent out staples and imported capital equipment and consumers' manufactured goods. From 1914 to 1918, foreign trade greatly increased because of the rise in prices and the export of food-stuffs, munitions and other materials for war purposes. After the deflation of 1920 our trade expanded with business revival. In addition Canada was under obligation to repay interest and principal of her heavy borrowings before the War. We did not borrow money but money's worth. English pounds are of no particular value in Canada, but railway equipment and factory machinery brought in from Britain or the United States are. After the War we repaid the debt not with Canadian dollars which the British did not especially desire but with wheat, pulpwood, copper and so on. The export of these commodities to repay borrowings from abroad boosted our foreign trade. During the 1930's trade fell off greatly in terms of value because of the precipitous decline in prices. It fell off also in terms of volume due to poor general business conditions throughout the world.

As already explained, Great Britain and the United States together account for about eighty per cent of our foreign trade. Normally the United States is by far our best supplier, providing us with nearly seventy per cent of our imports in 1957. Up to about 1940 our exports went to each nation about equally, although formerly Britain was more important than the United States as a market for Canadian goods. The reason for the shift was the rise in importance of such staples as pulp and paper and base metals sold mainly in the United States, with a relative decline in value of wheat which is sent chiefly to Britain. Especially after 1940 Canada's dependence on the United States as a market and a supplier grew enormously. Since Confederation the number of other countries with which Canada carries on direct trade has greatly increased, although the volume of trade conducted with them rarely exceeds twenty per cent of the total.

In the early years of the Dominion, our exports were almost entirely raw materials and our imports manufactured goods. In the 1950's our exports were classed as being about thirty per cent raw materials like wheat and copper ore, thirty per cent partly manufactured like flour, and nearly forty per cent fully manufactured. Of our imports, nearly eighty per cent were fully manufactured, an abnormally high proportion because our expanding factories needed to be equipped. Contrary to popular belief, Canada is an important exporter of manufactured goods.

Even during the 1920's, the value of Canadian exports of manufactured goods was over three times that of the United States on a per capita basis, and five times on a per wage-earner basis. It is only as an exporter that Canada is, relative to her population, more important than the United States for she does not, of course, rival the United States if the total volume of manufacturing is considered. The most important reason for this situation is the British preferential tariff which enables Canadian made goods to enter every part of the Empire on more favourable terms than those of the United States.

As a nation Canada is still very greatly dependent on external trade. The share of our gross national product (the sum total of the value of goods and services produced by Canadians) which is derived from exports was about one-third in the years 1918-39, one-fifth in the mid-1950's, and one-quarter in the early 1960's. The main markets for wheat, wood pulp, newsprint, lumber, base metals, potatoes and furs lie abroad. An important share of our manufactured goods is sent to other countries. The prosperity of great areas of the country and of the railways, financial, mercantile and industrial interests which serve these regions is dependent on foreign trade. This dependence is likely to continue. Canada, therefore, has an immediate interest in seeing that channels of world trade are kept open.

SELECTED READINGS

ELLIS, L. E., *Reciprocity, 1911*, Toronto, 1938.

HEATON, H., *The Story of Trade and Commerce, with special reference to Canada*, Toronto, 1955 (rev. ed.), pp. 267-71.

LOGAN, H. A. and INMAN, M. K., *A Social Approach to Economics*, Toronto, 1939, pp. 610-29.

MCDIARMID, O. J., *Commercial Policy in the Canadian Economy*, Cambridge, Mass., 1946.

SKELTON, O. D., "General economic history", Shortt, Adam, and Doughty, A. G., ed., *Canada and its Provinces*, vol. IX, pp. 93-274.

YOUNG, J. H., *Canadian Commercial Policy*, Ottawa, 1957 (Gordon Commission Study).

16

Labour

CANADA's original labour problem was that of securing workers. Once an immigrant arrived he usually found a good demand for his services. In the early years of English-speaking settlement in Eastern Canada, ordinary wages were about fifty cents a day but food costs were low. Land was cheap and little equipment was needed. If the immigrant did not wish to work for someone else he could farm or start a business of his own on a small scale. Opportunities were great and the man who did not earn a living and provide for his old age suffered because of his own shiftlessness, or because he had an extravagant wife. The unfortunate were cared for by private charity, or in city or county poor-houses.

These conditions changed with the relative increase in the supply of labour and the growth of large scale enterprises. Indeed the individual workman was largely helpless before the new industrial conditions. As one of hundreds, later of thousands, employed by a large corporation, he could not expect to have working conditions altered to suit his personal wishes. He was selling his labour to an employer who could easily secure another workman, whereas it was often difficult for a man to get another job. If the worker lost his job, he had nothing to fall back on, while the employer had a financial reserve in case some or even all his workmen quit. In brief, the worker in dealing with his employer was in a weak bargaining position. Unscrupulous employers often took advantage of this fact in order to force down wages and lengthen hours. Not only was the worker placed in a less advantageous position while on the job, but his avenues of escape were cut off. It became increasingly difficult to set up in business for oneself due to the competition of large factories and chain stores. Also the cost and degree of skill required in modern farming eliminated another outlet for the unemployed city worker.

Moreover, the large factories employed women and children. Of course women had worked before; in fact they did hard physical work about the pioneer farm. Children too had their tasks for there were plenty of jobs on a farm, and the attitude was that "Satan still finds mischief for idle hands to do". But work in a factory took these classes away from their homes and set them to work in poorly ventilated buildings and close to dangerous machinery. Also it was easier to beat down their wages than it was those of the men and hence they were usually poorly paid. In short, the problems of child and women labour associated with the Industrial Revolution in England quickly reproduced themselves with industrialization in Canada.

The Canadian labour movement has been greatly influenced by developments in the United States and Britain. The similarity in industrial conditions between the Republic and the Dominion, and the fact that many Canadian factories are branch plants of American corporations has led to affiliation of the unions in the two countries. American labour leaders are partly responsible for this association. If Canadian unions were completely independent or if Canadian workers were unorganized, they might accept lower wages or poorer working conditions than their American brethren and the export of goods to the United States would break down the standards which unions in that country had attained. Even where there is no legal affiliation, leaders of Canadian unions, and probably the public generally, feel that wages and hours of labour should be roughly as satisfactory to the workers in this country as those to the south. Compared with Britain, unionization in Canada made slow progress. The relatively higher living standard, the larger area, the importance of agriculture, the greater possibility of gaining admission to the executive or professional classes, difficulties of language and the presence of new immigrants accounted for the difference between the two countries. The influence of Britain on the Canadian labour movement has been mainly in the direction of legislation, whereas American influence has been strongest on the side of organization, though the social security measures of President F. D. Roosevelt have tended to modify this generalization.

The first labour unions in Canada were small, independent of each other, without money, and short-lived. They came into being to deal with a particular abuse. When their object was attained or they had lost out in the struggle with employers, they disbanded. In 1844 a union of printers, which still exists, was formed in Toronto. In the 1850's local craft unions of this kind increased their numbers, especially in Ontario. In the 1860's labour organizations in the United States set up branches in Canada or induced Canadian unions to affiliate with them.

In 1873 the Canadian Labour Union tried to bring together in one organization all the unions in the country. On account of poor leadership it lasted only three years. In the 1880's, however, unions grew in strength and cooperated with each other in city organizations. They joined together in a Canadian Assembly of the Knights of Labour, a militant American body which was fairly quickly discredited by the violence of the strikes in which it engaged. In 1886 the Trades and Labour Congress of

Canada was formed. Delegates to its annual conventions were elected by various groups but basically the organization represented international craft unions such as printers, plumbers, and carpenters. These crafts were also affiliated with similar craft unions in the United States. In other words, the crafts were international and, at the same time, united in a central labour body in each country, i.e., the Trades and Labour Congress of Canada and the American Federation of Labour.

Meanwhile, all workers in certain industries were organizing regardless of craft. For instance, the Western Federation of Miners (1895) appealed to all workers in coal mines without respect to the kind of work they did or the degree of skill they exercised. For the most part these labour unions have been more radical than the craft unions. After 1921 the Canadian Brotherhood of Railway Employees and Other Transport Workers, another industrial union though its members are mainly freight handlers and clerks, was active in promoting purely Canadian unions. But in 1939 it discarded its policy of opposition to international unions and helped form the Canadian Congress of Labour. This body drew inspiration from the Congress of Industrial Organizations, which had attracted a great deal of attention in the United States in the 1930's because of its aggressive leader, John L. Lewis, its policy of industrial not craft unionism, its campaign to enlist machine-tenders and general factory workers, and its insistent demands for higher wages and shorter hours. In 1956 the Trades and Labour Congress and the Canadian Congress of Labour united to form the Canadian Labour Congress. By 1961 this body had close to 75 per cent of all organized workers in Canada.

Some unions, especially the railway running trades (engineers, firemen, conductors and trainmen), stand aside from central labour bodies. Others are associated in the Confederation of National Trade Unions, which had 7 per cent of all Canada's union members in 1963. Called the Canadian and Catholic Confederation of Labour until 1960, this body is particularly strong among French-speaking workers in Quebec and New Brunswick. In general, members intend to put into practice the economic and social ideals of the Catholic Church as set forth in Papal Encyclicals. They emphasize that the interests of employers and employees are fundamentally the same, but recognize that some organization of workers is essential in view of man's present moral imperfection.

In 1911 roughly 133,000 Canadians were members of unions. The number grew to 400,000 in 1919, declined in the 1920's, but rose again to about 300,000 in the 1930's and then to 1,500,000 in 1963. Unions try to reach agreements with individual employers covering wages, hours and working conditions. This is, perhaps, their main task. But they also try to secure sympathetic attention on labour matters by the general public, and educate their own members to the needs of the working man. Some of the unions have built up financial reserves from which they pay benefits to their members in case of a strike.

Unions also agitate for legislation which they believe will benefit them. Up to 1959 organized labour in Canada, like that in the United States but not in Britain, had never officially had its own political party. To be sure from time to time in Canada, beginning as early as 1875, labour members have been elected to provincial legislatures and the House of Commons; for a while there was an Independent Labour Party; and after its formation in 1933 the Canadian Commonwealth Federation or C.C.F. made a special appeal to wage-earners. These members and organizations were often assisted by union members but they acted as private citizens supporting the platform which appeared to offer more to working men than did the Liberals or Conservatives. The unions, as such, preferred to lobby with all parties in Parliament for favourable legislation. For five or six years the Canadian Congress of Labour had its own political programme which broadly coincided with that of the C.C.F. Then in 1959 the C.C.F. along with leaders of the recently formed Canadian Labour Congress created the New Democratic Party. They also attempted to devise a platform which would be acceptable to farmers as well as urban wage-earners. Only time will tell what success will attend these efforts.

The enactment of labour legislation is both part of the general policy of unionism and an independent line of attack on the labour problem. Although the earliest labour laws were passed at the instigation of social reformers who were deeply concerned with low wages, and unhealthy living and working conditions particularly for women and children, the pressure for more recent legislation has come mainly from labour unions. It is significant that at one time "the dim inarticulate public" was almost completely indifferent to labour problems; now, large sections of it are acutely conscious of the need for social reform. At one time too, employers, with a few conspicuous exceptions, were unconcerned about conditions in their plants; now, most of them are genuinely interested in improving relations with their workers through voluntary pension schemes, vacations with pay, medical services, profit sharing and through the individual adjustment of the worker to his job. This change of attitude toward social problems is undoubtedly as important as the legislation designed to give it effect.

The specific legislation deals with a number of rather distinct topics, namely, working conditions, hours and wages, insurance and pensions, strikes, and the general condition of the labouring classes. Laws dealing with working conditions are numerous. They cover such matters as ventilation and lighting in factories, the provision of fire escapes, the guarding of dangerous machinery, the inspection of steam boilers, elevators and motor vehicles and certification of the ability of their operators, and so on. Separate and very elaborate codes regulate mines, railways, hydro-electric power plants, and factories making or using chemicals. The purpose of all these regulations is to preserve health and prevent accident.

Hours and wages of women and children are regulated in all the Provinces except Prince Edward Island. Most of this legislation was passed in the two years before 1920. Laws governing maximum working hours and minimum wages for men came later, because it was at first assumed that men were sufficiently well organized to protect themselves. In some provinces, male wages are governed by statute but since 1945 it is more common for provinces to create a Labour Relations Board. This body certifies which union is legally entitled to represent employees in a certain plant. Then wages and working conditions are arrived at through negotiation between the employer and the certified union. Negotiators cannot anticipate all the situations which may arise or frame their ideas in such precise language that, later on, it is not open to different meanings. Hence, once an agreement has been reached, it must be interpreted either by further negotiation between the parties or by arbitration under the Board. These Boards have developed an elaborate code of practice which is taken as precedent in subsequent cases. This so-called administrative law broadly resembles the common law which is enforced by regular courts.

The regulation of hours and wages, whether by direct legislation or by collective bargaining backed up by legislation, has steadily broadened out. Originally, wages and hours were controlled only in the "sweated" trades, that is, in those where conditions were so poor that the health of the workers was seriously and immediately endangered. Gradually the laws have been extended to cover more industries, raise minimum wages, reduce maximum hours, and provide vacations with pay. In short, the purpose has changed from preventing positive suffering to providing a decent standard of living. Most provinces have laws requiring that women be paid the same wage rates as men when they do the same or substantially identical work. Other laws forbid any employer or union from discriminating on grounds of race, colour, religion, or national origin.

Insurance and pensions legislation is designed to protect the workers from financial distress arising from accident, old age and involuntary unemployment. Before 1886 if a worker were accidentally injured in a factory, he could collect damages only in special cases and at great expense to himself. This situation was slowly modified by the legislation directed toward strengthening the legal position of the worker. Beginning in 1917, the Provinces started to pass Workmen's Compensation Acts which provide that a worker, accidentally injured in the course of his employment, receive without litigation a sum varying with his previous wages, the period of his incapacity and the extent of his injury. The payments are made from a central fund to which employers, and in some Provinces employees also, contribute and whose solvency is guaranteed by the Province concerned.

Legislation covering old age benefits begins with a Dominion Government annuity scheme in 1908. Under it, workers are encouraged to deposit regularly through their post-office a sum which, with interest, will give them something to live on when they reach the age of sixty-five or seventy. The sums deposited are as safe investments as government bonds and are not liable to seizure for debt. Unfortunately only comparatively few of the people who should have provided for their old age did so. Hence a non-contributory scheme was introduced in 1927, though not adopted in all Provinces until 1936 (Newfoundland, 1949). The original scheme provided for pensions, not exceeding $20 a month, to all British subjects of the age of seventy or over who were not in receipt of an income exceeding $365 a year. Beginning in 1952 old age pensions were payable to all persons over the age of 70, at the rate of $40 a month regardless of their other income. In 1957 the rate became $55 and in 1962, $65. It is now payable to persons of 65 to 70 who are in need. Money for these pensions is raised by special sales and income taxes. Civil servants, teachers, and employees of most companies pay into governmental or company pension schemes during their working lives and upon retirement, usually at 65, get monthly pensions which vary in amount with years of employment and previous wage or salary.

During the serious business depression of the 1930's, efforts were made to introduce in Canada a scheme of unemployment insurance which had been in operation in Britain since 1910 and was currently being adopted in the United States. Because it took some time to straighten out the constitutional difficulties, it was not until 1941 that the scheme became law. It does not cover such work as agriculture, domestic service and school teaching, or those who are paid each week or month and get over

$4,800 a year. All other workers (including fishermen since 1957) and their employers contribute each week to a fund managed by the Government. If a worker becomes involuntarily unemployed, i.e. if he is discharged for reasons beyond his control and cannot find another job, he receives an allowance varying with his previous wage and the number of his dependents. It is not expected that the scheme will eliminate all need for relief in a depression, for not all industries are covered by the arrangement and allowances are paid for only a limited time. The aim of the legislation is to tide the worker over until he can get another job.

In 1948 the Federal Government began to pay Family Allowances of $6 or $8 a month for each child under 16. As a result of taxes paid by parents on their personal income, Allowances benefit only families with fairly low incomes and will be especially helpful in depressions. Payments are made directly to mothers and are to be spent on food, medical attention, clothing and education beyond what the family could normally provide.

A strike is the withdrawal of a number of workers from a job with the object of returning to the same positions but on more satisfactory terms, e.g., shorter hours, higher wages or perhaps the same wages if the employer has threatened to cut them. A lock-out occurs when the employer refuses to allow his men to work because they will not accede to his terms. Sometimes it is difficult to distinguish a strike from a lock-out. Both are final weapons, used only after peaceful negotiations fail. The number of working days lost by strikes and lock-outs in any year in comparison with the total number of days worked by all the gainfully employed, is relatively small. Nevertheless, strikes and lock-outs are to be regretted since the loss to the individuals concerned may be very great, and in any event as they are appeals to force, essentially they are methods of war rather than of justice.

Legislation relative to strikes does not deal with them by denying the right to strike. Instead it tries to remove the causes of industrial conflict, facilitates agreement between the parties before the strike has actually occurred or while it is in progress, and attempts to delay strikes and lock-outs until hot tempers have had a chance to cool. Since 1900 Dominion and Provincial Departments of Labour have been empowered to act as conciliators. They try to get the parties voluntarily to arrive at an agreement regarding the matters in dispute, and frequently the mediation of the Government is successful either in forestalling a strike, or in shortening its length.

The Industrial Relations and Disputes Investigation Act was originally passed in 1907. The Act applies only to industries such as transportation and communication and mines, where the public as a whole would be very greatly inconvenienced by a strike. With the consent of both parties the Act may be applied to other industries also. The legislation provides for a Board consisting of one member appointed by the employer, one by the employees, and a chairman appointed by the two members or by the Minister of Labour. The Board makes an investigation into the points at issue and submits a fair solution, called an award, to the problem. Acceptance of the award is purely voluntary but no strike or lock-out may occur before the award is made, nor for thirty days thereafter. The theory of the legislation is that once the facts are known and a conclusion based on them is made by a competent, presumably unbiased body, public opinion will see that justice is done. The Act does not deny the right to strike or enforce a lock-out. It merely states that these must not occur until every opportunity has been taken to arrive at a peaceful settlement. The theory has worked reasonably well and the principles of the Act have been copied in other countries. In 1925 the Act was declared to be beyond the legal powers of the Dominion in certain respects, but it was so useful in dealing with industrial disputes that it has been retained in effect by almost all the provinces. The Act as revised in 1948 gives employees the right to organize into unions of their own choosing. It also requires employers to enter into agreements on wages, hours, and conditions of work with their employees. These agreements are legally binding on both parties. The Act defines and prohibits unfair labour practices on the part of management and union. Broadly speaking, the new legislation made permanent and extended to some civilian industries the arrangements made between the Federal Government and employees in munition plants and shipyards during World War II.

Legislation covering the general conditions of the working class deals with a variety of matters. Free education, particularly in its technical and commercial aspects, is designed to permit potential workers to become more useful members of society. Laws relative to hospitals, free clinics, the use of deleterious drugs, quarantine of easily communicable diseases and so on, protect the workers' health. The laws are supplemented by information distributed freely by government departments on health topics and the rearing of infants and children, and by the teaching of hygiene and temperance in the schools. The Federal and some of the Provincial Governments operate employment services where workers seeking jobs and employers wanting men are brought into contact with each other, without charge to either party. Up to 1940 the service was often looked down upon, for it chiefly handled unskilled workers and perhaps even the shiftless. Since then it has also proved helpful to unemployed craftsmen and executives. Finally, governments have financially aided in building houses and clearing slums.

From a study of this mass of labour legislation a few general conclusions may be drawn. In spite of conflicts in jurisdiction between the Dominion and the Provinces, an attempt has been made to deal with most of the disabilities under which the wage-earner whether man, woman or child, lives and works. A very great deal still remains to be done before the life of the bulk of the population is what it should be. But this at least, can be said: in social legislation Canada has not lagged far behind other Anglo-Saxon countries. The fact that we have such a volume of labour legislation is indicative of the strength of our social consciousness, and also of our industrial development.

Labour legislation on such an extensive scale raises difficult economic problems. The cost of social services increases taxes and may lessen the ability of our export industries to sell abroad. If taxes get too high people at home may be unwilling, as well as unable, to pay them. If the state performs too many services for its citizens, they may lose their initiative and eventually do little or nothing to improve their own conditions. If unions or legislation force wages too high, business men may use more machinery and fewer workers, thus adding to unemployment temporarily at least. Also as labour unions have grown in strength the possibility of abuse of power by labour leaders arises. This danger is paralleled by the danger of unscrupulous action by business executives in charge of large corporations. There are good and bad among both employers and employees. Neither side is always right or always wrong. Only one thing is certain: in every instance of conflict in labour matters, the public interest is paramount.

Partly as a result of legislation and union activity, mainly as a consequence of rising standards of living all over the world, the condition of the working population in Canada has greatly improved over the decades. Machines, once used mainly in production, are now used directly to make life more pleasant. The automobile, radio, telephone, electric light, electric washers, electric irons, vacuum cleaners, air conditioning systems and so on, are conveniences our forefathers never dreamed of. Then too, the modern family has clothes of superior texture, variety and style; it spends more on health; it spends more on education by keeping children in school longer and seeing that schools are better equipped; it also spends a great deal more on recreation—automobiles, moving pictures, summer and winter vacations. So insistent are the demands of the family for these comforts and pleasures, that the middle class wage earner probably finds it just as difficult to provide for the needs of his family to-day as his predecessor did fifty years ago. The change in living standards makes it virtually impossible statistically to compare real wages i.e., the relationship between dollar wages received and goods and services purchased. This much can be said, however: along with the reduction since 1875 of hours of work per week from sixty or more to approximately forty, the standard of living has greatly improved. Moreover, minimum wage laws, hospital insurance, old age pensions and the like, coupled with heavy succession duties and high taxes on large incomes, have spread these gains more equitably among all classes of the nation. If the findings of a Royal Commission are valid, the average Canadian can expect to have about 70 per cent more goods and services at his command in 1980 as in 1955. This conclusion assumes there will be no war, no devastating depression, and no runaway inflation but continued technological progress, normal growth in population and satisfactory world trade.

SELECTED READINGS

BLADEN, V. W., *An Introduction to Political Economy*, Toronto, 1956, Chap. VIII.

CASSIDY, H. M., *Public Health and Welfare Organization in Canada*, Toronto, 1945.
Social Security and Reconstruction in Canada, Toronto, 1943.

CLARK, S. D., *The Social Development of Canada*, Toronto, 1942, pp. 380-472.

DEPARTMENT OF LABOUR, *Labour Gazette*, 1901-
Labour Legislation in Canada, annual
Labour Organization in Canada, annual

EASTERBROOK, W. T. and AITKEN, H. G. J., *Canadian Economic History*, Toronto, 1956, pp. 558-71.

KOVACS, A. E., *ed.*, *Readings in Canadian Labour Economics*, Toronto, 1961.

LOGAN, H. A., *The History of Trade-Union Organization in Canada*, Chicago, 1928,
Trade Unions in Canada, Their Development and Functioning, Toronto, 1948.

LOGAN, H. A. and INMAN, M. K., *A Social Approach to Economics*, Toronto, 1939, pp. 495-565.

MACKINTOSH, M., *An Outline of Trade Union History in Great Britain, the United States and Canada*, Ottawa, 1946.

MARSH, L. C., *Canadians In and Out of Work*, Toronto, 1940.

ROWNTREE, B. M., *The Railway Worker*, Toronto, 1936.

Royal Commission on Canada's Economic Prospects, *Report*, Ottawa, 1957 (Gordon Commission).

SELEKMAN, B. M., *Postponing Strikes*, New York, 1927.
Law and Labor Relations, Cambridge, 1936.

WARE, N. J., LOGAN, H. A., and INNIS, H. A., *Labour in Canadian-American Relations*, Toronto, 1937.

17

Private Finance
after Confederation

THE development of banking in the colonies up to
1867 was formative. Most banks conducted a local
business and, despite the existence of a few sound
financial institutions, many of them were obviously weak,
as the failure in 1866 and 1867 of two of the St. Lawrence
Valley's largest and oldest banks had shown. Nevertheless some of the important features of the present banking system of Canada had already proven their value.

Although the British North America Act gave the
central government authority to regulate banking in the
Dominion, it was not until 1871 that the first comprehensive banking legislation was passed, the existing banks,
meanwhile, having continued to operate under their old
Provincial charters. In drawing up the new legislation,
the choice between adopting the American or the British
banking system presented itself. In the former, or unit
banking system, there were a great many banks with
small capitalization and without branches. Each of these
banks could issue its own bank notes with gold or government bonds as security. It had to maintain a fixed rate
(or better) between its gold and government bonds i.e.
its reserves, and the amount of its deposits and outstanding notes, i.e. its liabilities. On the other hand, under
the system of England or Scotland, there were only
a few large banks with branches scattered throughout the country. The note issue was based on general
assets, that is, the security for the notes was not specific

government bonds but the bank's general promise to pay. No fixed ratio of reserves to liabilities was required, and the responsibility was placed on the general manager of each bank to see that at all times he had on hand sufficient legal tender, i.e., gold, silver or government notes, to redeem the bank notes which might be presented to him for payment or to pay depositors who might ask for the return of their deposits in legal tender.

The differences between the two systems were great. The advantage of the American system was that it brought the bank and the local business man in close contact with each other, and made the bank more responsive to the needs of the community. Also, it had recently been improved upon in the United States and was apparently providing that country with the financial basis for a great expansion in trade and industry. On the other hand, the British system provided elasticity in the currency, that is, the bank note issue could be expanded or contracted readily in accordance with the needs of trade. Moreover, all the reserves were available if required whereas under the American plan, an irreducible minimum, fixed by law, had to be maintained and only the reserves above the minimum could be used in case of emergency, such as in a business depression when people might want to be paid in legal tender. Of course, under the British system the bank's general manager assumed great responsibilities. He did not have any legal reserve limits, and hence he might lend so extensively in good times that when people demanded legal tender he might not have it available. With cautious and experienced bankers, many of them trained in Scotland, this danger was minimized. Also the British plan made it possible for part of the profits of the larger branches to be used to offset the expenses of branches in smaller centres, and thus banking services might be given to communities which, under the unit system, would not have enough business to justify having a chartered bank of their own. On the whole the British system seemed to be more advantageous and in any case it was more in line with that to which the people were accustomed. As a matter of fact, the proposal to introduce the unit system of the United States raised a storm of protest from Canadian business men and farmers, and two of the individuals chiefly responsible for the proposal had to resign their positions.

The Bank Act of 1871 gave legal effect to the decision to follow the British system. Canadian experience with branch banking since that time has shown that our system has adequately met the demands of a rapidly expanding frontier of settlement. It has shifted savings quickly from places where they were made to points where they were needed to carry on trade. At the same time, the branch bank system has operated with a minimum number of serious failures, none since 1923. Although there are now only eight banks and all but one (the small Mercantile in Vancouver) have their head offices in Montreal or Toronto, this concentration of banking control has not led to neglect of the financial needs of outlying parts of the Dominion. On the whole branch banking has worked satisfactorily.

The Act of 1871 incorporated other principles still being followed. A large amount of capital (at present $500,000, at least half of which must actually be paid up in cash or government securities), a good deal of publicity and a special Act of Parliament are required before a new bank can be established. The difficulties of incorporation cut out many financially weak banks which might otherwise be formed. The incorporating Act or charter of every bank runs for a period of only ten years and since all charters come up for renewal at the same time, an opportunity is given to consider any shortcomings in bank legislation which the previous decade has revealed. The decennial revision of the Bank Act is a valuable provision carried over from the pre-Confederation period.

The 1871 Act also provided for double liability for shareholders, that is, in case of bankruptcy they lost their original investment and had to pay in as much as they had originally subscribed to the capital stock of the bank. This feature had previously been included in the charters of the Halifax Banking Company, the Bank of Nova Scotia, and, for all practical purposes, in the charters of English banks but not in those of the Province of Canada. Between 1935 and 1950 double liability was removed but when banks were not as strong as they are today, this provision was important. In addition, the Act required the submission periodically of certain information from the banks to the Government so that the public might keep itself informed of the financial position of any chartered bank. No bank was permitted to loan money on real estate, the intent of the law being to have the chartered banks confine their activities to short-term finance. Any bank might issue notes up to the amount of its capital and surplus. The amount of gold or legal tender to be kept as security against the notes and deposits was left to the discretion of the bank itself, but the bank notes constituted a first claim on the assets of a bank in case of liquidation.

After 1871 successive decennial revisions modified but did not fundamentally change the law covering chartered banks. In 1891 a "Bank Note Circulation Redemption Fund" was created by means of a levy on each bank of five per cent of its average note circulation. In case a bank in the process of liquidation did not redeem its notes promptly, this fund was available so that no note holder need suffer loss. A decade later control of this fund was shared by the Government with the Canadian Bankers' Association which had been formed a few years previously. The Association was also legally authorized to establish and regulate clearing houses and, in case of a bank failure, to appoint a curator who would take over and conserve the assets of the bank until a liquidator could be appointed by the court. As a result of the depression of 1907, a special amendment to the Bank Act in the following year, authorized a bank to increase its issue of bank notes to an amount not exceeding fifteen per cent more than its combined capital and surplus. Such excess note issue was available only during the crop-moving season, that is, from September to February inclusive.

The revision of 1913 provided appointment of auditors by shareholders and it authorized banks to lend to farmers upon security of their threshed grain. It also established the Central Gold Reserves in which banks might deposit gold or Dominion notes, for the purpose of providing security for the issue of their own notes to an equivalent amount. At the outbreak of War there was a wave of panic in certain cities and the withdrawals of gold were unusually heavy. To protect the banks, the Government authorized the Minister of Finance, in case of national emergency, to issue Dominion notes to banks up to the full value of certain Government and industrial bonds and other types of indebtedness which chartered banks might deposit with the Minister. The Government passed other regulations to cover the War time emergency but these were removed after the War. The power to issue Dominion notes to banks against approved securities was, however, continued in the Bank Act of 1923. The general revision of that year made more stringent the earlier laws regarding returns, auditors, loans to bank officers, the payment of directors and their attendance at bank meetings.

With the establishment in 1935 of the Bank of Canada, which is described later, a number of important changes came about. The law with respect to bank notes was altered. Double liability ceased, and bank shareholders became liable for only the par value of their stock. Each bank must carry a reserve of notes of, or deposits in, the Bank of Canada. The latter sets the reserve at from eight to twelve per cent of the deposits made by the public in chartered banks. As no bank is likely to try to operate on such a small reserve, considerable discretion is still allowed the general manager of a Canadian bank regarding what reserve he shall keep. In other words Canadian bank legislation has retained the British policy with respect to reserves as was decided in 1871.

The general tenor of the legislation since 1871 had been to preserve the branch banking system and give full responsibility for the determination of banking policy to the banks themselves, while attempting to prevent abuse of powers by means of publicity of accounts, auditing by expert accountants, government inspection, and so on. Bank deposits multiplied over 400 times between 1867 and 1961. The number of branches increased from 123 to over 5,200, not counting about 140 in Britain, France, United States, and the West Indies. The number of banks rose from 28 in 1867 to 38 in 1900 and then declined, because of mergers and a few failures, to 9 in 1950 and 8 in 1961. The three largest do approximately two-thirds of the total business. On the whole the efficacy of bank legislation has kept pace with the expansion of the banking system and the needs of Canadian business.

In the depression of the 1930's an important weakness in Canadian banking structure became apparent. The individual banks performed their operations satisfactorily and some co-operation between them was secured through the Canadian Bankers' Association. Nevertheless, a single institution seemed to be required effectively to handle the complicated monetary problems which the increased importance of the business cycle and public finance had thrust upon governments everywhere. A strong agitation for credit reform, monetary heresy it was called by some, had arisen in the West and a central bank might to some extent appease this attitude, though it would still insist on "sound money". In particular, some control over the right of the banks to get Dominion notes by presenting securities to the Minister of Finance was needed. Such transactions, originally authorized during a war time emergency, had risen in amount during peace time years and were made automatically with little consideration of their effect on the business life of the nation. Moreover, Canada lacked an agency which could co-operate with similar agencies, central banks, in other parts of the Commonwealth and the United States.

Accordingly the Bank of Canada was created, beginning operations on March 11, 1935. The Bank operates as the fiscal agent of the Dominion Government, that is, it helps to float public loans, transfers and holds Government funds, issues its own notes replacing those of the Dominion and, generally, does the Government's banking business formerly handled by the chartered banks. It also gives valuable service, as the financial and general economic adviser to the Government. More important, and more difficult, are the tasks of reducing the fluctuations of the business cycle within Canada, preventing pronounced changes in prices generally, and of maintaining a proper relationship between the Canadian dollar and the currencies of other countries. The bank may purchase or re-discount promissory notes of business men provided the notes have been endorsed by a commercial bank. By setting the re-discount rate very low, the Bank of Canada will encourage ordinary banks to borrow from it and then lend freely to businesses. This will stimulate revival. The central bank can buy and sell Government securities and so increase or reduce the amounts of the reserve which commercial banks have in their possession. Thus the Bank can enlarge or restrict the ability of ordinary banks to lend money to business. The degree to which the Bank of Canada can accomplish a greater measure of business stability can be determined only after many years have elapsed. As already intimated the Bank of Canada conducts its operations almost entirely with the Government and with chartered banks, not with the general public. In other words it does not compete with chartered banks in ordinary commercial transactions.

The coinage system of Canada will not be described in detail for full information is readily available elsewhere. It is sufficient to say that, by the Uniform Currency Act of 1871, decimal currency was introduced throughout Canada and the British sovereign, the United States eagle and a new coin, the Canadian five dollar gold piece (not minted until 1912) were made legal tender. A mint, established at Ottawa in 1908, and operated until 1931 as a branch of the Royal Mint and since then as the Royal Canadian Mint, issues gold and silver coins. With the rapid development of gold mining in Canada the mint does a great deal of refining. From 1871 to 1935 the Dominion, under authority of various pieces of legislation, issued its own notes chiefly of the denominations of 25c,

$1, $2, $5,000 and $50,000, while the chartered banks issued the denominations of $5 or multiples thereof. When the Bank of Canada was established, its notes were substituted for those of the Dominion Government and have gradually replaced those of the chartered banks. The amount of silver, nickel and bronze coins plus bank, Dominion and, since 1935, Bank of Canada notes in the hands of the public varies with the business cycle and with the general level of prices. The rapidity of circulation, that is, the speed with which the money passes from hand to hand fluctuates for the same reasons, but to a greater extent.

To sum up, the chartered banks and the Bank of Canada, along with the currency and coins they provide, are very important parts of the financial mechanism of Canada. The first provide facilities for the deposits of surplus funds, the transfer of funds from one area in the country to another and to foreign lands, and the collection of accounts from business men in other parts of Canada. In particular, the chartered banks make available loans for short terms, say from three months to a year taking as security the promissory note of an honest, capable business man, or some stocks and bonds which he owns, or grain in storage, or cattle, or some other asset which will likely be sold in the near future. The Bank of Canada acts as financial agent for the Government and tries to control the business cycle, the domestic price level, and foreign exchange. Notes and coins provide the ordinary medium of exchange, the mechanism through which we buy and sell though an increasing amount of business is carried on by cheque. Together, the chartered banks and the Bank of Canada supply facilities for day-to-day or short term business transactions.

The institutions dealing with short term finance are

supplemented by several organizations which are concerned more particularly with the longer term aspects of finance. The first of these are the savings banks which are operated by all chartered banks, by the Post-Office, by Newfoundland, Ontario and Alberta and by a few special savings institutions in Quebec. Strictly speaking, a savings bank receives deposits from a great many people and then invests these in Government bonds or in high grade mortgages. Depositors may withdraw their funds only after having given ten days' notice. Thus the savings bank, knowing exactly what demands will probably be made on it in the future, need keep only a small cash reserve on hand. The competition between chartered banks in Canada has been so keen, however, that depositors are able to withdraw their funds on demand and use their savings accounts, within limits, for chequing purposes. The distinction between a savings bank and a commercial bank is not clear-cut in Canada. Savings banks perform a useful function in encouraging thrift and in providing a safe place where surplus funds of individuals may be left until they are needed.

Loan and savings companies are institutions definitely associated with long term finance. They obtain money by selling their own stocks and bonds to the general public and by operating as a bank in accepting deposits of people with surplus funds on hand. This money they loan to individuals, taking as security a mortgage on some piece of real estate such as a farm, house or store. The investor can get his money out of the company only by selling his stocks or bonds to another member of the public, but the depositor may withdraw his funds by cheque, after giving the company the required notice. The first mortgage and loan company in Canada started in 1844. By 1867 there were nineteen such companies and in 1963 about seventy. Although primarily engaged in short-term finance, chartered banks lend on mortgages under the National Housing Act (1954) and the Farm Loans Improvement Act (1944). Central Mortgage and Housing Corporation administers the housing programme of the federal government and aided construction of about one-third of all housing units built since 1945.

Trust companies act as executors of estates, trustees of property, guardians of minors and agents of living persons who do not wish to assume the difficult task of managing their property and investments. Like the loan companies, some trust companies are local, others national in scope.

An investment trust is a company which raises funds by the sale of its own stock and then uses the funds to purchase stocks and bonds of other companies. The object is to earn dividends and interest from the securities purchased and distribute them to its own shareholders. By purchasing stock in an investment trust an individual presumably secures more expert financial management than he himself could provide. Also, because the trust invests money in a great many concerns in different lines of business and different parts of the country, the shareholder in the trust gets greater diversity and thus assumes less risk than if he had "put all his eggs in one basket". Highly successful in Britain, some investment trusts, which were formed in Canada during the 1920's, failed in the subsequent depression. Later on, others were started and all became very popular in the 1950's.

Small loan companies make loans, usually not exceeding $500 each, on the promissory notes of borrowers. Ordinarily these notes have the additional security of an endorsement by some other responsible person, or of a chattel mortgage. These companies lend to individuals and small businesses. As a rule they charge interest at two per cent per month but costs of investigating borrowers and collecting small amounts of money each month are high. The companies raise funds by borrowing from chartered banks and selling their own stocks to the public. Other finance companies take over the collection of chattel mortgages placed by dealers on automobiles, furniture, and household equipment. They pay the vendor at once and then collect the instalments from the purchaser. Credit unions had over two and a half million members and assets of nearly $1.3 billion in 1960. They lend to members to meet emergencies such as illness and to finance improvements to home, farm or small business. The first credit union in North America was started by Alphonse Desjardins at Levis in 1900.

The Federal Government set up a Farm Loan Board in 1929. It became the Farm Credit Corporation in 1962. It lends to young men who have at least five years experience in farming. Under the Farm Improvement Loans Act the Dominion in cooperation with chartered banks provides credit for implements, livestock, fences, drains and buildings on farms. The Government also insures Canadian exporters against loss caused by insolvency or protracted default of a buyer overseas, war, revolution, or exchange restrictions by other countries.

With the possible exception of the chartered banks, the financial institutions with which the average man has most contact are the life insurance companies. Life insurance was introduced into Canada about the middle of the nineteenth century from Great Britain and the United States. By 1869 insurance in force totalled about thirty-six million dollars, chiefly "straight life". In 1962 the total was fifty billion including endowment policies and group insurance. Besides, Canadian companies have taken over from British and United States companies a steadily growing proportion of the total insurance business written in Canada, and have also entered foreign countries on an extensive scale. As everyone knows the essential task of a life insurance company is annually to collect funds called premiums, from policy holders, invest these in various types of securities and then, at the date of decease, pay a stipulated amount, the face value of the policy, to the policy holders' beneficiaries. The companies have had an important influence on encouraging saving by the bulk of the people, and in making available enormous amounts of funds for investment in bonds of governments, public utilities and industries, thus aiding the nation's development. Insurance companies as well as the Dominion Government sell annuities by which one can provide for one's old age.

Another group of companies insure against fire. The first fire insurance in Canada was written by branches of British firms, the first agency being opened in Montreal in 1804. Although companies owned and operated by Canadians were started as early as 1809, the majority of the concerns are still British or foreign. In pioneer days fire was a terrible menace but use of brick and concrete instead of wood, the replacement of the coal oil lamp by electricity, the introduction of municipal water systems and the improvement of fire fighting equipment, have greatly reduced the hazard of fire and hence the rates. Insurance is now available for a wide variety of risks— accident, automobile, plate glass, hail, rain, explosion, fraud, even earthquake and falling aircraft. All insurance companies, life, fire, and casualty, are under strict government regulation. This control has developed not because of failures of Canadian companies but as a reflection of American conditions. Regulation of insurance is divided between provincial and federal governments, depending chiefly on whether the company has a provincial or Dominion charter.

One of the most important aspects of finance relates to raising of capital for corporate enterprises. With the growth of larger size businesses no one man is likely to have sufficient cash to finance say, a railway or a huge factory. Even if he had the funds he might not be willing to sink them all in one enterprise whose possible failure would ruin him entirely. Hence corporations were formed. They gather up the funds of a great many individuals by selling them stock in the company, and then give them control of the company by entitling them to vote at the annual meetings in proportion to the number of shares held. The investor of small means can buy a few shares, perhaps only one, thus giving him a chance to share in business profits while the person with larger resources, by buying shares in a number of different companies, can reduce his risk.

In addition, the corporation gives its investors limited liability. A person's responsibility for the debts of the company is restricted, usually, to the par value or stated value of his shares, whereas he is liable for all the debts of an individual business or partnership. This feature encourages new investment since the investor knows exactly the extent of his liability. In any case, he may easily sell his stocks or bonds to some other member of the public. Also the corporation has perpetual existence and thus can enter into contracts covering a much longer period of time than a man's life. It is not dissolved by the death, insolvency or lunacy of a shareholder as is the case with a proprietorship or partnership.

In view of all these advantages of incorporation, it is not surprising that business men increasingly resorted to limited liability companies to carry on banking, railway, trading and manufacturing enterprises. Obviously only the Government could create an institution with perpetual existence, legally distinct from the people who owned it and with the right of limited liability. Incorporation, therefore, involved securing a charter from the legislature. At first these charters were passed especially for each enterprise, as is still the case with banks, insurance, railways, telephone and telegraph companies. It was not until 1862 that a general act of incorporation was passed, that is, one setting forth the important clauses in the charters of all companies (except financial institutions and public utilities), and permitting such companies to incorporate by securing the approval of a government official without the necessity of going to parliament or a provincial legislature for a special Act. The Dominion and each of the provinces has its own Companies Act. A company incorporated in one province may, on payment of a fee, carry on business in another province. All of the Acts aim to guard the creditor and shareholder from the unscrupulous. Due to the principle of limited liability, a creditor can collect his debt only from the company and not from the individuals who compose it. In order to protect the creditor from the malicious wasting of the assets of the company, the law forbids payment of dividends except out of earned profits. To give protection to the existing shareholders, the law places great responsibility on the board of directors who really manage the company for the shareholders, and provides for the appointment of auditors and the supplying of detailed annual financial reports. To guard the prospective shareholder in a concern just being established, the law has licensed salesmen of corporation securities; it also tries to prevent fraud and ensure that the investor receives accurate information on the company and its promoters; finally, the law regulates stock exchanges and dealers in bonds and shares. The essential problem is to prevent the mulcting of creditors, shareholders and new investors by a few unprincipled persons, without hampering legitimate enterprise.

The number of incorporations increased slowly from 1816, when the first charter was issued, until the 1880's. The early charters were given mainly to banks and railways. With growing industrialization, factories, merchandising organizations, the mines, in fact all types of businesses were incorporated as soon as they got beyond the stage where one man could supply all the capital and managerial ability required.

The theory of these corporations is that the shareholders, through the board of directors which they elect, have full control over the policies of the company. The basic principle is democracy. Some of these corporations have grown to such a size, however, that no one, except perhaps the president and the higher executives of the concern, really understands its operations. The small shareholders would be bewildered if the complicated problems of the business were presented before them at the annual meeting. Shareholders, especially those with only a few shares, feel that the problems are too difficult and the expense and trouble of going to the annual meeting of the company too great to justify their attendance. All that is needed to control a company is a majority of the shares present at an annual meeting. If most small shareholders stay away, it is possible effectively to control without holding more than a relatively small portion of the total number of shares outstanding. Thus control of large companies tends to concentrate in the hands of a few persons, to become a kind of oligarchy. So long as these persons are motivated by high ethical standards, and a desire to establish for themselves reputations as good managers, no difficulty arises. But if these men wish to make a profit for themselves at the expense of the general shareholder, such as by paying themselves very high salaries, the opportunity is great. With the exception of a few notorious cases there has been relatively little abuse of this nature in Canada. It must be remembered that the vast majority of corporations are still relatively small in size and in close contact with all their shareholders.

The increase in the number and size of the corporations has created the need for financial machinery for the sale of their securities. At first, corporations sold their stock and bonds directly to the general public, or through bankers in England. In 1883-84 specialized institutions for raising funds for corporations came into being in Canada. These organizations, known as investment banks, make contact between individuals, insurance companies and other groups with money to invest and the corporations which need funds for long term purposes, such as building a factory or developing a mine.

Besides selling new securities, i.e. securities in concerns just being established or which are enlarging their plant, investment bankers and brokers arrange to transfer securities of going concerns from one member of the public to another. To facilitate this transfer, stock exchanges are in operation at Montreal, Toronto, Winnipeg, Calgary and Vancouver. Generally speaking, the exchanges may not be used for new securities but only for those already in the hands of the public. Securities of smaller companies are not "listed", that is officially traded in on the exchange but are handled less formally "over the counter". In an indirect way the exchanges assist the sale of new securities because the purchaser knows that he can find the value of his shares by consulting the selling prices of listed and usually, also, of unlisted securities as quoted in his daily newspaper. He knows too, that the exchange will provide a market for his stock in case he should like to sell later on.

Despite the variety of financial institutions functioning in Canada, it had long been recognized that inadequate provision was made for lending money for terms of five, ten, or fifteen years. In 1944 the Government established the Industrial Development Bank as a wholly owned subsidiary of the Bank of Canada. It is empowered to lend money or guarantee loans, to enter into underwriting arrangements for any issue of stocks, bonds or debentures, and to acquire securities of any corporation. It may accept any form of collateral against its advances, including real property. The Bank is specifically forbidden to engage in the business of receiving deposits and is not to compete with chartered banks in extending short term credit on the one hand or with investment bankers in selling stocks and bonds to the public on the other. The Industrial Development Bank is especially useful in helping relatively small but sound and rapidly growing manufacturing and trading enterprises.

The great increase in the amount invested in Canadian corporations since the 1850's and, especially since 1920, was supplied from three main sources. Initially, it came mainly from Great Britain whose investors owned the Canada and British America Land Companies, and later purchased all the bonds and stock of the Grand Trunk and almost all those of the Canadian Pacific. They also bought substantially all the bonds of the Federal and Provincial Governments. In particular, they supplied most of the capital behind the extraordinary railway and industrial expansion of Canada between 1897 and 1914.

During World War I, the Federal Government was forced to finance itself more and more within Canada because Britain and, after 1917, the United States were entirely concerned with their own war requirements. After the War the various Governments continued to finance themselves in Canada, though a few loans were placed in New York. Meanwhile the flow of investment in private businesses switched from Britain to the United States. American money was invested heavily in approximately 1500 branch plants of all types from cameras to agricultural implements, pulp and paper, iron and steel, electrical goods factories, telephones in Ontario and Quebec, in oil refineries and also in mines and smelters. In general, American investors put their money in the newer or more speculative industries whereas the British stuck to railway and government securities. In 1913 about three billion dollars was invested by persons abroad in Canadian Government and industrial securities. Most of the investment came from Britain. The total amount of British investment had not altered much by 1940 but in 1949 it had fallen to $1,750 million. The total investment of all countries was nearly four billion in 1941, over six billion in 1949, and twenty-eight billion in 1961. The increase since 1913 has been almost entirely from the United States whose share of the total outside investment in Canada which was about 40 per cent in 1940 had nearly doubled by the late 1950's.

The increase in American investment both in terms of percentage and in terms of dollars has created the fear in some parts of Canada that the United States is securing financial control of Canadian industry and commerce, and will eventually obtain political dominance also. Such fears overlook the fact that political intervention follows financial penetration only when the debt cannot be repaid, or the government is unstable or corrupt as in some of the countries of South or Central America. Moreover, if one takes into account investment in farms, homes, retail stores, banks, etc., and the Canadian holdings of government and corporation bonds and of stocks of public utilities and industrial concerns, Canadians have an enormous investment in their own country. Besides, it is to be noted that in 1937 Canada was an investor in other countries to the extent of over one and three-quarter billion, of which over sixty per cent was in the United States, two per cent in Britain and the remainder in the British West Indies and Latin America. Canadian investments abroad were mainly in railways, insurance companies and a few branch plants. By 1949 Canadian investment abroad had grown to over three and a half billion, in 1961 to ten billion of which four billion consisted of government loans to foreign countries, subscriptions to international financial organizations such as the World Bank, and holdings of gold and foreign exchange. Part of the objection to American investment is that Americans control the most dynamic parts of our economy, notably mining, petroleum and manufacturing. In these industries earnings are usually re-invested in the business instead of being paid out as dividends. Retention of earnings plus inflows of new capital from the United States has resulted in the very rapid growth of control by non-residents since 1945. Outside investments contributed greatly to the extraordinary prosperity of Canada in post-war years.

Notwithstanding the enormous investment by Americans after 1945, Canada is showing an increasing economic maturity, a better balance of agriculture, forestry, mining, fishing, lumbering, and manufacturing than has prevailed in the past. In addition, the Bank of Canada and our system of branch banks and various investment institutions with their head offices chiefly in Montreal and Toronto tend to bind the country into a financial unity. Even so, our prosperity is still closely tied to world trade and world peace, and financial integration of the various regions of the country cannot overcome their economic divergencies in other respects.

SELECTED READINGS

BECKHART, B. H., *The Banking System of Canada*, New York, 1929.

BLADEN, V. W., *An Introduction to Political Economy*, Chapter VII, Toronto, 1956.

CANADA, Royal Commission on banking and currency in Canada, *Report*, Ottawa, 1933.

EASTERBROOK, W. T., *Farm Credit in Canada*, Toronto, 1938.

HOOD, WM. C., *Financing Economic Activity in Canada*, Ottawa, 1958.

JAMIESON, A. B., *Chartered Banking in Canada*, Toronto, 1955.

LOGAN, H. A., and INMAN, M. K., *A Social Approach to Economics*, Toronto, 1939, pp. 389-428.

MARSHALL, H., SOUTHARD, F. A., and TAYLOR, K. W., *Canadian-American Industry — a study in international investment*, Toronto, 1936.

NEUFELD, E. P., *Bank of Canada Operations, 1935-1954*, Toronto, 1955.

PARKINSON, J. F., ed., *Canadian Investment and Foreign Exchange Problems*, part II, Toronto, 1940.

PLUMPTRE, A. F. W., *Central Banking in the British Dominions*, Toronto, 1939.

ROSS, V., *A History of the Canadian Bank of Commerce*, Toronto, 1920-34.

18

Public Finance

UNDER the French regime and the earlier part of British rule the functions of the Government were confined almost entirely to the administration of justice and the more or less casual regulation of trade. The funds necessary to carry on these functions were supplied by certain seigniorial dues, the proceeds of the sale of land and the collection of duties, chiefly on spirits. The task of national defence including the maintenance of garrisons, the erection of forts, the construction of roads and later of the Rideau Canal, involved considerable expense but this was borne almost entirely by the Governments in the mother countries.

Without attempting to detail the changes throughout the years, it can be said that by 1867 each of the colonies incorporated in the new Dominion had complete control of its finances without interference from Britain. The popularly elected legislatures had secured the power of the purse. An important factor behind the demand for responsible government was the insistence of the public that it should control the spending of money raised by taxation. The functions of the Government had greatly expanded though they were still modest, judged by modern standards. They included railways and canals, the post-office, education, immigration, the encouragement of agriculture and industry and a few other matters, besides the traditional ones of justice and national defence. All these responsibilities were conducted with frugality. In contrast with the present, the amounts expended on education were small because the demands of the people were largely limited to elementary schools. Expenditures by the Canadian colonies for national defence were restricted, since the garrisons were still maintained by the Imperial Government. Over half the total expenditures (including the interest on debts) of the four original provinces in Confederation were directly devoted to the development of the resources of the country, by providing transportation services. The revenues continued to be derived from the sale of land and, mainly, from customs duties and excise taxes. Finally it should be recalled that fiscal difficulties arising chiefly out of the construction of canals in the St. Lawrence basin, and the real or attempted construction of railways in all the provinces, were factors leading to Confederation.

At the inter-provincial conference which took place prior to Confederation, the most difficult problem which the delegates had to face was not so much the division of authority between the Provinces and the Dominion, as the division of taxing power. The delegates quickly agreed to give the Dominion most of the functions which were, by this time, considered properly to be within the scope of governments with the exception of education, the administration of justice and local public works. In order to carry on its tasks the Dominion would need the largest share of the revenue which then came mainly from customs duties. But to give the Central Government all the revenue from this source would deprive the Provinces of sufficient funds to carry on even their more limited functions. At the same time it seemed unwise to leave customs in the hands of the Provinces, since it was logical that the control of foreign trade should be in the hands of the Dominion Government. Also a province with unlimited control of customs might tax goods going through its ports to another province, giving rise to ill-feeling similar to that which arose from this cause in the early decades of the nineteenth century between Upper and Lower Canada. The essential difficulty was that the yield from different sources did not coincide with the logical division of powers.

This problem was solved at the inter-provincial conference by giving the Federal Government the largest immediate source of revenue, the customs, and the greatest potential source, the raising of money by any mode of taxation. At the same time, the Dominion became responsible for what the Fathers of Confederation felt were the more important and expensive duties of government; also it took over all the existing debts of the four original Provinces and in addition paid them annual subsidies in cash. For their part the Provinces undertook the less costly governmental tasks and got the right to secure revenue only by direct taxation, that is, taxes paid by the individual on whom they are levied and not passed on, like customs duties, to some one else. The arrangement regarding debts and subsidies was definitely stated in the British North America Act to be "in full Settlement of all future Demands on Canada".

In spite of the "finality clause", within two years of the date of Confederation an extra subsidy was given Nova Scotia as a result of the "better terms" agitation of that Province. The adjustment was made by Act of Parliament, not by amendment to the British North America Act as would have seemed logical in view of the fact that the original arrangement was written in the latter Act. Modification of the terms by ordinary enactment left the way open to exerting political pressure in a manner which would not have been so easy had the Act itself had to be amended, a matter which could be done only by the British Parliament after a vote by both Houses of the Canadian Parliament and probably also, after the consent of all the Provinces. As new provinces were admitted after 1867, they were able to bargain for different arrangements than the original four. This gave the older Provinces a chance to allege discrimination against them and gave rise to further concessions. It is scarcely necessary to set forth the details of the financial adjustments made from time to time. By 1907 the whole scheme of subsidies had become so haphazard that the system was re-arranged on a more logical basis. Again the intention was that this arrangement be final and, in fact, the scheme was incorporated in the British North America Act, by means of an amendment passed by the Imperial Parliament.

Meanwhile, the expenditures of governments were increasing due to the rapid development of the West and to some extent, of the Laurentian Shield. These new regions were remote from the seaports through which they could send their staples to the markets of the world. Capital equipment was needed and this could be supplied more cheaply with government aid than by private individuals alone. The assistance might be given in various ways. The Canadian Pacific received cash, land, and railway lines already built. The Canadian Northern, the Grand Trunk Pacific and the Pacific Great Eastern obtained bond guarantees and subsidies. The National Transcontinental, what is now called the Ontario Northland, and Alberta's railways north from Edmonton as well as highways, harbour works and municipal services were constructed outright by various governments. All this capital equipment was designed to develop the country. In a sense the governments were agencies "for creating conditions in which private enterprise might thrive".

As already intimated, most of these expenditures took place after 1897 for, before that date, the recurring depressions periodically cut down revenue and operated as wholesome checks on the possible extravagances of governments. But in the early part of the twentieth century, the steady increases in government revenue in spite of low rates of taxation, and the general optimism of the time seemed to place no limit on the extent to which governments ought to provide capital equipment. By 1913 the Dominion had advanced about $700,000,000 for canals, river improvements, harbours, and railways either directly or indirectly. In addition the Federal Government had guaranteed the interest on large amounts of railway securities. The provincial "investment" in transportation facilities was also very large and, in addition, municipalities had greatly extended their services. So long as times were good the cost of this equipment could be readily borne. The possibility of a drastic contraction of revenue at some future date with a consequent strain on government finance was never seriously considered.

These capital expenditures must be distinguished from current charges. The former are for assets of a more or less permanent nature, for outlays from which a revenue may be derived in future years, and from which future generations as well as the present one may be expected to benefit. On the other hand current expenses are those incurred for the day-to-day operations of the government such as interest, education, national defence, the maintenance of public works (but not their original cost), the administration of justice and so on. Like capital expenditures, current expenses increased rapidly after 1896. Because of the considerable growth in the population of Canada, the absolute figures are apt to be misleading.

Yet on a per capita basis expenditures of the Provinces and Dominion combined increased slowly until 1896, and then multiplied three times by 1913. The increase in current expenses was rather more rapid for the Dominion than for the Provinces. Data regarding municipal expenditures are not available but the per capita increase was undoubtedly as great as that of the two other types of taxing bodies.

As far as revenue is concerned, the Dominion continued to finance itself almost entirely from customs and excise duties. The westward expansion involved huge imports of capital equipment and consumers' goods on which duties were paid, usually at the highest tariff rates of the time, for the goods came largely from the United States. Excise taxes were levied on alcoholic liquors and tobacco. The Provinces as a group got about one-third of their revenue from federal subsidies, nearly one-third from the sale of land, timber and mining rights, and rather more than one-third from licenses and other direct taxes. Of course the position of the various provinces differed from one another. Municipalities secured their revenue solely and without difficulty by means of a tax on real property.

During the War of 1914-18 there was an enormous increase in expenditure and also in the public debt. Generally speaking, Canada's share of the cost of the War was met by borrowing mainly within Canada. Taxation was increased only sufficiently to cover the increased amount of interest on the debt. This policy was followed because people, especially in pioneer communities, object to paying heavy taxes. Also, in the early years it was felt that the War would be short and inexpensive. By the time this idea was shown to be false, expenses had risen so rapidly that tax revenue could not be increased fast

enough to keep up with them. Expenditures at war time
levels did not cease with the Armistice but continued until
1923, due to the cost of demobilization and soldiers' civil
re-establishment. Also, during and after the War the
various governments were obligated either to complete
projects in the process of construction when the outbreak
occurred, or to re-equip facilities acquired during the
War. Thus by 1921 not only had over one and three-
quarter billion dollars been added to the debt on account
of the War, but two billion more had been spent by
Federal, Provincial and Municipal Governments on capital
account. Of the capital expenditures the share of the
Dominion had multiplied nearly three times over 1913,
the Provinces twice and the Municipalities about sixty per
cent. On a per capita basis the combined debt of Federal,
Provincial and Municipal Governments was $555 in 1921,
or three and one-quarter times the per capita debt of 1913.

During the decade of the 1920's, capital expenditures
by governments were resumed but with a significant difference. The Dominion added to its investment in railways, canals and other public works only by about thirty
per cent over 1921, and the Municipalities increased their
capital expenditures only about forty-five per cent. On the
other hand, the Provinces nearly doubled their expenditures. The reason for the difference was that the Provinces had to construct broad, hard-surfaced, and therefore
expensive, highways for the use of motor vehicles, whereas the Dominion had fairly well finished its task of providing national transportation facilities. To be sure, the Federal Government had to complete the new Welland Canal
and the Hudson Bay Railway, erect harbour works at Vancouver, Montreal, Halifax and elsewhere and renovate
the Canadian National. Nevertheless, its main task as
far as capital equipment was concerned, had already been

done and the virtual absence of deficits on the publicly owned railway during the latter years of the decade materially relieved the financial burden on the Dominion. On the contrary, the Provinces were under continual pressure to take over more and more road mileage from the Municipalities, and to construct better quality highways for the use of a growing number of motor vehicles, including the tourist traffic.

Aside from capital expenditures there was a growth in current expenses of nearly one-third in the years 1921-30. Again there was a discrepancy in the rates of increase in the different types or jurisdictions. Current expenditures of the Federal Government increased ten per cent, of the Municipalities thirty per cent, but those of the Provinces rose more than one hundred per cent. To meet these increased expenditures on current account, revenues had to be increased also. During the War the Dominion had supplemented its receipts from customs and excise by taxing personal and corporation incomes, and by sales taxes on commodities. After the War these new taxes were continued, though at lower rates, and thirty-five per cent of the total revenues of the Federal Government was derived from them in 1930. The income of the Provinces was increased by means of new taxes on gasoline and, in some cases, on incomes and also by profits from the government sale of liquor. With the growth of revenues from other sources, the Federal subsidy occupied a minor position in the fiscal position of most Provinces. The revenue for the Municipalities came almost entirely from taxes on real property, augmented in a few jurisdictions by taxes on personal property, income and businesses.

It is apparent that the decade of the 1920's represented a re-alignment of the relative fiscal positions of Dominion,

Provincial and Municipal Governments. Generally speaking, during the ten years the Dominion had been able to prevent any large increase in its own debt or expenditures; the Municipalities had experienced a moderate increase but the Provinces had doubled their capital and current expenditures as well as their debts. To some extent the increase in provincial debt was justified because it was incurred largely for highways which partly pay for themselves. The Provinces get revenue from taxes on gasoline and diesel fuel and from licenses. They use this money to meet interest on highway debt and the cost of repairs and maintenance. In other words, the provincial debt, unlike war debts and a considerable proportion of the "investment" by the Dominion in railways, is represented by assets which pay for themselves and do not require assistance from taxes levied in the ordinary manner.

Nevertheless, the Provinces faced financial problems. Their responsibilities had been extended by decisions of the courts, and by the industrial and social changes which had taken place since Confederation. In short, their revenues and obligations got out of balance.

It will be recalled that the British North America Act had set forth a certain division of powers between the Dominion and the Provinces. Since 1867 these relations had been altered by custom and the courts. The Fathers of Confederation apparently assumed that the Dominion had authority over the Provinces and, in the early years of the new nation the central government had disallowed, or thrown out, certain provincial laws. The Provinces contended that, within their geographic borders and with respect to the subjects enumerated in the British North America Act as being under provincial control, they had complete legal authority. In the main the Judicial Committee of the Privy Council, then the highest court of appeal for Canadians, supported the Provincial view and by 1890, the use by the Dominion of its veto power, generally speaking, fell into abeyance, being resorted to only when the Dominion felt that its jurisdiction was clearly being infringed.

The Judicial Committee influenced the division of powers between the Provinces and the Dominion in another way. Almost any piece of legislation, say, a law dealing with strikes on railways, relates to more than one category in the division of powers, in this case to railways (Dominion) and civil rights (Provincial). The Judicial Committee must decide who has jurisdiction. If it considers that the real purpose, the very essence, the pith and substance of the legislation is the regulation of railways, then the Dominion has control even though incidentally to its real purpose the law may effect civil rights. If the essence is to control strikes, then the Provinces have control in spite of the fact that there is a casual interference with railways. Obviously disputes regarding the division of powers often give rise to nice legal distinctions. In deciding such questions the Privy Council tended to lean in the direction of strengthening the powers of the Provinces. In brief, the power of disallowance fell into disuse and the Provinces were given relatively more legislative power.

Not only did the Provinces have their powers enlarged so far as legal jurisdiction was concerned, they had their influence extended because of the steady growth of government functions. The construction and maintenance of highways represents an obvious widening of provincial responsibilities. So does the mass of labour legislation—factory inspection, minimum wages and so on. The expense of regulating modern industry and agriculture in order to protect the worker, assist trade and guard the consumer is very considerable. Even more important is the growth of social services. These come within the category of "property and civil rights" and therefore, are within provincial control. Social services include expenditures on health such as hospitals, the prevention and cure of tuberculosis and contagious diseases, cancer clinics, the provision of nursing and other medical services for the very poor and, more recently, medicare and hospital insurance for everyone. They also include the care of the needy aged, mothers' allowances, children's aid, the relief of the unemployed and the like. At one time all these expenses were borne either by private charity or, mainly, by other members of the family. Gradually, as the country became more highly industrialized the need for these services increased. People became less self-sufficient and therefore more subject to the evils of the business cycle. The concentration of population in cities made certain problems of health more acute. The advance of science raised the cost of medical services. The proportion of elderly persons in the total population rose. Hence more people had to be taken care of after their working life was over. While these changes were taking place, families became separated through moving away to cities or to the developing West. Consequently they lost some of their clannishness, became less conscious of responsibility to their less fortunate kinsmen. In short, the need for social services increased and the traditional method of meeting the contingencies was weakened. As a result governments, i.e. the Provincial Governments, had to assume a larger measure of responsibility for a growing volume of social services.

One other field of provincial control, education, also became more and more expensive as time went on. Before

the industrial revolution began to influence Canadian
economic life, formal education consisted almost literally
of the Three R's. A knowledge of farming, of a trade or
of a profession like the ministry, law or even medicine
was picked up by observation of those already in that
occupation. As time went on, life became more complex.
One needed more than the first few years of elementary
schooling in order to deal effectively with the problem of
earning a living and fulfilling the duties of citizenship.
Professional education involving several years' study
was required in preparation for work in the church, the
law courts and medicine and was becoming virtually
essential in teaching, pharmacy and engineering, and important in agriculture, architecture, commerce, forestry,
social service and so on. Moreover, vocational or technical education was given in a wide range of subjects.
More branches of learning were taught; more young
people attended schools and universities; expensive equipment was needed for teaching purposes and teachers,
being themselves more highly trained than before, were
better paid. Thus industrialization and the complexity
of modern economic life greatly added to the cost of
education. Since education is a type of governmental
activity which comes almost entirely within provincial
and municipal control, their expenses have increased on
this account.

To sum up, the activities of the Provinces grew in
legislative power by means of judicial decree; they grew
in expense because people demanded more and more social
services; on the contrary the field of provincial taxation
scarcely grew at all. The power to levy taxes directly,
the only taxing basis possessed by the Provinces under the
British North America Act, was used assiduously but,
except in the central provinces, exercise of the power

yielded returns inadequate to carry on the social services on the scale desired. On the other hand Dominion jurisdiction had not been enlarged significantly and it was able to prevent too rapid an increase in its expenditures during the 1920's. Also it cut down its debt slightly. To reach this strong financial position the Dominion had invaded the direct taxation field by levies on the sale prices of goods and on incomes. Although it had the legal right to do this, the Dominion was profiting by revenues which might otherwise have been available for collection by the Provinces, and doing so at the very time when the responsibilities of the Provinces were being enlarged. In brief, the division of legislative powers was out of line with the division of taxing powers. The condition which the Fathers of Confederation had wrestled with had recurred.

The problem of disparity of functions and revenues had been handled initially by the system of provincial subsidies. We have already seen how that system had been modified until by 1907 it had become completely illogical. In spite of the alleged finality of the settlement of that year, in 1912 the scheme was altered by giving Manitoba a bigger subsidy. The reason given was that the crown lands, which were a source of revenue to the other Provinces, had been retained by the Dominion in the case of Manitoba, Saskatchewan and Alberta. Adjustments in the case of the latter two Provinces had been made when they were admitted to Confederation in 1905. Manitoba considered it just that she be treated similarly, even to the extent of receiving arrears. In 1927, as a result of the Duncan Commission, extra subsidies were given the Maritimes and in the early 1930's, special arrangements involving the return of crown lands were made with all the Provinces west of the Great Lakes. By 1935 the subsidies followed no logical arrangement except for

Ontario and Quebec. Subsidies had again degenerated into a haphazard attempt to solve a fundamental difficulty.

The basic problem of disparity between functions and revenues was postponed by another make-shift, namely "conditional grants". The Federal Government made grants of money to the Provinces notably for technical education and old age pensions on condition that the Provinces make certain expenditures toward the same objectives out of their own funds. These grants were open to the objection that the citizens of every Province paid part of the cost of the Dominion grant, but did not receive any benefit from it unless their particular Province accepted the scheme. In effect, conditional grants are a means of forcing provinces to undertake social services which they may not want. The grants are objectionable on the further ground that some of the Provinces have not the funds to pay a large proportion of the expenses of the service. If the Dominion pays most of the costs, the Provinces may not exercise reasonable care in seeing that the money is spent economically and, under the British North America Act, the Dominion cannot administer the schemes itself.

During the 1930's the disparity between jurisdiction and revenue arose in even a more acute form. The depression greatly increased expenses for the direct relief of all the urban unemployed and for the drought stricken areas in the West. More money was spent on public works undertaken as relief measures, and for the deficits on the National Railways. These depression costs could not be offset by reducing government expenses in other directions. Interest costs, which in 1930 comprised over one-quarter of the total expenses of Dominion, Provincial and Municipal Governments combined, could be reduced only by the slow process of refunding at lower rates of interest.

The standard of social services, such as health and education, could not very easily be cut and existing public works, like highways, had to be maintained at a reasonable state of efficiency. Thus in spite of reduction in the salaries of government employees and, until 1938, in the budget on national defence, expenditures on regular services tended to continue at their old level at the same time that expenses on account of the depression were greatly increasing.

The increased total expenditures were met in part by heavier taxes, the existing rates being raised substantially. Business was so bad, however, that these higher rates often yielded less in total revenue than lower rates had in 1929. Of course improving business tended to change this but commonly, increases in expenditures outran gains in receipts. Thus public debt increased. Between 1930 and 1937, roughly one billion dollars was added to the Dominion debt, one-half billion to the debts of the Provinces and two hundred million to Municipal debts, a total increase of about twenty-seven per cent. The grand total of the public debt of the Dominion, its Provinces and Municipalities was over seven and one-half billion dollars, or approximately $700 per capita.

Although some of this debt is represented by earning assets, much of it is "dead weight" and interest on it must be secured from the general sources of taxation and paid whether times are good or bad. When times are good, people do not object to paying taxes and relatively low rates yield high returns. The interest and other government expenses can be borne easily. But when business is poor, the burden of governmental costs is severe. In all countries the changes of the business cycle are becoming more pronounced. In Canada, income fluctuates widely because of dependence on a relatively few staples. When the prices of these staples are low or markets fall off or crop yields are poor, governmental costs take a relatively larger share of the Canadian national income. An unstable income is coupled with comparatively fixed expenses on government services at all times and expenditures for relief and railway deficits which fluctuate contrari-wise to business prosperity. These factors create an almost intolerable burden when business conditions are depressed.

More than this, the burden of the depression is not spread evenly over the entire nation but, as will be shown later, strikes with peculiar force upon certain areas. In the Maritimes the feeling of family responsibility seems to be stronger than elsewhere in Canada with the exception of Quebec. In addition, it is relatively easy for people to shift from lumbering or fishing into part-time agriculture and thus make a living of sorts. The per capita income, though never reaching so high a level as in the previous decade, did not fall so far in the depression. The Maritimes had been under a financial strain in previous years and could "stand it" a little longer. Ontario and Quebec, with more mature economies and a protected market for many of their goods, did not suffer from the depression as badly as their western neighbours. As the centres of industry, banking and trade, they could tax the incomes of large corporations and of individuals, and the estates of deceased persons, and thus secure large revenues for themselves even though the profits giving rise to the incomes or estates were drawn from all parts of the country. The Prairie Provinces and British Columbia were not so fortunate. They derived a relatively larger proportion of their revenues from taxes on land and when the prices of staples fell, land-owners found it exceedingly difficult to pay their taxes. Other sources of revenue open to the Provinces and Municipalities were quickly explored and exhausted. Their expenses rapidly exceeded their revenues and debts increased. The central government had to come to their aid by assuming a larger share of the cost of old age pensions, giving direct loans to the more impecunious provinces and resorting to conditional grants for relief on a huge scale.

At the same time that the Dominion Government was paying more and more of the costs of the depression, it was handicapped in trying to cure the difficulty, in practising "depression therapeutics" as distinct from simply keeping the patient alive. Though it attempted to do so, the Dominion could not control the marketing of natural products, or regulate hours and wages, or introduce unemployment insurance for these were within the legislative scope of the Provinces. Whether these measures would have aided recovery is a debatable question but in any case, the Federal Government did not have available the powers it desired. In a word, the British North America Act needed re-examination.

Accordingly in 1937 the Dominion Government appointed a Royal Commission to re-examine the economic and financial basis of Confederation and the distribution of legislative powers in the light of the economic and social developments of the past seventy years. After long and careful study the Commissioners recommended that the Dominion take over all Provincial debts and assume full responsibility for unemployment relief. The Provinces were to withdraw entirely from taxing personal incomes, corporation incomes, and estates of deceased persons. However, they would continue to tax motor vehicles as well as gasoline and diesel fuel. They would get other revenues from timber and mining rights, the sale of liquor, and various minor sources. Besides,

they would be paid national adjustment grants by the
Dominion. These were designed to insure that provinces
with low taxing capacity would have adequate revenue to
provide a minimum standard of social services. The
wealthier provinces might, if they wished, give larger
benefits to the aged, to public health, and so on. In this
event they would have to pay for the additions out of
their own tax revenues.

The report of the Commission was considered at a conference between the Dominion and all the Provincial
Governments early in 1941. The Premiers of Ontario,
British Columbia and Alberta objected to the proposals,
chiefly on the ground that their Provinces lost relatively
more than their neighbours and gained much less. The
conference collapsed but during the War the Dominion
made temporary arrangements with all the provinces as
explained later.

Since 1945 the Dominion and the Provinces have tried
to work out various tax-sharing arrangements and the
federal government has taken on more of the obligations
which formerly rested entirely with the Provinces. For
instance, it has assumed the main burden of unemployment relief. It has not accepted responsibility for any of
the Provincial debts, as suggested by the Royal Commission of 1937, but it does make equalization payments to
those Provinces which for one reason or another cannot
reasonably be expected to collect in provincial taxes the
same revenue per capita as the wealthier provinces. The
formula for arriving at these payments takes into account
the amount received by the province from oil royalties
and timber dues as well as the yields from taxes on
incomes and estates within the province. In addition, the
Dominion makes a special adjustment grant to the Atlantic Provinces.

For a time the Dominion made tax rental agreements with several provinces. It paid them an agreed proportion of the revenues it collected from taxes on incomes and estates. In 1962, it replaced tax rentals with tax collection agreements. If a province wishes to impose a personal or corporation income tax and if it is prepared to define income in the same manner as the federal government, the latter will collect the tax and pay it over to the Province concerned. As a rule, succession duties are shared equally between the Dominion and the Province.

Conditional grants have increased in size and variety since 1945. They apply to the construction of hospitals, pensions to the blind, the trans-Canada highway, roads to resources, and so on. The Dominion also helps higher education by annually paying each province a sum based on its current population. This sum is then divided among the universities in the Province in proportion to the number of students registered for degrees. Moreover, in 1957 the Dominion gave the Canada Council $100 million, which it got from the succession duties levied on the estates of two wealthy men and which it might otherwise have used for general purposes. Half the sum has been spent on university buildings; the interest on the remainder is used to help painters, writers, musicians, etc., and to encourage drama, the ballet, and research in the humanities and social sciences.

Broadly speaking, rates of taxation have been somewhat reduced since 1945, but on account of the relatively high level of prosperity, the total amount paid to various levels of government in taxes has risen. The Dominion was able to reduce its debt by upwards of $2 billion between 1946 and 1957 but in the ensuing five years it increased by roughly the same amount. All provincial governments, except Alberta, increased their debts, although by ignoring its borrowings for the Provincially-owned railway and hydro-electric power system, the Premier of British Columbia claimed the elimination of the Provincial indebtedness. Most provinces found it necessary to introduce taxes on retail sales in order to bolster their revenues and balance their annual budgets.

The post-war movement of population from farms to cities and the influx of immigrants created financial difficulties for numerous communities. Several cities enlarged their boundaries and a metropolitan council was created for Greater Toronto.

SELECTED READINGS

BATES, STEWART, "Financial history of Canadian governments", *Royal Commission on Dominion-Provincial Relations*, (hereafter referred to as *Dom-Prov. Study*), Ottawa, 1940.

CORRY, J. A., "The growth of government activities since Confederation", *Dom-Prov. Study*.

EGGLESTON, W., *The Road to Nationhood*, Toronto, 1946.

GOLDENBERG, H. C., "Municipal finance in Canada", *Dom-Prov. Study*.

GOUIN, L. M., and CLAXTON, BROOKE, "Legislative expedients and devices adopted by the Dominion and the Provinces", *Dom-Prov. Study*.

LEMONTAGNE, M., *Le Fédéralism Canadien; Évolution et Problems*, Quebec, 1954.

LOGAN, H. A., and INMAN, M. K., *A Social Approach to Economics*, Toronto, 1939, pp. 566-609.

MAXWELL, J. A., *Federal Subsidies to Provincial Governments in Canada*, Cambridge, 1937.

PERRY, J. H., *Taxation in Canada*, Toronto, 1953.
Taxes, Tariffs and Subsidies, Toronto, 1955.

ROYAL COMMISSION ON DOMINION-PROVINCIAL RELATIONS, *Report, Recommendations*, Ottawa, 1940.

19

The Business Cycle

A CHARACTERISTIC feature of modern economic life is the alternating periods of good and poor business associated with the term "business cycle". Any book on the economic history of Canada would be incomplete if it did not give a good deal of attention to this phenomenon. A study of cyclical changes has the additional advantage, for our purposes, of binding together the specialized studies of particular regions and topics. It must be emphasized that Canadian economic development resembles not a series of still photographs nor even of "shorts", but rather a full length feature picture in which the "shots" of one industry have the other industries for a background, and in which for a time everything is bright with prosperity and then darkened by depression.

Confederation opened with a period of poor business occasioned by the abrogation of the Reciprocity Treaty in the previous year. Revival took place with the construction of the Intercolonial Railway and better business conditions abroad, only to become badly depressed again after 1873. A change of government and, later, the National Policy reflected the popular discontent of the time. During the next nearly twenty-five years, that is, until about 1896 or 1897, the business cycle followed a complicated course. Although there were some good business years such as the early 1880's, prosperity was spotty and on the whole, times were hard. It was only the fact that most people lived on farms where they could at least raise their own food that prevented the gloom becoming worse.

This situation was completely altered in the period from 1897 to 1920. This was a time of great prosperity; a period when the brightness of the economic picture seemed to justify the prophesy that the twentieth would be Canada's century, as the nineteenth had been that of the United States. The West was developing at an extraordinarily rapid rate. New mineral areas in the Yukon, British Columbia and Ontario were being opened up and the forest resources of British Columbia were being exploited. Manufacturing was expanding because of new industries, the transfer of tasks from home to factory, and the tariff. Power for the new factories was being provided by hydro-electricity in Ontario and cheap coal in the Maritimes. The transportation network was being extended, and low rates by rail and lake and ocean steamship simplified the selling of staples in foreign markets. World trade was relatively free from the restrictions of tariffs and quotas, and the fact that all countries were on the gold standard lent an element of stability to all international transactions. Capital was flowing into Canada, mainly from Great Britain. The interest of the Mother Country in her colonies had been stimulated by the Diamond Jubilee of Queen Victoria. In addition, Britain's concern for Canada had been strengthened by the offer of Imperial tariff preference made by Canada without asking anything in return, and by the great impression made on the British people by Sir Wilfrid Laurier. Bank credit was easy to secure and the prices of commodities were rising. All of these elements acted on one another. Once prosperity got under way, it kept piling up, so to speak. Although there were recessions in 1901, 1905,

1907 and the beginnings of one in 1913, the accumulated force of the previous prosperity was so great that the country was carried easily through the short periods of contraction.

Not only was the period from 1897 to 1920 one of expansion, it was also one of integration of Canada, of binding together the various economic regions of the country. The growth of inter-regional trade, the construction of transcontinental railways, the establishment of large businesses selling in the national markets were evidence of greater economic unification. Similarily, in political life a new spirit of unity was evident. The quarrels between different Provinces and between Province and Dominion such as those arising over the Ontario boundary, the Jesuit Estates, Manitoba's school question, Maritime union and the threatened secession of British Columbia, were largely forgotten. Provincial claims for better terms were easily settled by additional subsidies which a Dominion Government having ample revenues was glad to give. The spirit of loyalty was heightened in the early years of the War. On the other hand the naval question after 1910, the controversy over the use of the French language in Ontario schools, and the conscription issue in 1917 indicated that political unity was not yet complete. Nevertheless, during this period Canada approached economic and political integration more completely than she had ever been able to do in the past. The main reason for the integration was that the business life of the country was concentrated on the opening of the West and the export of wheat.

The Great War stimulated a tremendous boom in certain industries—base metal mining, pulp and paper, woollens, ships and, especially, in munitions. Farming was prosperous because of high prices and the great wartime demand from Europe. Taxes and the prices of commodities both rose to new high levels. The former, however, were not raised enough either to pay for any significant part of the cost of the War, or to prevent the growth of several large personal fortunes. Some persons, especially merchants with stocks of goods on hand, gained from the increases in prices. On the other hand, wage earners and recipients of salaries, interest and rent, tended to lose because their incomes did not rise as rapidly or to the same degree as their living costs. To some extent they were compensated by the fact that work was plentiful and no able bodied person needed to be without a job. Even so, the high cost of living became a serious problem during the latter years of the War.

The cessation of actual hostilities caused some hesitation in business but recovery was rapid. Europe continued to need food. Returning soldiers had to be provided with civilian clothing. The physical equipment of railways and factories had been allowed to run down during the War when the entire attention of the country was focused on providing munitions and satisfying other war needs. This capital now had to be repaired and replaced. Thus the good times of the War were followed by an immediate post-war boom.

Late in 1920, however, there was a crash, an immediate post-war depression. Prices generally fell by forty per cent, and wheat by sixty per cent. Thousands of Canadians went to the United States in the hope of finding jobs. Within Canada, agricultural and labour discontent was wide-spread expressing itself in the formation of new political parties and in strikes. Fortunately the depression was short lived and by 1923, except in the Maritimes, expansion had been resumed and in the last few years of the decade a considerable boom was again experienced.

The causes of this new expansion in part resembled those occasioning the boom after 1897. Conditions abroad were good, mainly because the United States lent heavily to Europe for reconstruction after the War. Within Canada the annual investment of capital almost doubled, in the period from 1925 to 1929, over the preceding five years. Some industries previously established such as pulp and paper, automobiles and electrical goods now expanded very rapidly. The construction industry thrived because of the erection of new plants, increased urbanization of the population and the demand for more and better highways. The tourist trade became important. Also more people became engaged in the professions and in the civil service.

In certain respects the new expansion differed from that prior to the war of 1914. It was based relatively less on staples and comparatively more on industrial goods. Although agriculture continued to be important, it occupied a relatively weaker position. Farming in the West was aided by a great reduction in railway freight rates to below the high level of the War, by low ocean rates due to the excess of shipping space after 1920, and by the opening of the Panama Canal. On the other hand, toward the end of the period, Western agriculture ran up against a steadily deteriorating situation in the world market. In the East agriculture was, for various reasons, only moderately prosperous. In comparison with 1913 manufacturing was more significant in the 'twenties, especially in the production of durable consumers' goods. These are articles like automobiles, radios and electric refrigerators used by the general public. They are more durable than other types of consumers goods such as clothing, and hence their purchase may be postponed if necessary when times are hard. On the contrary in periods of good business the use of a chattel mortgage, commonly called the instalment plan, allows their purchase before one has the full amount ready to pay for them. The effect of the instalment plan was to speed up business faster than would otherwise have been the case. In the 1920's, manufacturing of capital equipment within Canada also became significant whereas in the pre-war days most of the machinery, except farm implements, had been imported. Mining, except coal, had become much more important since the pre-war period. The exploitation of forest resources had largely shifted from lumber to pulp and paper, especially in Eastern Canada. In construction the emphasis was on highways instead of railways.

In comparison with the decade before the War immigration was much less, being only 1,125,000, in the years 1921-29. Organized labour, fearing that wages would be cut, opposed large scale immigration. The general public was skeptical of the ability of the country to assimilate the various racial elements. The Government encouraged *bona fide* farmers of Anglo-Saxon or Scandinavian descent but the people who were most anxious to come were discontented urban workers in Britain and, especially, Slavs and other Central Europeans. Immigration was offset by a considerable movement to the United States, partly of Canadian born attracted to American factories, and partly of Europeans who entered Canada and declared themselves to be *bona fide* immigrants but whose real intention was to enter the United States as soon as the quota restrictions of that country would permit them to do so. The net absolute increase in population, that is, the number of migrants plus natural increase during the 1920's, was not much lower than in the first decade of the century, but in terms of percentage it was eighteen compared with thirty-four. Unlike the first boom of the century, relatively little of the capital investment in the later prosperity came from Britain. A good deal was from the United States but most was supplied within Canada itself. Most important of all was the fact that the good times of the 1920's were not shared equally by all parts of the country. To a large extent the Maritimes were passed by, in spite of the fact that they were given concessions in railway rates and in other ways. The prosperity of the Prairies was considerable while Ontario and Quebec, the Laurentian Shield and especially British Columbia enjoyed, or suffered, a tremendous boom.

The great prosperity of the 1920's ended late in 1929. As a matter of fact, industrial production had turned down earlier in that year and agriculture had been slowly declining in prosperity for some time. The general public, however, believed that the good times would last forever and only the collapse of the New York stock market in October 1929 awakened it to reality. Immediately after the crash business contracted rapidly. Bank credit was hard to secure because the banks were calling in their loans. The purchase of durable consumers' goods and capital equipment was deferred. Men were discharged and in 1930, out of every hundred wage earners, thirteen were unemployed compared with four in 1929. Wages were cut. Prices of agricultural commodities, minerals (except gold), forestry products and fish fell to disastrously low levels though the prices of manufactured goods tended to be maintained. Foreign trade was definitely poor since the United States had ceased to loan abroad, and the fear of war had led European countries to erect even higher tariffs. The contraction in international trade was especially serious for Canada because in the 1920's about one-third of our income was derived directly from exports, and an indeterminate amount derived indirectly from selling manufactured goods, providing transportation or from rendering financial services for the export industries. By 1933 the value of our exports was only one-third its level in 1929. The cyclical depression dragged down all countries, but Canada was exceptionally hard hit due to the Western drought the like of which for extent and duration had never before been experienced.

The effects of the depression on the Canadian economy were accentuated also by the fact that the decline in business was worse in certain economic regions in Canada than in others. Saskatchewan and Alberta suffered severely: they were exposed to the full blast of a frigid depression. On the other hand the St. Lawrence Valley, Manitoba, the Pacific coast region and the Maritimes were affected less seriously: they suffered, in comparison, only a very cold chill. Finally, the Canadian Shield expanded for the rise in the price of gold stimulated development there. Measured statistically, the average income per capita declined between 1928-29 and 1932-33 by forty-eight per cent for Canada as a whole. In other words, an income of $1000 in 1928-29 had shrunk to $520 in 1932-33. The decline in real income, that is, goods and services, was not quite as great as the reduction in dollars for a dollar would "go farther" because the prices of goods were less. Nevertheless, the loss in real income *on the average* was very considerable and in certain regions it reached disastrous proportions. In Saskatchewan the decline in money income per capita was seventy-two per cent and in Alberta sixty-one. On the other hand declines in Ontario and Quebec were forty-four per cent, in New Brunswick and

Nova Scotia thirty-nine and thirty-six respectively, while in the three remaining Provinces the decline was just about the Dominion average.

Similarly certain income groups were more adversely affected than others. Indeed a few groups gained during the depression, for the prices of the goods which they purchased were much lower and their incomes were cut only moderately. In this class were most salaried workers and civil servants, and the railway employees who were able to retain their jobs but not those, a very considerable number, who were discharged. Generally speaking, in any particular industry the skilled workers suffered least and the unskilled most. Investors and owners of property were better off on the whole, but the position varied from one type of security holder to another. Investors with Government, Government guaranteed or high grade industrial bonds and chartered bank stock undoubtedly gained, but those who had their money in Canadian Pacific stocks, in pulp and paper and most other industrial common stock, and in farm mortgages were in the opposite position. The industries which were most adversely affected by the depression were those exporting most of their product such as wheat (but not nickel and gold) or producing capital goods. In short, the burden of the depression would have been serious enough if it had been spread evenly over the entire population, all areas and all industries. It was the inequality of incidence as much as the depression itself which created difficulties.

Canada's fundamental economic problem during the depression arose out of her dependence on a comparatively few staples. It has already been pointed out how the unconscious adoption of the staple theory has enabled Canada to enjoy a higher standard of living than would have been possible had the alternative of self-sufficiency been chosen. It is obvious that the maintenance of this living standard is contingent upon the continued sale of the staples in distant markets at satisfactory prices. When anything occurs to cause a collapse in markets or prices or both, the economy will suffer severely as would be the case in a business depression. In other words, a staple economy is peculiarly vulnerable to the business cycle.

This vulnerability shows itself in a number of different ways. So long as an industry produces and sells mainly within one country, that country presumably has considerable control over its production and marketing, but when the industry sells abroad that control is distinctly limited. More specifically, if other countries try to keep out Canadian staples by tariffs or quotas, we can do little to stop them. Of course we can protest and possibly retaliate by erecting tariff walls to keep out their goods. Unfortunately our protests and retaliations may be ineffective because, though foreign markets are very important to us, our own market is much less important to them. For example Canadian exports to the United Kingdom and the United States in the 1930's were, respectively, fifty and thirty per cent of Canada's total export trade. On the other hand British and American exports to Canada are only five and fifteen per cent, respectively, of all the foreign trade of these two countries. Therefore they can afford to ignore our retaliation whereas their actions are vital to us.

Another repercussion of our economic vulnerability was the fact that we had to pay annually substantial sums, perhaps 230 million dollars, abroad for principal and interest, not to mention payments for the importation of essential raw materials such as cotton, rubber and oil, and other goods such as tropical fruits which we cannot

heavy debt wouldn't help recovery

produce at home. The debts are payable in a fixed number of dollars or pounds sterling. When the prices of commodities decline, we must export relatively a larger volume of commodities to pay these debts. The payments have to be maintained but our wheat, lumber, pulp and paper, and so on, that is our means of payment, have become less. To look at the matter from a slightly different angle, we have borrowed heavily from abroad. Such borrowing was justified in as much as it enabled a pioneer or colonial economy to produce a large volume of staples. Of course, some of the borrowings were unprofitably invested but in the main, they enabled us to increase production. So long as we continued to borrow either for new investment or to pay the interest on previous loans, we remained prosperous but eventually we had to repay the loans. The capital equipment purchased with the loans ought to provide the goods for their repayment. If it does not, the country is in a bad way. In the life of every young country there occurs a kind of testing time when the value of previous investment is shown to be sound or not. Figuratively speaking the country has to "turn a corner" between a borrowing and a repaying nation. The "corner" for Canada came in the 1920's and 1930's. In the former decade it could be turned easily because of good prices and markets and considerable lending abroad by Canadians. In the 1930's, however, the road was more slippery and the corner could be turned only with difficulty, because the charges to be met were fixed in amount but the means of meeting them were less valuable.

The problem of repayment was also made more difficult by the fact that a great many of the fixed charges were on government account. It has already been shown how the resources of Canada are, as a rule, located remote from seaports and separated from each other by wide stretches of relatively barren rock. To exploit these resources requires a huge expenditure in railways, canals, harbour works and other transportation facilities, and also in farm equipment, pulp and paper mills, smelters, refineries and so on. Much of this enormous capital equipment, especially in transportation, was supplied by Governments, both Dominion and Provincial, because they could provide it, either directly or by guarantee, more cheaply than could private corporations. No matter how difficult it is to repay the borrowings a government—certainly not a government with British traditions—cannot default on its debts. Aside from the ethics involved, such repudiation would destroy the confidence of investors abroad and within the country as a whole, and prevent the inflow of additional capital which is needed to develop the resources further. Had more of the capital been supplied by private corporations such as the Canadian Pacific, the steamship lines on the Great Lakes, and the paper companies and mining concerns, the non-payment of interest would have been much less serious. In short, the magnitude of government investment made the problem of repayment especially intractable when the prices of staples fell.

The inter-related problems of lack of control over our markets, the problem of "turning the corner" and the heavy burden of fixed charges especially on government account seemed to coincide in the 1930's. The international world was particularly disturbed by tariff restrictions, monetary instability, fear of war and finally, war itself. The stream of foreign lending, so large before 1914 and in the 1920's, now dried up. The prices of commodities fell to exceptionally low levels, e.g., wheat, by fifty-seven per cent, cattle, by thirty-six, copper, by thirty-eight and Canadian exports generally by forty per cent. From 1897 to 1913, because of a conjuncture of favourable circumstances, Canada enjoyed great prosperity. The problem of repayment of principal and interest was just becoming acute when the first War and then the post-War boom postponed the day of reckoning. The result was that the Canadian economy was not accustomed to the contractions of the business cycle. In many respects Canada's first real depression occurred only in the 1930's and our economy was unfitted to stand the strain.

Within Canada herself the vulnerability of a staple economy showed itself in a different way. The prices of staples such as wheat, newsprint, base metals and so on are forced downwards in a depression much farther and faster than the prices of manufactured goods. This is true because the many consumers of finished products like food, clothing or newspapers are not likely to higgle over a difference of a cent in the price they pay for the article, even though in terms of percentage the saving may be considerable. The final consumer is inclined to keep on paying the usual price. Also the final processors being relatively few in number can hold up the price either because they agree among themselves to do so, or because no one wants to cut prices for fear of starting a "price war". Commonly these processors are protected by a tariff from competitors abroad who might otherwise undersell them.

On the other hand the wholesaler, manufacturer or importer buys in large amounts for resale and the difference of even a fraction of a cent makes a large profit or large loss to him. When business generally is poor, purchasers of raw materials for manufacture try to recoup their losses by bidding down the prices of staples. Producers of these basic commodities are unable to prevent the price being forced down because there are so many producers, and usually they are scattered among so many countries that agreement among them is impossible. In addition producers of staples typically have to meet large fixed expenses such as interest, taxes and freight. When the price of, say, wheat declines, producers must grow a larger number of bushels in order to meet these fixed charges which, of course, remain the same in terms of dollars. Thus in a depression, production of staples may actually increase and, if demand remains unchanged, the increase in production may force prices even lower than would otherwise have been the case. On the other hand manufacturers tend to maintain prices and, because the demand for their goods is less, they reduce output, throwing men out of work. In short, during a depression, producers in the staple industries suffer from low prices and a reduced standard of living but do not curtail output, i.e., there is no unemployment, whereas manufacturers follow the opposite course. There is therefore, a decided difference in the way in which the depression affects the staple producers selling in the world market, sometimes called the "exposed" industries, and the manufacturers or "protected" or "sheltered" industries. Both types of production suffer but they suffer in different ways.

To sum up, the Canadian economy was affected because of its unusual dependence on staples. Our vulnerability increased because of the unusual contraction in world trade, the reduction in lending abroad, the unprecedented decline in prices, the necessity of repaying heavy borrowings, and the differences of the incidence of the depression within the country. So long as the markets and prices of staples were good, Canada prospered. When staples could no longer be sold at profitable prices, economic problems became so acute that the Dominion, Provincial and Municipal Governments proved incapable of dealing with them effectively. Indeed the task was so enormous that the Governments could not follow a comprehensive policy of correction. Instead they had to adopt policies of expediency, of doing what the exigencies of the time seemed to require, or what the pressure of groups demanded.

The first effort, obviously, was to prevent suffering from hunger and cold. Private agencies did what they could but as the depression quickly deepened, Municipalities, then the Provinces and, by the autumn of 1930, the Federal Government had to lend their financial assistance. Most of the aid was in the form of direct relief, that is, cash payments, rent allowances, or the authority to purchase at public expense goods up to a certain value. In the dried out areas of the West direct relief had to be augmented by seed grain, feed for animals and other farm requirements so that farmers could plant their crops and eventually, if the weather were satisfactory, become self sustaining.

Late in 1930 there were about 470,000 persons on direct relief, a number which increased steadily to perhaps two million in 1933 and then gradually declined, though even after the outbreak of the second War there were still large numbers on the relief rolls. Of course the number on relief was much less than the number of the "unemployed", using that term in its proper sense, that is, the heads of families, individual persons and dependents over sixteen years of age (other than wives) presumably able and willing to work but for whom no jobs were available. In June, 1937, direct relief was provided for slightly over 930,000 persons in Canada of whom roughly twenty-seven per cent were farmers in the drought areas and their dependents, and about fifty-two per cent were dependents of urban workers, i.e., wives, children under sixteen, and aged persons. The "unemployed" as such numbered about 200,000 though this figure does not include a very considerable number of workers without jobs who were supported by friends or relatives, or their own savings, or by private charities. In any case the number of jobs needed was much less than the number on relief. Of course sustenance had to be given both to the unemployed and to their dependents. Between 1930 and 1937 Dominion, Provincial and Municipal Governments had spent not far short of one billion dollars on alleviating distress caused through drought and unemployment.

Assistance to the unemployed could not be confined to direct relief. When a man is out of a job for any length of time he begins to lose skill, morale, health and certainly his youth. Many men in their late 'fifties come to the stage where they can scarcely expect to hold down a steady job again, and little could be done to help them. On the other hand to assist the young in acquiring skill which it was hoped they might be able to use at some future time, an extensive system of youth training was begun, though not until 1937. Instruction was given in mining and forestry techniques, in all phases of agriculture, in motor mechanics, radio servicing, machine shop practice, carpentry and so on. Young women received instruction in commercial work, dressmaking, salesmanship and the like. The problem of a depression is not simply one of economic losses; it is one of human suffering. The solution is not simply one of sustenance; it is one of human rehabilitation.

A particularly serious aspect of the depression was the decline in construction because private individuals could see nothing to be gained from adding to plants which were even then being used at much less than capacity. To some extent the Government tried to offset the decline in building by private persons and corporations by increasing the construction of public buildings such as post-offices and schools, and by building highways, colonization roads and harbour improvements. This construction involved enormous expenditures of money and gave work to only a limited number of those on relief. If carried out on an extensive scale other disadvantages would have developed also, but in Canada the public works programme, though larger than in previous years, was still on a reasonably moderate scale.

As already indicated, some classes in the community were more adversely affected by the depression than others. To assist these groups, the Government tried to help bankrupt or semi-bankrupt firms get back in a position to carry on their businesses successfully by passing legislation to facilitate the re-organization of such concerns. To help farmers, some of the Provinces passed Moratorium Acts, and the Federal Government passed the Farmers' Creditors Arrangement Act. To facilitate the sale of farm products at prices and under conditions more satisfactory to the farmer, Marketing Acts were introduced. To help industrial workers, the tariff was increased. These efforts were of some help to the groups concerned but obviously failed to deal effectively with the fundamental problem of an economy based on the export of staples.

Because one of the essential difficulties in the 1930's was the contraction of foreign trade, the Government tried to enlarge markets for Canadian products in other countries. This was the basic purpose behind the Ottawa Agreements, and the treaties with the United States and other foreign nations. Prior to negotiating these agreements Canada had increased her protective tariff to a level higher than ever before with the object of keeping out foreign goods and encouraging their production in Canada. The paradox of asking other countries to buy more of our goods while we aimed to purchase less of theirs was typical of almost every other country in the world. Fundamentally, of course, world conditions were far too disturbed for action by a small country like Canada to be instrumental in freeing the barriers of international trade.

Another feature of depression was the decline, almost the complete cessation of capital investment. Business men refused to invest in new plants and equipment because they could not be reasonably sure that they would make a profit by so doing. The selling prices of their output were not high enough to cover costs and leave even a small profit. The Government tried to reduce costs by lowering interest rates. The appropriate mechanism for doing this was lacking in Canada and hence a central bank was established. Unfortunately low interest rates, even though accompanied by an offer to extend credit to all worth-while enterprises through the chartered banks, were not sufficient to induce investment. Business men were so discouraged about future prospects for profits that even negative interest, that is, requiring them to repay less than the principal, would probably not have led them to undertake capital expenditures. In part various governments themselves contributed to this pessimistic attitude. The cancellation of the Ontario power contracts, the technical repudiation of its debts by Alberta, which did not pay the principal amount of a bond issue when due though it continued to pay the interest on it, the threat of an arbitrary reduction of interest rates in Vancouver and elsewhere, these factors disturbed the security markets and led investors and business men to "sit tight". The paradoxical situation of governments pleading for investment, and then scaring it away by threatening repudiation or inflation, by increasing taxes or undertaking new social reforms, was more typical in the

United States than in Canada. The attitude of Canadian business men, however, is often more affected by actions of the American Government than by events in their own country.

On the whole the Government policy of low interest rates did not seem to exert much influence toward improving business conditions. Of course, once things began to pick up, once the business man started to recover confidence as he did about 1935 and again in 1938, low interest rates speeded up the process of recovery but in the depth of the depression they were of limited value. On the other hand government action, late though it was, helped the badly depressed building trades by making loans at low rates available for the construction of new homes and the renovation of old ones. Governments made no effort to reduce other business costs, notably wages, because of the opposition of numerous, strongly organized groups. In the main the Government had to wait for conditions in the world generally to improve so that a new relationship between costs and prices would occur and so that, with better prospects for profits, business would recover. Revival began in 1933 but it was so hesitant that the depression can be said to have lasted throughout the entire decade of the 1930's.

To conclude, the policies of the Government in dealing with the problem of the depression lacked comprehensiveness because no proper theoretical basis for action was available, for economists cannot agree on the cause or the causes of the cycle. Moreover government efforts seemed to lack reality. Canadian prosperity is very greatly dependent on foreign trade and is largely determined in world markets by conditions over which our Government has little control. It is difficult to prime the pump when other countries have the hold on the handle. Finally, and most important, government policies lacked consistency. Sometimes Ottawa was following one course of action, encouraging investment for example, while one or other of the Provincial Governments seemed to be doing the opposite. Some of the legislation of the Federal Government to deal with such matters as marketing, unemployment insurance and wages and hours was thrown out by the courts because the Provinces alone had jurisdiction over such affairs. The Dominion Government could not get the Provinces to work with it, nor was it legally able to do by itself all that it wished.

At the very time when constitutional difficulties were arising, the need for consistent action was becoming greater. This was true not merely because the depression generally was unusually severe, but because its regional incidence was unequal as already pointed out. Citizens in areas especially adversely affected by the depression looked with envy and not a little suspicion upon those in more favoured regions and the latter, in turn, suggested that a good many of the difficulties of the people in the depressed areas were due to their own extravagance in good times. Also, while some Provincial Governments were scarcely able to remain solvent, others were doing quite well financially. Finally the functions of government had changed greatly since Confederation. New tasks, especially the construction of highways and the provision of social services, came mainly under the Provinces whereas originally the more important tasks and therefore the greater taxing powers, had been under Dominion control. The Provinces, as a group, were expected to perform functions which they had no money to undertake.

Alberta, in particular, embarked on a novel financial programme. In 1935 Mr. William Aberhart, a Calgary school teacher who had attracted attention by his sermons over the air and at the Prophetic Bible Institute, was elected premier on a platform of Social Credit. This economic doctrine assumes that the cause of business depression is a deficiency of consumer purchasing power. To obtain the money necessary to take off the market all the goods which farms, factories, mines and forests need to sell in order to obtain full employment, the assets of the province were to be appraised and used as security for 'scrip'. This scrip could be tendered in payment of all debts, goods and services. The scrip would bear a tax of two per cent per week. The tax would keep the scrip circulating rapidly since no one would want to have scrip on hand at the end of the week when the tax was payable. Evidence that the tax had been paid was shown by stamps which were bought at Government offices and stuck on the scrip. In its cruder form Social Credit promised a dividend of $25 a month per person. The specific schemes varied from time to time but essentially 'fountain pen money' would prevent business depressions. Neither the public debt nor commodity prices were to be allowed to rise. Individual enterprise and private property would be preserved.

Whatever the merits of Social Credit may have been, the courts took the view that the legislation ran counter to the Dominion's exclusive jurisdiction over currency, banking, and interest under the British North America Act. The Dominion overruled some of the legislation by using its obsolescent but perfectly valid privilege of disallowing provincial laws. Meanwhile the Social Credit party was torn between the radicals who wanted to circumvent the courts and the Federal Government in introducing Social Credit, and the Conservative wing led by Mr. Aberhart who was ready to give business-like administration to the Province's affairs generally while looking forward to Social Credit as an ultimate objective.

In brief, during the depression serious political strains developed between the various economic regions of the country, and the financial relationships between the Dominion and the Provinces needed readjustment. Accordingly the Government appointed the Commission whose chief recommendations have already been examined. The significant matter is that the depression revealed the lack of integration in the Canadian economy. In part this centrifugal tendency was a reflection of the fact that since 1925, our economic efforts had been spread over a number of different staples rather than being concentrated so heavily on one as was the case before the first War. There was less agreement on the objectives of national policy than when the West was being developed. At all events the depression showed the need for a central government with powers adequate to handle the economic problems which the country has to face. One of the most difficult problems of Canada is how to unify the economic regions into one economic organism. This problem is paralleled in the political and cultural fields by the need for a greater spirit of unity and the development of a distinctive Canadian nationality. The problems of the depression quickly shrank into insignificance upon the outbreak of hostilities in 1939.

By the 1950's the problems of the depression of the 1930's seemed remote and perhaps unreal. Despite brief recessions, between 1939 and 1959 Gross National Product at current market prices rose from 5.7 billion to about 34 billion dollars. However, one has to take account of the rise in prices which occurred during this period, and the growth in population through natural increase, immigration, and the entry of Newfoundland. Even so, national income grew spectacularly. In terms of the average purchasing power of a dollar over the years 1939–55, per capita income rose from roughly $860 in 1939 to about $1,400 in 1955. In other words, the average Canadian was at least 60 per cent better off in 1955 than in 1939. He was also working fewer hours per week, in farming 55 instead of 59, in business 40 in place of 45, and in industry about 40 compared with over 50. Broadly speaking, during the years 1945–59 population grew at the rate of 2.7 per cent compounded per annum and national income in dollars of constant purchasing power at 3.5 per cent.

Unfortunately the tempo of business tended to slow down after 1957, especially if the growth in population and the rise in the price level is taken into account. In some years crops were poor, construction declined moderately, and the rate of industrial expansion in Britain and the United States levelled out somewhat. Unemployment at one time rose to about 10 per cent of the labour force and throughout the period there seemed to be a "hard core" of unemployed, chiefly among unskilled workers.

SELECTED READINGS

CASSIDY, H. M., *Unemployment and Relief in Ontario*, Toronto, 1932.

HOOD, WM. C., *Financing Economic Activity in Canada*, Ottawa, 1958 (A study prepared for the Gordon Commission).

LOGAN, H. A., and INMAN, M. K., *A Social Approach to Economics*, Toronto, 1939, pp. 429-74.

NATIONAL EMPLOYMENT COMMISSION, *Final Report*, Ottawa, 1938.

RICHTER, L., ed., *Canada's Unemployment Problem*, Toronto, 1939.

TAYLOR, K. W., "Problems of rigidity in the Canadian economic structure" in Innis, H. A. and Plumptre, A. F. W., ed., *The Canadian Economy and its Problems*, Toronto, 1934.

ROYAL COMMISSION ON DOMINION-PROVINCIAL RELATIONS, *Report*, Book 1, Ottawa, 1940.

SAFARIAN, A. E., *The Canadian Economy in the Great Depression*, Toronto, 1959.

20

The Wartime Economy

DURING the first nine months after the outbreak of war in September, 1939, Canadians considered their role would be relatively limited. The industrial and manpower resources of the British Commonwealth and France greatly exceeded the war potential of Germany. Their command of the sea was complete and the Maginot Line along the Franco-German border seemed impregnable. The allies felt that, given time, they would starve Germany into submission without the appalling loss of life and waste of physical resources associated with the first World War. Canada would supply foodstuffs and munitions, defend her own territory and shipping against sneak attacks by enemy submarines, and provide relatively limited numbers of men for navy, army, and air force. Otherwise the Canadian economy would not be drastically altered.

Within a few months after war was declared, many of the approximately 400,000 workers who were reported as unemployed were absorbed into industry or the armed services. Taxes on luxuries, ordinary incomes, and excess profits were increased or levied for the first time. The value of the Canadian dollar declined to about 91 cents in terms of United States money thus adding to the difficulty of meeting interest on debts owed by Canadians in the United States. But broadly speaking, economic conditions were not greatly changed from what they were in the last years of the depression.

The concept of a 'limited war' was completely out-moded after the fall of France and the Low Countries in June, 1940. Between that date and the entry of Russia and the United States into the conflict over a year later, Britain and the Commonwealth stood alone against Nazi Germany and Fascist Italy. The enemy overran all Europe (except Switzerland) from the Mediterranean to the North Sea and from the Pyrenees to beyond the Vistula. Later, enemy troops conquered Norway and north Africa. With shocking suddenness the 'phony war' turned into an all-out conflict. On the economic front the sole objective of the nation was to enlarge and re-direct its human and material resources toward winning the war. Every policy had to be appraised in the light of this ultimate end.

Men and women were vitally needed in the armed forces and in munition plants; they were required to raise food for ourselves and our allies; and they had to produce a wide variety of consumers' goods which civilians wanted to purchase because now that the depression was apparently over, they had plenty of money to spend. The labour force was increased by young people who left school earlier than they otherwise would have, by older men who kept on the job rather than retiring, and by married women who worked outside the home. The under-employed took on full-time work whereas formerly they had worked intermittently on farms, in lumber woods, in fishing and in odd jobs, or had been supported by relatives. The labour force, including military personnel, grew rapidly from 4,600,000 in October, 1941, and then to 5,100,000 in early 1943, remaining at about this figure until the end of the war in Europe.

By July, 1942, shortage of manpower became a problem. Workers in essential industries like transportation were frozen to their jobs, that is, they were forbidden to seek employment elsewhere. Other workers were directed away from non-essential industries such as the production of luxuries or fancy packages for goods and toward war industries such as aircraft or munitions. Though the navy and air force got all the men they needed by voluntary enlistments, conscription was required to keep the army up to strength. At the peak, the number of men and women in the fighting forces exceeded 784,000. Since skill was just as important as numbers, intensive vocational training courses were provided both in civilian industry and in the armed services.

Some areas increased in population while others declined. The Maritimes enjoyed full employment for the first time in twenty years. Industrial cities in Ontario and Quebec grew by leaps and bounds. The Prairies lost population but Vancouver and Victoria expanded. The numbers of the gainfully occupied in manufacturing nearly doubled between 1939 and 1945 but declines were shown in agriculture and in mining. Living accommodation was hard to get in the vicinity of army camps, air-force stations, seaports and munition plants. For a time the construction industry was allowed to hire as many men as it could get. By the end of the war, however, the shortage of lumber and plumbing, and the virtual completion of war plants and military training centres lead the Government to cut back its building programme and release men for other, more important jobs.

The increased demand for labour would normally have resulted in very much higher wages and heightened the possibility of strikes by employees who felt their incomes were not rising fast enough. Early in the war the Government set up a National War Labour Board to deal with wages in war plants and shipyards and later in all industry. In 1941 the Government froze wages to their prevailing levels. It permitted increases only if the Labour Board decided they were necessary to correct discrepancies. Some firms had granted wage increases between the outbreak of war and the imposition of controls. Other enterprises had the same wage rates when controls were applied as they had in 1939. In consequence wage rates varied from company to company for work of the same degree of skill. By adjusting some wages the Board brought about substantial uniformity within the same trade but kept wages generally under the ceiling set by the Government.

When wage controls were imposed, the prices of goods and of services such as rents, transportation tolls, motion picture admissions and electric rates were also frozen. Stability in living costs would remove one of the reasons for labour unions demanding higher pay. Nevertheless the Government provided that wages of persons receiving less than $3,000 per annum were to be raised 25 cents a week for every rise of one percentage point in the cost of living index. In other words it said that if it failed to 'keep the lid' on prices, wages would move up more or less concurrently with the cost of living. While labour would be protected against a marked rise in prices, in the long run it could not gain by higher wages because they would merely force up living costs. At the same time business men saw that higher selling prices would eventually involve heavier wages and higher production costs. Of course to the extent that increases in wages and other costs lagged behind rises in selling prices, business might gain but high rates of tax on excess profits would quickly bring net profits back to their previous level. Thus due to the inter-relationship of wages, prices and taxation, both business men and labour leaders were discouraged from trying to raise either selling prices or wage rates.

From time to time organized labour claimed that the official cost of living index was unsound. It did not adequately take into account the importance of rent and other services in the budgets of wage-earners. Also it did not properly recognize differences in the relative rate of increase in living costs in different parts of the country. In any event since the bonus was paid at the same weekly rate to all employees coming within the regulations, it was more significant percentage-wise to poorly paid than to well-paid employees. Hence it reduced the range between the wage rates of various classes of employees, and so had a permanent influence on the wage structure.

Organized labour pledged itself to avoid strikes for the duration of the war and to increase production. Notwithstanding this promise and the official conciliation machinery set up by the Government, serious strikes over wage rates and union recognition occurred in steel, aluminum and coal. The Government gave labour in war plants and shipyards the right to organize and to bargain collectively with their employers. Total union membership doubled during the war and spread out from the pre-war fields of transportation, coal-mining and clothing manufacture to the automotive, aircraft and general industrial fields.

Wartime control of the prices of commodities and services was necessary to keep down the cost of the war. If prices had sky-rocketed, the expense of providing each fighting man with food, quarters, clothing and arms would have reached fantastic amounts. Once prices begin to rise rapidly, cost of production increases too. This results in still higher prices and pressure for more wages. Thus after inflation gets well under way, prices spiral upward.

When goods are dear, only the wealthy can afford to buy them while the poor have to do without. This creates unrest and lowers civilian morale which is so important in winning a war. Some workers who are better organized or more aggressive than others get wage increases while people in other occupations get none. Merchants and manufacturers who have money invested in stocks of goods receive exhorbitant profits. Soon a sense of injustice pervades the community. To forestall these difficulties, the Government set up a Wartime Prices and Trade Board even before Canada had formally declared war.

During the first two years of its existence the Prices Board allocated scarce commodities like sugar, wool, leather and strategic minerals but did not otherwise interfere with the economy. Prices rose only slowly because there were surpluses of many commodities. Supplies of other goods could be easily increased for not all workers were employed and industry and agriculture had unused productive capacity. After April, 1941, however, prices started to soar. People had plenty of money to spend because almost everyone capable of working had a job at good wages. Factories and farms were concentrating on meeting war needs and could not devote resources to making goods for civilian consumption. The conjunction of buoyant spending power and the comparatively limited amounts of goods coming on the domestic market pushed up prices. To reduce the pressure, the Government drew off purchasing power by levying high taxes and encouraging people voluntarily to subscribe to Government loans.

Then in October, 1941, the Government ordered that goods and services might not be sold at prices higher than those prevailing in the period between September

15 and October 11, 1941. The Prices Board was directed to administer this sweeping regulation. By various devices it kept costs of production down. For instance, it forbade double-breasted suits and cuffs on men's trousers. It simplified packages and eliminated duplication in deliveries to households and retail establishments. It also restricted credit to consumers in order to prevent increases in the costs of operating retail stores and discourage the purchase of consumers' durable goods. The Prices Board rationed sugar, tea, coffee, preserves, butter, meat and gasoline in order to distribute them more equitably among the populace and keep consumption within the amounts available.

Because other countries were slower or less successful than Canada in applying price ceilings, the costs of imported goods tended to rise. Accordingly many imports had to be restricted or prohibited entirely. Essential imports like raw cotton, sugar, petroleum, tea, coffee, dried and citrus fruits had to be subsidized. Cash subsidies were paid on dairy products, canned fruits and vegetables, shoes, soap, synthetic rubber, and other items. Eventually these subsidies cost about $25 million dollars annually but the money was well spent considering that runaway inflation would have upset the entire war effort and cost infinitely more. At first the Prices Board was sparing in its authorizations of price increases on individual commodities. It feared that any rise, however minor, would provide a precedent for other demands. Later it approved increases on meats, potatoes, fresh fruit, and poultry principally on the ground that prices of these goods had been frozen at such low levels that producers would not raise them for the market.

The operations of the Wartime Prices and Trade Board reached into every corner of Canadian economic life. The official cost of living index (1935-39 = 100) stood at 115.8 when prices and wages were frozen. By May, 1945, it had risen to only 119.0. No other belligerent was as successful as Canada in holding prices down. The work of the Prices Board and the support given to it by all segments of the community must be included among our major war-time achievements.

On agriculture the war had far-reaching effects. Our pre-war markets in Germany, Italy and the vast areas of enemy occupied territory disappeared. On account of the need for conserving shipping space, British demands shifted from wheat, fresh beef, and apples to concentrated goods like bacon, dried eggs, condensed milk and cheese. As family incomes within Canada rose, the domestic demand for milk, eggs, and meat rose too. Farmers especially in Western Canada turned from wheat to hogs and dairy products. In 1939 sale of wheat provided Prairie farmers with 63 per cent of their cash income, in 1942 with only 30 per cent. In Alberta for two war years cash receipts from hogs were greater than from wheat.

The Government subsidized farmers to take land out of cereals and use it for pasture. Soil which had drifted during the drought would be conserved and the output of wheat for which overseas demand had declined would be reduced. By paying part of the freight rate, the Government assisted the movement of coarse grains from Western Canada to the East and British Columbia where they could be used for feeding hogs and dairy cattle. The Government bonused farmers for producing butter and cheese. Agricultural subsidies cost as much as $100 million in some years but were justified by the increases in output on the one hand and the maintenance of the price ceiling on the other.

Some farm prices had risen before overall price control was instituted. Other prices were allowed to rise by the Prices Board in order to induce farmers to increase their output of essential foods. Throughout the second World War the agricultural population feared a repetition of the price collapse which had occured in 1920. Sometimes they wished they could get rid of price control so that they could make enough money to withstand any post-war drop in prices. Yet they saw the value of price control in the overall policy of the nation and realized that while the ceiling on prices kept down their profits, it also held down their costs of production and of living. Moreover farmers are among the most patriotic groups in the nation and so they supported price control as loyally as any other class.

Between 1939 and 1945 the output of pork, evaporated milk, barley and seed crops doubled and the supply of cheese, eggs, poultry, meat, and most vegetables rose by 50 per cent or more. These and other increases were accomplished by about 25 per cent fewer full-time farmers and without any appreciable increase in machinery. The long-established movement of man from farms to cities was accelerated by the demand for labour in war industries. Moreover, enlistments from rural English-speaking areas were heavy. In consequence, agriculture suffered from shortages of labour especially during the harvest. The Government encouraged those who remained on farms to work harder. It also arranged for students, urban residents and the Japanese who were removed from the Pacific Coast areas for strategic reasons to help out on farms during seasonal emergencies. Eventually the Government had to defer enlistments of *bona fide* farm workers. Relatively little farm machinery was manufactured during the war because the implement plants made tanks, guns and parts of ships. The existing farm implements had to be used more intensively or shared among several neighbours.

Canada's munition production was slow to get under way because of the attitude of the Government and the people during the 'phony war'. The 'shooting war' threw the machinery into high gear. Before long aircraft, ships, guns and rifles of all types, armoured fighting vehicles, explosives and machine tools poured out in a steady stream. A synthetic rubber plant at Sarnia, Ontario, was established in record time and an enormous power project developed at Shipshaw on the Saguenay. Although Canadians lacked previous experience, our factories turned out radar equipment, anti-submarine detection devices, machine tools of many kinds, and optical instruments like gunsights and range-finders. Canadian scientists co-operated with those of Great Britain and the United States in 'splitting the atom'. The mining of uranium at Great Bear Lake and a huge plant at Chalk River, 100 miles west of Ottawa were further contributions of Canada to the atom bomb. Only about 30 per cent of Canada's output of war equipment was used by Canadian troops; the rest of our production went to many countries, chiefly Great Britain, the United States, China and Russia.

Most of the goods were manufactured by private industrialists working under contract with the Government. Nonetheless, several publicly-owned corporations or crown companies were formed to operate steamships, erect houses for war workers, and to produce and distribute artificial rubber, wool, scientific instruments, machine tools, uranium and so forth. The munitions programme had to be synchronized with price control, the manpower situation, and the supply of scarce materials. A huge organization, the Department of Munitions and Supply, was created to run what was sometimes called the industrial front.

Because the economies of Canada and the United States are closely interconnected even in peace-time, it became necessary to take steps to prevent the two countries competing with each other for scarce goods during the war and overlapping their productive efforts. Before the United States declared war in December, 1941, many of her plants were working below capacity and were glad to accept orders from Canada. Later, as the physical and human resources of both countries came to be used more fully, a scramble for scarce supplies with resultant price increases seemed likely to develop. To avoid this interference with the common effort toward victory, a number of joint boards were set up and channels of daily, almost hourly, communication between 'opposite numbers' in Ottawa and Washington were cleared. Before the war was over, production authorities in both capitals worked as a well-trained team.

When a nation is at war, capital tends to be transferred to non-belligerent countries which are apparently safer. This flight makes it difficult for the belligerent to meet its obligations abroad such as remitting interest on past loans and paying for raw materials which must be brought in to make aircraft, ships and other implements of war. Consequently foreign exchange, which represents claims by citizens of the belligerent on the currencies of foreign countries, must be conserved for the purchase of things which are really needed to win the war. It should not be wasted on luxuries that people in a country at war can do without.

What is more, foreign exchange must be acquired abroad. This can be done only by exporting goods and services to other countries or by loans. Although any export will add to the amount of foreign exchange owned by Canadians, some exports could be produced in Canada only by diverting labour and capital from producing munitions, military uniforms, or fighter planes. Other exports might deprive civilians within Canada of articles needed for their health and comfort. Still other exports will fit well into the war programme. They do not divert resources from essential needs because the belligerent is an efficient producer of them, and they will provide foreign exchange which can be used directly to further the war effort. In a word, the effective prosecution of a war necessitates some control of the exports and imports of goods and of stocks and bonds, and some supervision of foreign exchange balances.

To deal with these and related problems the Government created the Foreign Exchange Control Board. Canadians were required to obtain permits from this Board before they could transfer goods or securities across Canada's borders. Despite the Board's efforts, the problem of foreign exchange soon became acute. Prior to the war, Canada typically had a favourable balance of trade (value of exports in excess of value of physical imports) with Great Britain and an unfavourable balance with the United States. Through the complicated mechanism of foreign exchange, Canada was able to use her surplus of pounds sterling to meet her deficit of American dollars. After war broke out, Britain needed all the United States dollars she could lay her hands on in order to pay for her purchase of military supplies and raw materials in the United States. Indeed, to add to her American balances, the British Government took over most of the investments in American companies owned by residents of the United Kingdom. Britain compensated her own citizens by giving them British Government bonds for their American securities. Then she sold the securities in New York. With the dollars so obtained, she paid for the war supplies she had purchased.

Eventually Britain used up almost all her holdings of American stocks and bonds. Thereafter she would have found it nearly impossible to buy goods made in the United States and her war effort and the cause of democracy would have suffered. Early in 1941 the United States arranged to transfer 50 over-age destroyers to Britain for convoy duty in exchange for 99-year leases on bases in Newfoundland, Bermuda and other British colonies in the Western Hemisphere. Later the United States worked out a scheme of lend-lease. War supplies could be transferred from the United States to any of the countries fighting against Nazi aggression. These supplies might have to be returned to the United States after the war was over but as the post-war arrangements were never clearly formulated by American officials, it was assumed that the goods were part of the American contribution to the common war effort. In any event this lend-lease arrangement solved the British problem of American exchange.

Inasmuch as Britain needed American dollars so badly, she could not allow Canada to convert her surplus of pounds into dollars and so make up for her unfavourable balance in New York. Britain's action was especially understandable before the introduction of lend-lease. Later it was justified by her natural pride in being able to pay in cash for as many American goods as she could and by the fact that lend-lease used by Britain ate into the amounts available to other countries. Technically Canada was eligible for lend-lease. Some goods such as parts for planes were acquired by Britain in the States under lend-lease, brought into Canada, incorporated into aircraft made in this country, and then re-exported to Britain. This kind of lend-lease was solely on British account. Canada did not herself take advantage of lend-lease. Instead she paid in cash for everything she bought in the United States during the war. She preferred not to use funds when other countries seemed to have greater need of them and she did not want to store up possible financial difficulties with the United States after the war was over.

At first Canada transferred her reserves of gold to New York to pay for American goods. But Canada's purchases of essential war supplies and of consumers' goods not produced at home grew so rapidly that the gold reserves approached exhaustion. To prevent this, a special excise tax was placed on goods from non-Empire countries and the importation of goods such as electric refrigerators prohibited. Canadians were not allowed to take money out of Canada for travelling in the United States except for reasons of health or business and then only under carefully controlled conditions. Conversely American tourists were urged to come to Canada and thus add to our supply of United States dollars. The Canadian Government encouraged the output of newsprint and the mining of gold because both articles are sold chiefly in the United States. Thus in various ways the supply of American dollars owned by Canadians was increased and their use restricted to the purchase of goods which could make a direct contribution to the successful prosecution of the war.

Though these efforts greatly eased the situation, they did not solve it. Early in 1941 President F. D. Roosevelt and Prime Minister King signed an agreement at Hyde Park whereby the United States bought from Canada

aluminum, ships and certain kinds of shells in which
Canadian output was far in advance of immediate anticipated requirements and American production was
below her current needs. Some Americans were surprised
that Canada was in a position to supply the United States
with manufactured goods for her war effort. The Hyde
Park Agreement was of fundamental importance in helping Canada solve her war-time problem of foreign exchange and, of course, the Americans received physical
assets for the money they advanced. Despite the Agreement, the restrictions on travel and the importation of
goods by Canadians could not be relaxed.

As explained, even before the war Canada had exported
more to Britain than she imported from that country.
Her exports grew tremendously during the war since
Canada possessed foodstuffs, nickel, lead, copper, and a
variety of other materials of strategic importance. Moreover many ships, aircraft, guns and the like were being
made in Canada under orders from the United Kingdom.
At the same time Britain was spending so much of her
effort directly on the war that she could not expand her
pre-war volume of exports to Canada without cutting
down on the amount of labour and capital which she was
using so nobly to defend herself and carry the war to the
enemy. In short, Britain's need for Canadian dollars
grew while her ability to export goods and services to
earn those dollars declined.

At first, the British Government used the securities of
Canadian companies, railways, and governments which
were owned by her citizens to pay for some of the goods
she bought in Canada. In other words, she sold securities
in Montreal to pay for Canadian goods just as she sold
stocks and bonds in New York to pay for supplies bought
in the United States. But before long, the British had

sold substantially all their Canadian securities, and other arrangements were necessary. For a time the Canadian Government bought up the Canadian securities formerly owned by British subjects. Then she sold these securities for about $800 million in New York, thus acquiring American dollars. The major part, about $700 million, of the accumulated sterling balances in London, that is, the excess in the value of goods and services exported by Canada to Britain over the value of goods and services bought by Canada from Britain, was offset by a Canadian loan to the United Kingdom. In effect, the Canadian Government told the British they need not send $700 million worth of goods and services to Canada to pay this country for what we had already sent to Britain and had not yet been paid for. After the war Britain would repay Canada but in the meantime the Dominion would pay the Canadian exporters.

Later on, the Canadian Government made an outright gift of one billion dollars to the United Kingdom for the purchase of foodstuffs and war supplies within Canada. Still later it loaned money to Britain with the understanding that plans for repaying the loan were to be worked out after hostilities ceased. Subsequently this arrangement, which went under the title of Mutual Aid, was extended to Russia, China, France, Australia, New Zealand, and India. Mutual Aid was the Canadian equivalent of American lend-lease. The total of Mutual Aid, about $1,800 million, exceeded the amount of lend-lease if differences in population and in the values of the Canadian and United States dollars are taken into account.

Canada's war finance is a simple story of stiff taxation, huge victory loans, and mounting public debt. Early in the war the Government announced a pay-as-you-go policy. So far as possible, the cost of the war was to be met out of current tax revenues. The cost of modern mechanized warfare was so heavy, however, that in the latter years of the struggle tax receipts equalled only about half the expenditures. The balance had to be raised by borrowing. By March, 1946, when demobilization was reasonably complete, the debt of the Federal Government, direct and guaranteed, stood at $17.3 billion compared with less than $5 billion at the outbreak. In May, 1947, the Government announced that the total monetary cost of the Second World War to Canada was about $20 billion or $1,688 per capita. Pensions to nearly 100,000 veterans were running at roughly $35 million dollars annually. Experience after the First World War indicates that the cost of pensions rises as veterans become older and reaches a peak fifteen or twenty years after hostilities cease. The cost of pensions plus interest on war debt will raise the 1947 estimate.

Taxes were imposed on all luxuries, on transportation tickets and long distance telephone calls, on the sale of hydro-electric power, and so on. The Federal Government entered fields of taxation previously used entirely by the provinces such as succession duties and gasoline taxes. It laid very heavy taxes on excess profits, i.e., those in excess of what the companies had earned in the period just before the war. The purpose of excess profits taxation was partly to ensure that no one made exhorbitant profits out of the sacrifice of men on the field of battle. Rates of taxation on personal incomes were increased materially. In the case of the single men, only the first $600 was exempt from tax compared with $1,200 in 1939. On a gross income of $3,000 per annum, a single person paid $104 before the war and $824 in 1943. On an income of $10,000 the corresponding figures for persons without dependents were $946 and $4,312. The general sales tax remained at its 1939 level of 8 per cent throughout the war but high taxes were levied on specified commodities. For example, 30 per cent was charged on chewing gum and candy, 35 per cent on luggage and handbags, and 25 per cent on cameras, film, radios, phonographs, electrical goods, clocks, watches and jewellery. The tax per cigarette was raised from four-tenths of a cent to one cent, and on toilet soaps and cosmetics from 10 to 25 per cent. All these rates were in addition to the eight per cent levied on substantially all goods except foods.

Gross national product, which is the estimated value of all goods and services produced by Canadians, rose from about $5.5 billions in 1939 to $11.7 billion in 1945. Since these figures are stated in the prices prevailing during the years in question, 1945 data have to be reduced by about 20 per cent to take account of rises in prices and wages and make it more strictly comparable with the 1939 figure. Broadly speaking, during the war, the Government took in taxes and borrowing half the national income. Yet the amount remaining in the hands of the public for spending on consumers' goods of all kinds was large enough to permit a definite rise in the standard of living. Work was easy to get, prices were held down, and on the whole Canadians were better off in a material sense than they were in 1939.

Disputes between provinces and the Federal Government which had been prominent in the late 1930's shrank in importance during the war. In time of real or apprehended emergency by virtue of its general power under the British North America Act of passing laws for the "peace, order and good government of Canada", the Government in Ottawa may legally regulate wages, hours, prices and other matters. Normally these and similar questions come solely within the jurisdiction of the Provinces because they are included under the section of the Act reserving to the Provinces 'property and civil rights within the Province'. Before the war the Provinces had been getting a large portion of their revenues from taxes on gasoline and profits on the sale of intoxicants. During the war the Federal Government rationed gasoline and took steps to cut down the sale of liquor. Its action though desirable in the national interest, reduced provincial revenues. To compensate the Provinces for their loss in income, the Dominion paid them additional subsidies. The Provinces, in their turn, agreed not to raise their tax rates. Many citizens had enough difficulty paying the heavy taxes levied by the Dominion without being required to pay taxes on the same income to the provinces. Notwithstanding the country's preoccupation with the war, it did not neglect social security. As already explained, the Federal Government set up an unemployment insurance scheme in 1942 and three years later began to pay children's allowances.

The conduct of the war on the economic front involved the integration of a number of different policies—the allocation of manpower, wage and price control, the settlement of labour disputes, increased production of foodstuffs, the munitions programme, foreign exchange control, taxation, borrowing money, and so forth. Any description of the overall effort tends to create a feeling of orderliness which was far from existing in practice. While the war was being fought at home on farms and in factories, with price control and with taxes, by governments, labour unions and business men, it was also being fought in Europe, Africa, the Far East, on land, on sea, and in the air, by diplomats, and by preventing strategic war materials from reaching the enemy either directly or by way of normal trade channels through neutral countries. Disaster or victory abroad inevitably had their effect on the morale of the Canadian people. The long controversy over conscription for overseas active service was another disturbing influence. At times it appeared that the country was tottering uncertainly from one crisis to another. But always, though sometimes apparently more by good luck than good management, the immediate difficulty was solved and the nation moved on to greater efforts and to final victory.

The ultimate results were most impressive. Canada emerged from the war more unified in spirit than anyone had believed possible when war broke out. Among the Allied Nations she had the third largest navy and was fourth in air power. In 1939 she had virtually no physical facilities for producing naval ships, aircraft, tanks, heavy guns, optical instruments, machine tools, and a host of other articles. During the war Canada became the world's second largest exporter having shipped abroad enormous quantities of base metals, lumber, foodstuffs, weapons and a multitude of other goods for the use of our own servicemen and women and for the civilian population and the armed forces of our allies. Mutual Aid alone represented a remarkable achievement for a nation of thirteen million people. All in all, Canada had carried a full load in attaining victory over the Axis.

SELECTED READINGS

CURRIE, A. W., "Canada—Economic and Political" in Yust, W., ed., *Ten Eventful Years*, Chicago, 1947, vol. I, pp. 512-22.

PARKINSON, J. F., *Canadian War Economics*, Toronto, 1941.

SMITH, J. M., *Canadian Economic Growth and Development from 1939 to 1955*, Ottawa, 1957 (A study prepared for the Gordon Commission).

WADE, MASON, *The French-Canadian Outlook*, New York, 1946.

21

The Present Economy

WHILE Canadians were proud of what they had done during the War, they were rather dismayed by the problems of peace. They realized that modern war creates more difficulties than it solves and that two world wars within a generation stand as a terrible condemnation of our so-called civilization. Consequently Canada entered with high hopes into world organizations like the United Nations which were designed to bring peace to a weary world. She was also prepared to co-operate with other countries in raising the standard of living of backward lands and in freeing the barriers to international trade.

Within Canada people were well fed and well clothed but many were inadequately housed. They wanted automobiles, refrigerators and other consumer durable goods which for several years they had been unable to buy freely. Our farms and factories had not been damaged by bombing nor had they been ravaged by modern tank and artillery warfare. They were, however, producing for some markets which had disappeared or changed. Warships, torpedos, rifles and uniforms were no longer needed but the semi-starved population of Europe were nearly desperate for food and lacked the money to pay for it. During six years of war Canada had become relatively highly industrialized, the numbers gainfully occupied in manufacturing having grown from 652,000 to 1,162,000, or from 31 to 41 per cent of the non-agricultural wage and salary recipients. In many lines Canada could produce far more than her own requirements. To maintain her industrial position, she would have to sell abroad. In doing so, she would face intense competition from the United States and eventually Britain, continental Europe and Japan. Every other major war had been followed by the collapse of prices and by unemployment. Everyone feared that the course of economic development after the Second World War would follow the typical pattern.

Even before the end of hostilities, the Government had declared "unequivocally its adoption of a high and stable level of employment and income, and thereby higher standards of living, as a major aim of Government policy". The Government's plan was to give the widest possible scope to private enterprise and individual initiative. But it also intended to regulate and direct the economy so that everyone would have the opportunity of working for fair wages, so that none would be impoverished during periods of ill health, old age or involuntary unemployment, and so that the standard of living in all parts of Canada would rise steadily. Full employment would make it possible for the Government to derive from taxes enough revenue to finance unemployment insurance, old age pensions, family allowances, hospitalization and other social services which the public now demand. People who are periodically unemployed through no fault of their own are susceptible to the blandishment of dictators. Thus reasonably full employment is basic to the continuance of economic well-being, social welfare, and political freedom.

Now in a country like Canada employment is the result of three factors—consumer spending, capital investment, and exports. In 1946 (data for 1961 are in brackets) consumers had roughly $8.9 ($24.3) billion to spend or save after they had paid nearly $800 ($2,500) million in income taxes, succession duties, and miscellaneous direct taxes. Consumer disposable income was derived from a number of sources: wages and salaries, 55 (65) per cent; military pay and allowances, 3 (2) per cent; net income from farms, i.e., the value of farm products which are sold by farmers or consumed by them and their families, less the cost of seed, tractor fuel, agricultural machinery, taxes, and the like, 11 (3) per cent; net income of non-farm unincorporated businesses such as retail stores, barber shops, and service stations owned by individuals, 11 (8) per cent; interest, dividends, and net rental income of individuals, 8 (10) per cent; and transfer payments, e.g., old age pensions, family allowances and unemployment insurance but not interest on government bonds, 12 (12) per cent.

The income received by individuals is used in a variety of ways. As already explained, in 1946 (1961) about 8 (9) per cent went to the government in various direct taxes. Individuals saved roughly 9 (5) per cent of their incomes. They spent the rest on non-durable goods, mainly food, clothing, fuel, and tobacco, 50 (43) per cent; on durables like houses, radios, motor-boats, automobiles, and refrigerators, 8 (10) per cent; and, finally, on services approximately 27 (34) per cent. The service industry includes those who work as barbers, hairdressers, actors, musicians, lawyers, medical doctors, teachers, etc.

In addition to the savings made by individuals, corporations save large sums. As a rule they do not pay out all their net earnings as dividends. They reinvest these retained earnings in the business, along with the annual allowances for depreciation. Moreover, governments add to the nation's capital, that is, to its fixed assets which are used in further production. Instead of paying out all their current revenue for interest, old age pensions, national defence, and a host of other things, they put money in highways, schools, harbours, airports, and public buildings of all sorts. Sometimes, they borrow money for these capital works.

Although governments use their money in various ways and tax away some of the potential spending power of consumers, in the last analysis it is the individual Canadian who decides what he will do with his money. In conjunction with other Canadians, he determines what segments of the economy will thrive and what ones will shrivel in importance. Indeed, if consumers as a group slow down their purchases, they may precipitate a business depression. If they step up their rate of buying, they will encourage recovery and may even, under certain conditions, touch off an inflationary boom. Consequently, it is important to understand the factors affecting the disposition of personal income. The elements which have a bearing on the size or total amount of personal disposable income will be discussed later.

In the first place, governments have an influence. They determine how much they will collect in taxes from year to year. A government agency, the Bank of Canada, through its control of the money market can ease or tighten up on credit. In this way it can stimulate or discourage consumers from buying on the instalment plan and influence the level of employment, of prices and of the export trade.

The rate of personal saving is related to whether or not the individual is confident he will have a job next week or next year, whether his family is young or grown up, whether he is just starting to work, has reached his maximum earning power, or has retired, and whether he works for an organization which has a compulsory pension plan. Most of all, perhaps, his rate of saving hinges on whether he is by nature thrifty or improvident.

Personal spending on goods is, in large part, set by the same factors as those just mentioned. Each family decides how it will spend the family income, or at least what remains of it after the government has collected its taxes. Some families like expensive foods, flashy clothes, the latest model car, and the most pretentious house in the block. Others are not so materialistic. Some consumers are suspectible to the blandishments of salesmen and the subtle appeals of advertisers. Some people want the latest of everything and manufacturers appeal to them by bringing out both new products, such as television and hi-fi sets, and new models of existing products. Without these innovations our economy would tend to stagnate. In short, people vary in their tastes but a reasonably high level of consumer spending is necessary to a high level of prosperity.

There is, however, an important difference between personal spending on durable and non-durable goods. As a rule, the purchase of durables may be more easily postponed than the buying of food, clothing, and the like. Therefore, in so far as business prosperity hinges on the level of consumer spending on durables, postponement of these purchases may slow down the rate of recovery. Besides, most families find it easier to spend a lot of money on electrical appliances, household furniture, and phonograph records than to get rid of the same amount of money on new clothes and fancier foods. Hence, expenditures on non-durables fluctuate more than spending on durables. This partly accounts for the swings in the business cycle.

As for consumer spending on services, it seems clear that Canadians are spending an increasing proportion of their incomes on professional and amateur sports, vacations, medical and dental care, and so forth. It is not likely that variations in the total amount of these expenditures from one year to another are sufficiently large to have much of an effect on the course of the business cycle or the general level of employment.

In 1945, there was no question of the willingness of consumers to spend. During the war they had gone without many goods, especially durables like cars and household appliances. Moreover, they had put their money in savings accounts and victory bonds, and were waiting for a chance to spend it. Indeed, many observers were inclined to fear that spending by consumers would be so far in excess of the supply of goods coming on the market that prices would rise precipitously. But most Canadians, and particularly the manufacturers, felt that if prices were allowed to rise moderately, business men and farmers would immediately raise their output. The hope of a somewhat larger profit would induce producers to expand operations. As the supply of goods on the market increased, prices would decline though they would never reach disastrously low levels as long as capital expenditures and exports (the other factors in maintaining full employment) continued at a high level. It was confidently asserted that not harm but much benefit would come from relaxing price control. Moreover as the war-time patriotic fervor evaporated, the public would support price control less enthusiastically, black markets would develop, organized labour and farmers would become restless, and the cost of policing the regulations would increase. It was generally believed that price control in peacetime was impractical.

Acting on this assumption the Government eased the regulations on prices beginning in August, 1945, shortly after the capitulation of Japan. By January, 1946, price controls had been removed on 300 items and by the end of the year on all goods and services except butter, bread, flour, fruit, rent and transportation. Sugar, butter, meat, and all other commodities had all been de-rationed by early 1949 and the restrictions on buying on the installment plan removed. Controls over salaries and wages were lifted in November, 1945. Although the cost of living which was 119.9 on November 1, 1945, stood at 127.1 a year later, not many Canadians were alarmed because they believed that the supply of goods would go on increasing and prices level off.

Capital investment, the second important factor in sustaining Canadian prosperity, continued at a high level immediately after the war. Plants which had produced war goods had to be re-equipped for civilian output. Since machinery was hard to get in wartime, some equipment had become obsolete and now had to be replaced. During the war shortage of hydro-electricity developed in Ontario and British Columbia. After hostilities, enormous power plants were constructed in both Provinces. Inventories of repair parts had become depleted and had to be replenished. In particular houses had to be built. Due to low incomes and lack of jobs in the depression, young men and women often had to postpone marriage. During the war the marriage rate jumped up but if the husband were overseas, couples did not need a self-contained dwelling. In many instances couples moved in with relatives or lived in a few rooms in converted houses. This make-shift living accommodation was unsatisfactory from many points of view. Consequently after the war the demand for housing became persistent, especially in industrial centres which had grown so rapidly during the preceding few years.

The Government encouraged capital expansion by reducing some taxes, by establishing the Industrial Development Bank, and by keeping down the rate of interest.

It also made loans available at low rates and on long terms to responsible persons for constructing their own homes, to individuals and insurance companies for building homes and apartments for rent, and to municipalities for slum clearance. It increased the supplies of some assets by rapidly disposing of publicly owned buildings previously used for war purposes and selling machinery, machine tools, trucks and ships owned by crown companies. For several months after the cessation of hostilities Government officials allocated steel, lumber and other basic products so as to ensure a large and increasing flow of capital goods to both foreign and domestic markets.

The Federal Government refrained from constructing public works except veterans' hospitals. Had the Government put up many buildings, it would have competed with private industry for men and materials and forced up the prices of both. So far as possible, governments should erect buildings and construct docks and highways only in periods of depression. The cost to the taxpayer is lower then and the need for finding jobs for men and women is urgent. In anticipation of a possible depression, the Government completed construction plans which could be taken "off the shelf" and executed whenever needed to iron out cyclical fluctuations in employment. It should be emphasized that in all these endeavours the Government placed its main reliance for maintaining employment on private enterprise which would invest in capital assets of all kinds and on consumers who would spend rather than hoard their incomes.

Foreign trade, the third chief determinant of the level of Canadian prosperity, reached record heights during the War. When hostilities ceased, Canadians realized that unless Britain and other European countries quickly got back on their feet, our export markets would shrivel, perhaps permanently. Aside altogether from sentiment or from a desire to contribute to world peace, our economic interest lay in helping rehabilitate Europe. Our first effort was through the United Nations Relief and Rehabilitation Administration (UNRRA) whereby we gave foodstuffs and clothing to destitute people in Greece, Italy, France and Germany and China. Then we lent roughly $1.8 billion to various democratic nations including $1,250 million to the United Kingdom. These loans bore low interest rates and were to be repaid in relatively small installments over a long period of time. Most of the loans were spent by early 1951. The United States made rather similar arrangements. Their loans, the Marshall Plan, continued until 1952. By that time Europe, though not yet firmly on its feet, was in a position to finance its own trade. At first the loans were used mainly to buy foodstuffs. Later they were spent more largely on industrial raw materials, machinery for farm and factory, and rearmament. These loans were instrumental in sustaining the flow of international trade.

When open warfare ceased, the nations expected they could disarm although they would have to keep some occupation troops in Germany, Austria and Japan until democratic governments were firmly established in these countries. The United States and the British Commonwealth including Canada cut down their armed forces as quickly as they could, but as the relations between the democratic West and Russia soon became strained they had to increase them again. Fighting between communist and anti-communist troops broke out in Malaya, French Indo-China, China proper, and Korea. At one time Russians refused to permit Britain and the United States to send supplies to troops and civilians in their sections of Berlin by rail or highway. Airplanes had to be resorted to and though the cost was huge, the democracies won a moral victory. As a result of the 'cold war', countries went back on a war footing in an economic sense. They made large purchases of military equipment and began to store or stock-pile base metals which might be unobtainable if normal trade channels were interrupted by war. All this government spending added greatly to the peacetime demands for goods.

In brief, all three factors—consumer spending, capital investment, and foreign trade—were favourable to continued prosperity. To be sure, within six months of the end of active fighting, the numbers of unemployed approached 300,000. This was due mainly to the fact that men had to be laid off until plants could be re-tooled from war to peacetime production. On the whole, conversion took place quickly and with relatively little dislocation. By law, firms had to reinstate in at least as good positions as they held upon enlistment, all men who left their employ to join the armed services. But some men had joined up directly from school and others came from the ranks of the unemployed. Having no job of their own to return to, they had to compete for work with men and women who were already employed. Some veterans, though competent in navy, army and air force, had few skills of any real value in civilian life. To help these men fit themselves for peacetime occupations and make up for interrupted schooling, the Government paid their fees at universities and trade schools and gave them allowances for books and living expenses. Despite the apparent certainty of a surplus of labour after the war was over, men and women in the fighting forces were quickly absorbed into industry and trade.

Economic history is not like a series of snapshots, with

each picture separated from the next by time and content. Instead, it resembles a motion picture with episodes blending into each other and every scene crowded with actors. Consequently, it is impossible to state precisely when post-war reconstruction ceased and normality, or something approaching it, was restored. The best one can do is to call attention to the main themes in Canada's economic history in the late 1940's, the 1950's and the early 1960's. The topics include labour, agriculture, fishing, manufacturing, transportation, mining, and northern development, along with inflation, foreign exchange, world trade and the business cycle.

The population of Canada, which was barely 14,000,000 in 1951, rose by about 13 per cent to 18,200,000 ten years later. About 75 per cent of the increase was accounted for by the excess of births (4,470,000) over deaths (1,320,000). The remaining 25 per cent was net migration, i.e., immigration (1,540,000) less emigration (460,000).

The growth in population had two important economic effects: first, a larger labour force could produce more goods and services for export and domestic consumption; second, more people increased the demand for food, clothing, houses, automobiles, highways, schools, churches, medical care, and a host of other products and services. Thus, a greater population might, if all went well, add enormously to the supply of goods and services available to Canadians and, at the same time, provide a market. Unfortunately, if too many members of the labour force are unemployed, their demand for goods and services declines, and other workers may be thrown out of jobs. On the other hand, if the purchasing power of consumers grows at too rapid a pace, their demands may outrun the supply of goods coming on the market. It must be remembered that ultimate consumers, like you and me, are only part of the market. Manufacturers, farmers, miners, and the government in their capacity as producers and as suppliers of such "social goods" as schools and roads are also in the market for goods and labour. In any event, if demand is too high in relation to supply, prices will rise and the economy will suffer from inflation. In so far as governments can control the economy, they must avoid too much unemployment on the one hand and runaway inflation on the other. They must try to get the best of both worlds: full employment and a fairly stable price level.

Though it is possible for immigration to add to the problems of the economy by creating or aggravating a condition of unemployment, Canada unquestionably gained from the influx of people and the rise in the birth rate after 1945. In the 1930's not many settlers had entered Canada. Prospective immigrants lacked money to pay fares and re-establish themselves in a new land. As long as Canadian-born workers were on relief, the nation did not welcome additional settlers. During the War many thousand Europeans had been displaced from their homes. They were anxious to start life anew in Canada and by the end of 1949 approximately 75,000 had arrived. While overseas, some Canadian servicemen had married and after the war approximately 45,000 war brides and their 21,000 children entered Canada.

The influx of other immigrants, not displaced persons, fluctuated with economic and political factors at home and abroad. The number was high in 1948 because Europe was still in the throes of reconstruction while Canada was prosperous. The inflow declined over the next two years with a slow-down in the rate of Canada's expansion. It picked up in the early 1950's because the

Korean War and the influx of American capital stimulated Canadian business, created a shortage of labour, and led to higher wages. Immigration was heaviest in 1957 when the Hungarian revolt and the crisis over Suez gave rise to fears of another war in Europe. For the next two or three years, immigration fell off because Europe's economic position improved while Canada's worsened. In view of the growing number of unemployed in Canada, we stressed immigration only by those who had capital to establish their own businesses, or skills which would permit them to enter the Canadian labour force without delay. Though some Canadian citizens went to the United States to find work, the number of such emigrants was very much smaller than in the first quarter of the century, an indication of the growing industrial maturity of Canada.

The composition of the labour force changed after the war. The proportion of female workers dropped slightly and then rose to about 29 per cent of the labour force. In 1946 married women constituted 27 per cent of all women who were grainfully occupied, i.e., those who worked for wages, salaries, and profits. In 1961 nearly half of the gainfully occupied women were married.

Almost 25 per cent of all Canadian workers were employed in manufacturing in 1946 and 1961 compared with 15 per cent in 1901. Employment in the service industries rose from 14 per cent in 1901 to 17 per cent in 1946 and then jumped to over 25 per cent in 1961. The numbers in agriculture showed a remarkable shift, from 40 per cent of Canada's total labour force in 1901 to 25 per cent in 1946 and then a sharp decline to 11 per cent in 1961. The proportion of workers in construction (7 per cent), mining, fishing and lumbering (3 or 4), and transportation (8) did not show much change over the years 1946-61, while the percentage in finance, insurance and real estate rose moderately to 4 per cent, and in trade from 12 to 16 per cent.

Over the years the degree of skill and the amount of formal education possessed by a typical Canadian worker has greatly improved. Moreover, in a rapidly changing economy workers have to be prepared to adapt their existing skills to new techniques of production and, if necessary, to learn quite different jobs. The unskilled labourer has increasing difficulty finding regular work and he is among the first to be laid off when business turns down.

Weekly wages rose pretty steadily after 1945 and by 1961 the average had more than doubled. Inevitably the rate of increase was not uniform in all industries and in all parts of the country. For instance, wages on railways and in the Maritimes tended to lag behind other wages. Of course, in all sections of the nation prices had risen as well as wage rates. Nevertheless the average wage-earner could buy many more goods and services with his income in 1961 than he could in 1946. This is another way of saying that his real income had increased or that his standard of living had risen.

The average number of hours worked per week was nearly 43 in 1945 and barely 40 in 1961. Thus, scientific advances, better management of factories and offices, and increased productivity brought two kinds of gain to the labour force: higher real incomes, and shorter hours. Besides, workers got relatively more of their incomes in fringe benefits such as company pensions, vacations with pay, sick leave, time-and-a-half and even double-time for overtime, and job security.

By the early 1960's, however, organized labour began to be concerned about the probable effects of automation, or the increased mechanization of factory operations and office work. It was also apprehensive that, even without automation, the working population would increase faster than the number of jobs. For a few years after 1945 the birth rate had been much higher than during the depression and the war. When these 'post-war babies' reach working age, the number of young men and women seeking jobs will be abnormally high.

After 1945 the Federal Government strengthened the National Employment Service. Its function is to place workers including unskilled, technically trained and professional men and women in suitable jobs. The Service paid particular attention to elderly and partially disabled persons who as a rule have more difficulty in finding work than the young and physically fit.

Up to about 1950 agriculture thrived on good prices and the strong demand for food both at home and abroad. Thereafter it went through an almost revolutionary change. In Eastern Canada fewer acres were planted in cereals for sale abroad and more effort was spent on raising dairy products and vegetables for sale in the large nearby cities. On the Prairies the wartime shift from cereals to livestock and its products proved to be largely temporary. Under favourable conditions farmers can make more money from wheat than from cattle and hogs, and can make it more quickly and with less work. Except in the northern sections with more rainfall and less evaporation, dairying has declined in importance since 1945.

Most Canadian farmers used their relatively high incomes during and after the War to liquidate debts incurred in the depression, acquire the latest implements, and purchase more land. Modern machinery makes it possible for a farmer and his immediate family to seed and harvest many more acres than even thirty years ago. Hence farms have grown in size, declined in numbers, and increased in cost. Broadly speaking, the amount of capital invested in farming doubled between 1945 and 1961, sales of farm implements increased three-fold, and the size of the agricultural labour force declined from over 1,000,000 to 675,000.

Changes in methods of producing and marketing farm products have been numerous: greater mechanization of cultivation, seeding, harvesting, and preparation for market; improved breeds of plants, animals and poultry; more insecticides and pesticides; expanded sales of fertilizers; mechanical and more scientific methods of raising eggs, broilers, and even hogs and milk; the purchase of feed off the farm instead of its production by the same farmer who finishes the livestock or who markets eggs or fresh milk; dependence on ready-mixed feeds; improved or new products such as quick frozen vegetables, powdered milk, canned apple juice, and instant potatoes; the transport of fluid milk in tank trucks rather than in cans by rail or truck; the trend towards self-service grocery stores and hence greater emphasis on putting meat, vegetables and fruit in packages so that the housewife and the retailer can handle them conveniently; the tendency of chain stores to put out their own brands of tinned goods and thus displace the products of independent canners; vertical integration whereby the production of hogs, poultry and eggs is financed and directed by a meat-packing company; and the ever-increasing importance of education and research in agriculture. Finally, in the ten years after 1951 the proportion of farms serviced by electricity rose from 51 to nearly 80 per cent.

Some small farms are occupied during the summer by city dwellers. Many more are owned by well-to-do business men, gentleman farmers who like to have a country estate which, under their general direction and with their capital, will pay for itself. Still other farms are worked on a part-time basis by wage-earners who, for one reason or another, like to live in the country and drive to and from their jobs in a nearby city. At the same time, more and more farmers and their wives do their shopping in urban super-markets and department stores. As a result, the old distinction between urban and rural life is becoming somewhat blurred.

In the West schemes for irrigating comparatively large sections along the St. Mary's, Bow, Red Deer and South Saskatchewan rivers are being undertaken. The irrigated areas will grow fodder so that livestock can be finished for market even in years of rainfall deficiency. Irrigation is too expensive for wheat, especially because too much moisture lowers the quality of the grain. Fresh and canned vegetables for consumption and sugar beets are important on irrigated lands.

Western grain is pooled by a federal Board but companies owned co-operatively by farmers have about 2,000 elevators at country points throughout the West. They also own terminal elevators at Lakehead and Vancouver, an oil refinery in Regina and are important in handling livestock, dairy products, wool, honey, seed, and farm implements. Scientists have waged an endless battle on pests which periodically devastate western crops. They have made progress in developing oats and wheat which will resist rust, in destroying plagues of grasshoppers, and in overcoming the saw-fly.

After 1945 the Government renewed its war-time contracts with Britain whereby it undertook to supply wheat, bacon, cheese and other products to Britain at prices fixed by negotiation. Although contract prices were rather lower than the going price in the world market, farmers were prepared to forego a large immediate profit for the assurance of protection in case world prices declined. By 1951, however, farmers saw they would have been much better off if, instead of selling at contract prices in an assured market, they had sold their goods in the world market for whatever price they would bring. Moreover, Britain lacked Canadian dollars and therefore was reluctant to renew old contracts or reimburse farmers for some of the profits they had foregone by the relatively low prices on the previous contracts. Unsettled economic and political conditions throughout the world were disheartening to Canadian farmers who depended on overseas markets. In the early 1960's Canada began to extend credit to mainland China, Russia, and some other Communist countries for the purchase of grain. This is hardly a permanent or dependable method of dealing with recurring surpluses of wheat. The alternative, reductions in the size of surpluses by drought, is even less acceptable.

Several steps have been taken, however, to protect agriculture against the worst evils of a collapse of prices or failure of crops by drought. The Federal Government assures farmers of a minimum price for bacon, butter, cheese, eggs and so on. It guarantees payment of loans made by banks for farm improvements. In the West any farmer who does not reap so many bushels of wheat, oats, barley or rye per acre is entitled to cash assistance up to $500 in any one year. The scheme is financed by a levy of one per cent of the selling prices of each of the cereals named. Any difference between receipts from the levy and payments from the fund is met from general tax revenues. These schemes are expensive and, by artificially raising the amount of money received by farmers, they may encourage the continuance of production and the perpetuation of the surplus. On the other hand, it is difficult for farmers to organize themselves into strong labour unions. Hence, the programme of price supports tends to equalize the incomes of industrial and of farm workers. Besides, the payments serve to minimize the loss, and even hardship, which is sometimes suffered by small farmers caught up in what is virtually a new agricultural revolution. One problem is how to ensure that the aid goes to farmers who are in need and not mainly to the large, efficient, and well financed operators who can get along without it.

Price support arrangements have also been applied to the fishing industry. On account of the need for proteins and the shortage of meat during the war, fishermen on the Atlantic and Pacific coasts prospered, quite a change from the intolerably depressed conditions of the 1930's. The British market for canned and frozen fish was particularly good while Caribbean and Mediterranean purchasers were willing to pay satisfactory prices for salt fish.

After 1945 diesel trawlers displaced almost all the schooners. Processing plants have taken over most of the curing of fish from the fisherman and his family. They have perfected quick freezing and provide rapid delivery to market. In many instances they convert low grade fish, formerly unsaleable, into feed for household pets and other animals. The canning of lobsters and sardines on the Atlantic Coast and of salmon on the Pacific has continued to be important. For several years commercial fishing on the Great Lakes was hurt by the depredations of lamprey until, by 1960, scientists discovered methods of controlling them. Catching fish for sale has expanded on numerous lakes of the Shield. Angling is a popular sport almost everywhere in Canada. The Dominion and Provincial Governments conduct research in the conservation and utilization of fish. They operate hatcheries on inland waters and they try to stimulate the consumption of fish by advertising them at home and overseas and by inspection of fish and fish products before sale to the public. The co-operative movement has made considerable progress in fishing communities along both coasts, especially in Nova Scotia.

In manufacturing, many significant changes occurred after 1945. The conversion of industry from military to civilian production was accomplished with comparative ease. Post-war demands for consumer goods were well sustained, first by the backlog of requirements which could not be satisfied during hostilities, and then by the high level of consumer spending, capital investment, and foreign trade. Furthermore, new machinery was needed to replace what had been worn out during the war or had become obsolete through technological advance. More equipment was also needed to produce the growing quantities of goods demanded by a larger population at home and by the export market. Although some of the equipment was purchased abroad, mainly in the United States, much of it was made in Canada. This was particularly true of farm implements, machine tools, railway rolling stock, trucks, hardware, and steel for construction. Similarly, while Canada continued to import some kinds of consumer goods, she was also able to export others. In the external market she faced competition from American, British, West German, Japanese, and other producers. As time went on, the struggle for markets became keener. Nevertheless, Canadian manufacturers were able to hold their own.

Because of competition at home and abroad, Canadian manufacturers had to be alert to the demands of consumers. They continued to make standardized goods like flour, footwear, bedsheets, newsprint, and gasoline. They manufactured new products such as television sets, detergents, home freezers, pressure cookers, and Salk vaccine. They also made articles, e.g., synthetic fibres, record players, and instant coffee, which had been known before the war but greatly improved after it. In hundreds of instances our manufacturers were able to make within Canada things which we had formerly got from external suppliers. Often we used newly discovered resources to make these goods. For example, from petroleum and natural gas we produce synthetic rubber, sulphur, ammonia for explosives and fertilizers, plastics, cellulose acetates for textiles, and carbon black for the tire industry.

Manufacturers were also alert to the need for continued efficiency in production and the reduction of costs. This is essential if they are to expand external sales and hold the domestic market in the face of competition from abroad. Between 1945 and 1959 the number of persons employed in manufacturing rose by 16 per cent and the volume of production by 61 per cent. Thus productivity increased nearly four times as fast as employment. The advance in efficiency has not been as great among office and administrative employees as among so-called production workers. This is because work is not as readily mechanized in the one case as in the other. For Canada as a whole, weekly earnings in the manufacturing industry advanced by 121 per cent between 1946 and 1959.

The railways like all other segments of the economy suffered from the 'high cost of living' after 1945. Wages rose as did the prices of rails, ties, coal, freight cars, lubricants, paints and the hundreds of other commodities bought by carriers. Increases in the general level of freight rates authorized by the Board of Transport Commissioners amounted to over 150 per cent between 1945 and 1958. However the rates on grain from the West for export were not raised at all, while rates on coal and on traffic between Canada and the United States were lifted by varying percentages. Higher freight rates were persistently opposed by all the provinces except Ontario and Quebec and by numerous shippers. The general level of tolls was alleged to be higher in Western Canada than elsewhere. The same percentage increase was applied to tolls which were already high as to those, mainly in the St. Lawrence Valley, which were held down by competition from trucks and inland steamships. The West argued that a horizontal increase would widen the discrepancies between the various parts of Canada.

The West and the Maritimes are dependent on selling relatively bulky articles in distant markets. Often they must bring in consumers' goods and capital equipment from distant sources of supply. The St. Lawrence Valley, on the other hand, is more self-contained, the distances to and from market being comparatively short as a rule. The various regions of Canada differ in the relative level of existing tolls, the comparative strength of competition from other transportation agencies, and in average length of haul. Thus railway freight rates involve two problems: the need for covering the operating expenses, interest and dividends of the railway companies; and the necessity for having rates which will apply equitably to different parts of the country. In 1951 following the report of a Royal Commission, the government required railways to publish the same rate per mile on each class of freight in all parts of Canada west of Levis except on Western grain, exports, imports, competitive traffic, and so forth.

Although some progress was made in carrying out this policy of equalization, by the late 1950's the railway problem had taken a different form. Federal and Provincial Governments had spent vast sums on highways, airports, the St. Lawrence Seaway, the trans-Canada

Highway, and so on. They made the expensive investments in fixed assets, and left individuals and companies
with the relatively easy task of financing the purchase of
automobiles, trucks, airplanes, and ships. As a rule users
of highways, airports and the Seaway pay at least part
of their cost but they pay mainly in proportion to use.
If their business declines or ceases to grow, they are not
obligated to meet the entire cost of interest and maintenance of the fixed assets. By contrast, railways must
raise the capital for both rolling stock and track, and
they are expected to bear the full cost of interest and
maintenance come what may. Thus, one effect of government spending on transportation facilities is to put railways at a relative disadvantage.

The various agencies of transport differ in the quality
of service which they offer to the shipping and travelling
public. Service includes such matters as speed of delivery,
convenience of time of departure and arrival, risk of
injury or damage, courtesy of employees, and cost. Obviously, shippers and travellers have to take into account
many factors before deciding what agency to use. Although railways have many competitive advantages for
certain kinds of freight, particularly bulky, relatively
low-valued goods moving for long distances at fairly low
rates of speed, the large increase in the volume of traffic
handled by trucks, pipelines, airplanes and private automobiles after 1950 suggests that railways will have increasing difficulty in getting enough revenue to meet their
expenses.

With a view to enabling railways to reduce their costs,
in 1961 a Royal Commission recommended that they be
allowed to abandon their unprofitable branches and
passenger trains at a more rapid rate than in the past.
But the Commission feared that a policy of accelerated
abandonment of branches and trains might cause eco-

nomic distress in the communities concerned. So it proposed that the Dominion Government should subsidize railways to continue operation until a programme of gradual withdrawal could be implemented. In addition, the Commission proposed that the carriers be subsidized for their losses on the carriage of Western grain to Lakehead, Vancouver, etc., for export.

Meanwhile, the railways had been acting vigorously to retain traffic which was in danger of going to competitors and, if possible, to recover what they had already lost. They reduced expenses by replacing steam locomotives with diesels, constructing more efficient marshalling yards, mechanizing their accounting, and eliminating firemen except on passenger trains. Then, too, they published rates which, they hoped, would keep traffic to the rails. Finally, they purchased trucking companies and introduced a trailer-on-flatcar service, commonly called piggy-back.

After 1945 various levels of government modernized their existing highways and built new ones. The ownership of trucks and passenger cars increased so rapidly, however, that congestion was common on city streets during the morning and evening rush to and from work. It was also bad at week-ends during the summer on roads which connect metropolitan areas with resorts. Beginning in 1958 the Dominion and Provincial Governments cooperated in the finance and construction of roads-to-resources. These provide access to mines, fishing grounds, and tourist attractions. In the Northwest and Yukon Territories, the Dominion assumes full responsibility for the programme.

Although civil aviation got started in Canada in the 1920's and Trans-Canada Air Lines was created in 1938, the main development came after 1945. In the late 1950's the larger companies began to use jet aircraft instead of piston or turbo-prop planes, i.e., those with propellors which are driven by either gasoline engines or jet turbines. Jets cost about three times as much as turbo-props and six times piston aircraft. Consequently, the charges for interest, depreciation and insurance are heavy. If seats are unoccupied, the airline receives less revenue while its expenses, broadly speaking, are the same as if every seat were filled. Hence, if the airline is to cover its costs, it must have a high load factor, or ratio of seats occupied to seat capacity.

During the 1950's air travel quadrupled but jet aircraft are so much bigger and speedier than their predecessors that in the early 1960's capacity had expanded far in advance of demand, the load factor fell, and airline companies lost money. The growing popularity of economy class and of charter flights indicates that airlines have a huge potential market, provided they can reduce their fares. If they can simultaneously cut their costs by reducing expenses or increasing their load factor, they can recover their earning power. Air cargo increased rapidly after 1960 and will expand still further if costs and rates can be lowered.

In another basic Canadian industry, mining, post-war changes were based on wartime developments which both helped and hindered. The industry benefitted because during hostilities the mining of lead, copper, zinc, nickel and iron was treated in the same way as the production of guns, ships and planes as far as allocation of labour and productive machinery was concerned. The Government assisted the exploitation of a large reserve of high quality iron ore at Steeprock, 135 miles west of Port Arthur. It also encouraged the mining of gold, not because the gold itself could be used to make munitions but because it could be exported to the United States to pay for steel, raw cotton, parts for aircraft, and other things which we badly needed in the all-out war effort. The mining of uranium was especially important. Offsetting these gains was the fact that during the war prospecting for precious metals had to be minimized since men and materials could be used more advantageously elsewhere.

After the war the Government assisted gold mining by tax concessions. Gold is sold at a price fixed by the Government. Although the price paid by the mint does not rise and fall with the business cycle, wages of miners and other expenses change with other prices. Gold mining tends to be more profitable in periods of general business depression when wages and supplies are low in price, and to decline in profitability in times of inflation. Hence in order to provide work for hard-rock miners and foreign exchange for the country at large, the federal government gives financial aid to gold mines.

The mining industry has proceeded apace since 1945. Prospecting has been speeded up by using the Geiger counter which emits a clicking sound in the presence of uranium and by the magnetometer which indicates base metals even when flown in an aeroplane over the surface of the earth. Many new deposits of potential value have been discovered in the Shield, New Brunswick, and Newfoundland. Railways have been built to Lynn Lake and Chisel Lake, north of Flin Flon, in northern Manitoba. Another line is being constructed in northern Alberta. New lines also run from the former National Transcontinental to mining areas in northern Quebec. A railway 350 miles long has been constructed from Sept Iles on the north shore of the Gulf of St. Lawrence to the huge iron deposits on the Quebec-Labrador boundary. Ontario's iron output grew because of beneficiation, a process for improving the quality of low grade ore by means of pulverization and then treament by chemicals. British Columbia's iron mines on Vancouver and Texada Islands find their chief market in Japan. The output of silver, platinum, cobalt, gypsum, asbestos and salt increased after 1945. The highest rate of expansion, however, was shown by Portland cement. Road-building, domestic construction and exports to the United States absorbed large quantities.

On the other hand there were some declines. Some of the gold mines at Kirkland Lake have seen their best days and are being closed. The output of uranium fell off after 1959 when the Atomic Energy Commission of the United States decided to reduce its purchases in Canada. The atomic energy plants which we established at Chalk River, and at Douglas Point on Lake Huron can absorb only a small fraction of our potential output of uranium. Coal-mining was especially hard hit after 1945 due to competition from fuel oil, diesel fuel, and natural gas.

Salt at Malagash, N.S., titanium not far from Quebec City, magnesium at Haley near Renfrew, Ont., nickel at Moak Lake, Man., and at Rankin Inlet on the west shore of Hudson Bay are some new finds of great potential importance. The huge reserve of potash in southern Saskatchewan is being exploited. But perhaps the greatest post-war discovery has been petroleum at Leduc, just south of Edmonton, and at other places in central Alberta. Several million barrels of petroleum and billions of cubic feet of natural gas are believed to underlie these areas. The Leduc field is supplying British Columbia, the Prairies, northern Ontario and part of the St. Lawrence Lowlands as well as nearby states with crude oil and natural gas. The tar sands at McMurray at the end of steel near the Athabaska river are another potential source of crude oil. A cheap method for extracting the oil from the sands in which it is imbedded has not yet been perfected, though an atomic blast will be tried. Starting in 1954 Canada became an important producer of sulphur. It is extracted from natural gas in Western Canada.

Another significant feature of post-war Canada is the accelerated rate of development of the northern areas. Uranium on Great Bear and gold at Yellowknife on Great Slave are good examples. More uranium has been found elsewhere in the North West Territories. Lead has been discovered near Coronation Gulf and nickel in Ungava, northern Quebec. Between 1942 and 1945 the American Government financed the construction of a pipe-line from Norman, on the Mackenzie River not far from the Arctic Circle, to Whitehorse in the Yukon where a refinery was built. The development was intended to supply relatively cheap fuel to aircraft flying between the United States and Alaska and beyond. Before the facilities were put into operation, the war with Japan ended and the scheme was abandoned. The refinery was bought by a Canadian company and re-erected at Edmonton.

Meanwhile Americans had built a road from Dawson Creek, B.C., at the end of steel in the Peace River country, to Whitehorse and Fairbanks, Alaska. The road was used for carrying war supplies to Alaska and for servicing the airfields which were constructed along it. After the War the highway, airfields and the adjoining communication system, in so far as they lay in Canada, were purchased by the Dominion from the United States.

During the War an air route was constructed to Europe via Southampton Island using Churchill, Man., as its rail base. This route has been abandoned but several air force, radar and weather stations are maintained throughout the north. The airports at Goose Bay in Labrador, Gander, Nfld., and more recently at Frobisher on Baffin

Island are used by planes of all nations flying between North America and northwestern Europe. In general, these bases are not used as much as formerly. Jet aircraft are capable of flying longer distances between refueling stops than piston or turbo-prop planes. So they fly over the above airports which, however, are still essential for emergency landings and servicing.

Notwithstanding the importance of labour, agriculture, manufacturing, mining, transportation and northern development in our economy, no one can get an adequate picture of post-war Canadian economic development by looking at the pieces. Factors affecting the economy as a whole must be studied. These include inflation, foreign exchange, world trade, and capital investment.

One of our national objectives is to provide jobs for everyone who is willing and able to work and yet avoid a continuous rise in prices. Expressed in different terms, Canada, like other countries, wants economic growth along with reasonable stability in prices. This objective cannot be reached without hard work, thrift, honesty, and such virtues on the one hand, and willingness of consumers to spend, of capitalists to invest, and of foreigners to buy our goods and services on the other. Moreover, the attainment of this objective necessitates sound policies on the part of all levels of government.

The problem of inflation was effectively handled during the war. Afterwards price and wage controls were removed as quickly as possible in the belief that the way to keep prices down was to give enterprise a chance to produce an abundance of goods. This hope proved unfounded, mainly because the 'cold war' led democratic nations to step up their purchases of war goods, and to take men from civilian production into the armed services. The cost of living index which was apparently levelling off at about 160 in the early part of 1950 had risen to 172.5 at the end of the year. The Government believed that an over-all price and wage freeze, the kind which had been so successful during the war, would fail in peace-time. The American price level appeared to be out of control. It would be hard to hold down prices in Canada when they were rising sharply in a nearby country which was at once our chief foreign source of supply and an important customer. In 1949 the government changed the basis on which it computed its index of consumer prices. Between 1949 and 1962 the new index rose from 100 to about 132. Nearly two-thirds of the increase came in 1951-2 during the Korean War and in 1955-7 during a boom in investment.

Inflation was particularly hard on recipients of old age and veterans' pensions, mothers' allowances, workmen's compensation, retirement allowances, and interest. It was almost as hard on professional men and women like teachers and clergymen who worked for salaries. Wage-earners, merchants and professional men such as lawyers, accountants, dentists and doctors who are paid fees did not suffer much. In short, the incomes of some economic groups rose more or less in unison with prices whereas the incomes of pensioners became adjusted slowly, if at all, to the cost of living. In peacetime, governments find it hard to "hold the lid" on prices without discouraging business men from adding to their plant and their inventories. When expansion ceases, men lose their jobs and price control is blamed.

Another complex post-war problem was the shortage of American dollars. In 1947 the value of our exports, aided by the loans discussed elsewhere, was three times their value in 1939 but our imports had risen fourfold. About four-fifths of our imports came from the United States as against two-thirds before the War. The value of our exports to the United States had dropped from the pre-war level of one-third of the total to one-quarter. There was a large 'gap' between receipts and payments on international account and so the shortage of American dollars became acute. For a time our Government forbade importation of some goods and allowed the others to come in only under permit. An importer had to prove he really needed the article and that he could not obtain it within Canada. For the most part the goods selected for permit were those which could not be produced in Canada. In this respect the import restrictions acted in the same manner as a protective tariff. They kept out foreign goods and gave Canadian suppliers a great advantage. Simultaneously the Government encouraged exports to the United States and purchases from non-dollar countries. By diverting Canadian imports from the United States to the Commonwealth, France, the Low Countries and so on, Canada eased her own problem of American foreign exchange and provided other countries with Canadian dollars to buy goods in the Dominion.

While these conscious controls were unquestionably important, the normal trend of events helped us out of our difficulties. American investors were unwilling to sink their money in parts of the world where political affairs were in a turmoil. But the Canadian Government was stable and foreign investors were welcomed. The discovery of new resources, especially petroleum at Leduc and iron ore on the Labrador-Quebec boundary, were the initial post-war stimulants to the influx of American capital.

For the sake of simplicity let us assume that all Canada's external trade is with the United States. Americans who ship goods to Canada are paid in Canadian dollars which of course they want to change into United States dollars. Conversely Canadians who sell goods in the United States receive United States currency and want Canadian dollars. In other words, American exporters to Canada and Canadian exporters to the United States are in exactly the reverse position as far as dollars are concerned. Obviously the thing to do is for exporters to Canada to sell the Canadian dollars they have to the exporters from Canada who want these dollars. Similarly the exporters from Canada will sell the United States dollars which they have been paid, to the American exporters to Canada who want this kind of currency. The two groups buy and sell currency, or as it is usually called foreign exchange, in substantially the same way as a merchant trades in groceries. Dealing in foreign exchange is carried on mainly by banks.

When imports into Canada exceed the value of exports from this country, the amount of Canadian dollars coming on the international exchange market will be large relative to the demand for these dollars which arises, as explained, from people who sell Canadian goods abroad. Everyone understands that when the supply of an article increases relative to the demand for it, its price will fall. The same thing happens in foreign exchange. When Canadian imports exceed Canadian exports, the value of the Canadian dollar in New York will decline when expressed in terms of the United States dollar. The Canadian dollar will sell at a discount in New York. This is what happened in 1948–9.

In the 1950's the situation was reversed. It is convenient to think of international trade in terms of physical articles like citrus fruits, copper, canned goods and cotton print. In fact services are also exchanged—such services as transporting freight by sea, royalties on motion picture films, remittances by immigrants to their relatives who have remained at home, interest and dividends, and so on. These invisibles are just as significant in the balance of international payments as physical assets. Once Americans began to invest large sums in Canada, Canadian dollars became scarce relative to American. Therefore, the Canadian dollar was quoted at a premium in New York.

By 1960 the situation was again reversed. American investment in Canada was tending to decline. The Federal Government had had a budgetary deficit since 1958. Canadians were buying American goods at an enormous rate. For these reasons the Canadian dollar fell from a premium of roughly five cents in March, 1960, to par in mid-1961 and then to a discount of five cents in December, 1961. In May, 1962, the Government announced that it would stabilize the Canadian dollar at 92.5 cents in terms of United States currency. By the end of June, when the Canadian dollar showed signs of further weakness, the Government raised a number of customs duties with the object of reducing imports from the United States and the drain of Canadian dollars to that country. It also cut back its expenditures so as to reduce the amount of its deficit. Simultaneously, the Bank of Canada raised the interest rate in order to encourage more investment by Americans in Canada. This monetary "tool" had to be used sparingly because higher interest rates influence business men not to expand operations in view of the increased cost of money. In other words, the Bank had to take care that by encouraging lenders it did not discourage borrowers.

The Bank of Canada was also able to assist in the stabilization of the Canadian dollar by using its Exchange Fund Account. This was created partly with Canadian gold reserves in Ottawa and New York, partly with funds lent Canada by countries which were in a stronger foreign exchange position than we were, and partly from the International Monetary Fund. The latter had been established in 1945 to promote exchange stability and eliminate exchange restrictions between countries of the Western World. Details about how the Bank of Canada operates the Account are rather too technical to be explained here. In effect, Canadian dollars will be exchanged for American dollars in the ratio of 92.5 : 100 instead of 100 : 100 which was the traditional par of exchange.

After 1945, other countries were also short of foreign exchange. The War left some belligerents prostrated and poverty stricken. European farmers lacked machinery, chemical fertilizers, livestock and seed. Factories had been destroyed outright or were capable of producing only war goods. The people were in dire need of food and clothing, of shelter and medical supplies. Europeans required many machines and raw materials which could be supplied only by the New World with its vast resources unravaged by war. But until European lands got back into production they could not export goods to pay for the imports they needed so badly. Temporarily loans from the United States and Canada filled the gap. Many nations, notably Britain, embarked on austerity programmes, whereby they limited both purchases from abroad and made more goods available for export by restricting the amount of domestically produced goods which could be used at home. Unfortunately, Britain's austerity programme was not sufficient to meet her financial difficulties and so in 1948 she arbitrarily set the value of the pound at $2.80. This compared with about $4.00 which was the price quoted by dealers in foreign exchange after the War and with $4.86⅔ which was the exchange value based on the relative gold content of the pound and the dollar. The devaluation of 1949 had the effect of lowering the price of British goods being sold in the United States and other dollar markets, and in making American goods relatively dearer in Britain. Accordingly, it helped alleviate, at least temporarily, Britain's shortage of dollars, both American and Canadian.

In view of her economic history and ner natural resources, Canada has been active in promoting world trade. She has agreed with other nations to conduct international trade without discrimination, to reduce some tariffs provided other countries will do the same, and to refrain from raising tariffs on a wide variety of imports. Canada has also participated in the Bretton Woods agreement whereby various countries agreed not to devalue their currencies without the consent of the various parties to the agreement. She has taken part in the International Bank for Reconstruction and Development, the so-called World Bank with headquarters in Washington which lends to underdeveloped lands for the purchase of equipment or the construction of hydro-electric power plants, irrigation and drainage systems, and similar undertakings which will add to their productive ability. Loans are made only if private capital is not available on reasonable terms. The Colombo Plan, a scheme of the British Commonwealth for the development of India, Ceylon, and southeast Asia, has the same objectives as the International Bank except that some of the contributions are outright gifts, for example, the Canadian donation to India of a huge dam for hydro-electricity and irrigation. Furthermore, Canada has been an active member of the Food and Agricultural Organization (FAO). This international body exchanges information on farm practices. Above all, it tries to raise the standard of living of underdeveloped areas like most of Asia, Africa and South America.

International agencies for aiding under-developed countries have proliferated since 1945. Canada has taken part in many of them: the United Nations, the U.N. Children's Fund (UNICEF), U.N. Technical Assistance, the U.N. Refugee Programme, the Organization for Economic Cooperation and Development, the Canada-West Indies Aid Programme, Commonwealth Aid to Africa, and in conjunction with authorities in Quebec, educational assistance to French-speaking States in Africa. Though this list is impressive, Canada has given a smaller percentage of her gross national product to underdeveloped countries than several other countries.

Conditions in these countries seem all the more deplorable because of the post-war boom in Canada. The reasons for our prosperity are not difficult to find but the relative weight to be attached to the various factors is indeterminate. First of all, during the War some articles were unobtainable. These included some consumers' durables such as automobiles, refrigerators, and houses. At the same time the public was encouraged to save through the purchase of Victory Bonds. Besides, they built up cash balances in banks, largely as a result of plenty of work at good wages and of inability to spend money on such things as new cars or even on gasoline for older models. For a few months immediately after the War consumers seemed reluctant to spend. They feared another depression and therefore held on to cash. Before long, however, they were spending freely and beginning to buy on the installment plan. In effect, they mortgaged future earnings in order to get articles at once, rather than wait until they had the cash to pay for them. New kinds of goods such as television sets and oil furnaces added another fillip to demand.

Though Canadians continued to save a fair proportion of their income, they showed a stronger propensity to spend on consumers' goods of all sorts after about 1947 than throughout most of their history. This shift in spending habits is hard to explain and may not be permanent. Part of the explanation lies in rapidly rising incomes, growing confidence of workers in their ability to get jobs, unemployment insurance in case of loss of work, Family Allowances, and a more equable dispersion of income over all classes of the community.

The purchasing power which consumers had accumulated in banks and government bonds or which they got from current income and installment credit was coupled with deferred demands and with the urge to buy new or more attractive kinds of goods that were coming on the market. Growing expenditures by consumers led to greater output by factories, more purchase of raw materials, more employment, good wages for other workers, and so forth. In other words, active buyers meant busy factories and good domestic markets for farm products.

The growth of demand would have been significant even if the goods had been produced by the same methods and with the same equipment as before the War. But to a large extent the construction of factory and office buildings, the purchase of lathes and looms and locomotives, of tractors and combines, had been deferred during the War in the same way as consumers' durables. Our industrial and agricultural equipment was obsolescent because it had been allowed to deteriorate during a decade and a half of depression and war. Old machinery and buildings had to be replaced with modern facilities. The necessity for modernization was urgent, especially in view of lively spending by consumers.

Fortunately, capital to undertake the modernization and expansion could be readily secured. Business corporations, like individuals, had accumulated cash after 1940 since they sometimes could not buy machinery which they needed. More especially, high wartime and post-war profits were available for re-investment in new equipment. Businesses could also borrow from banks on the strength of orders on their books or sell new securities to the public which had become more interested in buying industrial bonds and shares than at any time since 1929. Then too, farmers had been able during the War greatly to reduce their mortgage debt. After 1945 they felt that it was reasonably safe for them to incur other debts for machinery or the purchase of larger farms. The Federal Government was helping smaller and newer businesses through the Industrial Development Bank and it was providing financial backing for the construction of dwellings through the Central Mortgage and Housing Corporation. Finally, new capital was flowing in to Canada from the United States and to some extent from Britain.

Investment in assets was unquestionably stimulated by the low rate of interest which prevailed from the end of the War, and indeed from 1940, to about 1957. Such a stimulus is particularly strong when business is booming and business men are optimistic about the future. Moreover, up to a point low interest rates encourage saving. A person who wants, let us say, $1,000 a year in his old age, will have to accumulate $20,000 when the interest rate is 5 per cent per annum and over $33,000 when it falls to 3 per cent. Inflation also affects saving. When the cost of goods and services goes up, a man needs more life insurance to give adequate protection to his dependents. The important point is that conditions of saving and interest after 1945 strongly favoured expansion in the Canadian economy.

Another buoyant influence of the period arose out of population trends—a relatively high rate of marriages and births, immigration, and the movement of people away from farms and villages and into large cities. The growth and re-distribution of the population necessitated more houses, furniture, streets, highways, schools, and the like; larger urban transit systems; more restaurants and super-markets; more beauty parlours and barber shops; more clothing and food; more of almost everything. Some farm houses which would otherwise have been abandoned were moved bodily to cities and towns, thus reducing the monetary loss of the farm owner. Even so, the shifts in population involved heavy social costs, especially the loss of neighbourliness. Besides, population changes aggravated the problem of municipal finance. Suburbs of large cities had to cope with a relatively sudden influx of new citizens. Rural areas were faced with the need of maintaining schools, highways, and other essential social services with a relatively smaller assessment on which taxes could be levied.

In the post-war world the external demand for Canadian products continued strong, notwithstanding the accumulation of unsold grain and the difficulty which many potential buyers experienced in getting Canadian dollars as outlined above. Canadian exports grew steadily to 1948 when other countries began to feel pinched by the lack of dollars. The outbreak of the Korean War in 1950, coming on top of a generally expanding world economy, led to a sudden increase in demand and sharp rises in world prices. Subsequently, prices of some goods, especially farm products, declined somewhat but the long run outlook continued favourable. By 1975 American consumption of raw materials, except foodstuffs, will be almost two-thirds greater than in 1950. Her domestic resources, particularly of base metals and iron ore, are becoming depleted. In 1975 she may have to import about 20 per cent of a much larger consumption compared with 9 per cent of her smaller requirements in 1950. Canada is, from the American point of view, the most satisfactory source

of supply since her government is stable, supplies are un-
likely to be interrupted in time of war, and costs of
transportation are relatively low. Hence, the United
States will turn to Canada even more than in the past,
not merely for asbestos and nickel in which we already
have a veritable monopoly, but for copper, lead, zinc, iron
ore, even petroleum and natural gas, and possibly for
foodstuffs. Moreover, the United States is an important
market for Canadian newsprint, aluminum, and so on.
In a word, economic trends since 1945, especially in the
United States, have brought rising demands for Canada's
exports. This growth favoured the inflow of American
capital and encouraged the search for new mineral and
petroleum resources.

Expenditures on defence were another ingredient in
the post-war boom. By 1949 Western democracies were
beginning to realize that they had been short-sighted in
rapidly cutting back their defence spending after 1945.
In particular, the Korean War led to a marked increase
in outlays on defence by Canada and other countries as
well as an upsurge in external demand, mainly by the
United States, for strategic raw materials from Canada.
Moreover, loans by the United States to its allies overseas largely solved the problem of foreign exchange faced
by these countries. The loans aided economic rehabilitation abroad and thereby expanded the markets for Canadian goods.

Of course, there is danger that a large reduction in
defence spending will precipitate a serious depression.
Yet the growing propensity of Canadians to consume and
the ingenuity of business men in searching out and developing new products and services suggest that consumer
spending would, before long, take up any slack brought
about by lessened expenditures on preparations for war.
Slight recessions, or slower-than-average advances were

noticed in 1948, again in 1954. Fortunately recovery was rapid, chiefly because the United States led the way. Between 1957 and 1962 the Gross National Product grew 30 per cent but most of the increase occurred in 1962. If one corrects for the rise in prices, the increase was of the order of 15 per cent over the six years. During this period employment rose 11 per cent but it failed to keep pace with the increase in the labour force which was 14 per cent. As a result the number of unemployed averaged 6.3 per cent of the labour force over the years 1957-62, or roughly twice the average rate of the period 1952-7. It is obvious that Canada has not yet solved the problem of full employment in a free society. It is equally obvious that it has made enormous strides in raising its standard of living.

SELECTED READINGS

BREWIS, T. N., ENGLISH, H. E., SCOTT, ANTHONY, and JEWITT, PAULINE, *Canadian Economic Policy*, Toronto, 1961.

BROWN, G. W., ed., *Canada*, Toronto, 1950.

COATS, R. H., ed., "Features of Present-day Canada", *The Annals of the American Academy of Political and Social Sciences*, vol. 253, September, 1947.

FIRESTONE, O. J., *Canada's Economic Development, 1867-1953*, Cambridge, 1958.

HEATON, H., *The Story of Trade and Commerce, with special reference to Canada*, Toronto, 1955 (rev. ed.), pp. 277-89.

LOWER, A. R. M., *Colony to Nation*, Toronto, 1946.

Royal Commission on Prices, *Report*, Ottawa, 1949 (Curtis Commission).

Royal Commission on Canada's Economic Prospects, *Report*, Ottawa, 1957 (Gordon Commission).

SMITH, J. M., *Canadian Economic Growth and Development from 1939 to 1955*, Ottawa, 1957 (A study prepared for the Gordon Commission).

22

A Summary

THE economic development of Canada has proceeded generally from East to West. Beginning with fish on the Atlantic coast, development went on by exploiting furs in the St. Lawrence Valley. After the Conquest three new staples—potash, lumber and wheat—were introduced. Lumbering had ship-building as a sort of appendage, and the exploitation of wheat soon destroyed the fur-trade and forced it back into the Nelson-Saskatchewan River basins where it was already being developed through Hudson Bay and, until about 1821, by lake and river from Montreal. All the development up to 1885, except for agriculture in the St. Lawrence Valley after 1850, was based on the use of water-ways.

The barren rocks of the Laurentian Shield dammed back the westward movement of agriculture and diverted population to the United States. Only the pooling of colonial strength and the construction of railways gave the country the figurative seven league boots needed to reach the Prairies. New types of wheat and a conjuncture of other favourable circumstances permitted rapid development in the West and greatly speeded up manufacturing in the St. Lawrence Valley and, to a lesser extent, in Nova Scotia. Meanwhile development on the Pacific coast started with furs and fish and spread to lumbering, farming and mining. At the same time the economic life of the area, though retaining much of its original outlook on the sea, struck its roots deeply into the interior. After 1920 the mineral, pulp and paper, and hydro-electric resources of the Laurentian Shield began to be exploited and the entire north cracked open. Having thus stretched itself across the Continent and then northward in a physical sense, the country had to integrate itself, to pull all the geographic areas into a unified economy. Also it tried to broaden out economically from a few staples to a more well-rounded development, to proceed from a colonial to a more mature economy.

Canadian economic history can be looked at from the point of view of a real estate agent who discovered a piece of property 450 years ago. For the first hundred years he bothered only to look at it occasionally and then for the following two hundred was concerned merely with gathering the fish around its shores, securing the furs from its wild animals and exploring all its area superficially. Only in the last slightly more than one hundred years has he done much to develop its other resources. During the long period of development, the mythical real estate agent has opened up the area in five smaller blocks, two of them concurrently after 1785 on the basis of wood and wheat, two since 1897 on a foundation of wheat, and of lumber, fish and mines and the last since 1920 with metals and newsprint. While he was opening these new regions he went back, this imaginary realtor, to repair and build additions to the older properties in the form of mixed farming, manufacturing, coal and hydro-electric power. Also he has tried to keep each of the four "blocks" from breaking away and becoming separate economic municipalities. He has done this by installing national transportation systems and encouraging all to do business at the same store and the same bank, figuratively speaking, and decide questions around the same council table. He has tried to erect new and more solidly built economic houses than those of fish, fur, wheat, lumber and mineral products. He wants to have his property cease being a financial and trading suburb of London or New York. He wants the homes of all the citizens to be fit for human habitation, and desires everyone to get a decent wage but he does not know exactly how to tackle this problem. In fact, he never has been absolutely certain at any time in the lengthy development of this property exactly how he was to go about doing anything. The reason for this is that he has had to work through thousands of humble men and women, each of whom had his own ideas on what needed to be done and whose immediate problem was to get as much as he could for himself and let the rest of the world, or of the parts of the project, fend for themselves. Nevertheless, this real estate operator is confident that somehow, working through his subjects, he can promote a more prosperous community than has existed in the past. If Canadians are prepared to learn from their past successes and failures, they need not fear the future but will have every confidence in it.

INDEX